W9-BAS-265

Contents

Much Ado about Culture

Much Ado about Culture

North American Trade Disputes

Keith Acheson and Christopher Maule

Ann Arbor

THE UNIVERSITY OF MICHIGAN PRESS

Copyright © by the University of Michigan 1999
All rights reserved
Published in the United States of America by
The University of Michigan Press
Manufactured in the United States of America
⊖ Printed on acid-free paper

2002   2001   2000   1999   4   3   2   1

*A CIP catalog record for this book is available
from the British Library.*

Library of Congress Cataloging-in-Publication data applied for
ISBN 0-472-11048-9

Figures

Tables

Preface

The cultural-entertainment industries have always been international in the scope of their activities. They have also been politically sensitive. At first, copyright regimes evolved to address both the author's and the sovereign's concerns with book publishing and the other print media. As technology led to the development of films, radio, sound recordings, and television, opportunities opened up for the production and distribution of material in domestic and foreign markets. Various domestic regimes evolved for the print and broadcast media, but these activities never fitted comfortably into international trade agreements, in part because of the peculiarities of the modes of organization and contracting and in part because governments wanted to maintain a controlling hand. Over the years frictions developed with respect to trade, investment, intellectual property, and the movement of persons in these industries. During the Uruguay negotiations, the cultural and entertainment industries nearly derailed the completion of an agreement, and in NAFTA special wording was introduced in an attempt to satisfy the three parties. The European Union has also struggled with developing an appropriate framework for cultural activities.

The purpose of this book is to examine these industries, their modes of organization and underlying technology, related domestic policies and their interface with international agreements. By examining the evolution of particular disputes that have arisen between Canada and the United States, we look for lessons and implications for developing an international governance structure for this sector of the economy, one that will be flexible enough to accommodate convergence and the Internet.

The research has been conducted over a decade and has benefited from the input of many people, as we tried to develop an understanding not only of the economics of these industries and the legal intricacies of trade policy but the implications of changing technology that meant that most of what we wrote was continually being dated. We spoke to many people in the industries and in government who helped immensely in increasing our understanding and forcing us to sharpen our arguments. Many of them will not agree with our conclusions, which are ours alone, but we thank them for sharing their knowledge and experience with us.

The research was supported initially by a grant from the Donner Canadian Foundation and subsequently by grants from the Social Science and Humanities Research Council of Canada. We very much appreciate this assistance.

Persons who must be named are Judith van Walsum, Killaine Sharman, and Ginette Harte, all of whom undertook invaluable research assistance at different stages of the project. Elizabet Filleul co-authored articles with us, and Leslie Milton and Stephen Whitehead clarified our understanding of legal issues. All provided insights into our work. Others who provided invaluable input are Judith Alexander, Tom Borcherding, Richard Collins, Roger de la Garde, Michael Dorland, Adam Finn, Fil Fraser, Peter Harcourt, Michael Hart, Colin Hoskins, Gary Hufbauer, Pierre Lalonde, Jorge Uriarte Landa, Roland Lorimer, Stuart McFadyen, Don McRae, Gilles Paquet, Gaetan Tremblay, and Bob Tritt. At Carleton University, we are grateful to Judy Poole and Brenda Sutherland for assisting us in many ways to complete the manuscript. At the University of Michigan Press, Ellen McCarthy guided us through the publication process ably assisted by Alja Kooistra, Mary Meade, and Roxanne Hoch.

Finally we would like to thank our wives and families who doubted that we would ever finish the book and have listened to more about the cultural industries and the arcane details of trade policy than any person reasonably expects to hear in a lifetime.

Abbreviations

ACP	Association of Canadian Publishers
ACTRA	Alliance of Canadian Cinema, Television, and Radio Artists
ADSL	asymmetric digital subscriber line
A&E	Arts & Entertainment
AMA	American Medical Association
ASCM	Agreement on Subsidies and Countervailing Measures
BBC	British Broadcasting Corporation
BBG	Board of Broadcast Governors
BCE	Bell Canada Enterprises
BET	Black Entertainment Television
BPIDP	Book Publishing Industry Development Program
CAB	Canadian Association of Broadcasters
CAC	Consumers Association of Canada
Cancom	Canadian Satellite Communications, Inc.
CBC	Canadian Broadcasting Corporation
CBSC	Canadian Broadcast Standards Council
CCA	capital cost allowance
CFDC	Canadian Film Development Corporation
CFTPA	Canadian Film and Television Producers Association
CIDF	Cultural Industries Development Fund
CMPA	Canadian Magazine Publishers Association
CMPDA	Canadian Motion Pictures Distributors Association
CMRRA	Canadian Musical Reproduction Rights Agency
CMT	Country Music Television
CNBC	Cablevision National Broadcasting Company
CNN	Cable News Network
COE	Council of Europe
CPF	Cable Production Fund
CRTC	Canadian Radio-Television and Telecommunications Commission
CTCPF	Canadian Television and Cable Production Fund
CTF	Canadian Television Fund
CUSFTA	Canada-United States Free Trade Agreement
DBS	direct broadcasting satellite

DCH	Department of Canadian Heritage
DGs	directorates general
DTH	direct-to-home
DVD	digital video disk
EBU	European Broadcasting Union
EC	European Community
EU	European Union
FACTOR	Foundation to Assist Canadian Talent on Records
FCC	Federal Communications Commission
FTC	Federal Trade Commission
GATS	General Agreement on Trade in Services
GATT	General Agreement on Tariffs and Trade
GDP	gross domestic product
GSO	geostationary orbit
HBO	Home Box Office
ICI	International Cablecasting Industries Incorporated
INS	Immigration and Naturalization Service
IRM	international raw materials
ITU	International Telecommunications Union
MAI	Multilateral Agreement on Investment
MEDIA	action program to encourage the development of the European audiovisual industry
MFN	most favored nation
MGM	Metro-Goldwyn-Mayer
MOW	movie of the week
MPA	Motion Picture Association
MPAA	Motion Picture Association of America
MPDEC	Motion Picture Distributors and Exhibitors of Canada
MPEA	Motion Pictures Export Association
MPEAA	Motion Pictures Export Association of America
MPPDA	Motion Picture Producers and Distributors of America
MSO	multiple systems operator
NAB	National Association of Broadcasters
NAFTA	North American Free Trade Agreement
NBC	National Broadcasting Company
NCN	New Country Network
NFB	National Film Board
OECD	Organization for Economic Cooperation and Development
OFRB	Ontario Film Review Board
PBS	Public Broadcasting Service
PCA	Production Code Administration

PICS	Platform for Internet Content Selection
PPV	pay-per-view
PTC	production tax credit
RDI	Réseau de l'information
RIAA	Recording Industry Association of America
ROBTV	Report on Business Television
RTPC	Restrictive Trade Practices Commission
SOCAN	Society of Composers, Authors, and Music Publishers of Canada
TCI	Tele-Communications Inc.
TNN	The Nashville Network
TRIMs	trade-related investment measures
TRIPs	trade-related aspects of intellectual property rights
TWF	television without frontiers
UIP	United International Pictures
UNESCO	United Nations Educational, Scientific, and Cultural Organization
USSB	United States Satellite Broadcasting
USTR	United States Trade Representative
VCR	videocassette recorder
WIPO	World Intellectual Property Organization
WP	Webb Pomerene Act
WTO	World Trade Organization
WWW	World Wide Web

Part I

The Issues and Setting

Part I presents the issues and setting for debate over the international governance structure for the cultural industries. Chapter 1 examines the nature of culture and the opposing views of its significance for and treatment by nation-states. As a result of these views, countries have adopted policies that range from allowing an open flow of cultural goods and services to restrictions on their entry and interventionist measures to support domestic producers and distributors. These differences have led to widespread disagreement on how culture should be treated in international agreements, especially those affecting trade.

Chapter 2 recognizes that this debate is taking place at the same time that technology is rapidly changing the way in which cultural goods and services are produced and distributed. Any agreed upon rules will have to be flexible enough to accommodate future changes such as use of the Internet, satellites, and wireless-cable to transmit content. One aspect of convergence is the way in which different platforms, wireless, cable, telephone, and hard copy formats such as records, books, and tapes are being used to distribute cultural content.

The discussion of possible governance structures is informed by material in the public domain, some of it supplied by official government agencies and some by industry associations and trade publications. Chapter 3 identifies the sources of information, noting both the conceptual difficulties of measuring inputs and outputs and the unsatisfactory nature of the data about the cultural industries published in official sources. The continuing lack of reliable data, which at times appears to be deliberate, impedes the development of satisfactory agreements.

The final two chapters in part I trace the way in which cultural issues arose prior to the General Agreement on Tariffs and Trade (GATT) in 1947 as well as in the context of Europe, regional trade agreements, and the World Trade Organization (WTO). Together these chapters provide background to a discussion of the economic organization of each cultural sector and related policies in Canada in part II and the actual and impending disputes in part III.

CHAPTER 1

Culture and the Cultural Industries

The Diversity of Cultural Policies

In Canadian policy circles, film, radio and television programming, records, books, and magazines are cultural products, and the industries that produce, distribute, exhibit, broadcast, or sell them are the cultural industries. In contrast, Americans, official and otherwise, call these activities—which generate a substantial trade surplus for the United States—the entertainment industries. The choice of words reflects significant differences in domestic policies and political discourses. The United States has relatively open policies toward these activities while Canada has adopted inward-looking protectionist policies. In Canada, the protectionist policies applied to the cultural industries contrast with the increasingly liberal and open policy regimes covering other sectors of the economy.

Over the past 20 years, new technology has made a greater variety of foreign cultural products available over a diverse set of distributional alternatives. Foreign markets and finance have also become increasingly important for most of the cultural industries, particularly for the audiovisual sector. During this period, Canada has maintained the same negotiating position—everything but culture is on the table—at any formal talks concerning regional or international trade policy. In contrast, in its list of trade irritants and in its trade diplomacy generally, the United States has increasingly raised the profile of trade barriers imposed on its cultural products by a number of countries, including Canada. This American diplomatic offensive has been accompanied by actions, undertaken within the present set of international arrangements, that make continuation or extension of current policies by Canada and like-minded countries more costly. The parties at the recent Uruguay round of the GATT negotiations failed to negotiate an accord on audiovisual trade. The signs are clear that addressing the thorny issues raised by trade in cultural products will be a priority in the next round of WTO negotiations.

After listening to the political discourse, not even Pangloss would be optimistic that a mutually acceptable agreement on this topic can be reached by WTO members. Consider the Canadian reaction to one of the recent initiatives by the United States, a complaint registered with the WTO concerning a new prohibitive excise tax on magazine split-runs and postal subsidies granted to Canadian magazines. The decision of the WTO resolution dispute panel and the appellate body together supported the position of the United States in ruling that the new tax and postal subsidy structure contradicted Canada's treaty obligations. Immediately after the panel's decision was released, a front page story in Toronto's *Globe and Mail*,[1] arguably Canada's most influential English-language newspaper, quoted a senior federal official as stating that the U.S. position "is just classic 19th-century white man's burden—they've got to bring us their ways and their language. They'll only be happy when we have drive-by shootings or something." Such emotional and largely incoherent responses, especially from a civil servant, are rare in Canadian federal politics, but they do reveal the passion aroused by cultural policy.

Canada is not alone in this regard. Many countries have adopted inward-looking policies that are publicly justified as an antidote to the cultural effect of the availability and popularity of American cultural products. Among English-speaking countries, Australia is currently a spiritual and policy ally of Canada. For non-English-speaking countries, language both weakens and strengthens public concern with the availability of foreign cultural products. For language-intensive media, the use of a foreign language insulates listeners, readers, and viewers from cultural messages. With books and magazines the insulation is great. With instrumental recordings there is no insulation. In between lie recordings of music with lyrics and film or television programming. Without the key of language, the door to full understanding of the lyrics of a song or the plot of a movie is locked. The more important dialogue is to the media experience, the less attractive to the audience will be content in a foreign language.

There is a flip side to the natural protection provided by language. The images and other qualities of a film may more than compensate for what is lost by dialogue so that a significant foreign audience is attracted to an English-language film or television program. If this experience is repeated, viewers will assimilate some English and blend some English words into their own languages. Such small steps toward the development of a street Esperanto is threatening to some in society. Linguistic nationalists believe that the availability and popularity of English-language shows over a sustained period of time pose a long-term cultural threat to the paramountcy of the local language. For them, language is the sustaining life support system of the national culture and must be protected.

As well as language, a country's policy stance toward foreign cultural products depends on its economic situation, the policies of others, the values and traditions of its citizens, and the internal political resonance of different

---

1. *Globe and Mail,* January 17, 1997, A1.

arguments. Since policy decisions are made by governments, they will also be subject to strategic considerations arising from domestic political concerns. For example, the government may be a dictatorship, as is currently the case in China, and be concerned with liberal democratic themes stressed or taken for granted in imported cultural products. How these effects interact to determine a policy position varies.

Of the non-English-speaking countries, France is at the activist end of the spectrum. The French government's concern with foreign records, films, and television shows embraces both their cultural content and their effect on the national and international role of the French language. In contrast, Japan, Germany, and Mexico are currently in the more open camp with respect to trade in cultural products. The volatility of public opinion and the ease with which a country's policy can change is illustrated by the German and Japanese protectionism of the 1930s. France, Canada, and Australia mainly support protectionist policies for cultural or industrial purposes. Ideology and religion are important additional determinants of cultural imports for some countries. Before the 1959 revolution, about 70 percent of the films shown in Cuba were of American origin. After a period of churning following the revolution, Cuba embraced Marxism-Leninism and joined the Comecon in 1972. Despite this reorientation, about 50 percent of the films shown in Cuba still originated in capitalist countries in 1980 (Colina 1986, 238).

International Governance Alternatives

An international agreement on trade in cultural products can only be successfully negotiated if the underlying situation among the different countries is less polarized than the current rhetorical exchanges. To assess the gap in views, we examine the evolving commercial relations in cultural products between Canada and the United States. The Canadian-American situation is representative of the divide that must be bridged by a set of rules if it is to gain international acceptance.

In parts I and II we examine the logic of the case for Canada's current policies and their actual impact over the past 25 years. More specifically, in the remainder of this chapter we develop a pluralistic framework for examining the connection between the cultural industries, the rich and diverse cultures embraced by most citizens, and the government policies affecting access to content related to this set of cultures. The chapter concludes with a discussion of two stylized perspectives on cultural policy, which we label cultural nationalism and the open access view. Each perspective prescribes a different policy course.

Which of these views receives more weight in guiding policy in countries like Canada is critical for assessing whether trade involving the cultural industries can be integrated into existing international arrangements or will require a formal or informal framework of its own. The cultural nationalism argument supports protectionist policies, but it is more than a simple protectionist plea. Every industry association with which we are familiar would argue for protectionism, using all the rhetorical tools that have been developed over the ages in support of that position. The cultural industries have succeeded in attracting overt political support for clearly protectionist policies whereas other Canadian industries have, by and large, failed to do so. The difference is that the emotional appeal of the cultural nationalist case has been decisive. The discussion of the two perspectives identifies the emotionally appealing aspects of the cultural nationalist arguments and the counterarguments of the alternative open view. Whether on closer examination of the nationalist argument the Canadian electorate will reconsider its support is moot.

A more tangible factor affecting the political assessment is the impact of an integrated set of technological developments on the cultural industries. In chapter 2 we explore these new technologies and argue that they are having and will have a profound effect on the production and delivery of content. Distinctions among media are becoming blurred. The new technologies are making international trade and investment economically more important for these industries. Inward-looking policies that are protective of existing players retard creative responses to these new opportunities. If, as seems likely, inward-looking policies result in retaliation and restricted access to foreign markets for our creative professionals and businesspeople, their participation in cutting edge developments will be reduced. For some Canadian firms, groups, and individuals in the cultural industries, the losses from not having access to foreign markets, capital, and professional opportunities outweigh the gains from protection today. They will generally prefer both open access abroad and protection at home. If this is not sustainable, as we believe it is not, those interests have a commercial incentive to abandon overt support for cultural nationalist policies in return for continuing access to markets abroad.

Clearly showing that an increasing part of Canada's creative community has more to gain from access abroad than protectionism at home would also affect the way in which Canadians not involved in the industry thought about cultural policy. Unfortunately, finding out what is happening in these industries is extremely difficult. It is surprising that for an emotional topic that has generated much heated debate the official data are poor. In chapter 3 we discuss the weaknesses in these data and provide an illustration of how an unsubstantiated assertion—that Canada is the world's second largest exporter of television programming—became a "fact" in the Canadian public debate. It is not that this claim is wrong, although it probably is, but that the data to support it are not available. The absence of comprehensive official data creates an environment in which assertion becomes fact. We spend a chapter on this topic for two reasons. Better information will allow a less emotional examination of what Canadian policies have achieved and at what cost. Second, adoption of an international regime that constrains national cultural policy options for mutual advantage requires decent data for assessing compliance and monitoring its effectiveness.

The measures affecting the cultural industries that have been included in various international agreements are discussed in the last two chapters of part I. To the extent that trade in cultural products represents the international movement of goods, GATT rules have always applied, with some specific exceptions. For whatever reasons, no cultural industry complaints were adjudicated under the old GATT. The ground rules for cultural trade have received more detailed attention in the European Community (EC) and in the North American regional pacts. Countries other than the United States are also linked by a set of bilateral treaties granting national content status and access to subsidized funds for film and television coproductions that meet a number of staffing and financing requirements. In the last decade, the United States has served notice that it will react to discriminatory treatment against its entertainment industries. This agenda was pursued with increased intensity as the United States took bilateral copyright initiatives and participated in negotiating the Canada-United States Free Trade Agreement (CUSFTA) and the North American Free Trade Agreement (NAFTA). It culminated in the WTO agreement, which integrates copyright, investment, and trade concerns within a single agreement. The impact of the WTO on the cultural industries was not clear since the WTO members failed to reach an audiovisual compact. As a result, a number of members did not include that sector in the most favored nation, national treatment, and market access commitments of the WTO's General Agreement on Trade in Services (GATS).

In this book, Canadian policies are explored, not because of their stand-alone importance but because Canada's policies are representative of those of a number of countries. We begin part II with a general discussion of the idiosyncratic economic features of production, distribution, and finance for the cultural industries and how the resulting coordination challenges have been met by private and governmental responses. Both domestic and international policy must be formulated with an understanding of the production and transactional characteristics of these industries. When we began to write this book, we thought that a brief description of the Canadian industries and policies would suffice. We are now convinced that such a concise description would be misleading. The problem for drafting a meaningful and sensible international agreement governing the cultural industries is the proliferation of national subsidies, taxes, licensing, ownership regulations, and detailed regulatory interventions that support the cultural industries in most countries. In chapters 6, 7, 8, and 9, we provide an integrated account of the ways in which Canada's cultural industries are organized, financed, and regulated either by policy or by an agency with discretionary powers. We quantify wherever possible so that the reader can assess the overall importance of the different policies.[2] We also assess the extent to which technological changes are impacting or threaten to impact each sector of the cultural industries. The complexity of policy and the lack of good data combine to make policy anything but transparent.

Parts I and II provide a context for the discussion in part III of a number of disputes, largely between Canada and the United States but also between Canada and the EC, that have recently occurred or are proceeding. These disputes concern: *Sports Illustrated* and policies regarding the tax on split-runs of magazines; Country Music Television (CMT) and the status of American cable networks on the Canadian system; the status of American satellite broadcasting in Canada; the Borders case and foreign participation in book retailing and distribution; neighboring rights, copyright, and blank tape levies; censorship, program classifications, and the V-chip; and film distribution and language dubbing. We conclude in part IV by drawing lessons from these disputes about domestic policy and the alternative structures for an international agreement covering the cultural industries.

In discussing these structures, we argue that in the long run small countries have much to gain by coalescing to bargain for an international set of rules granting reciprocal access. For industries with the economic characteristics of the cultural industries, the go-it-alone option is particularly costly for small countries. That said, small countries will bear considerable costs in transforming their cultural activities along more specialized lines. More importantly, once transformed, small countries are vulnerable to large countries taking advantage of the smaller countries' relatively high cost of exiting the agreement to extract concessions concerning their obligations. An international agreement covering the cultural industries must provide credible safeguards against such contingencies in order to generate support from small countries with lingering doubts about the wisdom of "putting culture on the table."

Culture, National Culture, and Cultural Products

Culture is an elastic word. To us, a culture embodies a group of people engaged in communicating, sharing experiences, and interacting under a mixed structure

---

2. A reader who skips chapter 3 is warned that the numbers used in subsequent chapters are sometimes questionable. They are in our opinion, however, the best available.

of formal rules, values, and uncodified norms of behavior. Rules are interpreted and conflicts resolved by reference to formal and informal institutions within the culture. History matters, and cultures generally thicken over time as a relevant past develops to constrain and inform.

From our perspective, everybody is multicultural in the sense that they are overlays of many separate cultures. An individual's mix of cultures typically embraces many specialized allegiances with very different geographical boundaries. He or she may be born to a Scottish clan and later become a naturalized Canadian, a physicist, and a volunteer for the United Way. Membership may not be a matter of choice, as in the family or clan; require formal acceptance by the relevant group, as in receiving citizenship in an adopted country; be realized by a mixture of degrees and self-proclamation, as in the physics profession; or be chosen, as in charitable work. Of all these cultures only citizenship coincides with national boundaries. Interest in solutions to problems in physics is universal. Charitable works affect the local community, and family matters have an intense impact on a relatively small set of people who may or may not be scattered geographically. Typically, individuals are not only multicultural but local, national, and international in their cultural allegiances.

Competition is ubiquitous among cultures that are open to new members: clubs vie for members, evangelical religions seek converts, and embassies advertise the advantages of immigration. This competition spurs change and accommodation to members' interests, but it can also have a dark side such as the false denigration of rivals. Even those cultures that do not actively recruit new members must compete to remain viable.

The National Culture's Relationship to Other Cultures

A person's nationality imposes obligations, entitlements, values, shared knowledge, a menu of cultural choices, and an environment for making those choices. What nationals know better than foreigners are the sometimes subtle differences within their country and how communication bridges can be built in their presence. A regional accent, an occupation, the schools one went to, and the identity of a hometown generally convey more about a person to another national than to a foreigner. To a foreigner, the variations within the nation are usually not appreciated. From this perspective, and simplifying considerably, national culture has two dimensions: how outsiders see the insiders, often a stereotypical image, and how the insiders see each other, a complex and richer view

One of the most important roles of a national culture is to establish effective rules and norms for direct competition among the cultures operating within the country's borders. The current Canadian "hate" laws, for example, are part of the governance structure of this competition.[3] These laws are reinforced by a tradition of relative civility in public debate. A set of sometimes implicit taxes and subsidies affect the activities of different cultures. These vary from subsidies to finance a regulatory intervention by an association representing low-income individuals to restricting the rights of or banning some collectivities. This regulatory power of the nation-state makes national cultures extremely important for other cultures. It also creates an imperative for the competing cultures to curry the favor of the state to subsidize them or tax their rivals. Since the government may have an incentive to reward groups that have supported it electorally, many countries either have a constitution or norms limiting, but not eliminating, the ability of a government to act opportunistically in this regard.

As in most developed countries, Canada's citizens have highly diverse cultural allegiances, but the nature of that diversity has changed markedly in the past three decades with changing birth rates, patterns of immigration, and improved communications.[4] The country's formal governance institutions are making deliberate attempts to adapt to these changes. At the same time, less formal initiatives of exploration and education about the changing realities are occurring in firms, universities, government bureaucracies, and voluntary organizations throughout the country.

Increasingly the integrative role of national cultures has been augmented by the effects of transnational cultures. Religious allegiances have always represented an organized transnational overlay imposed on national cultures. With modern communications, individuals participate in a dizzying array of transnational cultures and these cultures have become more subtle and complex. The organizational reflection of this development is the emergence of a rich set of institutions, histories, and norms at the international level for inter alia amateur sports, art exhibition, environmental initiatives, bird-watching, and

---

3. See Canadian Human Rights Act, section 13(1); and Criminal Code VIII, section 19.

4. The ethnic and language composition of Canada's major cities has changed markedly over the past 15 years. Forty-two percent of Toronto's population in 1996 was composed of immigrants. Twenty-one percent of Toronto's total population were immigrants who came to Canada in the past 15 years. Immigrants represented over a third of Vancouver's population in 1996 (Statistics Canada, The Daily of November 4, 1997). Between 1971 and 1996, the proportion of people with a mother tongue other than English or French (allophones) increased from 13 percent of the Canadian population to nearly 17 percent. In 1986, nearly 60 percent of Canadians had English as a mother tongue (anglophones) and less than 24 percent had French as a mother tongue (Statistics Canada, The Daily of December 2, 1997).

education as well as for commercial activities such as shipping, telecommunications, and aviation.

Links to the Cultural Industries

What does all this have to do with an animated television series or soap operas? What is the connection among cultures in general, the national culture in particular, and the cultural industries? How do international agreements governing trade and investment in book and magazine publishing, sound recording, film, broadcasting, and cable fit into this cultural matrix?

The cultural industries produce and disseminate images, sounds, and narratives that support and enrich many of the different cultures embraced by individuals. These inputs influence how individuals participate and develop in the cultures to which they are committed—sports, science, music, and so on—and to which cultures they join. Within each household and between households, the same texts, images, and sounds provided by the cultural industries are processed, discussed, and interpreted. Of course, much of an individual's cultural development is stimulated by activities outside the cultural industries as he or she participates in a host of spontaneous family and community events. In some instances, a passive participation with the programming provided by the cultural industries may substitute rather than complement spontaneous and unorganized activities. In short, cultural products are a part of many of our cultural activities. As they become more attractive and cheaper, activities that are intensive in their use become more popular.

People's actions reveal that they believe cultural products influence their development and, perhaps more fervently, that of others. How would someone who did not believe in this connection behave? They would not care what their children read or watched on television. They would not worry that the lyrics of popular songs might influence young listeners. They would not make New Year's resolutions promising to do more of activity X and watch less television. They would have difficulty explaining why any company advertises, except to list the different properties of its product and the price, or why election strategists fight to get their candidate's latest sound bite, but no more, on the evening news. They would not be like most of us.

The debate over cultural policy cannot be understood without recognizing that films, television shows, pop music, books, and magazines are generally viewed as important inputs in the development of people. Unfortunately, there is little agreement on the causal relationships. Casual impressions rule, and behavioral inconsistencies abound. Most parents are not concerned if their teenage son goes to see the local theater's production of *Oedipus Rex*. They do not anticipate that he will return home, marry his mother, kill his father, and, overcome with guilt, tear out his eyes. On the other hand, if the same lad wants to watch a program of which they do not approve, they will often justify a denial based on the program leading to some mixture of drugs, gang membership, and apprenticeship as a serial killer.

An added twist to this theme is that cultural products are crucial to developing a strong national culture as well as affecting individual development. In this view, the national culture is nurtured as a by-product of consuming cultural products. When the individual is not able to consume the right cultural products, the national culture suffers. Suppose that one of an individual's cultures is ballet. In the opinion of a cultural nationalist, it is better that this individual watch the National Ballet of Canada on television than watch the Bolshoi. In the former case, the ballet is presented with a "Canadian sensibility" that in the long run instills a national identity as well as satisfying the aesthetic taste of the viewer. The general message of the cultural nationalists is that foreign product crowds out "national voices telling national stories." The cultural nationalism sentiment is powerful in Canada and in many other countries. Later in this chapter we examine this position in more detail. At this juncture, it suffices to note that there is as little agreement of what the causal link is between cultural product and a national culture as there is between cultural product and an individual's development. There is even less agreement about what a desirable national culture is than what a desirable individual might be.

Cultural policies often reflect both the reasonably widespread concern that access to these products matters for individual development and national identity and the equally widespread differences in opinion as to what should be done, if anything, about either of these concerns. The former consensus means that doing something can garner reasonably widespread political support. The latter feature, the lack of agreement on the details about what products to keep out, increases the chances that groups with a focused view of which cultural products are "appropriate" will disproportionately influence the direction of policy.

There are a number of religious and educational groups that express strong feelings about content in general but, with some exceptions, have had difficulty in mobilizing their memberships in support of specific policies. They are sporadic participants in the public debate. The two types of groups that have had a sustained interest in cultural policy are industry associations and cultural nationalist organizations. The position of industry groups on protection depends on whether members foresee more profit from protection than from being able to invest and sell in foreign markets. Those members that are motivated by commercial considerations obviously prefer both protection and foreign access, but if that is not available they will choose depending on the balance of advantage. An association speaks with a clear voice when there is near unanimity among its members. If most domestic players consider protection superior, the association will lobby for it. Cultural nationalist supporters also favor protection. When the industry and the cultural nationalists' interests are in line their position has considerable weight in determining how cultural policy is shaped. If the interests of the cultural industries begin to change because of technical change and their learning and development over time, that alliance will come under pressure. In Canada, there are emerging signs of conflicting policy interests between some segments of the cultural industries and the cultural nationalists, as the probability of access being restricted abroad rises, in the absence of a change in domestic policy.

The political economy of policy-making is also affected by the government's interest in presenting a favorable image of itself and the national culture under its tutelage. The cultural industries produce a joint product—commercially valuable properties and politically valued output. The political effects are the positive or negative image of the government created as a by-product of developing commercially successful products. The industry is in the position of "trading" favorable images for either policy changes or the cooperation of the government.

Political exchange of this type is ubiquitous. An automobile firm contemplating a large investment in an employment-intensive assembly plant publicly dickers with the different levels of government, which are concerned with unemployment, for a package of tax breaks and subsidies. In a democratic society, the automotive industry is unlikely to become a propaganda wing of the government. That is a possibility with the cultural industries, but subtle changes in "spin" and tiptoeing around the skeletons in the government's closet are more likely.

To gain an understanding of the "terms of trade" between the cultural industries and the government, consider the *Killing Fields,* a film about the efforts of an American reporter to find a Cambodian colleague incarcerated during the Pol Pot era. The scriptwriter, Bruce Robinson, recalls that David Puttnam, the British producer, changed 20 percent of the original script, including additions and cuts intended to "dilute a measure of anti-Americanism in the script" (Yule 1989, 134). Jake Eberts of England's Goldcrest Films, which was heavily involved in the financing of the film, writes that Puttnam "had to change the portrayal of the American Ambassador." In this matter he was under severe pressure from the U.S. State Department, which had been very helpful in securing the cooperation of all the relevant American authorities (Eberts and Ilott 1990, 63). Although a common phenomenon, this type of exchange raises particularly difficult issues when unconscious changes in media coverage occur as the quid for the quo of favorable policy changes.

The Role of the State

There is a wide consensus that the access of children to cultural products should be monitored and controlled. In Canada and the United States, parents are the main gatekeepers. Social and technological developments influence the effective control that can be exercised by a parent. The ability of parents to control the access of children to television is limited by their other responsibilities and by the fact that their children are able to watch shows in other homes. The rise in the number of single-parent homes, and the increasing incidence of both parents in two-parent families working, have made the exercise of parental control more difficult.

On the technology side, the proliferation of channels and the consequent broader fare available on television have exacerbated the parents' problem. On the other hand, technology offers some parental aids. The V-chip is a hardware example, whereby the parent will be able to filter out programming in various categories. Another is subscription television or reliance on videos. A further device is the brand name reputation of particular broadcasters, publishers, or recording companies for making good quality products for children. Another instrument is to make the public broadcaster responsible for producing good children's programming. Many parents have availed themselves of these solutions. The sell-through market for children's movies and television videos, for example, is very active, and specialized children's cable and pay channels have been popular with parents. Private brands are important guides for parents but so are some public initiatives and public brands. Public Broadcasting Service's (PBS) *Sesame Street* was and is a huge success in the United States and internationally. The Canadian Broadcasting Corporation (CBC) also has a reputation for good children's programming. With respect to television content and children, the state's involvement includes mandating aids to a parent in limiting their children's choices, for example, the V-chip initiative, requiring more adult programs to be aired later in the night, and regulating private broadcasters or funding public broadcasters to provide more or better children's programming.

With other media, the control of parents is even more limited. Monitoring what is heard on a Walkman or what magazines are read is not often feasible. Parents rely on their own judgment and a number of other gatekeepers to control as well as they can the access to such cultural products by their children. Supporting mechanisms include laws controlling how sexually explicit magazines are displayed in stores and campaigns to influence record companies to regulate the messages on songs or rap discs.

The state's involvement with content goes beyond parenting aids to measures of censorship and other controls aimed at adults. Censorship boundaries are determined by community values, which change and are fuzzy at best, and the accessibility of the medium. A more permissive array of content is available on videos than on over-the-air television. For societies that value free expression, the existence of censorship and its application have always aroused public debate, usually focused on some example of exclusion or inclusion that is controversial. The V-chip is a self-censoring device, but the rating system that is an integral part of its functioning raises questions of freedom of expression and side effects of the classification system. Censorship can also be a mask for excluding foreign products for industrial policy purposes. In chapter 14 we discuss some international aspects of censorship and the V-chip initiatives.

As well as censorship, some states, like Canada, have introduced quotas and preferences that explicitly discriminate against foreign cultural products. These measures are not conditioned on content but solely on the source of the content. Many of them raise the costs of a Canadian gaining access to foreign content. For example, subscriptions to American magazines in Canada are more expensive than for Canadian periodicals. Others deny legal access to the content. For example, the Home Box Office (HBO) service cannot legally be watched in Canada. Investment controls accompany many of these trade measures.

Almost every country imposes foreign ownership constraints on the cultural industries that are more severe than those generally applied to other sectors. The Canadian controls cover a wider set of cultural activities than those imposed by the United States, which are restricted to over-the-air broadcast outlets. The Canadian restrictions are based on the assumption that ownership by foreigners would result in inappropriate programming for developing an informed and wise citizenry. In the public debate, the quotas, preferences, and ownership rules are always justified in part as culturally, rather than industrially, motivated. An assessment of that controversial link is one of the focuses of this study.

Cultural Nationalism versus the Open Option

Within the constraints set by policy, economic forces determine the qualities and quantities of cultural products consumed and produced. The policy framework is determined politically. In the political process, competition occurs along a number of dimensions. One area of competition is among accounts of what consequences will follow from adopting different policies. Often that competition appears to occur only at the level of exchanging sound bites and slogans at election time. In the longer run, we believe that the contesting of ideas at a more complex level is extremely important.

In this book, we discuss a variety of aspects of cultural policy in detail. As economists we pay attention to scarcity. Changes in cultural policy domestically and internationally will alter what we read, listen to, and watch and what we have to forgo in order to achieve that mix. What makes cultural policy particularly interesting and difficult to assess is that one of the "products" affected is either the reality or the perception of ourselves as individuals and as a part of different communities. This is a production process that economists generally neglect, but it cannot be ignored in this context. To be more concrete about the policy choices, we provide a general account of two polar views on cultural policy, the cultural nationalist perspective and the open alternative. This account includes how each of the two polar views assesses the different policy instruments typically employed in an activist cultural policy.[5]

Cultural Nationalism

Cultural nationalists believe that commercial cultural products made by Canadians differ significantly from those made by foreigners. American shows in particular are commercially driven and corrupting of the soul and sense of communal identity of Canadians. State support is necessary because the costs of Canadian cultural products exceed their value in the marketplace. The necessary implicit or explicit subsidies are a good investment because they are substantially exceeded by the nonmarket value of these products for promoting national identity, unity, and sovereignty as well as creating employment in Canada. The cultural nationalists favor an array of policies to support the displacement of foreign cultural products. These include: federal and provincial subsidies and tax incentives for the production and distribution of film and television programming; the "encouragement" of licensed cable companies to establish additional production funds for Canadian production of audiovisual material; content quotas for broadcasting; the continuous monitoring of television to determine categories of programming that are not sufficiently Canadian in order to initiate "import substitution" policies; the subsidization of postal rates provided to Canadian periodical publishers; limits on foreign ownership and control; and funding to support the Canadian record and book-publishing industries.

There are two official languages in Canada and two major markets for language-intensive media. The French-language market receives more natural protection from American productions for linguistic reasons but requires the same level of per capita support because it is smaller than the English-speaking market. Although there may be differences in the commercial responses to policy, a common policy initiative helps bind the two linguistic communities and contributes to national unity.

---

5. We warn the reader that we find the open view more persuasive. Our purpose here is to present as neutrally as possible the two alternatives, but the reader should know the most likely direction of any unintended bias.

Canadian producers provide an identifiable sensibility in the products they make. It follows that a point system based on the nationality of inputs, the ownership of resources, and the percentage of expenditures made in Canada is a legitimate way of identifying Canadian content for the purposes of subsidy, tax credits, and quotas.

Canadians have to bear the costs of an unnatural advantage held by their American counterparts, who recover the costs of expensive products in their home market and then sell them at low prices in Canada. This dumping prevents Canadian producers from getting a toehold in their own market even with substantial subsidies. Canadian English-language films and television productions are particularly vulnerable to American competition because of the language similarity, but in some media dubbed material reduces the difference between the French- and English-language experience. Subsidization of domestic output and limitations on the entry of foreign product is necessary because of these unfair advantages.

Access of foreign product to the Canadian market must be limited in order to release "shelf space" for Canadian cultural products. Without such shelf space Canadians are denied an opportunity to choose their own products. Canadian protective policies are a measured response to the problem. With them in place, Canada remains among the most open of countries in permitting access to foreign material. Statistics such as those presented by the assistant deputy minister (for cultural development and heritage) of the Department of Canadian Heritage (DCH) in 1997 support that position:

- 70% of the music on Canadian radio stations is foreign in content.
- 60% of all English-language television programming available in Canada is non-Canadian, reflecting the importation of many American channels and programs; 33% of all French-language television programming available in Canada is foreign.
- 70% of the Canadian book market consists of imported books.
- 83% of the Canadian newsstand market for magazines is made up of foreign magazines.
- 84% of retail sales of sound recordings in Canada feature foreign content (including 69% of French-language retail sales).
- 95% of the feature films screened in theaters in Canada are foreign.
- 85% of prime-time English-language drama on Canadian television is foreign, mostly from the United States; 75% of prime-time drama on French-language television originates outside Canada. (Rabinovitch 1998, 30)

Walk into a magazine shop or a megabookstore and one finds a bewildering array of products from every part of the world. All of the major networks in the United States are available through either over-the-air spillovers or cable television. A long list of American cable networks and superstations are also available on Canadian cable. Geography and technology result in a deluge of American media products. American distributors in the various media are biased against foreign productions, so the flow is one way. Whereas American distributors operate in both countries, they apply a set of blinkers to a rich menu of Canadian materials and distribute product with no sensitivity to Canadian differences. To them, Canada is the fifty-first state.

Without the various policies in place for television, cable, and book and magazine publishing, the situation in these industries would be similar to that of film distribution. In film, there are subsidies but no special policies to reduce the overwhelming flow of American product. As a result, Canadian films are invisible.

Ensuring access requires that the means of distribution be Canadian owned. The cultural nationalist approves of the set of foreign ownership and in some cases control restrictions on book and periodical publishing, book retailing, film distribution, recording, broadcasting, and eligibility of advertising in certain media for tax deductions. Canadian products have a special national sensitivity and Canadian distributors have a special sensitivity to that fact. If foreign firms are active in an area of the cultural industries in Canada and a Canadian firm is prepared to offer the service, the foreign firm should be evicted.

The ultimate defense against foreign ownership is Canadian public ownership. Public ownership involves the community and preserves a public space that enhances the quality of Canadian life and public debate. The CBC and various public provincial educational channels are examples of corporations dedicated to producing and delivering Canadian programming. As public broadcasters they will not be tempted to sell out their mandate for short-term profit from showing popular American programs. The other direct government presence in the cultural industries is the National Film Board (NFB), a producer of mainly documentary films funded by the federal government. The CBC and the NFB are cultural icons that are untouchable.

With respect to international trade arrangements, the Canadian nationalists support exempting culture from the domain of comprehensive agreements. If trade has to occur, the cultural nationalists support the nexus of mostly bilateral coproduction treaties negotiated with a number of countries. These agreements grant Canadian status for the purposes of quota, subsidy, and tax policies to coproductions between the partners. They properly regulate the personnel decisions and financing arrangements that are necessary for qualification.

The Open Option

In contrast, the open position maintains that the control of content should rest on the shoulders of individuals and groups. There is no justification for the government to influence the content menu with the exception of censorship laws, in particular those aimed at protecting children. The personal development of individuals depends on their becoming informed through their associations with different communities and by exercising responsibility.

It is a myth that there are stories of interest to all Canadians and to no one beyond Canada's borders. A well-written Canadian story with interesting relations, a strong plot, and good dramatic values will be of interest to many, but not all, Canadians and to a significant audience abroad. International programming "travels" not because it mentions the main street of every city in the world but because of a strong story line, tight production, and themes that relate to a diverse set of people. In the mass market television drama category, *Anne of Green Gables* provides a good example. The story is Canadian in its setting and characters, Avonlea being a thinly disguised Cavendish, Prince Edward Island, but universal in its themes. The television series based on Lucy Maud Montgomery's books and produced in Canada has sold widely in many countries. Japanese women in particular relate to the fictional Anne's *gambaru,* or pluck, and her free spirit. Consequently, a large number of Japanese tourists now travel to Prince Edward Island to see the various sites connected with both Montgomery's and the fictional Anne's life. Japanese couples may purchase a symbolic marriage conducted by a United Church of Canada minister followed by a horse and buggy ride around the Lake of Shining Waters (Trilling 1996).

Anne of Green Gables is not an exception. Canadian producers of television programming are selling series, movies of the week, and children's programming successfully in Canada and abroad. In children's animation, *Madeline, Babar, the Richard Scarry Stories, TinTin, The Little Lulu Story, Beetlejuice, Paddington Bear, Rupert,* and *Franklin* are among the many successful Canadian animated series that are selling, or have recently been sold, to Canadian and foreign buyers. The international success of Canadian recording artists—Bryan Adams, Céline Dion, Joni Mitchell, Anne Murray, Shania Twain, k.d. lang, Alanis Morissette, Robert Charlebois, Dianne Dufresne, and Roch Voisine—and authors—Margaret Atwood, Timothy Findlay, Mavis Gallant, Alice Munro, Michael Ondaatje, Mordecai Richler, Carole Shields, Anne Hébert, Roch Carrier, and Michel Tremblay—confirms that the works of Canada's creative community enjoy impressive support from abroad.[6]

---

6. The lists are incomplete and are intended only as indicators of international success.

Canadian content restrictions have done little to generate national unity. Indeed, they have accentuated the French-English divide. Rather than building bridges between the two linguistic solitudes of Canada, the CBC runs distinct and insular broadcasting operations in each language. Subsidy programs are typically split in a fixed ratio among French and English projects regardless of the merit of submissions. Other linguistic and ethnic communities in Canada are assured that Canada is a multicultural society but are shortchanged in discretionary allocations of funds and licensing decisions.

The plea for "Canadian stories told by Canadian voices" is an emotional wrapping for an industrial policy. The points system for determining Canadian content has nothing to do with content and everything to do with the nationality of the personnel and the owners of capital and where money is spent. The incentives are perverse given the ostensible goals of cultural policy. By producing international content with the requisite points, Canadian producers receive subsidies and favorable access to broadcasting in Canada and the possibility of substantial international sales. Typical of films judged to be Canadian by the points criterion is *Prom Night,* starring Jamie Lee Curtis, which is set in an American town but garnered sufficient points to be classified as Canadian. The climatic scene, in which the villain of the piece is beheaded, occurs at the high school prom and is staged in a Canadian building decked out as Alexander Hamilton High.

The rigidity of the points system, particularly when the producer has to adjust to a key player suddenly leaving the production team, raises costs and offsets part of the subsidy. The system invites deception and nominal sharing of key positions to acquire the requisite points.

There is no lack of "shelf space" for Canadian audiovisual material. Multiple radio and television channels, a comprehensive video distribution system, and pay-per-view (PPV) mechanisms provide space for Canadian programs and films inside and outside a rapidly expanding broadcasting system. Canadians are posting content and participating in multimedia dialogue through the unplanned, largely unregulated, and rapidly expanding Internet. Federal and provincial public broadcasters are there to serve any neglected programming segment of the Canadian market. That they carry old foreign movies or sporting events indicates that the failure is not in the availability of shelf space but in the scarcity of good audiovisual content to put on them.

Indiscriminate subsidies of all projects passing the point system test is wasteful. Subsidies should be targeted directly on content that is valued by the community and is not currently being provided by the public institutions with a mandate to fill this gap. Public funds are scarce. Money spent on telling stories reinforcing Canadians' sense of civility and mutual concern might be better spent directly on those goals. A disproportionate number of the "Canadian" movies supported by tax shelters and subsidies involve a small set of Canadian actors and directors, many of whom spend a portion of the year in Los Angeles. Some of the effect of the subsidies is increased production, but another part is reflected in rising incomes for critical Canadian inputs in inelastic supply. These are often individuals who are already established in the international industry. Nor is the current environment supportive of commercial creativity in the long run. Too much time and effort are diverted to manipulating and preserving the system rather than producing better product.

It is not credible that Americans who are buying foreign cars and other goods in unprecedented numbers have formed an implicit conspiracy not to consume foreign cultural products. If existing cultural product distributors fail to respond to favorable trading opportunities, new entrants will take advantage of their oversight. The American cable networks have successfully attracted market share from the traditional networks with program schedules that include much more foreign content. Part of the response of the traditional networks has been to develop new relations with foreign producers and explore joint ventures with them. These actions and responses have resulted in rising imports from other countries, including Canada. There is no question that the American film and television industry has been extremely successful domestically and internationally despite the protectionist policies of many countries (Acheson and Maule 1994c). Over half of the revenue earned by a typical studio film is derived from foreign countries. The importance of access to foreign markets is even greater for a country with a small domestic market than it is for the United States.

The charge of dumping by American distributors in foreign markets reflects a misunderstanding of how cultural products are financed and priced. In film financing, for example, the producer assesses all the markets for programming rights—domestic and foreign markets, theatrical, first-run television, pay television, syndication or second-run markets, video, and cross marketing of merchandising—in establishing a financing and marketing plan. Some of these rights are presold to distributors or directly to the end user. The challenge to the producer is to presell only those rights necessary to finance the production and keep as many rights unencumbered as possible. These can be commercially exploited at the most opportune time. The costs of serving any rights are low and establish the reservation price of the producer for those rights. The price that the producer can obtain depends on this reservation price and the demand price of buyers in that market. Clearly the producer attempts to obtain as much for these rights as possible and on average must obtain more than would have been obtainable from a presale of the same rights.

Licensing prices for different areas reflect the size and value of the viewing market. Consequently the price of Canadian rights for an American-produced program is less than that of the American rights. Similarly, the Bermuda rights for a Canadian-made program typically earn a producer less than the Canadian rights. In neither case is the difference in price evidence of dumping.

In arguing their case, Canadian nationalists choose figures that create an impression of cultural dependence resulting from a system that makes Canadian creative and commercial efforts impotent. The government has implicitly colluded with the nationalist position, which is supportive of official rationales for those policies, by not producing better statistics and obscuring what the available statistics reveal. Statistics on foreign penetration are given with no sense of what is a reasonable benchmark against which to compare Canadian performance. The unsuspecting listener to the usual litany of numbers might assume that a 100 percent figure for the Canadian share is desirable. This is clearly a silly target. If Canadian policy succeeded in making culturally Canadian, as compared to industrially Canadian, 100 percent of the books sold, there would be no literature from the seventeenth, eighteenth, or two-thirds of the nineteenth century, not to mention the classical period. Such parochialism is hardly conducive to the development of an attractive national identity. For internationally traded product, Canada's relative size in the particular market is a more revealing benchmark than 100 percent. For some cultural products, like English-language feature films, the proportion of world revenue generated by Canadian cinemas relative to that generated by cinemas in the rest of the world is very low. Measured against that origin, the performance of Canada's creators and producers is something to celebrate rather than deprecate.

Foreign ownership policies are counterproductive, as there is no evidence that there is a systematic connection between ownership and content. Canadian ownership of Cineplex-Odeon, a significant exhibitor of films in Canada, has not led to an appreciable increase in the number of Canadian films appearing on Canadian screens. Similarly, the fact that Universal, a major Hollywood studio, is now owned by Seagram, a Canadian company, is unlikely to alter the "nationality" of its output. Japanese ownership of Columbia and formerly of Universal has not resulted in a series of films reflecting a Japanese sensibility. While it was recovering from bankruptcy, Metro-Goldwyn-Mayer (MGM) was owned by a French bank but operated as before. Rupert Murdoch, an Australian, has not changed the scheduled output of Fox, which is owned by the Murdoch-controlled News Corp., to the interesting but quirky films typical of Australia. The causation in this case was clearly in the other direction. To meet American ownership restrictions in broadcasting Murdoch became an American. For a small growing country to impose ownership controls in this area reflects a victory of emotion over economic logic and the evidence.

Canada's policy of exempting trade in cultural products from the CUSFTA, the NAFTA, and the WTO was a mistake. First, it is not clear that Canada's negotiators achieved that objective. Second, to the extent that they did the policy puts disputes about policy between Canada and other countries into the law of the jungle rather than the negotiated rules of an international agreement. An escalating number of disputes between Canada and the United States or Europe, which are explored in part III, have been initiated or threatened. As the process of dealing with each of these disputes reaches a conclusion, either Canadian policy will be altered or access to foreign markets will be restricted. If the latter, Canadian consumers will face higher prices or taxes and less desirable choices and Canadian producers will have more restricted opportunities.

Conclusion

The credibility of these two views is affected by technology and the ability to assess and judge the current situation. In the next chapter we address the impact of significant technological innovations affecting both the production of content and its dissemination. In chapter 3 the statistical numbers are addressed in a more thorough and less rhetorical manner than in either of the two views just outlined. How international agreements have dealt with the cultural industries to date, discussed in chapters 4 and 5, has been influenced by the relative valence of these two perspectives in the past. Judging how the changing technological base and an appropriate economic framework alter the persuasiveness of the two views is critical for predicting the possibilities for future international agreements governing the cultural industries.

CHAPTER 2

The Changing Technological Setting

The organizational and contractual dynamics of the cultural industries and the evolution of its policy structure cannot be understood without a general knowledge of the technological forces affecting the industry. From the printing press to direct satellite broadcasts, technological changes have created new opportunities for presenting and communicating content. Innovations in distribution have also expanded the demand for content. Both production and distribution generate a demand for specialized equipment by producers and consumers and for specialized training and learning by employees. Difficult transitional challenges and redistributions have often accompanied the reaction to these opportunities.

The boundaries of the traditional cultural industries are defined by their originating technology. The publishing industries imprint content on paper, bind it, and distribute copies through stores or lending libraries. Radio began as the dissemination of sound information inserted through modulation on a carrier wave. Records provided a fixation of sound information that could be played back at the convenience of the listener. Film creates a technological illusion of continuity from a set of still pictures. Television is a complex extension of the principles of radio and film. The commitment of the consumer in each case also varies. Records and radio can provide a background space, while film and television require greater attention.

In part II, we examine the significance of the economic characteristics of the cultural industries on their organization and finance and on government policy and the legal environment in Canada. The mix of Canadian policies is unique and such policies differ considerably from their American counterparts. The differences in the contractual and organizational structure are more similar. In each country, the technological base is similar.

Known and emerging technologies affect organization through their impact on the costs of organization and contracting. The nonrivalrous nature of content is one constant over time, but other economically relevant characteristics of content and those of the media through which content is delivered to consumers vary with different technologies. For example, the durability of books and records coupled with the exhaustion principle reduce the ability of copyright holders to earn money and affect the activities of rental outlets, secondhand markets, and lending libraries. As a consequence, copyright holders lobby for legal barriers to these activities or compensating remuneration. The situation also elicits private responses such as price discrimination by booksellers between bookstores and libraries. The technological developments that we discuss in this chapter are altering and will alter these economic characteristics of the cultural industries and induce new public and private organizational responses. Our focus in this chapter is on the nature of the new technological developments, their ability to spawn new ways of presenting content, and their impact on the costs of extending distribution internationally.

Technology is permissive, not determinative. What happens in private institutions depends on the energy and initiative of individuals and on the wisdom embodied in the organizational structures within which they interact. Similarly, policies depend on the quality of the people attracted into government service and on the wisdom embodied in political decision-making processes. Policy determination differs in each society, but democratically based processes share many features. One is the importance of the interplay of affected parties in providing information and influencing policymakers. In most industries, suppliers create an association, which hires public affairs and other professionals. These associations both act behind the scenes to provide detailed advice on legislation and policy and act publicly through sound bites and slogans to influence political opinion.

In contrast to most industries, the everyday activities of the cultural industries crucially affect electoral prospects. The steel industry cannot enhance the probabilities of the government's reelection by altering the composition of its steel, but the cultural industries can do so by changing its selection of issues and the way they are reported. Modern governments "lobby" the cultural industries as intensely as the industries lobby it. For this reason, the cultural industries' pressure groups have a competitive advantage over those of other industries in influencing policy and public opinion.

The objectives of the different stakeholders in the cultural industries—owners, content providers, skilled workers, and hardware suppliers—are sometimes in harmony and sometimes not. When a uniformity of interest exists among the cultural industries one expects policy to be particularly industry friendly. In contrast, policy issues that arise when new technologies threaten rather than complement older ones create discord among the different interests within the sector and generate particularly intense and divisive domestic and international debates. Whether policy becomes supportive of or opposed to beneficial change depends to a great degree on how the various groups in the industry assess the impact. By creating alternative sources of content and means of distribution, technological innovation also makes collusion between the government and dominant elements of the cultural industries more difficult and less rewarding.[1]

Technological Innovations

A Capsule Account of the Traditional Industries

Publishing

Each of the traditional media has experienced continual developments and improvements in quality as a result of computer technology. In publishing, this technology has significantly reduced the costs of preparing material for printing. The process begins with a transformation of the information into a digital format. The American Standard Code for Information Interchange (ASCII) code provides a widely recognized means of representing letters, numbers and standard symbols in binary codes. The functions of editing, formatting, and typesetting are done on computers and require less expertise than before. Increasingly these functions are migrating to the author from the publisher. Printing has become more decentralized, and the relative advantage of in-house printing rather than contracting out has shifted. Many users of information prefer to obtain material in electronic form and do their own printing. For example, complex business forms that once were bought from specialized producers are now often developed and printed in-house or filled out electronically on workstations.

Radio

The quality and fidelity of radio signals have been improved, as has the ability of receivers to lock onto signals and filter out noise. The FM band of frequencies has been developed, and slots on it are now more valuable than on the original AM band. Analogue radio signals still dominate, but the introduction of terrestrial digital radio broadcasting is proceeding as standards are set and ground rules developed. In the 1990s, satellites deliver scrambled radio signals directly to subscribers or indirectly through cable systems. Scrambling turns broadcasts into narrowcasts. Car radios and miniaturized portables have taken the radio out of the living room and onto the roads, sidewalks, and jogging

---

1. The impact of changing technology on trade is being studied by a number of organizations, including the WTO. See World Trade Organization (1998).

paths. The peripatetic habits of many radio listeners pose a difficulty for subscription radio that is much less pronounced for subscription television. Correspondingly, subscription radio has not had the same impact as subscription television.

Sound Recording

The fragile 78 rpm or more robust 33 and 45 rpm recordings of the 1950s are now found in garage sales or the homes of collectors. A listener no longer has to cope with the mysteries of cartridges, needles, and scratched vinyl, as lasers read digital sound information encoded on the surface contours of compact discs. Compact discs offer a robustness, portability, and flexibility that was absent in the older technologies. Just over a decade after the introduction of the compact disc, the minidisc and digital compact cassette have also entered the market. The digitalization of sound adds new editing and mixing possibilities. For reproduction or as a medium for carrying original content, digital audio tapes outperform their analogue predecessors. The modern sound system continues to have analogue components. For example, the digital information from the compact disc is transferred to the amplifier, which converts it into analogue signals that are sent to the speakers.

Film

Developments in cameras and their mobility have continuously extended the options of cinematographers. Sound was added to films in the late 1920s, and color was first introduced on a commercial basis in the 1930s. Improvements in sound and color techniques continued after their introduction. More recently, the special effects departments of movie and television programming studios have been revolutionized by the advent of digital content. The producers of animated television series and feature films are increasingly dependent on computer techniques, and some shows are almost totally created by means of them. What was a labor-intensive activity is becoming computer and software intensive, with considerable implications for international trade related to production.

Distribution and exhibition have also evolved. Multiplex cinemas, often integrated into suburban malls or downtown office complexes, have replaced many of the palatial cinemas of the pre–World War II period. This current standard of commercial exhibition is flanked, at one end of the spectrum, by expensive IMAX theaters, which offer higher resolution and a three-dimensional effect, and, at the other end, by the videocassette recorder (VCR), which has transformed living rooms into household cinemas. Many technical innovations require the refitting of cinemas. Currently, many theaters have been or are being modified for digital sound, which surrounds the moviegoer.[2] The video rental store has become as ubiquitous as the corner convenience store. In some cases, the two have merged. As well, home video libraries have expanded, particularly in households with children. Currently, digital video disc (DVD) players, which can display a film over standard and advanced television sets (in a different aspect ratio), are beginning their product cycles in North American markets.

Television

In many homes, color television sets have either replaced or banished the original black and white ones to the guest room. Better pictures and stereophonic sound are received on larger, brighter, and flatter screens. Cable and satellite systems have significantly extended the domain and quality of reception and the variety of offerings. They have also altered the commercial base for financing television by adding subscription fees to advertising revenue and public grants. The capacity of these systems has steadily risen and promises to increase at a more rapid rate in the near future. Advanced digital television sets with much higher definition, more eye-pleasing aspect ratios, and more intelligence are beginning their product cycle. Currently, we are on the threshold of the digitalization of traditional over-the-air television. Compressed digitalized signals will eventually economize the spectrum. The bandwidth of a single analogue television channel will carry five or six compressed digital channels. Digital television will also offer enhanced signals with a much improved picture. On the production side, digital techniques in both the television and film industries make the editing and adaptation of content easier.

A simple convergence of television and film has already occurred in the use of television sets as the screen when a videocassette or disc is shown. Another manifestation of convergence is the rising popularity of pay movie channels and PPV services provided by cable and the new satellite broadcasters.

Despite these examples of convergence, the above changes have generally occurred within the boundaries of publishing, recorded music, film, and broadcasting. The common digital base of many of these innovations indicates that the blurring of the divisions among the traditional media will accelerate. The common digital form of content encourages the development of new,

---

2. These changes have not been universally welcomed. In commenting on surround sound, Michael Posner, the arts reporter of the *Globe and Mail,* wrote: "Thanks to the wonders of modern science, you no longer have to leave home to lose your hearing" (October 3, 1998, C6).

multimedia communications, which combine text, sound, and image in novel ways. Digitalization allows all content to be more easily adapted to different linguistic and cultural markets. Behind the scenes there is more conversion than meets the consumer's eye. For example, the book trade seems distinct from television because of the difference between how the user consumes a novel and a television show, but below the surface there is much that is similar. Before embedding the content in a medium, both industries depend on the digitalization of content and its transfer along electronic networks. In one context, the on-off signals represent text, while in the other they represent pictures and sound. In both cases, there is much greater flexibility and economy in adapting the content to different markets and in transporting the content to local printing and broadcasting entities. That has already happened.

A conversion that is more visible to the public looms, as the means of presenting and delivering the content over the last stage are affected, for example, when text becomes more frequently delivered on an electronic palette than on paper. In addition to the development of different stand-alone readers of musical, text, and visual content, much innovation is occurring on traditional and new communications networks.

Convergence in Communications Networks

Greater Capacity

Electronic and optical innovations have broadened the channels along which information can be transmitted on a communications network. Fiber optic cables carry more information, by a very large factor, than coaxial cable, which in turn dominates the copper wire local loop of a traditional telephone system. These advances in the capacity of physical linkages have been accompanied by rapid development in wireless connections. Wireless and physical links are close but not perfect substitutes. The comparative advantage of one or the other depends on the circumstances, and most networks are a mix of the two. Terrestrial microwave and cellular technology coupled with the use of satellites as a base for redirecting microwave signals back to earth have become an integral part of delivery systems. The introduction of lasers, fiber, and optical readers into parts of the system creates the need, and an associated cost, of conversion from optical to electronic mode, or the other way around, at the relevant boundaries.

Increasingly the informational content of pictures, sound, computer programs, and data are transformed and transmitted as a set of binary signals. Digitalization of content has been accompanied by means of compressing the quantity of binary bits required to represent content. Compression includes both reducing the amount of information transmitted and the number of binary bits necessary to transmit a given amount of information. The former is done by intelligent sampling. The latter requires more compact code and the identification and transmission of only the incremental change from one frame to another. With sampling, image quality deteriorates as the information transmitted is reduced. Determining the size of the sample requires assessing a tradeoff between required bandwidth and quality.

With digital signals, the condensed bits of information representing content can be grouped into packets. The packets from different content sources can be mixed and delivered along different routes. Computers "read" the network and calculate the least congested way to send the packets from their current location to the destination. Along parts of the path, the digitalized information may be transmitted electronically, while at others it will be converted and transmitted in optical form. Optical signals are not subject to the interference problems experienced by microwave or coaxial carriage. At the nodes of the network, packet switchers redirect the components along the appropriate outgoing connections. At the final destination, all the packets from a given message, which may have taken different routes, are gathered and put back in order. Digitalization, compression, and packet switching have had and will have an extraordinary effect on communication capacity because they improve all of the elements in the networks, not just the new ones.

To appreciate the joint impact of the increase in the size of the new "pipes" and the developments associated with digitalization and compression, which affect all transmission media, imagine the effect on traffic congestion of a dramatic increase in the size of new highways combined with an equally dramatic shrinking of all vehicles. Further imagine that some clever transportation engineer notices that there are still gaps between the vehicles on the road. He or she develops a method of deconstructing the vehicles into fenders, motors, and the like. With an identifier attached, the pieces are packed in the most compact way. Traffic now consists of a constant flow of components. Network benefits are then exploited by sending the pieces of the vehicle along different routes to their destination, where they are reassembled. Unlike present traffic flows, but like a modern, unmanned, urban transportation system, decision making does not occur in the vehicle, or its parts, but at the nodes of the network.

The Emergence of the Internet

The mail, telegraph, and telephone systems were the pioneering communications networks for exchanging information. The systems vary in the immediacy of the interaction among users. They are substitutes in some dimensions and complements in others. The telephone system has largely absorbed the telegraph system and is increasingly intruding into the turf of the mail system. It has spawned a telecommunications system that is commercially the most important of the three. An interconnected dynamic of falling usage prices, rising density of subscriptions within an area, and the geographic linking of a wider and wider set of terminal apparatuses has resulted in universal telecommunications service in many developed countries. National telephone systems have always been interconnected. The boundaries between national telecommunications systems are increasingly notional rather than physical.

The nature of usage along any network is affected by the level and structure of prices. Today, e-mail, which does not charge by the word, is a medium for text "conversations," a popular use that never developed on the telegraph system, which charged by the word. Capacity has increased on the specialized cable and telephone networks, and a wider range of services are offered. Telephone systems, for example, now carry both text and pictures from fax to fax and masses of data and other information among computers.

These extensions of traditional services only absorb a fraction of the capacity and intelligence of a modern communications network. New uses are being explored with profound possibilities for altering the way we communicate, shop, organize business and finance, and distribute information and cultural products. The capacity and intelligence of the network available to provide services germane to the cultural industries will depend on the total value created by digital communications for all of these activities. We are in a period of experimentation. It is almost certain that some initiatives will not fulfill the hopes that launched them while others, which appeared marginal at their inception, will turn out to be important.

One of the important new developments for the cultural industries is the Internet/World Wide Web (WWW; we will use the term Internet for both), an international network of interconnected computers and computer networks that is also connected to telephone and cable networks. The unique management system of the Internet has provided an ordered environment for experimentation and international participation in communications. A key aspect of this environment is the set of software, standards, and protocols that permits computers and computer networks with different operating systems to communicate. The Internet is comprised of a rapidly rising number of member computer networks. Traffic among them travels along a system of leased lines and backbone communications corridors and is directed by a set of router computers situated at key nodes in the system.

Currently, charges paid by the connected computer sites on the Internet and various public funds support its operation. As the system becomes more complex, diverse means of adding value and charging users are being considered. System and hardware evolution are overseen by an idiosyncratic set of committees and processes (Comer 1995). Behind the seeming anarchy of the Internet is a complex software, a set of rules allowing that software to facilitate the seamless interaction of different operating systems, high-capacity backbones, and a sophisticated packet-switching architecture.

Access to the current Internet is available from the computers on member networks. On-line services, such as the internationally available versions of services such as America Online and the regional services offered by telephone, cable, nonprofit freenets, and independent companies, provide entry to the Internet for any member of the public who subscribes. A member network provides visitors from other Internet sites access to specific parts of their networks.

The Internet supports a number of services: e-mail communications, bulletin boards, newsgroups, file transfers, search engines, and discretionary linkages. The World Wide Web refers to the collection of Internet sites that post material in formats readable by graphic web browsers. The content can be text, images, audio, video, or a mix of the four. It may also be stored or created in real time. The material is transmitted from the site being visited to the computer screen of the initiating searcher. The searcher can read, view, or listen to the content or download components for subsequent editing, playing, or printing. The target site will typically have a number of hyperlinks, or "hot buttons," which will, if initialized, transfer the user to other files at the same location or to other locations. The experience is interactive and responsive to the purposes of the particular searcher.

At this early stage in the evolution of the WWW, the capacity of the typical personal computer modem and the telephone lines that connect many of the users to the system limit the information that can be effectively transferred. Video requires a very large number of bits of information. Currently, even with a high-end personal computer, video clips are small and jerky. Sound requires less bandwidth, and so a crude but reasonable form of radio broadcasting, songs, and telephone conversations are currently feasible. The Internet provides effective distribution for an increasing array of text and images provided by businesses, associations, groups, governments, and individuals.

If sufficient bandwidth can be efficiently brought to the home, the Internet will be able to provide video on demand, live and taped television shows, recorded music, and an array of print material. There will be much greater flexibility of timing for viewing, as content can either be called on demand or downloaded, stored, and viewed when convenient. If similar content is provided through both the Internet and traditional routes, viewers will migrate to the less regulated media.

Broadband to the Home: Cable, Telephone,
and Other Responses

A number of technical solutions of the remaining barrier to extending broadband capacity to the home are being explored. Cable systems have an advantage in already having hybrid coaxial and fiber systems with broadband capacity passing near the homes and offices of most urban residents. Where these systems have been upgraded, at considerable cost, to carry two-way traffic, their cable modem services provide superior connections to the Internet. With compression techniques, cable systems that have been upgraded will be able to deliver hundreds of channels of information. By repeating their movie transmissions with different timing they can offer a close substitute for video on demand.

Telephone companies and others have been making substantial progress in developing hardware and software means of upgrading the capacity of the traditional copper loops that join customers to central offices. The best developed system is the asymmetric digital subscriber line (ADSL) service, which reportedly will be able to deliver video on demand. Technological improvements continue to increase the length of local loops to which it can be applied. The quality of cable modem service is sensitive to the traffic on the cable system since all the signals are pooled in one large pipe. ADSL works with the largely dedicated capacity of the local loop and is not vulnerable to crowding. Another solution is for the telephone companies to replace local loops with shared pipes to neighborhoods. Each house would be connected to the pipe by a wireless broadband connection.

A solution independent of the current networks is the development of a wireless broadband network capable of delivering broadcasting or two-way connections to the Internet. A local multipoint communications service network can move information at 10 megabytes per second, 350 times faster than current telephone modems.[3] Terrestrial cellular systems are and will be complemented by international systems based on satellite communications. Iridium, an international project led by Motorola, uses 66 satellites as the backbone of a global cellular network. The new-style satellite broadcasters are having a significant impact on the PPV and movie channel business, but without two-way capability they can only provide part of a modem system. The other parts of the system would be supplied or leased from existing carriers.

Terrestrial broadband wireless networks may provide additional competition for existing cable companies or telephone companies in their traditional business

---

3. Three companies have been awarded licenses to operate local multipoint communications systems in 66 larger markets across Canada as well as in 127 rural communities.

as well as in connecting to the Internet. One viable technology is the multichannel, multipoint, distribution service, which covers an area with signals beamed from towers or the tops of tall buildings. A signal similar to those of digital satellite broadcasting systems is received with a small antenna. The weakness of the system is that not all homes are covered. The wireless systems are cheaper to build than wired alternatives. They may even be cheaper than upgrading the wired systems. In total, very large investments will be required to transform existing delivery systems or create alternatives.

Access to and Regulation of the Internet

Arranging the financing of these investments raises the issue of the terms of access to the Internet. The ability to charge for access is always potentially beneficial for public or commercial providers. The option may not be exercised. Even if a charge is feasible and more than covers the costs attributable to the service, a commercial provider may decide to "give" the service away. The increase in profits of other services caused by the increase in subscriptions to the "free" service more than compensates for the lost profit due to not charging. Commercial concerns almost always leave some dimension of their service uncharged. Restaurants do not typically charge for water or utensils, although both enhance the value of a meal. There is no technical or legal reason for not doing so. It is just deemed not to be good business.

Although pricing structures are complicated and contain many "free" dimensions, the ability to charge is crucial for the viability of commercial providers. For entities that cannot depend on the public purse, charges or imputed benefits must at least cover their costs. If commercial users are to pay for the infrastructure of the Internet, charges will have to cover their operating and infrastructure costs.

Complete reliance on commercial provision may be deemed by the government to be inefficient or unfair. It may provide the service directly or subsidize private suppliers. In the first case, the government must decide on the mix of taxpayer or user finance. In the second, it must decide on both the extent of the subsidy and the conditions imposed on access to the subsidized facilities. Alternatively, the government may subsidize the access of selected groups—for example, students—through commercial services or provide public gateways through terminals at libraries and schools. It may also limit or regulate the ability to build commercial fences around information in order to make it more widely available. To protect children, the government may want to build some fences of its own. Pornographic or hate literature sites may be prohibited or access restricted. The technology of the Internet, broadly conceived, is sufficiently flexible to permit fences, or partial fences, to be built or removed.

Caution in regulating the Internet is warranted given its rapid rise and its encouragement of decentralized experimentation. National content regulation will be difficult to implement and make effective because of the Internet's international character. In any case, national regulation is likely to spawn international repercussions. From its own governance structure to its architecture, the Internet is an extremely open system. Content in any language and with an infinite variety of spin is available. This openness and its popularity provide a deep challenge to the inward-looking cultural policies of Canada and many other countries.

Impact on the Traditional Cultural Industries

Songs can be down loaded from the Internet and played on a home computer with a sound card and attached speakers. Radio broadcasts can also be accessed over the Internet, and there have been experiments to offer a crude form of television programming. Small-dimension video clips are now standard fare on Internet sites and on the interfaces of some on-line services.

The 500 channel cable universe and the ability of ADSL to provide video on demand stand out as two of the few aspects of the current technological revolution for which reality has lagged behind expectations. Their realization or the maturing of satellite broadcasting will potentially have a dramatic effect on the movie and broadcast businesses. The ability of these systems to provide effective video on demand and broadband links to the Internet depends not only on the capacity of these systems but on the ability to provide an intelligence that curbs piracy of signals and copyrighted material and ensures security of payment.

Publishing is also being affected. All the regional variations of magazines or newspapers can be made available on the Internet or an on-line service. The Internet user can unbundle different magazines and download a portfolio of articles on a given subject. If the reader is pressed for time, intermediary services will find and download to his or her computer all articles covering a specified topic. News services are commonly available that search the Internet for articles on topics specified by a subscriber and send the results of the search to him or her on a daily basis.

Different or additional advertising may accompany the electronic version of a magazine or newspaper. A blend of advertising, product information, and company information is available on the many home pages of the WWW. In this sense, the Internet is already an important vehicle for advertising. The effectiveness of third-party advertising on the Internet is still being assessed, but its volume is growing rapidly.[4]

Convergence is evident in the web sites created by broadcasters that provide clips of broadcasts and summaries of news. They are provided under the broadcaster's brand name, and advertising is sold according to a rate card. Are these sites subject to the regulatory constraints included in the relevant broadcasting license? For example, the *Globe and Mail,* an influential Canadian newspaper, has a web page carrying selected content and advertising. A new specialty Canadian business news channel Report on Business Television (ROBTV), named after the *Globe and Mail's* business section and supported by its information sources, was licensed in 1996. Will the newspaper's web site be unregulated but the site of ROBTV be regulated as to content, as is the service itself?

Conventional media are limited in their interactivity and in being able to combine types of content. With digitalization these constraints are significantly relaxed. Digital multimedia works mix sound, text, pictures, and video in new combinations. Consumers can either enjoy the productions in a default pattern or participate by making choices of story lines or other aspects of the presentation. Random elements can be incorporated through the computer's ability to generate random numbers. Viewers have the options of browsing and sampling multimedia postings.

The future of multimedia content on networks is unclear, but significant developments in the stand-alone multimedia video game industry may foreshadow what is coming. The computer or video game industry barely existed 15 years ago. In that period, an international industry with annual sales of over C$10 billion, according to the trade press,[5] has emerged along the seams of the cultural industries. Sony's PlayStation division developed from almost no sales in 1994 to revenues exceeding $5 billion in 1997 realized on gross retail sales of $9 billion.[6]

Impact on Appropriability

The new technologies have paradoxically made piracy easier while creating the potential for building more effective fences. For example, unlike analogue taping, digital audio taping makes an identical copy of a digital original. There

---

4. Global spending on Internet advertising in 1996 was estimated at US$260 million. This contrasts with US$173 billion spent in the United States on all forms of advertising in the same year (see Survey of Electronic Commerce in the *Economist,* May 10, 1997, after p. 57).

5. See *Playback,* October 24, 1994, as cited in Magder (1996, 173).

6. *Fast Company,* August–September 1997, 118.

is no loss of information in the duplication process regardless of how many copies are made. The same digital technology also allows defences to be incorporated into the taping system, which makes piracy more difficult. For example, the Audio Home Taping Act of the United States requires that digital tape recorders have the serial copy management system or its equivalent installed and forbids the importation, manufacture, or distribution of any device designed to circumvent this safeguard. The operation of this system requires that every recording be encoded with a category code and copyright status. Complying tape recorders allow only one copy to be made of each original.[7]

Photocopiers, scanners, and tape recorders extend the reach of distributional systems and provide consumers with considerable value, but from the producers' perspective they are "burglary tools." They affect business strategies of how to distribute and price their content. For all media, a strategic "game" between builders of security systems and creators of burglary tools is likely to develop, as has occurred with software and the black boxes used in marketing subscription television services. This game has international implications that will heighten already existing tensions about the enforcement of copyright.

Relatedly, the new technologies make possible new combinations of pricing and delivery. Software can be integrated with existing programs on a CD-ROM that automatically connects the user to an Internet site that sends back a signal allowing access for a limited amount of time for a fee. This arrangement allows the software access to be rented. Copying of the software presents no problem because the bootleg version has to gain approval and the user must pay for usage. This approach has considerable promise in distributing software for games. Similar schemes are being developed and introduced for DVD discs of movies. They allow the movie to be "rented" by distributing for no charge many low-price discs, which circulate and generate payments whenever access occurs. These schemes are vulnerable to the development of "burglary" tools that allow the program to run by circumventing the approval and payment process.

Impact on Concentration and Market Power

Traditional transnational players in the media industry are broadening their portfolio of interests and investing heavily in other countries. Important multinational media companies operate from a number of European countries, Canada, and Australia as well as the United States. At the same time, new firms with multimedia, communications, or related hardware interests have, in a relatively short period of time, grown from modest beginnings to become

---

7. Trade-related issues raised by national initiatives to counter either the practice or the effects of piracy are discussed in chapter 14.

extremely important players, domestically and globally. For example, 3-Comm, Cisco Systems, Compaq, Intel, Microsoft, Oracle, Scientific Atlantic, Silicon Graphics, Sun, and WorldCom are an impressive, albeit nonrandom, sample of the new American hardware and software giants developing and extending the new technologies that were either small or nonexistent 25 years ago. A large number of entries, many exits, but a significant proportion of rapidly growing survivors are also characteristic of the cultural industries in a number of European countries, Canada, Australia, Mexico, Venezuela, and Brazil.

Internationalization reduces the ability of any single government to monitor the activities of these firms and intelligently apply antitrust measures. Although there are large international firms and merger activity is intense, the potential for entry by new players created by the new technologies and the number of potential international competitors promise to make any exercise of market power temporary in the absence of protection. To the extent that there are persisting problems of market power in this context, internationally coordinated responses may be more effective than national ones. One area that merits attention in this regard is the tolerance of the law in many countries, including the United States and Canada, with regard to legal cartels for exporting, an issue discussed in chapter 16.

Conclusion

The impact of technology on trade and investment in the cultural industries is pervasive and ongoing. Anything written today will be dated tomorrow. Certain trends are nevertheless apparent. First, technology is altering the way in which content is produced and delivered from producers to consumers. To the extent that costs are reduced for any given output—book, film, or record—entry is facilitated and competition increased in both domestic and foreign markets. Second, greater capacity of distribution systems allows more material to be delivered so that producers can supply both mass and specialized audiences. Audiences are empowered where pick and pay systems are used, while government influence on content is reduced.

Third, the traditional boundaries between the cultural industries are dissolving. Newspapers, periodicals, and books can be transmitted electronically, frequently bypassing intermediaries such as printers, wholesalers, and retailers. Audiovisual material can be distributed in theaters and concert halls, by radio and television, and by videotapes and compact discs. These distribution systems coalesce in the evolution of the Internet, which is an organizational arrangement associated with the use of digitalization to convey different kinds of content.

Government policies for each of the cultural industries were developed for a set of conditions that once existed. As technology changed, for example, from broadcast to cablecast transmission, the policy framework was adapted. Recent and ongoing changes are placing more severe pressures on these frameworks and contributing to many of the frictions that we examine in part III. Agreement has yet to be reached on a framework for the Internet.

CHAPTER 3

Information Sources

Trade disputes are informed by statements of opinion and fact about particular circumstances. While attention is given to published data, a wide variety of sources and official, industry, and special reports are used to support opposing positions. There is a general professional willingness to treat the official numbers reported by governments in the case of wheat and automobile production, imports, and exports as reliable. This faith is not and in our opinion should not be extended to similar facts about the cultural industries.

Two factors plague the statistics. One is the conceptual difficulty of measuring the attributes of cultural production and distribution, including the difficulty of deciding what should be included in the definition of culture. The second is the deliberate avoidance of developing one set of numbers since the various parties think they can best further their interests by using and sometimes inventing figures that support their causes. This is not new. In describing the European quota system for imported films in Europe in the 1940s and 1950s, Guback (1969, 37) writes that "each nation selects and makes available only the information it considers important." Over 30 years later, in assessing feature film activity in Canada, Globerman shows how three different definitions of a Canadian film provide different production estimates.[1] The one chosen suits the argument of the day.

Our experience in trying to describe the nature and operations of the various cultural industries, and especially their international dimensions, has alerted us to the problems. We have found official reports failing to warn the reader about the limitations of the data recorded, opportunistic use made of published data, and facts reported for which there is no sound basis. We can only provide selected examples of why and where this has occurred, but it is a topic that in our view will need careful attention as disputes in this sector proliferate. Illustrative of the situation is the existence of an interdepartmental committee

---

1. A Canadian film can be defined as one that has some part of its budget spent in Canada; as one that uses Canadian screenwriters, directors, actors, and producers; or one that has a Canadian plotline or locale. Production activity in Canada varies according to whether a foreign firm shooting in Canada does or does not use a Canadian subsidiary. Only with the latter does film production get recorded in official statistics (Globerman 1987, 3–4, 6).

of the Canadian federal government examining the conceptual problems of measuring cultural activities. Despite the fact that a section of Statistics Canada has for many years been assigned the task of collecting cultural statistics, the committee is at the stage of deciding what activities should be included as culture, and whether a definition like that of the United Nations Educational, Scientific, and Cultural Organization (UNESCO) should be used, including sports and education, or a more limited boundary drawn. By the time agreement has been reached on this definition and surveys developed to collect the relevant information for each subsector, perhaps five years hence, numerous disputes are likely to have arisen and been settled using existing unreliable surveys and data sources.[2]

Conceptual Problems

First, we examine some conceptual problems. Cultural content such as films, television programs, sound recordings, and books all have public-good aspects, as discussed in chapter 5, and incur large up-front costs before any revenues can be collected. Once produced, they may earn revenues over a short time period like a daily newspaper or a much longer period like Shakespearean plays, the *Wizard of Oz,* or reruns of *Cheers* and *Monty Python* in syndication markets. For a product like copper bar, quantity can be measured in weight and quality in the percentage of purity. Market forces will give each bar of the same weight and purity approximately the same value. For new books of the same page length, covering similar topics, and involving the same advances to authors, there will be a wide range of valuations imposed by the market. The same is true for records, films, and television programs.

In order to produce these works, firms must engage in a wide range of contractual agreements to raise the financing and produce and distribute the end product. Films, for example, are financed by a mixture of equity investment, loans, government subsidies, tax credits, and presales of the final product in different formats (theaters, television, and home video) and different geographic and linguistic markets. Some of the financing may involve promises to pay in the future, such as presales, which may be used on a discounted basis as collateral to borrow from financial institutions. Some of the artists and creative personnel may be paid a fixed sum or hourly rate and a share in profits or revenues that

---

2. Our understanding is that agreement has been reached in the interdepartmental committee to compile the statistics according to the definition of *culture* provided by each department requesting information. This will merely confound the problem by proliferating the numbers used in public debate to represent similar aggregated cultural activities and by making time series and international comparisons impossible to compile. Statistics Canada is due to report on these developments in 1999.

may accrue in the future. Payments to them are both for the costs of their professional services and for their roles as investors. Licensing fees for audiovisual products or recording masters are tailored to the demand conditions in the market. Discrimination is the rule rather than the exception. Licenses may cover a different set of rights with varied constraints and may apply to different periods of time. Royalties may depend on a number of conditions such as ratings or box office success. Separating annual flows is a daunting task.

Data gatherers are faced with the problems of designing surveys that can collect this information in ways that answer such questions as: how big is country X's film industry; what are its costs, revenues, profits, exports, and imports; what impact does it have on the overall economy; and how much does it receive in government support? While the questions are easy to ask, they are difficult to answer in a meaningful way, or because there are a number of answers users can and do take their pick to suit their interests.

This is not to argue that similar problems do not arise in other industries. Pharmaceutical research and development have to be financed before revenues are realized. Profit sharing takes place in many industries, and revenues accrue over a long period for activities with high fixed costs such as petroleum refining and hydroelectricity production. Each industry has a particular configuration of contractual and organizational arrangements that have to be addressed in designing surveys, but the peculiarities of some of the cultural industries have been especially challenging because of the rights structure that is attached to the item produced and traded. A film, for example, is not sold as a physical item by a distributor to a theater but rented for use in a number of showings. This is in contrast to books or magazines, tangible items that tend to be sold to consumers or libraries for their personal or collective use.

In recording cultural activities, new complexities will arise with changing technology. Animation used to be highly labor intensive, employing persons under sweatshop conditions to draw and color the sequences that were later filmed. All the work tended to be concentrated in one place. Now the drawings are often made on computer screens and the work can be distributed anywhere in the world where there are telecommunications links that will transmit the data of those working on different frames.[3] Recording the volume and value of the digital information that constitutes the intermediate or final work presents a number of challenges for determining domestic production, exports, and imports.

---

3. One low-budget feature film, *Conceiving Ada,* is reported to have been made by combining live action shots of performers taken against a blue screen with computer-created backgrounds of rooms with furniture, carpets, and pictures (*Globe and Mail,* October 4, 1997, C3).

Trade data are at the center of trade negotiations and disputes. How should film, tape, compact discs, newspapers, periodicals, and books be valued for customs purposes? The value of the physical medium is often trivial. The value of its content is revealed individually in the market and may be very high or low. How to assess that value bedevils the imposition of traditional border taxes and makes the assessment of traditional trade concepts such as dumping unfeasible. Again, this is not a unique problem for the cultural industries, but it is particularly acute in their case. If agencies in different countries use different procedures, then there may be little agreement on the extent of trade flows in cases in which injury to domestic industries has to be assessed.[4]

A review of selected published data reveals some of the problems of measurement and reporting. First, we examine three Canadian government surveys. One measures the economic impact of the arts and culture sector, another government expenditures in support of culture, and the third cultural exports. All are the most recent published figures as of October 1998.

Canadian Examples

Economic Impact of Arts and Culture, 1993–94

Statistics Canada measured the direct and indirect impact of arts and culture on gross domestic product (GDP) and employment in 1993–94.[5] The sector's share of total GDP is 4.7 percent (direct plus indirect 6.8 percent), and the share of total employment is 6.9 percent (direct plus indirect 9.2 percent). The UNESCO framework for cultural statistics was used but modified to exclude sports. Comparability with surveys of other countries depends on where the boundaries of arts and culture are drawn. Within Canada the survey's coverage is not comparable to related surveys either for government support or for exports (described below).

The measurement of indirect impact is misleading for this and other sectors, since, if it is done for all industries, the sum of direct and indirect employment, for example, would lead to an employment figure in excess of the country's labor force. This occurs because the jobs assigned as indirect for arts and culture will

---

4. We have argued elsewhere that with the structure of the industry and the demand conditions it faces there is little incentive to dump product in the sense of selling it at a price below the cost of distribution or at a price equal to what the market will bear. Because each market has a different rental price or license fee for a film, record master, or book publishing right, comparisons across markets provide no information on predation (Acheson and Maule, 1997a, 71–72).

5. Statistics Canada, Cat. 87–004, vol. 8 (2), Summer 1996, 6.

be direct employment for some other activity and therefore if done for the whole economy would lead to double counting. Calculations like this are often made by those interested in inflating the importance of a sector.

Government Expenditures on Culture, 1996–97

A total of C$5.9 billion was spent at all levels of government, including about C$289 million on intergovernmental transfers in 1996–97.[6] The federal government accounted for 47 percent, provincial and territorial governments for 29 percent, and municipal governments for 24 percent. Over half the federal share went to broadcasting and the largest part to the public broadcaster, the CBC. Out of total federal and provincial spending, broadcasting accounted for about 37 percent; film and video 8 percent; literary arts, including publishing, 4 percent; and sound recording 0.2 percent. Over 75 percent of municipal spending is on libraries. In constant dollars, total government expenditures on culture have declined by over 9 percent from 1989–90 to 1996–97.

Included in these totals are cash outlays by individual departments and agencies. Excluded are funds that accrue to these activities as a result of tax expenditures and credits as well as benefits received from other types of policies.[7] For example, in 1996 Alliance Communications noted that "Canadian incentives typically account for 10% to 12% of the budget for Alliance's productions (except in the case of coproductions, or culturally driven programs such as *North of 60*, where they can go as high as 50% . . .)."[8] Only a part of these financial incentives would appear in the survey of government expenditures, as some arise from federal and provincial tax credits. Other examples of excluded government benefits, although more difficult to quantify, would be provisions of the Copyright Act that give Canadian publishers the right to distribute foreign-published books in the Canadian market and provisions of the Income Tax Act that direct advertising to Canadian periodicals and newspapers.[9] This official survey of Canadian spending on culture provides only part of the

---

6. Statistics Canada, Cat. 87F0001XPB, 1998 (Surveys of Government Expenditure on Culture, Cultural Statistics Program).

7. The lack of information on the tax cost of film tax shelters is noted in Poddar and English (1994, 34–35).

8. Alliance Communications Prospectus, August 1, 1996, 33.

9. Section 19 of the Income Tax Act states that "no deduction shall be made in respect of an otherwise deductible outlay or expense of a taxpayer for advertising space in an issue of a newspaper or periodical for an advertisement directed primarily to a market in Canada unless" the newspaper or periodical is 75 percent or more Canadian owned.

picture and may not be comparable to the way other countries quantify similar support.

International Trade in the Arts and Culture Sector, 1995

This Statistics Canada survey is not comparable to activities covered in the previous surveys of either economic impact or government spending.[10] Included in the total exports of C\$12.4 billion in 1995 are cultural tourism, exports of cultural equipment such as photographic and video equipment, and location shooting by foreigners in Canada. If the subtotal of cultural goods and services, C\$3 billion of the total C\$12 billion, are examined, the items covered become more closely aligned to the previous two surveys but a number of concerns remain.

The survey has led to criticism that the C\$3 billion figure for cultural exports is far too high and measures items that should not be included under culture, for example, visits by foreigners to festivals, performing arts and heritage institutions in Canada, and the manufacture of audiocassettes and CDs (Audley 1997, 3). Government officials are now suggesting that the figure is closer to C\$1 billion than C\$3 billion but are generally reluctant to discuss the data for fear of sending the wrong signal. A high number and rapid export growth suggests the cultural industries are doing well. From a political perspective, this plays well before a domestic audience, as it shows the viability of these industries and the success of government policies, but badly to a foreign one, as it inevitably raises questions about the need for continued Canadian protection.[11]

---

10. Statistics Canada, Cat. 87–004, vol. 8 (3), Autumn 1996, 1–4.

11. A footnote (fn. 2, p. 3) in this survey of international trade highlights a persistent measurement problem, the determination of national content. In the case of film production, this survey includes as Canadian any film meeting one of the following criteria: "1. certified for 30% capital cost allowance (CCA) since 1988; 2. certified under the film and video tax credit regulation; 3. produced with Telefilm Canada assistance; 4. made by Canadians prior to the CCA program; 5. produced by the NFB; 6. an official coproduction; 7. certified by the Canadian Radio-Television and Telecommunications Commission (CRTC); or 8. produced with financial assistance of the Canada Council, the CBC, or with provincial government assistance (Film Development Corporations, Departments or Agencies)." In effect, this survey states that any film is to be considered Canadian if it qualifies according to one of many policy initiatives past or present. Many of these policies used the Canadianess of inputs or money spent in Canada to qualify productions as Canadian content. Any film production in Canada that did not interact with one of these policies would not be considered to have Canadian content.

By reviewing these surveys, we do not intend to imply that Canada is the only country facing reporting difficulties.[12] Rather, the surveys reveal some of the difficulties of measurement and interpretation as well as the volume of data available from a variety of sources. In one sense there are too many data available, allowing each to use a source to support a particular position or policy. Some particular examples of the selection and use of data are illustrated below.

An Array of Measures

A study of the Canadian periodical industry reports three alternative calculations for the share of the Canadian industry captured by the publishers of Canadian as opposed to foreign magazines, 67.6 percent, 54.8 percent, and 25.5 percent in 1991. The first is based on the number of physical copies of magazines distributed, the second on Statistics Canada's estimate of advertising and circulation revenue, and the third on estimates of circulation revenue only. Problems are noted in accounting for the number of magazine subscriptions imported by mail and in the value attached to these subscriptions. It is estimated that more than three million subscriptions to American periodicals are not included in the Statistics Canada data (Cebryk et al. 1994, 1–11, 1–13, appendix A). In the future, the measurement of cross-border trade in periodicals such as *Hotwired* that are distributed via the Internet will present an additional challenge. Electronic trade will also highlight another problem that exists with the traditional magazine trade—the failure to measure the advertising services provided by one country and consumed by readers in another. If the electronic periodicals are not charged but the readers are consuming advertising services on the web site, no intercountry transaction is likely to be recorded.[13]

A second example concerns exports recorded by Statistics Canada for the film and television production industry in 1993–94 of C$149 million. Foreign earnings reported in annual reports of three film companies (Alliance, Atlantis,

---

12. Two studies are noted for their questionable use of statistics to measure the importance of the music industry and the cultural sector in the United Kingdom (Towse 1997).

13. Canada's proposed legislation, discussed in chapter 10, which prohibits advertising by Canadians in foreign periodicals where the advertising is aimed at the Canadian market, has defined a periodical as a printed publication, thereby exempting advertising in magazines supplied electronically. See Bill C–55, An Act Respecting Advertising Services Supplied by Foreign Periodicals Publishers, October 8, 1998, on <http://www.parl.gc.ca/36/1/parlbus/cham>.

and Nelvana) whose shares are publicly traded in Canada exceed that amount.[14] A study prepared for the Canadian Film and Television Producers Association in Canada (CFTPA) (Nordicity 1996) lists a figure of C$1.2 billion as the "export contribution" of the industry, about half of which is accounted for by location shooting of foreign firms in Canada, where some of the expenditures may already be included in payments by foreigners for hotels and meals in Canada. Even with this sum removed, there is a disturbing difference between it and the C$149 million figure reported by Statistics Canada. Part of the discrepancy is caused by comparing exports that relate to balance of payments concepts and to "export contribution" based on other sources of information and other ways of viewing foreign activity.

The data difficulties are illustrated by the circulation in official speeches, commissioned studies, and industry presentations of "facts" that receive their credibility solely from frequent repetition. One example is the now standard assertion that Canada is the second largest exporter after the United States of television programs in the world. To the best of our knowledge there is no source that can provide the basis for such a calculation. If there was a source it is highly unlikely that it could provide an accurate statement.[15] In order to calculate any country's share, it is necessary to have a global total broken down by countries or at least those countries that are major film and television producers. No such data exist. UNESCO has tried from time to time and some figures are published in *Screen Digest,* but none of these provides a complete tally. Nor is it clear that the figures for each country are calculated in the same way. The problems outlined for Canada being one example of the discrepancies that may arise, another is how to determine the value of program rights traded. A study published by the Organization for Economic Cooperation and Development (OECD) reports on the available data on trade in film and television services for 14 countries. By these figures, Canada ranks behind the United States, the United Kingdom, France, and Italy in each of the years from 1990 to 1993 (OECD 1994, 109).

We checked on the veracity of the claim with officials of Statistics Canada, the DCH, the CFTPA, and persons who have used this "fact" in presentations. None can provide the source or verify its authenticity. Why then is it stated? First, it is used to argue that government support has been necessary to promote

14. Figures were taken for the 1993–94 financial years of the three companies: Alliance Annual Report, 1996, 31; and Atlantis Annual Report, 1995, 34; and Nelvana Annual Report, 1995, 20. Financial year-end reporting may not coincide exactly with Statistics Canada reporting of exports for 1993–94.

15. The first appearance of this "fact" that we have found is on June 5, 1995, in "Speaking notes for a Member of Parliament on behalf of the Honourable Michel Dupuy," where it is written that "Canada is now positioned as the world's number two exporter of entertainment programming" (material obtained from the DCH).

and sustain the industry's success. Second, it inflates the economic importance of the industry and is used to argue for continuing the support by way of subsidies, tax credits, and other measures. What it also does, perhaps unconsciously, is support those who view it as evidence that the industry has matured and content quotas are no longer required.[16]

U.S. Examples

For the United States, a similar statement is frequently made, namely, that audiovisual exports are the second largest export item or account for a large trade surplus. Undoubtedly these are important export items, but the precise ranking depends on what categories of products are used for comparative purposes. More difficult is determining the foreign sales of American audiovisual products because some are exported directly from the United States and some are sold abroad by U.S. subsidiaries in foreign countries. Compounding these difficulties is the fact that a number of major American distributors are owned by foreign firms. Below we refer to some of the statements made and numbers used and compare them to data published in official sources.

Attention was drawn to the importance of the entertainment industry for U.S. trade in *Forbes* magazine,[17] which reported, without identifying a source, that in 1986 entertainment contributed the second largest trade surplus (US$4.9 billion) to the balance of payments after aircraft (US$10.8 billion).[18] Entertainment included television programming, motion pictures, videocassette recordings and music recordings. A check of trade data for 1986 shows that chemicals also had a larger trade surplus than entertainment at US$7.8 billion. And net investment income at US$20.8 billion made an even larger contribution to the balance of payments.[19]

By the 1990s, the "fact" had been established in public debate that American entertainment exports were second only to aircraft. The distinction between

---

16. A similar comment has been made for the United Kingdom: "Publications such as *Culture as Commodity* . . . are schizophrenic; on the one hand, they seek to show that attendance is buoyant and consumer spending high, with organizations clued in to the market; on the other they show how *necessary* subsidy is, as it provides half the income of organizations large and small" (*Journal of Cultural Economics* 21, no. 4 [1997]: 359).

17. Forbes, September 21, 1987, 122.

18. A similar statement was made in *Fortune*, December 31, 1990, 50; and *Time*, December 24, 1990, 56. Another claim using a different but related industry grouping is that the content/copyright industries are the third largest export industry after agriculture and autos (see Richardson 1998, 42).

19. U.S. Bureau of the Census, *Statistical Abstract of the United States 1988* (Washington, DC, 1987 [sic]), 755, 769.

gross and net exports was seldom made. What do the figures show? In 1995, the United States had merchandise exports of US$574.9 billion and services exports of US$208.8 billion. Within these categories ranking ahead of film and television entertainment on a gross export basis are a large number of products, including automobiles, office machines, and cereals. On a net export basis in 1995, the surplus on film sales and tape rentals abroad of US$4.5 billion was exceeded not only by aircraft but by agricultural products, processed foods, and chemicals. The net positive balance of income earned from foreign direct investments was about US$60 billion.[20] No doubt it is possible to compile some category of entertainment goods and services that ranks it highly on a gross or net export basis, but unless the basis for the comparison is known the usefulness of this information is unclear.

The estimate of film and television exports is arrived at by combining two sets of figures, reported by the U.S. Department of Commerce, as data on international services transactions. One set records the cross-border transactions between U.S. and foreign residents that are counted as exports and imports in the services account of the balance of payments. The second set records sales of services abroad (export equivalents) by affiliates of U.S. companies and sales of services in the United States (import equivalents) by affiliates of foreign companies in the United States that are not counted in the balance of payments (but represent part of the activities included under the GATS because they deal with the way in which services are delivered across borders).

Cross-border transactions for 1995 show, for film sales and tape rentals, U.S. exports of $4,662 million and imports of $172 million.[21] These are the only relevant items included in the balance of payments, showing, as expected, that the United States is a net exporter in this entertainment category. Affiliate sales for 1995 for motion pictures, including television, tape, and film, show U.S. affiliate sales abroad of $8,048 million and foreign affiliate sales in the United States of $8,658 million, revealing that the United States is a net importer of this component of filmed entertainment.[22] This is contrary to conventional wisdom. An explanation centers on the fact of foreign ownership of major entertainment producers in the United States, for example, by Seagram, Bertelsmann, EMI, and Sony Entertainment. Any sale by Sony Entertainment in the United States would

20. See U.S. Department of Commerce, *Survey of Current Business* 77, no. 10 (October 1997): 124–25; and U.S. Bureau of Census, *Statistical Abstract of the United States* (1996): 784 and 807.

21. U.S. Department of Commerce, *Survey of Current Business* 77, no. 10 (October 1997): 124–25, table 5.3.

22. U.S. Department of Commerce, *Survey of Current Business* 77, no. 10 (October 1997): 137–38, tables 10 and 11.

appear as part of the foreign affiliate sales of $8,658 million in the United States.[23]

There is another problem in interpreting these data. Sales by foreign affiliates in the United States or abroad may be preceded by cross-border sales to these affiliates. Thus, MGM might sell film rights to an affiliate in Europe, which then resells the rights to other countries. This could get counted twice and appear in both the export and affiliate sales data.[24] Clearly, the ranking of sectors by trade performance can be undertaken using a variety of numbers that give different results.

Conclusion

Comparing the published data to the statements made in public discussion reveals some of the liberties taken when describing these industries but also some of the conceptual difficulties that arise in measuring the extent of foreign trade and foreign impact. Part of the measurement difficulty occurs because of the way cultural rights are traded and part because of the involvement of foreign-owned firms in different jurisdictions. In order to achieve transparency in debate and to avoid politically opportunistic behavior, a set of statistics is needed that is generally agreed to describe conditions in the industry. A workable trade agreement will require the parallel development of comparable figures and the norms of statistical probity characteristic of other sectors of the economy.

The preceding examples are illustrative of the problems that arise in measuring cultural trade. By no means are we suggesting that this is an exhaustive treatment of the topic. In fact, we expect that there are many more horror stories to be revealed and that the problems associated with measuring Internet-related activity have hardly been touched. We consider the efforts made in the past by official agencies to have been inadequate in pointing out the difficulties and less than forthright in reporting on the quality of the data published.[25] Some users have benefited from being able to present numbers that

---

23. For 1996, an official of the Department of Commerce estimates that U.S. film and television exports were approximately US$10 billion made up of exports of US$3.8 billion and affiliate sales of US$6.0 billion.

24. The Bureau of Economic Analysis in the U.S. Department of Commerce is aware of this problem and has moved from reporting sales on a gross to a net basis (U.S. Department of Commerce, *Survey of Current Business* 77, no. 10, October 1997, 95).

25. Our opinion of the published statistics is not unique. Ernst and Young state: "The data reported by Statistics Canada are of concern in a number of respects. First, while the trends shown in the data over the past five years are difficult to reconcile with those from other sources, Statistics Canada remains the only source of comprehensive data on the industry. Second, some of the data are difficult to interpret and cannot be

support their arguments but do not represent reality. The extensive domestic and international debates over culture that have taken place have not been well served by the available official statistics. In the subsequent sections on individual sectors we use data from a variety of sources to describe the current situation but caution the reader on the quality of the information.

---

reconciled with other sources (e.g., in respect of mechanical royalties and payments for foreign masters). Third, the import data on the industry are not at all useful because they do not distinguish between sound recording products related to this industry (such as CDs and pre-recorded cassettes) and those used by other industries (educational products, books on cassette, etc.)" (1995, 3). As noted in chapter 9, similar reservations have been expressed about the reliability of official data on Canadian book publishing.

CHAPTER 4

Issues, Regimes, and Culture in GATT and the EC

In 1998, the WTO's Council on Trade in Services held discussions on issues to be examined in future negotiations, one of which is trade in audiovisual services.[1] These deliberations are part of a determination of the future international governance structure for the cultural industries. In commenting on cultural trade and investment negotiations, a senior Canadian official stated that "no one should doubt that cultural policy issues in the future will become more difficult not easier to resolve."[2]

The current treatment of culture is illustrated by the resolution of particular disputes, such as those discussed in part III, in the context of a number of formal and informal regimes. This environment for resolving conflicts has evolved from relatively modest roots since World War II. The development of more formal international governance as a means of coping with different impediments to realizing gains from international economic integration has been uneven. After tariff walls were significantly reduced, attention shifted to nontariff barriers and trade in services. Issues of investment, copyright, and antitrust coordination began to be systematically addressed. As rules and reinforcing institutions began to be codified and developed in new areas, more stubborn problems concerning tariffs, quotas, and subsidies in sectors such as textiles and agriculture, which were bypassed in the first wave, have been constructively revisited. Sectoral and regional experiments have provided information that has often accelerated international developments or in some instances delayed initiatives while the implications of unanticipated difficulties were absorbed. At the same time as formal international governance was developing, informal norms and channels

---

1. Article XIX of the GATS requires that future negotiations on services begin within five years of the date of entry into force of the WTO or by January 1, 2000. The Council for Trade in Services has developed an information exchange program to facilitate such negotiations. As part of this process, the WTO Secretariat issued a "Background Note on Audiovisual Services" (WTO S/C/W/40, 15 June 1998).

2. Remarks entitled "Culture: The Issue and the Paradox" by Bill Dymond, Canada's chief negotiator for the MAI, to a conference at Michigan State University, September 12, 1998.

of communication were evolving as complements or substitutes in areas in which the formal scarcely exists.

The largely North American disputes that we examine in detail in part III are building blocks in the untidy but so far effective process of developing a better architecture of formal structures and their relationship to the informal. Along with other influences, these experiences will determine how the environment in which the business of culture will be conducted in the future evolves. In this chapter, we first examine the different issues that international governance, either formal or informal, has to address. We then explore how trade and investment in cultural products was treated in the informal environment immediately after World War II, in GATT before its absorption into the WTO framework, and in the world's most ambitious regional initiative, Europe's Economic Community. With this background, the following chapter describes the overlapping regional and international structures currently impacting on the trade and investment flows of the cultural industries in Canada and the United States—a web of bilateral coproduction treaties involving Canada, CUSFTA and NAFTA, and the WTO, including trade-related aspects of intellectual property rights (TRIPs) and trade-related investment measures (TRIMs).

Issues

Since the end of World War II, trade agreements have liberalized the international economy in steps. After tariffs were lowered in a series of multilateral negotiations, attention shifted to nontariff barriers, such as government purchasing, licensing, standards, subsidies, and trade-distorting tax incentives, and the conduct of antidumping and countervailing duty policies. This expansion required the development of constraints over procedures as well as decisions made within those processes. The coverage was next extended from trade in goods to trade in services, making it necessary to define a service and describe the way services can be delivered. Copyright issues recently have been integrated into regional and international trade agreements. With respect to investment, the OECD is currently digesting a less than enthusiastic response to a proposed Multilateral Agreement on Investment (MAI).

In these steps, negotiation procedures were adapted to the nature of the problem. The mode of organizing negotiations in the tariff-reducing rounds differed from that adopted for incorporating services in the recent Uruguay Round. Within the negotiation for services, different procedures governed the commitments to most favored nation status (MFN), national treatment, and market access obligations.

Even within a mode of negotiation, the impact on different sectors of the economy varies, leading interest groups to lobby for special treatment.

Sometimes the resulting political pressure has eliminated or slowed down the pace of liberalization in particular sectors. For example, agriculture, textiles, steel, and aircraft have been sheltered from the extensive liberalization experienced by the rest of manufacturing. In other cases, special arrangements such as those recently negotiated for financial services, telecommunications, and information technology have allowed these sectors to liberalize more quickly than other services. The addition of a special agreement for culture, if this is the chosen route in the future, would be an extension of this customization process.

As well as special treatment of sectors, groups of countries have experimented with regional agreements and international agreements have made distinctions among countries such as the granting of preferential arrangements to developing countries. The coexistence of bilateral and regional with multilateral agreements has allowed experimentation at the less comprehensive level to inform initiatives at the international level. There nevertheless exists a continuing tension between interests that champion a regional agreement as a way of avoiding international commitments and those that support it as a bridge to more broadly based agreements. The forces leading to this tension manifest themselves in international agreements through demands for finer distinctions among members.

In addition to trade in goods and services, investment has become an issue since investment and trade are often complementary and barriers to investment may lead to barriers to trade. This is especially the case with services, where an important way to provide the service in another market is through the commercial presence of the provider. Issues of market access for investors, ownership restrictions, and confiscation of foreign assets have become part of the negotiations, as have various incentives that attract investment or try to attach certain trade-related performance measures to particular investments.

Once investment is included, restrictive business practices such as mergers, cartels, and boycotts have to be considered since these are actions by private decision makers that may restrict market access, in contrast to tariffs and quotas, which are actions undertaken by governments. This concern has triggered interest in coordinating national antitrust policies. Sanctions are an example of government-sponsored measures affecting trade that supersede trade agreement obligations. Private sector initiatives such as boycotts to protest against a failure of a member country to enforce an international obligation often morph into public initiatives when the relevant government aligns itself with the industry association. This informal enforcement by unilateral action occurred frequently in the copyright area before the recent development of a formal dispute resolution mechanism under the WTO for adjudicating such disputes.

Disputes concerning copyright were also made more likely by a variety of different legal structures for the treatment of intellectual property rights. Some diversity occurred because members of the Berne convention could sign on to different protocols embodying different commitments. Nor was Berne effective in disciplining members that were delinquent. As well, a number of important countries were not members either of Berne or the Universal Copyright Convention. Some countries had no laws protecting intellectual property or had laws that were not enforced. Either way, trade distortions occurred. Recent regional and international initiatives have addressed the reduction of the differences in copyright law and the establishment of effective enforcement procedures.

A final set of issues deals with the cross-border movement of labor services. Government issuance of work permits and private measures enforced by unions and associations of professionals can affect trade depending on how they are administered. At times the government effectively transfers responsibility to the individual union or association and outsiders have difficulty determining how the process works.

Addressing the governance of interrelated issues of tariffs, nontariff barriers, investment constraints, restrictive business practices, the coordination of national intellectual property policies, and the movement of labor in the context of the cultural industries is the emerging challenge. Distinguishing between formal and informal regimes facilitates assessing the structure that is currently in place.

Formal and Informal Regimes and the Cultural Industries

Accompanying the foregoing topics is an array of governing regimes that have evolved to address the issues. These include multilateral regimes like the GATT/WTO and United Nations organizations, regional regimes like NAFTA and the European Union (EU), clublike groupings such as the member countries of the OECD, and bilateral agreements such as coproduction treaties that provide special conditions for investors.

Each regime covers a particular set of countries, sectors, and topics, and each sets out commitments to which the participating countries agree to adhere. These may be binding or in the form of guidelines. Binding commitments may be associated with an independent dispute settlement mechanism, as in the WTO, requiring each country to implement decisions of an international tribunal. Guidelines imply the use of moral suasion but may be effective in drawing attention to desired behavior and conditioning future actions.

Over time these formal regimes change, either as a result of scheduled negotiations, as in the case of the GATT, or due to interpretation of the wording of the agreement or to the emergence of a dispute and a ruling leading to its resolution. The latter results in the creation of a type of case law precedent that provides both flexibility and certainty to the regime.

Aside from these formal regimes, there is a category of informal regimes or ways in which issues are addressed in the political arena, where there are few rules and the stronger party tends to have the upper hand. *Aggressive unilateralism* is a term applied to this kind of behavior when a national government is able to use credible threats of retaliation against foreign firms or governments whose actions are seen to be harmful. The threats may be transmitted via regular political and diplomatic interactions and through cross-border meetings between government officials outside the diplomatic service. They may also be communicated by representatives of business, unions, and organizations such as consumer associations and those concerned with issues like the environment and human rights. Lobbying as well as marketing and production have become more globalized. Using instruments at its disposal and anticipating responses and counterresponses, one country will attempt to persuade another to alter its policies. The CMT case examined in chapter 11 provides an example of the resolution of a cultural dispute between Canada and the United States through the informal regime.

Other effective political bargaining techniques are to threaten retaliation and to exploit the uncertainty caused by differing interpretations of wording in an agreement. By escalating the number of complaints in a given area such as culture, larger governments can put pressure on others to resolve the issues to their advantage.

Informal regimes have the advantage of flexibility, but they are often unpredictable in terms of their outcomes since no formal rules and no dispute settlement mechanisms apply. Many disputes are solved through this process with little publicity, but there is often an incentive for one of the parties to politicize the process. The media can suddenly focus mass attention on an issue and distort its relative importance. Complex issues are reduced to slogans. Negotiations are reported in rhetoric suitable to sporting events but not to diplomacy. While this tends to benefit the strong over the weak, less wealthy interest groups have also discovered ways to combine their forces across borders using information technology. Opponents of the MAI created an effective ad hoc international coalition to oppose the creation of another formal regime. These grassroots movements tend to simplify and manipulate emotions with the same abandon as do some of their corporate and governmental counterparts.

While there has been no comprehensive formal regime to address international cultural issues, when disputes arise they have been dealt with either within the context of existing general agreements or through informal arrangements. The former have recently become more important, but the informal processes still dominate. In the next section we present an illustrative example of how cultural industry disputes were resolved informally before the negotiation of the GATT in 1947 initiated the development of a set of post–World War II formal agreements.

Pre-1947 Conflict over Film Distribution: The United Kingdom and the United States

When GATT was negotiated in 1947, screen quotas were exempted from the general prohibition against quotas as an instrument of commercial policy. Demand for the exemption of theatrical screen quotas can be traced back to concerns expressed by European countries and Canada toward the American film industry during the interwar period and chronicled in detail by Jarvie (1992, 213–46). Throughout Europe, American films dominated theatrical screens after 1918, leading these countries to devise measures to restore the viability of their film industries and to promote, by quotas and other means, the production and exhibition of locally made films. A discussion paper entitled "Exhibition within the Empire of Empire Films"[3] was distributed prior to the Imperial Conference of 1926 in London. It lists for the countries of the British Empire the problems common to themselves and other European countries, namely, that only about 5 percent of the films shown are made by British companies employing British artists; theatrical screens are dominated by American films; non-British views and opinions are being spread throughout the empire; displaying British goods in films is a way of promoting trade; and there is a need to revitalize the British film industry and consider the creation of a quota for British films to be shown by exhibitors. The last came to pass with the passage of the Cinematograph Films Act in 1927.

Similar to the situation today, a mix of cultural, political, and commercial factors motivated these concerns. Espousal of British views and stories was as much a concern with spreading British political views and promoting trade as it was with boosting British culture. In the debate, note was taken of the prominence given in films to American roles in world events and to the influence films might have on American exports. The response by the U.S. film industry to measures that would limit the distribution of their films was a combination of lobbying to reduce their impact and the establishment of American firms behind the quota walls to qualify as local production, a move often encouraged by the host countries.

Resistance to competition from American films remained an issue at the end of World War II, which saw the American industry emerge unscathed and the European industry in dire straits. In addition, a general shortage of foreign

---

3. Reprinted in Jarvie (1992, 68–74).

exchange forced the U.K. government to seek remedial measures. One of these was a 75 percent ad valorem duty imposed on imported films, which sharply reduced the revenues accruing to American film distributors. In response, the American distributors organized a boycott of the U.K. market, which lasted from August 1947 to March 1948. When the duty was repealed, the British government permitted repatriation to the United States of US$17 million annually plus an amount equal to the earnings of British films in the United States.

The positions taken by various parties at the time of the boycott provide an example of how interest groups lined up in connection with this cultural trade dispute. Some lessons in how an informal system operates are applicable to the present. Two countries were involved, the United States and the United Kingdom. Both produced films for domestic and foreign distribution, but the balance of film trade was heavily in favor of the United States.

Within each country's industry, the principal players consisted of film producers, distributors, and exhibitors. Distributors and exhibitors, who derived a living from showing commercially successful films regardless of national origin, tended to be divided from the national producers, who saw benefits in protection. Thus, in the United Kingdom, distributors and theater owners opposed the boycott since it cut them off from lucrative American films and forced them to rely almost entirely on British films. British film producers, on the other hand, saw benefits from the boycott, which like the earlier quota scheme generated a larger proportion of screen time for their films. Some divisions occurred among British producers because of a preexisting policy that required part of the revenues from American distribution to be retained in the United Kingdom for local film production. Over time, a part of the British film production industry had come to depend on the revenues from American films. A boycott meant the loss of this revenue.

In the United States, the major producers and distributors were vertically integrated and through membership in the Motion Pictures Export Association of America (MPEAA) combined to organize the boycott of the United Kingdom film market. American exhibitors were unaffected. They exhibited some British films, but these would continue to be available, as the need for foreign currency meant that there was little chance of a counter British boycott. The eight members of the MPEAA worked closely with each other and with the government to administer the boycott and pressure the British government to withdraw the duty. The MPEAA had been registered as an approved export cartel in 1945 under the 1918 Webb Pomerene Act (WP).

While the positions taken by the commercial players can be clearly established once their circumstances are known, the positions taken by the governments were often ambiguous. At the highest political level, the British government supported the duty and opposed the boycott, while the opposite was true for the American government. Within each government, however, there were conflicting opinions held by different departments. In the British government, those concerned with coping with the exchange crisis and dollar shortage saw the duty as one of several measures intended to conserve American dollars. Those responsible for promoting industrial growth felt that a boycott would harm the industry and create unemployment.

In the United States, a different set of pressures was at work. Those in favor of promoting open markets and freer trade, in line with the negotiations concurrently taking place which would lead to the GATT, argued for the boycott as a way of putting pressure on the United Kingdom. They were anxious to end the prewar British preferential tariff arrangements, and any new measure of protection (such as the duty) was given a hostile reception. Elsewhere in the government there was concern that the industry was already cartelized and in need of vertical divestment between distribution and exhibition.[4] The U.S. Department of Justice saw the actions of the member firms of the MPEAA in organizing the foreign boycott as a possible restraint of trade that might reinforce its hold on distribution in the domestic market. Even though antitrust statutes in other countries have provisions exempting agreements that apply only to foreign markets, there is always a concern that these agreements may spill over into domestic markets.

While each cultural trade policy dispute is embedded in a unique set of circumstances affecting the commercial and governmental players, some commonalities emerge. Protectionist forces tend to be strongest among producers of content such as authors, film and television producers, and music composers, especially when they face import competition. Those providing carriage services tend to seek out the content that will earn them the most money. They have little incentive to distribute national content unless it is financially rewarding. Thus booksellers, broadcasters, newspaper publishers, and theater owners tend to favor open markets unless they are offered subsidies or tax incentives to distribute national content.

It is less easy to make generalizations about governments except to note that there are divergent views within them and these tend to separate those departments and agencies charged with responsibilities for content and those charged with responsibilities for carriage. The former tend to be more protectionist than the latter. Difficulties arise where agencies mandated to license carriers are instructed to ensure that they carry a certain amount of domestic content, leaving them with divided loyalties toward openness and protection.

---

4. The original complaint concerning vertical integration between production, distribution, and exhibition was lodged by the Federal Trade Commission in 1921. The Supreme Court decision that finally led to divestment was handed down in 1948 (*United States v. Paramount Pictures Inc.*, 344, U.S. 131).

The forgotten voice in these debates is frequently the consumer (reader, viewer, listener), although it is often consumer preference for foreign content that drives the policy process to try to alter that choice by promoting domestic content. When domestic content is subsidized, the taxpayer is left to pay for the outcome and told that national unity, identity, and sovereignty are being enhanced.

In sum, before any reference was made to cultural trade in the GATT, there was evidence of a series of public and private actions to restrict market access and promote domestic production of films. Government quotas and taxes restricted trade, as did private boycotts, while governments provided funding to assist local production.

GATT: From 1947 to the Uruguay Round

The circumstances surrounding the United Kingdom's duty and the MPEAA's boycott contributed to the inclusion in the GATT of article IV, "Special Provisions Relating to Cinematograph Films," allowing for the imposition of theatrical screen quotas. Article XX of GATT also permitted exceptions to be taken for measures "imposed for the protection of national treasures of artistic, historic and archaeological value." To the extent that traded cultural items are goods, they have been subject to GATT obligations since 1947. Only policy measures in place in 1947 would have been grandfathered. Measures introduced by countries since that date could have been challenged earlier but have been only recently.

Representing the first major trade agreement to make explicit reference to culture, the GATT provides a convenient starting point for an examination of a number of the current international agreements that address cultural issues. As the major world economies recovered and grew in the postwar period, there was an expansion in production and trade in services. Rising income levels provided discretionary income that was spent in part on films, television programs, music, books, magazines, and newspapers. After the introduction of commercial television services in the 1950s, the United States attempted without success to amend the GATT to address restrictions placed by countries on television programming (Wildman and Siwek 1988, 136). Part of the debate concerned the question of whether trade in television programming concerned a good or a service, since the GATT dealt only with goods except for the mention of film screen quotas, which provided some ambiguity.

The boundary problem between a cultural good and a service arose in a different arena and spilled over into the GATT. Three European court cases concluded that aspects of television broadcasts, film videos, and newspapers were subject to the EC regime related to goods. The Sacchi case ruled that the transmission of television signals, including those containing advertising, come under the rules of the Treaty of Rome related to services but that trade in material, sound recordings, films, and other apparatuses used to diffuse television signals is subject to rules related to the freedom of movement of goods. In the Cinéthèque case, the importation of audiovisual material in the form of videocassettes was ruled to involve a good not a service, and in a case involving favorable treatment given to French printers of newspapers the ruling stated that "printing work cannot be described as a service, since it leads directly to the manufacture of a physical article which, as such, is classified in the Common Customs Tariff." Later the MPEAA used the Sacchi case to argue that television programs and films are products within the meaning of article XI:1 of the GATT.[5]

The decisions in the European courts began the difficult task of defining the boundary between goods and services and how products that comprised elements of both would be treated in trade law. On a broader front the Europeans were, at first reluctantly and then with greater resolution, addressing cultural issues in an increasingly diverse regional group.

Europe

The politics and economics of commercial integration in Europe after World War II were significantly different from those that faced the United States, Canada, and Mexico in the late 1980s. Europe is made up of a relatively large number of countries of different sizes with different languages, histories, and views as to the nature and role of culture in society. Some favor more openness than others. Because of the configuration of countries, debate has been intense between those favoring the creation of a single European market and those prepared to mix unification with broader interventions because of the alleged failure of market forces to effect desired national cultural objectives. Interventionist proposals tend to be restrictive not only of trade within Europe but of trade between Europe and other countries. Attention here will be given to actions taken within the EC and by certain European institutions that have a cultural mandate.

---

5. *Sacchi v. Italian Republic, European Communities, Court of Justice, Report of Cases before the Court,* Case 155/73 (1974) 409; *Cinéthèque SA v. Fédération Nationale des Cinémas Français,* Case 60–61/84, (1986) *Common Market Reporter, Court Decisions,* 1985–86, paras. 14,220, 16,344; *E.E.C. Commission v. France,* Case 18/84, (1986) *Common Market Reporter, Court Decisions,* 1985–86, paras. 14,207, 16,259. The argument by the MPEAA is made in the "Request of the MPEAA for Designation of the EC as a Priority Country under Section 182 of the Omnibus Trade Act of 1988," filed by Jane K. Albrecht, February 15, 1991.

Two world wars provide the backdrop to the post-1945 creation of European economic and political institutions. The aim of the architects of postwar Europe has been to establish conditions that will reduce the likelihood of future hostilities. In the economic and political arenas, the 1957 Treaty of Rome, signed by six countries and later joined by nine others plus associate members, provides a landmark. Our emphasis here will be to trace how a treaty that dealt primarily with measures to promote economic and political unification approached the issue of culture and to identify trade, investment, and intellectual property issues that have arisen in a number of European forums.

The Treaty of Rome led to the establishment of the European Atomic Energy Community and the European Economic Community. A forerunner had been the creation in 1951 of the European Coal and Steel Community. Cultural policy has evolved mainly through actions taken by the European Economic Community, now known as the EC since passage of the Treaty on EU (the Maastricht Treaty) in 1991 as well as through reports of the European Parliament and decisions of the European Court of Justice. Elsewhere in Europe, the European Broadcasting Union (EBU) and the Council of Europe (COE) have been important players in the development of cultural policies that have affected not only economic relations within Europe but between Europe and other countries.

A series of tensions existing within Europe help to explain the tortuous evolution of cultural policies.[6] The goal of the EC has been to create a single market within Europe without barriers to trade in cultural as well as other goods and services. At the same time, countries can retain their political institutions except for the exercise of powers that have to be relinquished to make the single market possible. Externally, the single European market has a border as far as all other countries are concerned, and for culture the particular aim has been to ensure that there is a border between Europe and the United States. Because member countries of the EC have different views about the extent of the American threat to European culture, tension exists between these countries concerning the treatment of the production and distribution of cultural goods and services.

A second related tension arises because some EC countries want to introduce more interventionist cultural policies than others. France, for example, supports the view that what it perceives to be deficiencies of market forces to determine outcomes can be corrected by measures such as subsidies and quotas. At the other extreme, the United Kingdom favors creation of a single market with less emphasis on the introduction of proactive or restrictive measures.

---

6. These are ably described by Richard Collins (1994) with respect to broadcasting and audiovisual policies and help to explain the position taken by the EC in trade negotiations.

Because of a common language market with the United States, the U.K. has been increasingly realizing opportunities for the sale of films and television programs outside Europe.[7]

Paralleling the open versus interventionist views at the national level are similar opposing views within the bureaucracy of the EC in Brussels. These divisions are reflected in the development of audiovisual policy in which originally four directorates general (DGs) were involved, those responsible for the internal market (DGIII), competition (DGIV), culture and audiovisual (DGX), and telecommunications and information technology (DGXIII). A liberal approach to cultural policy has been espoused by DGIII and DGIV and an interventionist approach by DGX and DGXIII.

In part, the tensions have been caused by the conflicting roles that culture has played in the creation of a united Europe. Europeans view a different world when they look outward than when they look inward. On the one hand promotion of a European culture is seen to be unifying and necessary to provide a force able to compete with American culture. On the other hand, the governments of individual countries within Europe consider themselves to be the guardians of separate cultures and often different languages. Should cultural policy promote unity or diversity? The question provokes heated debate but defies a logical answer. The sound and fury of different positions turn into thorny issues when national policy actions conflict. Verbal compromises like "unity in diversity" provide little guidance as to how they should be achieved.

Framed by these tensions, the evolution of cultural policies has been played out within the legal agreements establishing the EC. No mention of culture appeared in the founding treaty, the 1957 Treaty of Rome, meaning that article 235 applied, stating that the Council of Ministers, after receiving a proposal from the commission and after consulting the European Parliament, must agree unanimously on taking action on anything not explicitly mentioned in the treaty. This suited later entrants to the union like the United Kingdom and Denmark, which argued that cultural policy should remain an exclusively national competence.

Changes came with the 1991 approval of the Maastricht Treaty of European Union. Article 128 provides for cultural cooperation by member states while "respecting their national and regional diversity." The wording recognizes the compromise struck between the advocates of unity and diversity, but it is not enough for some. In the 1997 draft Treaty of Amsterdam, which contains further

---

7. British programming from both public and private television suppliers is ubiquitous on American public broadcasting and specialized cable channels such as Arts & Entertainment (A&E), Bravo, and Discovery. American series have occasionally been based on formats first developed in the United Kingdom.

proposals to revise the founding treaty, paragraph 4 of article 128 has proposed new wording (shown in italics):[8]

The Community shall take cultural aspects into account in its action under other provisions of this Treaty, *in particular in order to respect and to promote the diversity of its cultures.*

The roots of post-Maastricht policy were developed in the preceding decade without any cultural mandate but under the impetus of expanding the domain of a pan-European market. From 1981 on there were numerous inquiries, reports, directives, and court cases that pertained to the governance of the cultural industries in the Common Market. The European Parliament, the commission, and the Council of Ministers were all involved in the process. Initiatives were also undertaken by the EBU and the COE, agencies outside of the formal EC administration. Despite the provisions of article 235, ways were found to introduce policies affecting culture within the wording of the Treaty of Rome or through the actions of non-EC institutions. A list of some of the important initiatives undertaken include the following:[9]

- 1981. Report of the European Parliament (Schall report) proposes creation of a European television company and television channel to promote the EC. (European Parliament 1981)
- 1982. Report of a committee of the European Parliament on radio and television broadcasting (Hahn report) reiterates the need for a European television channel, plus production of a full range of European programs and protection of young viewers. (European Parliament 1982)
- 1983. The European Commission in a report entitled *Realities and Tendencies* responds to the Hahn report, noting the impact of satellites, cable, and video on broadcasting policy. Expanded distribution systems are contrasted with limited European programming material, leading to the likelihood of expanded imports of American programming. (Commission of the European Communities 1983)
- 1984. The European Parliament (Arfe report) replies to *Realities and Tendencies.* It supports the introduction of a legal framework for European broadcasting, technical and industrial cooperation, a European television channel broadcast by satellite, and financial assistance for the

---

8. Draft wording from web site <http://ue.eu.int/Amsterdam/en/treaty.html>.
9. A detailed discussion of the period up to 1992 can be found in Collins (1994).

production of European programs. It asks the EC to ensure that public broadcasting monopolies do not compete unfairly against private broadcasters and program producers. (European Parliament 1984)

- 1984. An EC Green Paper is followed by a 1989 directive of what came to be called the Television without Frontiers (TWF) initiative. (Commission of the European Communities 1984)[10]

Television without Frontiers

The TWF green paper and subsequent directive provided the impetus for establishing a single market for broadcasting within the EC. The green paper argued that, although there was no reference in the Treaty of Rome, broadcasting was an economic activity for which the EC had the power to introduce measures. TWF stressed the need to remove measures that restricted broadcasting between member states, affirmed the need to ensure the right of reply and to protect children, and noted that rules on copyright in particular created obstacles to the cross-border flow of programs.

Throughout the period between the green paper and the final TWF directive extensive debate and discussion took place as the various interests argued their cases. Advocates of both a more open market and interventionism could point to some aspect of the directive that met their needs. Amendments were again made in May 1995 when the EC presented a proposal to increase the legal certainty and update the wording of the 1989 TWF directive. The new directive came into force in 1997 and required national legislation by the end of 1998.

While the TWF directive as a whole relates to the creation of a single television market within Europe, we note here those provisions that may give rise to possible trade distortions or restrictions:[11]

- Events of major importance, particularly sport—member states can draw up a list of events such as the Olympic Games and World Cup that must be broadcast unencrypted even if exclusive rights have been bought by pay television stations.

---

10. The directive is entitled Directive on the Coordination of Certain Provisions Laid Down by Law, Regulation, or Administrative Action in Member States concerning the Pursuit of Television Broadcasting Activities (89/552/EEC, *Official Journal L*, 298, 17.10.1989, 23–30).

11. This summary is based on the 1997 revisions to the wording of the 1989 TWF Directive—see *Official Journal L* 202 1997, no. 60; and *Official Journal L* 298, 1989, no. 23.

- Measures to promote European programs—where practicable, television stations must reserve a majority proportion of their time for broadcasting European works. Some flexibility is allowed in implementing this provision and the definition of *European works* has been extended to include some coproductions involving member states and third countries.
- Independent productions—10 percent of transmission time or program budgets must be reserved for independent productions, with member states introducing a definition of *independent producer*.[12]
- Film broadcasting—periods for which films may not be broadcast on television after first being shown in cinemas have been abolished. Member states are required to ensure that periods agreed to between broadcasters and rights holders are respected.
- Television advertising—a limit placed on advertising of 20 percent of any given clock hour. Public service messages and charity appeals are not included in this total.
- Sponsorship—pharmaceutical companies can sponsor broadcasts but not promote specific medicines or medical treatments.

Copyright Initiatives

Initiatives were also undertaken in Europe with respect to copyright. Sacchi and subsequent court cases established that the owners of copyrighted works embodied in a good had exhausted their rights at the time of a first sale. This decision removed the possibility of restricting European trade in records, books, and videocassettes by discriminatory national copyright licensing. Although Sacchi had classified broadcasting as subject to the European service regime, the decision permitted retransmission of a signal from one member country by the cable company of another without compensation. In contrast, in two decisions made in the early 1980s, Cotidel I and Cotidel II, the European Court of Justice ruled that owners of intellectual property rights in a film or television program were able to restrict the distribution by cable of the film or program in another member state.[13] A copyright owner's right to sanction the broadcast of a film or

---

12. In 1996, 214 European channels were surveyed to determine whether they fulfilled the TWF quotas for European programs and programs by independent producers. The survey concluded that the majority of broadcasters had fulfilled their quotas. Large satellite channels tended not to comply (information from Notes from EC IP/98/317, Brussels, April 3, 1998).

13. Case 62/79, *Cotidel SA, Compagnie Générale pour la Diffusion de la Télévision, Cotidel & Others v. SA Ciné-Vog & Others*, (1980) ECR 881; and Case 262/81, *Cotidel SA, Compagnie Générale pour la Diffusion de la Télévision, Cotidel & Others v. SA Ciné-Vog & Others*, (1982) ECR 3381.

program was not exhausted by its original broadcast. A retransmitter had to obtain permission to carry the film or program on its service. As Porter comments:

owners of the copyright in cinematograph films could continue to subdivide the common market into geographical areas, provided that their application did not constitute a means of arbitrary discrimination, or a disguised restriction on trade between member states. (1991, 31)

The European Commission subsequently abandoned an attempt to impose a compulsory retransmission license as part of the TWF initiative (Orf 1990, 270). The commission's concerns that in the absence of a compulsory licensing arrangement transaction costs would impede retransmission underestimated the efficiency of contracting responses between collectives of copyright holders and cable interests.

The Satellite and Cable Directive of 1993 (Commission of the European Communities 1993a) addresses the issue of satellite broadcasting. A debate about whether the copyright law of the receiving country or the sending country prevailed preceded the issue of the directive. The directive determines that a satellite broadcast is covered by the laws of the country of origin. Groups representing the recording producers and performers opposed this solution. They feared that satellite transmissions would gravitate to European countries that did not grant public performing rights to producers and performers (or if they did were less generous in their support).

This concern was in part assuaged by the EC Directive on Rental and Lending Rights (Commission of the European Communities 1992). Article 1 of this directive creates exclusive rental rights and public lending rights for all copyright works. Article 5 contains an option by which a member state can derogate from an exclusive public lending right as long as it provides for a remuneration right for authors affected by the derogation.[14] This directive also addresses the harmonization of neighboring rights with copyright in the EC.

The Term of Copyright Directive (Commission of the European Communities 1993b) was another of the recent spate of copyright directives issued by the

14. "Member states shall be free to determine this remuneration taking account of their cultural promotion objectives." Subsection 3 of article 5 relaxes the constraint on national policy of article 1 even further by giving the member states the right to exempt certain categories of establishments from the payment of the remuneration right. Reinbothe and von Lewinski (1993) provide a fascinating account of the negotiation process affecting the structure of this directive. They discuss subsection 3 of article 5 on page 82.

Commission. In response to a decision by the European Court of Justice in 1989 that disparate terms of copyright protection among member countries provided a legal justification for imposing restrictions on intermember trade, the directive established the duration of copyright at 70 years. The term of related rights was generally set at 50 years. The harmonization of duration reduces the costs of developing trade in multimedia products.

Financial Support and Other Measures

While the TWF directive sets out the conditions for a single European market, other, more proactive measures exist. A common feature of the film and television industries is the provision of government subsidies and/or tax incentives. The countries of Europe are no exception. Two regional schemes in Europe include the action program to encourage the development of the European audiovisual industry (MEDIA) of the EC and the Eurimages programs of the COE. In addition, actions taken by the EBU have affected trade between member countries and have been challenged by DGIV, the EC directorate in charge of competition policy. Cultural governance, in addition to the DGs, has involved institutions such as the COE and the EBU that are distinct from the EC.

The MEDIA initiative provides support for pre- and postproduction of films and television programs as well as their distribution using a number of programs such as BABEL (Broadcasting across the Barriers of European Language), SCRIPT (Support for Creative Independent Production Talent), CARTOON (support for animation), and EFDO (European Film Distribution Office).

The pilot phase of the MEDIA program was launched in 1986. It has been reviewed and revised with the current five-year program known as MEDIA II, which expires in the year 2000. Aside from aiding the development and distribution of audiovisual products, MEDIA II supports the training of audiovisual professionals.[15] The EC has been able to provide support by using its powers to assist the industries of member countries. Emphasis on the cultural dimensions of the program have therefore been downplayed somewhat in order to permit the EC to act.

Another source of funding is the Eurimages program administered by the COE. Established in 1949 with 10 member countries, the COE now has 40 member states, some of which are EC members. Its original mandate was to promote European unity through a variety of measures. As far as broadcasting is concerned, the COE promotes the freedom of reception by viewers of transfrontier signals through the Convention on Transfrontier Television and

---

15. Information from EC web site <http://europa.eu.int/s97.vts>.

requires that where practicable broadcasters must reserve a majority of their transmission time for European works. Europe in this case includes more countries than those affected by the TWF quota arrangements.

The Eurimages program began operation in 1989, providing support to film and television programming that was complementary to the MEDIA program. Its emphasis has been on assisting coproductions and distribution in areas such as dubbing and subtitling since language is a major barrier to the creation of a single market. Originally concluded between 12 member states of the COE, Eurimages now consists of 24 member states. Support is provided for feature film and documentary coproductions. Feature films require independent producers from at least three member states and documentaries must be presold to distributors in at least three member states. Distribution support is available to countries that cannot access the MEDIA program, that is, European countries that are not members of the EC.[16]

The EBU was established in 1950 with 23 members, mainly public service broadcasters. It has grown to 66 active members from 49 European and Mediterranean countries and 51 associate members in 30 countries in Africa, the Americas, and Asia.[17] On a Europe-wide basis, the EBU's responsibilities have included the provision of a network of program exchanges such as news and the collective acquisition of television rights, especially sports, for its member companies.

Public service broadcasters have been reluctant to support a single European market initiative that might undermine their status in national markets, and they have attempted to protect the monopoly position they enjoyed prior to the entry of commercial broadcasters. While extensive entry has occurred since the 1980s, actions of the public broadcasters have been challenged by DGIV, the competition authority of the EC. In particular, DGIV has acted when it has viewed the public broadcasters as behaving like a cartel in the acquisition of certain film and television rights that are restrictive of competition and affect trade between member states. Public broadcasters are concerned that increased competition for programming would raise the price of programs at their expense and to the benefit of the owners of program rights.[18]

---

16. Information from the COE web site <http://culture.coe.fr/Eurimages/eng/eleaflet.html>.

17. Information from the EBU web site <http://www.ebu.ch/welcome.3html>.

18. Cases include the acquisition by Arbeitsgemeinschaft der Offentlich-rechtlichen Rundfunkanstalten der Bundesrepublik Deutschland in Germany of exclusive television rights for films and television programs in MGM-United Artists library for exclusive transmission not just for Germany but for all German-speaking regions of member countries of the EC (see *Official Journal L* 284, 36–44, 3.10.89); and the preferential access obtained by a group of EBU member broadcasters to certain sports rights to the detriment of nonmember companies (see *Official Journal L* 63, 32–44, 9.3.91).

Audiovisual policy in Europe is very much a work in progress. It was the topic of a report from the EC to the Council of Ministers in July 1998—*Audiovisual Policy: Next Steps* (Commission of the European Communities 1998a)—where the regulatory framework is described as including the TWF directive as well as directives and initiatives related to the harmonization of certain aspects of copyright and related rights, standards, and regulations for Information Society Services and standards for the transmission of television signals.

While the emphasis here has been on audiovisual aspects of culture, the EC is active in the support of other cultural activities—the Kaleidoscope program to support artistic and cultural creation and cooperation; the Ariane program to promote books and reading; and the Raphael program to support the European cultural heritage. Our purpose here is not to provide an exhaustive examination of the cultural programs and policies within Europe at the national and regional levels. That would require duplicating for Europe the topics addressed in part II of this book for Canada. Rather we aim to identify areas where trade, investment, and intellectual property issues relevant to the cultural industries have been addressed in a major regional structure and where developments may have influenced policy discussions, especially in North America.

A recent assessment has been made of the progress toward a single market in audiovisual services for the 12 member states that formed the EC prior to 1995. It notes that the "basic principle of freedom of movement has been restricted in practice" in regard to the TWF Directive. Cross-frontier transmission of programs has been restricted where local or national licensing requirements have been imposed, attempts have been made to prevent cross-border channels from selling air time, and there has been denial of access to carriage on cable systems by the exercise of "must-carry" rules (Commission of the European Communities 1998b, 3).[19]

Coproduction Treaties

Aside from multilateral and regional agreements and cooperative clubs, such as the OECD, the European countries have negotiated bilateral coproduction treaties for films and television programs. While most audiovisual productions involve cooperative financial arrangements in that financing is obtained from different sources as a result of presales in different markets, equity investment, and loans, some more formal arrangements have been negotiated between countries to provide a framework for coproductions. These coproduction

---

19. We are grateful to Professor Patrick Messerlin for bringing this study to our attention.

agreements facilitate the acquisition of funding from official sources and the approval of the programming as local content in each of the partner countries.

Coproductions have been a ubiquitous form of organizational arrangement in Europe since 1949 (see table 1). They remain popular today. According to *Screen Digest,*[20] between 33 and 43 percent of all films produced each year from 1991 to 1996 in the 15 countries of the EU were coproductions. The treaties were originally created to support film production but have been extended to cover television. For example, production partners for *Baywatch* include American, Italian, German, and Spanish firms. In the United Kingdom, this program is counted as having 50 percent European content, while in the remaining member states of the EC it is 100 percent European content (Commission of the European Communities 1998b, 115).

Informal Regimes

The EC negotiates for its member countries in international commercial agreements and acts on behalf of its members in registering formal complaints related to those agreements. A number of DGs, the European Parliament, the Council of Ministers, and the Court of Justice, as well as non-EC organizations such as the COE and the EBU, often participate in policy formulation. European negotiators can use the tactic of agreeing to settle a dispute subject to the agreement of some organization that may not be present at the negotiations but whose agreement is claimed to be necessary in order to reach a settlement. The ultrafederal character of the European political structure in which responsibility is shared among EC institutions, national governments, and, in areas such as broadcasting in Germany, state governments makes negotiations and the monitoring of compliance with obligations difficult. The informal processes of reconciling conflicts are as a result active but extremely complex. Like the United States, the EC has the powers to take unilateral action on the part of member governments to offset "unfair" acts of other countries affecting trade and investment.

TABLE 1. Film Coproductions in Europe, 1950–66

Country	Total Films Produced	Percentage Coproduced
France	2054	53.7
Italy	2892	42.3
Spain	1316	31.3
West Germany	1522	19.2

Source: Guback (1969, 183).

20. May 1997, 105. India and Egypt are also important producers of films, but the extent of their coproductions is not recorded.

Conclusion

In this chapter we have discussed the evolving issues addressed by existing international agreements during the post–World War II period. There have been impressive achievements in liberalizing international trade. Extending these gains by developing mutually acceptable governance structures for the deeper issues concerning trade and copyright as well as extending coverage to investment and labor movements present a formidable but attainable challenge. The cultural industries have received some attention in the formal arrangements, but trading has been governed more by the existing informal regime than for most other sectors of the economy.

The discussion has explored the extent to which GATT dealt with cultural trade before the recent agreement of the WTO and how Europe has focused attention on crafting rules disciplining trade of the cultural industries within Europe and the national copyright policies of its members. By the time the Uruguay Round negotiations took place, most of the issues affecting culture had arisen in one forum or another—culture as a good or service, public and private measures that restrict market access, the relationship of trade to investment and intellectual property, and the use of subsidies and the impact of technology. In the next chapter we examine the prevailing formal and informal structures currently governing the commercial relations in these industries between Canada and the United States.

CHAPTER 5

Governance of Cultural Commerce in Canada and the United States

There are two prerèquisites for understanding the trade disputes addressed in part III of this book. One is a knowledge of the complex of support and regulatory programs for the cultural industries in Canada. These programs differ significantly from those of the United States. The second prerequisite is knowledge of the formal agreements and informal processes governing trade in the cultural industries between the two countries addressed in this chapter.

We begin with a discussion of a set of coproduction treaties that Canada has negotiated with a large number of countries. Although Canada has defended these treaties as nurturing the sourcing of cultural products from countries other than the United States, privileges similar to those included in the treaties have been extended to producers from the United States on an informal basis. The second section describes the array of instruments available to American policymakers for use in disputes that occur outside formal channels. We then address the treatment of cultural trade in the agreements to which the two countries are parties. These are the regional CUSFTA and NAFTA, which are considered as a piece, and the international WTO. After examining the significant changes in formal governance introduced with the WTO, we briefly discuss the informal processes within which talent moves between Canada and the Untied States. We conclude with an analysis of a recent attempt by the OECD, a club of developed countries that includes Canada and the United States, to gain approval of a MAI.

Canada's Coproduction Treaties

In 1963, Canada signed its first formal coproduction treaty with France. The agreement was modeled on the bilateral treaties that had been negotiated among European countries.[1] Since that time over 40 treaties have been signed. Most deal with film and television productions, but a few deal with film or television

---

1. France and Italy signed the first coproduction agreement in 1949. It is reprinted in Guback (1969, 209–14), revealing the complexity of the interpretations required. For example, details are laid out as to whether a person should be considered a national of the country of citizenship or of residency.

only. The principal purpose of coproductions is to give producers access to new sources of funding and to facilitate access to foreign markets. In order to achieve this end, a complex administrative structure is put in place, permitting national authorities to certify coproductions and to monitor them over time so that some sort of balance of benefits is received by each country. The problem of overall balance arises because each production does not have to be structured so that each partner has an equal share.

In an attempt to clarify some of these complexities, we will outline three types of arrangements: official coproductions and twinning arrangements, both of which take place within a bilateral treaty; and coventures, which are coproductions not meeting the conditions of an existing treaty or undertaken with partners outside a treaty country. The procedures associated with each illustrate their purposes and possible consequences. From an investment and trade point of view, they constitute preferential arrangements for the production and distribution of audiovisual works and were treated as such in the GATS.

Official Coproductions

Under the principles and rules governing official coproductions, wherein one party may be a majority or minority partner, the coproducers must make an effective creative, artistic, and technical contribution to the production, which should be in proportion to their financial contributions.[2] The minimum financial participation in the budget varies from 15 to 30 percent, depending on the agreement, and the coproducers will share in domestic and international revenues according to their investment shares. Each country facilitates the entry of personnel and equipment from the other country. The shooting and postproduction should normally be done in the country of the majority partner, but provisions are made to relax this requirement and permit shooting in third countries. Tradeoffs can occur between the location of shooting and postproduction and the employment of personnel so that flexibility is maintained and administrative discretion used. Provisions are also made for financing to be provided by third parties.[3]

Twinning

A twinning arrangement is a package of two properties, each of which is developed by separate national production teams in each of the treaty countries.

---

2. See Telefilm Canada, Official Coproductions, Policies 1994–95, and Telefilm Canada (printed materials), September 1996.

3. A detailed review of how a coproduction project would be evaluated in Canada is discussed in *Playback*, September 30, 1991, 26. A series of eight articles in *Playback* from August 19 to November 25, 1991, examines a range of coproduction issues.

The projects must be of equal size and type. Thus, the Canadian production costs may be zero percent of the foreign budget but 100 percent of the Canadian budget. There may be no Canadian content in the foreign production and no foreign content in the Canadian production, but under the coproduction treaties each work enjoys domestic production status in each country and thus qualifies under domestic content rules.[4] Twinned projects benefit from government grants and tax incentives. Whereas coproductions involve artistic cooperation between two parties, twinning can be quite separate and merely give the parties reciprocal access to the other market. An example of a twinned project is *Loyalties,* produced by Lauron International Inc. of Canada, and *No Surrender,* produced by Dunbarton Films Ltd. of the United Kingdom. One was a 97-minute and the other a 104-minute film.

Coventures

Coventures as defined by the CRTC are coproductions made without a treaty. They must have a Canadian producer or coproducer. By providing a series of funding and content incentives outside treaty arrangements they provide further financing flexibility.

Most of the coventure activity occurs with American firms. The participating firms contribute their producing expertise and their reputations and marketing connections in their respective markets. The Canadian producers also provide access to Canadian government funding. Both the twinning arrangements and coventures are clearly industrial policies aimed at promoting the industry rather than Canadian culture. The same is true for Canadian federal and provincial tax credits available to foreign firms working on location in Canada.

Business and artistic creativity are restricted by the bilateral focus of coproductions and the requirement of balance in financial and creative inputs. The treaty structure has been stretched over time to ease this constraint by including twinnings as well as official coproductions and relaxations of the rules to include stars from nontreaty countries and some locational shooting in nonparticipating countries. A further relaxation has occurred through the extension of the content status earned by treaty coproductions to coventures. With coproductions, the output is often vetted and influenced by the granting processes in the partner countries, each hoping to support a program reflective of its own society. The result can be a drab compromise. In Europe, the expression *Europudding* emerged to describe such works. We have assessed a sample of different "Canadian" films supported by tax shelters, many of which were also coproductions. A few of these creative works supported by low budgets

---

4. If a project is twinned, it is assured of domestic production status only in Canada.

might otherwise not have been made, but most of the fare is "industrial." The creative works are not typically tied to national culture issues (Acheson and Maule 1991b).

The coproduction treaty with France has stimulated the most activity and the most complex governance structure, but this activity is still less than that which occurs under the less formal coventure arrangements. The activity under other treaties has been highly variable and in many instances insignificant. The adoption of EC quotas for television has affected the relatively important treaties with European countries. Currently, the Canadian share of a majority Canadian coproduction, with France, for example, does not qualify as European content, although it may qualify as French content for the purposes of any additional content restrictions adopted by France. The language of the film has become an issue on occasion when a large number of films made under the accord with France featured the second of Canada's official languages, English (see Acheson and Maule 1989), underlining the fact that commerce rather than culture was driving at least some and perhaps much of the coproduction activity.

The Unilateral Trade Instruments of the United States

The general provisions of U.S. law covering unilateral trade policy initiatives are set out in section 301 of the Trade Act of 1974 as amended in 1979, 1984, and 1988. In addition to section 301, there now exist special 301 provisions dealing with intellectual property issues and super 301 provisions designed to force the executive branch of government to initiate section 301 proceedings against certain priority nations. The EC introduced a similar measure in 1984, permitting unilateral action when a person "has suffered injury as a result of illicit commercial practices."[5]

Under section 301, the U.S. Trade Representative (USTR) has flexibility in initiating retaliation against goods and services in the affected sector or a different sector, and in its response it can choose whether to obey the MFN principle or not. The process can be very political, described by a lawyer who has used it as follows (Fisher and Steinhardt 1982, 577):

> Indeed, astutely using the threat of filing a Section 301 complaint as leverage to achieve a desired end may lead to better results than casually filing a complaint and pursuing the case through administrative channels. . . . More than any other U.S. trade law, Section 301 works through feints and threats, rather than through formal legal processes.

---

5. A detailed discussion of the law and cases is found in Jackson, Davey, and Sykes (1995, 815–43).

The USTR's approach is supported by submissions made by interested parties. For example, the Motion Picture Association (MPA) makes an annual report to the USTR entitled *Trade Barriers to Exports of U.S. Filmed Entertainment,* detailing the nine categories of measures, one of which is lack of intellectual property protection.

In using special 301 provisions regarding intellectual property, unilateral action is combined with formal agreements like NAFTA or TRIPs. The USTR is instructed to determine whether the rights granted under the agreement are being denied as a result of the action taken by the foreign party. Deadlines are specified, and the USTR is given both mandatory and discretionary powers to pressure countries to alter their policies (McIlroy 1998).

The North American Free Trade Agreement

Treatment of culture in the CUSFTA and NAFTA can be considered together, as wording from the first carries over to the second with respect to the United States and Canada. The sectors covered are specified and allow little flexibility for new measures of content production and new delivery mechanisms.[6] Thus, multimedia productions and the Internet would have to be squeezed into existing cultural categories in order to be covered by the cultural exemption.

Canada attempted to exempt or exclude culture entirely from the CUSFTA. A complete exemption was Canada's preferred position in contrast to that of the United States, which wanted its inclusion. The final wording was a compromise that has led to ambiguity and to date no test of the agreed wording. Two articles set out the terms of the agreement:[7] article 2005(1) states that "cultural industries are exempt from the provisions of this agreement except as specifically provided"; article 2005(2) states that notwithstanding any other provision of the agreement "a party may take measures of equivalent commercial effect in response to actions that would have been inconsistent with this Agreement but for paragraph 1."

The exceptions to article 2005(1) that relate to trade and investment are a commitment to eliminate tariffs for goods that are inputs to the cultural industries; a requirement that those foreign companies that had to divest themselves of certain assets in Canada because of foreign ownership restrictions in the cultural industries be assured of fair market value for their assets; and the

---

6. The NAFTA cultural exemption relates solely to enterprises engaged in the print media, film and video recordings, audio or video music recordings, music in print or machine readable form, and broadcasting. Developments in multimedia are too new to have been listed separately.

7. Articles 2005(1) and 2005(2) provide the general exemption and retaliation provisions of the CUSFTA, which are carried over into the NAFTA in article 2106, annex 2106. The cultural industries are listed in article 2107.

removal of a restriction that magazines must be typeset and printed in Canada for a company to be able to deduct advertising in the magazine as a business expense in Canada.

At the time of signing, there was a difference of views as to the circumstances under which the United States could retaliate under article 2005(2). Neither side has initiated action that might lead to an interpretation of the wording even though the United States could have done so in the *Sports Illustrated* and CMT cases (see chapters 10 and 11). The reasons are probably twofold. Neither side was sure that its opinion was correct, and there existed other forums in which the dispute might be resolved, the informal political forum in the case of CMT and the WTO in the case of *Sports Illustrated*. The decision resulting from the choice of the WTO for the periodical case has allowed the United States to create a precedent for its dealings with other countries in matters related to culture.

At this time, we can only speculate on possible interpretations of articles 2005(1) and 2005(2) based on the discussions of trade specialists. Aside from not fulfilling the three trade commitments and one copyright commitment that would be contrary to Canada's NAFTA obligations, one extreme view is that Canada can do anything it wants in the cultural sector. At the other extreme is the view that the United States can retaliate for any cultural measure that is introduced by Canada. In a presentation before the Congress, the USTR stated:

> The Canadians have taken a cultural derogation just as they took a cultural derogation in the Canadian free trade agreement. . . . We for our government have said, if we suffer any economic harm as a result of their exercising any rights pursuant to that cultural derogation, we reserve the right to retaliate.[8]

In the NAFTA Statement of Administrative Action, the administration stated that it

> will consult with the Canadian Government regarding any proposed Canadian measures or policies that might lead to the exercise of, or reliance on, the "cultural industries" exemption. Should Canada choose to institute such measures, the Administration in consultation with the relevant industries, is prepared to exercise fully the right to respond granted in the Agreement. At such time as the Administration takes remedial action in response to a Canadian measure, it will endeavor to

---

8. NAFTA: Hearings before the Committee on Finance, U.S. Senate, 102nd Cong., 2d sess., September 8, 1992, 23.

fashion a response in such a manner as to discourage the creation of a similar nontariff barrier in other countries.[9]

The key wording in article 2005(2) concerns "actions that would have been inconsistent with this agreement but for paragraph 1" when a "party may take measures of equivalent commercial effect." According to Bernier (1998, 123):

> Taken literally, this contradicts the affirmation of paragraph 1 in that it penalizes the non-respect of obligations from which the Parties are exempted. As a matter of fact, in order to determine whether measures of equivalent effect can be used, one must necessarily proceed as if cultural industries were covered by the Agreement and consider whether measures applicable to them are in violation of the agreement. What Article 2005 says, in reality, is that if a Party is ready to pay the price, it can maintain cultural measures that are incompatible with the Agreement.

This interpretation suggests that because cultural industries and related policies are not part of the agreement both countries can do what they want. The price would be whatever economic damage each party could inflict and sustain on the other, a situation that favors the stronger.

Another interpretation suggests that, apart from the listed exceptions, the cultural industries have been carved out of the NAFTA but would be governed by whatever general international trade law applies. In this case, culture would be governed by WTO law. The question then remains as to what is meant by article 2005(2). It gives the United States the right to retaliate against cultural measures taken by Canada, providing that it abides by its WTO commitments. The USTR, by suggesting that it might retaliate against Canadian telecommunications interests in the CMT case, was pinpointing an area where, at the time, the United States had no treaty obligations.

Both these interpretations seem to favor the United States' position but conflict with the view of the Canadian negotiators. Because of the uncertainty involved, no party is likely to want to test the meaning of the two articles. It is not surprising that the United States presented the periodical dispute as a trade-in-goods case in which the known disciplines of GATT 1994 apply.

In the case of investment, chapter 11 of NAFTA extends nondiscrimination provisions to investors of other parties through MFN and national treatment

---

9. The Statement of Administrative Action was submitted by President Clinton to the Congress on November 3, 1993. It is reprinted in "North American Free Trade Agreement, Texts of Agreement, Implementing Bill, Statement of Administrative Action, and Required Supporting Statements," 103d Cong., 1st sess,, H. Doc. 103–59, 1: 670–71.

obligations as in the case of trade in goods and services. These provisions would apply to Canada's cultural policies in the absence of the cultural exemption in article 1105. Existing investment restrictions under the Investment Canada Act, for example, have been grandfathered and could not be made more restrictive. Investment issues that could become contentious in the future are foreign ownership restrictions, reciprocal ownership regulations, and cross-media ownership regulations.

The CUSFTA included one important copyright provision, Canada's commitment to create a distant signal copyright regime that would be nondiscriminatory.[10] Canadian cable companies now pay royalties into a fund that is in turn divided among collectives representing owners of programming. A large proportion of the fund is disbursed to American program providers. The NAFTA chapter on copyright brought Mexico's law into greater conformity with that of the United States. Although Canada exempted its cultural industries in the NAFTA negotiations, its laws were already in compliance with the copyright aspects of the intellectual property chapter except for a provision to provide a rental right for sound recordings. Canada adopted such a provision in the legislation implementing NAFTA but did not treat this measure as a cultural policy concession, as it would likely have adopted a rental right for records had there been no treaty.

The World Trade Organization

The treatment of culture in the WTO depends on whether it is considered a good or a service. To the extent culture is traded as a good, the disciplines of GATT 1994 apply regarding issues such as MFN, national treatment, and market access. In addition, the subsidies code applies to these items. If culture is traded as a service, the provisions of the GATS prevail. GATS is structured so that countries such as Canada and France can protect their audiovisual service sectors from trade-liberalizing measures, and the disciplines of the subsidies code do not apply.

---

10. After passage of enabling legislation, the Copyright Board of Canada set a royalty rate of 70 cents per month per cable subscriber in large systems and lower rates for small systems. Subsequently, the board was persuaded by evidence that distant signals were of lower value to Francophone systems and halved the benchmark royalty for such systems. In the decision announcing the revision, the board reported: "The figures advanced by various parties may differ; however, they all confirm that whether one looks at prime time, off-prime or full time, distant signal viewing as a percentage of hours tuned to cable is between 14.9% and 17.7% for Canada, 18.3% and 21.5% for Canada excluding Quebec, and only between 4.4% and 5.2% in Quebec" (Copyright Board of Canada, January 14, 1993, 48).

All services are subject to the GATS provisions regarding MFN and transparency, but reservations can be taken for MFN that are intended to be phased out over time. For each service sector, a country must then opt in or commit itself for the sector with regard to national treatment and market access. If it does not opt in, then the sector is not subject to the trade-liberalizing provisions of the agreement. Canada took MFN reservations with respect to its film and television coproduction treaties, which provide more favorable treatment for certain partner countries. The reason given was the need to preserve the Canadian and Québécois cultures. Canada did not take MFN reservations for its film distribution policy, which has given preferred status to the Hollywood majors relative to any new foreign distributor. This decision led the EC to complain to the Canadian authorities that its policies were not in accord with its MFN commitments under GATS. The complaint was lodged on behalf of Polygram, at the time a large Dutch film distribution company, which sought the same status in Canada as had been granted the Hollywood majors. The action is in abeyance, as Polygram was subsequently taken over by a Canadian firm, and the fate of its film distribution assets has yet to be decided, as is discussed in chapter 17.[11]

By not opting into the GATS for audiovisual services, Canada also protected this sector from the market access and national treatment disciplines of the agreement. France, for example, made no commitments for audiovisual works and included eight MFN reservations, all for an indefinite time period. One of these permitted the imposition of "redressive duties against third countries with unfair trade practices against a member country" in order "to counteract alleged unfair pricing."[12]

Countries that opt in for particular service sectors do so for four different methods of delivering a service, one of which is providing it through maintaining a commercial presence in the foreign country, which in effect means investing in the foreign country.[13] Qualifications can be made to each of the four delivery mechanisms so that even if a country does opt in for a sector it can still make significant reservations regarding national treatment and market access. For example, it may commit a sector and then place a limit on market access by

---

11. In October 1998, the EC complaint re Polygram was still listed as a "pending consultation" on the WTO web site.

12. U.S. International Trade Commission, "General Agreement on Trade in Services: Examination of Major Trading Partners' Schedules of Commitments," December 1995. The contents of this document are examined in Bedore (1997, 26–33).

13. The others are cross-border supply, consumption abroad, and presence of natural persons. It is estimated that after discounting for the effects of qualifications made to sector-specific commitments, high-income countries have commitments for about 36 percent of their service sectors and developing countries for about 10 percent (Hoekman and Braga 1997, 303).

declaring that acquisition by nonnationals of a firm above a certain size in the sector is subject to approval. A country is bound to any commitments made unless it declares that it is unbound, meaning that it can introduce limitations at a later date.[14] The United States made commitments for audiovisual services but included as a limitation grants from the National Endowment for the Arts, which are only available to Americans and therefore do not provide national treatment (Bernier 1998, 129). A summary of the audiovisual commitments by WTO member countries is shown in box 1.

Box 1
Country Commitments on Audiovisual Services under the GATS

Audiovisual services is subsector D of Communication Services in the GATS Services Sectoral Classification List. Six subcategories of audiovisual services are listed:

a.   Motion picture and videotape production and distribution services
b.   Motion picture projection service
c.   Radio and television services
d.   Radio and television transmission services
e.   Sound recording
f.   Other

Thirteen countries made commitments in the audiovisual sector at the end of the Uruguay Round. As a result of accessions, 19 countries have now made commitments. Only the United States and the Central African Republic have made commitments in all six subcategories; New Zealand in five; Panama and Gambia in four; and Hong Kong and Japan in three. The most commitments, 17, have been made in category a followed by 10 in category b.

Where commitments are made, countries may bind themselves completely or partially. Numerous restrictions exist. Typically they include limits on foreign ownership, limits on screen time for foreign productions, and exclusion from national treatment of domestic subsidies. Thirty-three countries have taken MFN exemptions for audiovisual services, and another eight for all service sectors, potentially including audiovisual services. Most of these exemptions are for film and television coproduction agreements.

Source: Audiovisual Services, Background Note by the Secretariat of the Council for Trade in Services, WTO S/C/W/40, 15 June 1998.

---

14. For details, see Uruguay Round of Multilateral Trade Negotiations, Legal Instruments Embodying the Results of the Uruguay Round of Multilateral Trade Negotiations Done at Marrakesh on April 15, 1994, annex 1b, GATS.

The net effect is that in the WTO, a country can protect its culture if it is considered a service such as audiovisual services and is subject to the GATS. It does so by a combination of taking reservations for MFN and not making any national treatment and market access commitments for the sector or by making only qualified commitments. If culture is traded as a good, then the disciplines of GATT 1994 apply. One implication of this distinction is revealed by the periodical case (chap. 10), in which a magazine was considered to embody a good and a service, the hard copy plus the advertising contained in it. When the good and service are jointly supplied, the WTO decision declares that the defendant cannot hide behind that part of the agreement providing the desired protection since GATT 1994 and GATS must be considered as part of a whole WTO agreement.[15] To the extent that other services are combined with goods, the GATS may not provide the protection for services that some parties to the agreement anticipated.[16] The imprecision of the goods-service boundary remains an unsettled issue for culture and other traded items.

Subsidies

A second implication for culture concerns subsidies. If the traded items are conside ed to be goods, as is certainly the case for hard copies of books, newspapers, and magazines, then GATT article III.8 applies and permits "the payment of subsidies exclusively to domestic producers." These must be paid directly to domestic goods producers in a transparent way. Since subsidies can be provided in a number of different ways—direct grants, loans on favorable terms, loan guarantees, equity investments, government purchases, tax credits, deductions, or remissions—care has to be taken in structuring the subsidy arrangement.

The subsidy must also be in conformity with the WTO Agreement on Subsidies and Countervailing Measures (ASCM). The subsidies agreement relates to three types of subsidies, those that are prohibited, nonactionable, and actionable. Prohibited subsidies (article III) are those that are contingent on export performance or the use of domestic over imported goods. Nonactionable subsidies (article VIII) are those that are termed not specific and do not limit access to the subsidy to certain enterprises. Examples of nonactionable subsidies are listed as those dealing with research, disadvantaged regions, and assistance

---

15. See World Trade Organization (1997a). This decision was confirmed on appeal as far as advertising in periodicals being a service is concerned in WTO (1997b).

16. In a subsequent decision, EC—Regime for the Importation, Sale, and Distribut.on of Bananas, the Appellate Body of the World Trade Organization refers to the good-service problem in a different industry context and states that it will have to be dealt with on a case by case basis (Bernier 1997, 3).

to promote adaptation of existing facilities. Actionable subsidies (article V) are those that are specific or have adverse effects on other member countries such as causing injury or serious prejudice to their domestic industry.[17]

Subsidies of any type can be offered to cultural services, as opposed to goods, and not be contrary to trade obligations providing they do not affect trade in goods. A postal subsidy was one issue in the periodical dispute. It was found to be contrary to GATT obligations because of the way in which it was delivered, indirectly through Canada Post as opposed to directly to publishers.

Subsidies as they relate to services are mentioned in article XV of the GATS, noting that they may distort trade. Member countries are required to enter into negotiations with a view to developing multilateral disciplines to avoid trade-distortive effects and to address the appropriateness of countervailing procedures. Members are also required to exchange information concerning all subsides related to trade in services. For culture, this will be an important issue because of the numerous ways in which countries provide subsidies.

The Council for Trade in Services met for the first time on March 1, 1995, and since then a working party has been addressing the issues, which include the following:[18]

- Creation of a balance between the use of subsidies as a tool of social and economic policy and their trade-distorting effects.
- Emphasis to be placed on disciplines to regulate the use of subsidies versus the development of unilateral remedies such as countervailing measures.
- Development of a list of subsidies related to services in order to determine whether a general discipline can be developed for all services as opposed to designing subsidy disciplines for individual service sectors.
- The definition of subsidy used and the extent to which it should extend to regulatory interventions that have the effect of imparting a subsidy on services or service suppliers.
- The applicability of the ASCM for goods to trade in services.
- The applicability of the special subsidy rules for agricultural goods to trade in services.
- The impact of the MFN commitment in the GATS in cases in which there are no domestic suppliers and differential treatment of foreign suppliers may be an issue.

---

17. Article XV outlines the ways in which injury is determined. Procedures for dealing with serious prejudice are dealt with in annex V of the ASCM.

18. For details, see Working Party on GATS Rules, Subsidies and Trade in Services, S/WPGR/W/9, March 6, 1996, and S/WPGR/W/12, May 20, 1996.

- The impact of the national treatment commitment in the GATS and how it might relate to the four different modes of supply especially where differential commitments are made for each mode. Different types of subsidies—for production, investment, export, and consumption—also have to be considered for each mode of supply.
- The type of remedies to be used.
- The provisions on subsidies relating to trade in services in 137 regional trade agreements. Relatively few of these agreements have relevant provisions.

Only after these issues are resolved will it be possible to determine how different measures, including regulatory interventions used in the case of film, audiovisual services, sound recordings, and publishing industries will be affected. The issues are complex, but, as noted, they have already arisen in the case of the periodical dispute referred to the WTO.

Investment and Intellectual Property

Unlike NAFTA, the WTO does not have an investment chapter. Investment considerations, however, emerge from the GATS, where commercial presence is one of the ways cross-border services are supplied. If no commitments are made for the coverage of cultural services, these disciplines do not apply. Elsewhere in the WTO agreement reference to investment is made through the provisions of TRIMs, which limits the tying of trade performance requirements to foreign investment. These disciplines apply only in the case of trade in goods. Exempt services under the GATS are not affected.

The Uruguay Round negotiations also resulted in TRIPs, in which member countries of GATT agreed to various measures strengthening copyright protection while committing "to ensure that measures and procedures to enforce intellectual property rights do not themselves become barriers to legitimate trade." More specifically, the parties agreed to comply with the 1971 Paris protocol of Berne, except for the moral rights provisions. In addition, copyright coverage was extended to include computer software. The minimum duration of copyright was extended for some works. An MFN clause was introduced into international copyright relations. Any neighboring right commitment made by a country as a member of the Rome Convention that was conditional on reciprocal treatment was exempted from the MFN requirement. A member country's treatment of parallel imports was also exempted from both national treatment and MFN. Both of these exemptions from MFN play a role in the trade disputes discussed in subsequent chapters.

A rental right was granted for both computer software and cinematographic works (prerecorded videos). This right allows the copyright holder to prevent rental of its product and is designed to curb unauthorized copying. A country is exempted from introducing the video rental right if illegal copying is not "widespread." A rental right is also required for sound recordings unless a country had in place at the time of the conclusion of the Uruguay Round a system for making equitable payments to the right holders of a recording that is rented and copying in that country is not leading to material impairment of the interests of those right holders.

TRIPs also tackled the difficult issue of limiting exceptions from copyright obligations that permit users to copy a work, or a part of it, for specified purposes such as educational or personal scholarship. The wording in this case is too vague to be of practical importance, but the agreement at least flagged a concern that exceptions might be widened so as to avoid a country's copyright obligations. A GATT-style dispute resolution mechanism was instituted. The parties to GATT also agreed to adopt more transparent processes for adjudicating copyright and to enhance their enforcement efforts.

With the accession of the United States to the Berne Convention in 1989, it became the dominant international copyright agreement. Under Berne, members often adhered to different protocols. The United States put pressure on Canada to accede to the more demanding Paris protocol in the CUSFTA negotiations.[19] Although Canada did not make this commitment in the CUSFTA and NAFTA, it did so in the WTO negotiations.

Labor Movement

Unlike the formal provisions of the NAFTA and WTO, the issuance of work permits is an example of an issue conditioned by an informal type of arrangement. In the cultural industries the cross-border delivery of services occurs when, for example, firms engage in location shooting in foreign countries and artists and performers work abroad.

The policies that allow for location shooting in Canada are somewhat opaque. Before a work permit can be issued to a foreigner to work in Canada, permission has to be received from the affiliated local union, guild, or association working on the project. In the case of a performer, the Alliance of Canadian Cinema, Television, and Radio Artists (ACTRA) has to issue a permit.[20] Because

---

19. See quotation from the statement by the USTR Clayton Yeutter of July 23, 1987, in Keyes (1993).

20. An ACTRA official indicated that a foreign performer would pay for a permit for the right to work in Canada and a similar arrangement would take place with the counterpart organization in the United States when a Canadian performer worked there.

there are no international regimes, local authorities are free to use their discretion in determining some of the conditions under which foreigners can work. This process can be used opportunistically when local authorities restrict the employment of foreigners on a project that is partially completed.[21]

Some coverage under a formal regime occurs in the case of chapter 16 of NAFTA, which provides for the temporary entry of businesspersons who are citizens of the three countries. Those permitted entry into one of the other countries as professionals are listed by profession in schedule II of chapter 16. Over 50 professions are identified together with the qualifications that signify professional status from architect through hotel manager and nutritionist to zoologist. Almost all the occupations require as a minimum a baccalaureate or Licenciatura degree. A management consultant with several years of experience can qualify. Missing from schedule II is any mention of artists, performers, and those associated with the cultural industries and not represented in one of these listed professions.

Since there is considerable cross-border movement of artists between Canada and the United States, one most look elsewhere for the prevailing entry procedures.[22] Our understanding of the process is as follows. For those performers who are established and have a performance or series of performances booked in different locations in the United States, there is little difficulty in obtaining a temporary entry visa. These persons are already employed, have a reason for being in the United States other than looking for work, and can be expected to leave within a short period of time. In contrast, those individuals who want to enter to engage in a self-promotion tour but have no fixed commitments and may be unemployed will have great difficulty in obtaining a visa, and in fact dealing with the visa authorities in the various American embassies will often be a frustrating experience. Consequently, these persons will tend to cross the border on some other pretext, work, if they can, without a visa, and hope that they are not apprehended. If they find a permanent employment opportunity, they then look for an employer to sponsor their immigration application.

In effect labor organizations issued work permits to foreign performers (telephone conversation with ACTRA official, Ottawa, September 11, 1997).

21. Director John Boorman (1985), while shooting *The Emerald Forest* in Brazil, described the conditions imposed by the Brazilian authorities on the use of foreign technicians and actors, which raised shooting costs.

22. Special attention is given to performers and artists in a pamphlet distributed by the Department of Foreign Affairs and International Trade entitled "Guide for Canadian Performing Artists Entering the United States." It addresses the major provisions of the U.S. Immigration Act of 1990, together with amendments and regulations instituted in September 1994.

In examining the procedures used by the U.S. Immigration and Naturalization Service (INS) to process temporary visas for musicians to perform in the United States, Jones (1996, 333–35) draws attention to the de facto quota arrangement that limits the entry of foreign musicians. Pressured by the combination of powerful unions and an unemployed army of aspiring artists, the INS has tightened its rules for issuing work permits to performers. Canadian performers were caught in the revisions to the U.S. Immigration Act in 1991, but representation by the Canadian government appears to have limited any damaging consequences.

Absent any formal regime for the cross-border movement of labor in the cultural industries, union pressure groups and industry associations appear to exert considerable influence in determining the issuance of work permits and visas. They often act as advisers to the authorities in managing a process that lacks transparency. Access to the U.S. market is important for artists from smaller countries who wish to raise their profiles at home as well as abroad. In a magazine interview, Canadian Margo Timmins of the Cowboy Junkies is quoted as saying: "I think that if this [U.S.] law had been in place in 1988, we might not have been given visas . . . and I probably wouldn't be sitting here."[23]

OECD and the MAI

Culture again proved to be a stumbling block in the completion of an international regime for investment, the MAI in the OECD in the spring of 1998. In part the objections stemmed from the feeling that a small group of 29 mainly wealthy countries was negotiating a set of rules that would be to their benefit and the detriment of others. Opponents existed not only in developing countries but among groups in the industrialized countries that coordinated their opposition using the Internet. With respect to culture, one view was that unless an exemption similar to NAFTA could be achieved, countries such as France and Canada would be disadvantaged. In one sense the MAI can be ignored since it does not yet exist for culture or any other sector, but the issues are important because they point to the areas that will have to be dealt with in the future in either the OECD or the WTO.

The MAI negotiations represented the continuation of a process that began at the time of the postwar negotiations for an International Trade Organization, which would have covered investment and restrictive business practices as well as trade (Diebold 1952). Only the GATT emerged from these deliberations. Subsequently, an attempt was made to resurrect the investment and restrictive

---

23. *Canadian Musician,* October 1991, 12.

business practice issues in various United Nations organizations and to develop a comprehensive code of conduct for multinational enterprises.

At the same time, the OECD worked on developing a number of related measures. An OECD Code of Liberalization of Capital Movements and of Current Invisible Operations was adopted in 1961 and a Declaration on International Investment and Multinational Enterprises in 1976. While promoting the free movement of capital, the Code of Liberalization of Capital Movements permits countries to list reservations. For example, Canada's reservations include direct investment in "activities related to Canada's cultural heritage or national identity, in particular those areas involving publication, distribution and sale of books, magazines and newspapers; films; music; video and audio recordings; and radio and television." In the Code on Current Invisible Transactions, Canada took reservations for content quotas and production subsidies in the audiovisual services sector and for split-run editions of magazines.

The OECD Declaration on International Investment and Multinational Enterprises contains an instrument entitled "National Treatment for Foreign Controlled Enterprises." Each country lists exceptions to national treatment. Canada has taken exceptions for foreign takeovers above a certain size and for policies related to broadcasting, cable television, book publishing and distribution, and film distribution. Reservations have been taken for provincial as well as federal policies.[24]

In the MAI, as for the GATS, draft wording was proposed stating that countries could shield sectors, culture and others, from the obligations of the agreement. France proposed wording aimed at inserting a general exemption for culture in the agreement. This approach, which was supported by Canada and some other countries, reads as follows:[25]

> Nothing in this agreement shall be construed to prevent any contracting party to take any measure to regulate investment of foreign companies and the conditions of activity of these companies, in the framework of policies designed to preserve and promote cultural and linguistic diversity.

The United States objected to a broad cultural exemption leaving countries the option of taking national reservations.[26] In the absence of an exemption, two

---

24. Reservations taken by countries for these three OECD agreements are listed at <http://www.oecd.org/>.

25. See OECD, Introduction of an Exception Clause for Cultural Industries in the MAI, DAFFE/MAI/RD(96), OLIS, April 25, 1996.

26. See <http://www/state.gov/www/issues/economic/multilateral.html/>.

types of reservation were discussed, bound and unbound. A bound reservation occurs when a country agrees to "stand still," meaning that it will not make the measure more restrictive. In future rounds of negotiations, bound reservations are likely to be the subject of "rollback" or amendments that make the measure less restrictive. An unbound reservation occurs when a country makes no commitments to either "stand still" or "roll back." In legal terms, an exemption and an unbound reservation for culture are similar in that a country would accept no present or future obligations with respect to culture. Politically they differ. An exemption would apply to all 29 countries, while an unbound reservation would be identifiable to a particular country and could be subject to political pressure to relax the reservation in future rounds of negotiations.

A second aspect of the MAI negotiations is of interest for the cultural industries. Discussion took place over ways in which the definition of *cultural industries* could be updated and amended to take into account distribution of print and audiovisual material over the Internet. The Society of Composers, Authors, and Music Publishers of Canada (SOCAN) proposed that the MAI incorporate the NAFTA definition of the cultural industries with one important difference.[27] The definition would include the phrase "communication by telecommunication" in connection with each cultural subsector. The aim was both to make the definition technologically neutral and to permit the Internet to be made subject to domestic cultural sector regulation as opposed to domestic telecommunications regimes. As part of the broadcasting regime, material carried on the Internet would become subject to domestic content policies for those countries with such policies. Whether this was practically feasible was not examined.

The MAI negotiations were scheduled to resume late in 1998. In October 1998, France announced that it would not participate in future negotiations at the OECD while Canada has indicated that it will continue to meet with the other countries. Whatever the outcome at the OECD, the issues are likely to become part of future WTO negotiations. Both the definition of *culture* and the process of exempting or excluding it from the obligations of an agreement are important for how an investment regime will handle disputes, especially those that combine trade and investment issues.

---

27. The original wording submitted by SOCAN for a cultural exemption was presented in SOCAN's brief to the Canadian House of Commons Standing Committee on Foreign Affairs and International Trade on November 20, 1997. The revised wording was contained in a letter sent by Keith Kelly, national director of the Canadian Conference of the Arts, to International Trade Minister Marchi, dated December 12, 1997.

Conclusion

In the past, international trade and investment in the cultural industries have taken place within an informal international regime. Despite some explicit references in GATT that remained unchanged until the EC and the NAFTA on a regional level and the WTO on an international level addressed issues of trade in services and in copyright, the legal backbone of contracting in these industries was largely disciplined by national laws, not international rules. Currently, more aspects of trade in these industries are disciplined by international constraints to which countries have voluntarily acceded, but much still remains on the outside.

The disputes examined in part III reflect the influence of the new arrangements and the efficacy or lack thereof of the old processes of ad hoc compromises influenced by immediate political concerns. International rules-based systems, the supporting institutions of adjudication, the norms governing diplomatic interactions, and informal processes of dispute resolution are constantly evolving. To creatively influence the future, the present must be assessed with reference to the past. The achievements in international governance of commerce since World War II have been both remarkable and insignificant in comparison with the challenges ahead.

One of those many challenges is incorporating more fully the cultural industries into a mutually advantageous international governance framework. An important step in achieving that goal is to develop an understanding of both the details of domestic cultural policies in a country like Canada and of their impact currently and in the future on commercial opportunities within these industries. That is the task of part II.

International governance will be accompanied by imperatives for change domestically. That inescapable fact scares many in these creative industries and in Canadian society as a whole. In our opinion, there are a number of elements in the current Canadian policy framework that are unsustainable in either an informal setting or a negotiated agreement. A viable rules-based system for these industries, which have important international commercial imperatives, is important to all countries but is especially critical to smaller countries. The alternative is an exodus of talent, a failure to participate in the opportunities created by the new technologies, and the abandonment of the emerging organizations capable of managing creativity while maintaining commercial viability

Part II

Economic Dimensions and Policies

The existing formal and informal governance structure for the cultural industries is in the process of change. A new structure will evolve, taking into account the domestic policies of individual countries and the responses of their trading partners within the context of changing technology. In the following chapters we examine first, in chapter 6, the idiosyncratic economic dimensions of cultural production and distribution and the organizational and contractual arrangements that have evolved for each of the sectors: film, broadcasting, print, and sound recordings. Each is made up of a mix of public and private organizations operating under a complex set of laws and policies. Because of the role that the media play in the functioning of democratic societies, these policies are of interest to a number of groups and tend to be vigorously debated.

The detailed characteristics of film and television production in Canada are set out in chapter 7, including the range of subsidies and incentives used to promote production on behalf of commercial firms and the role played by the public broadcaster and public filmmaking. In chapter 8, the industry structures associated with the distribution and exhibition of films and television programs are described along with another set of policies. Chapter 9 undertakes a similar task for publishing, sound recording, and radio. Notable are the cumulative effects of discretionary policies, which have lead to exceptions, contradictions, inconsistencies, and sometimes absurdities. Although specific to Canada, the chapters provide general insights into industry structure in a smaller economy that has adopted a complex set of inward-looking policies. While Canada's geography is unique in being located next to the United States, the introduction of satellites makes foreign content spillover a feature experienced by all countries.

The policies discussed in part II have given rise to the disputes examined in detail in part III. Any future set of trade negotiations will have to develop a similar inventory of policies for each country in order to determine where common ground can be reached for international agreement. The inventory is the starting point. Because many of the policies provide for discretion to be exercised in actual implementation, examples are necessary in order to determine their effects on trade and investment flows.

CHAPTER 6

The Economic Characteristics of the Cultural Industries and Their Organizational Implications

The cultural industries address the interrelated challenges of creating content, packaging that content in an appropriate format, distributing the result, and generating sufficient revenue, grants, or gifts to meet costs. The process of reproducing the transformed content into "copies" for distribution varies with the media. It is very different for a book than for a television show. Some media depend on physical networks for distribution, while others distribute "hard copies" through retail and rental systems. Content is always nonrivalrous, in the sense that once it exists it does not have to be re-created in order to make it available to someone else. Some distribution systems are also nonrivalrous along particular dimensions. For almost all media an increase in volume lowers the unit costs of production and distribution. Content can also be altered at relatively low cost to better serve different markets. The cultural industries distribute content that is typically novel. The marketing challenge is to provide predictability without divulging content. Demand is influenced by word of mouth and other social processing of information. The rewards of success with a new novel, movie, or record are large, but the odds of success are correspondingly low.

These characteristics elicit organizational responses. Cultural industries are vertically and horizontally integrated through both ownership and complex contracting. This structure creates incentives for creative inputs, aids in the financing of projects, and distributes risk. Contracting to realize the economic value of content is facilitated by the legal substructure of copyright and related or neighboring rights. The low costs of extending distribution to a wider audience and differentiating content to better serve segments of that audience create a commercial imperative to market cultural products widely. The parties to contracts can designate which national contract law will govern their agreement, but enforcement is made more difficult when the obligations are dispersed geographically and over time. One constant across different countries is the reliance on promotion of the cultural industries. They attempt to manipulate the social processes determining what is currently fashionable in music, television, or film but are also subject to their capriciousness.

In this chapter, we survey the economic characteristics of the cultural industries. These are shared by each of the industries, but the mix varies. There is both a common element and distinctive features in the organization of the film, television, broadcasting, publishing, and recording industries. We first present a generic outline of the organizational structure of each of these industries. In chapters 7 through 9, we provide a detailed description of the Canadian organizational and policy framework for each sector. The detail is necessary to convey the tension between the international imperatives and the inward-looking Canadian policy structure. These accounts also reveal a further contradiction between the set of different policies covering different media, which developed when their technologies were distinct, and the blurring of these differences by recent technological developments.

Economic Attributes of the Cultural Industries

Effect of Nonrivalry and Durability on Content

A manifestation of scarcity is that generally, if one person consumes a good, say, an apple, it is not available for another person to consume. Economists call that quality "rivalrous in consumption." This type of scarcity is absent for the content of cultural products. The consumption of the content of a book, record, or audiovisual presentation by one person does not make it unavailable to another.

Magazines and books illustrate a distinction between nonrivalry and the durability of a fixation of content. After one person has read a book another can borrow it and enjoy the same story. Repeated satisfaction over time from one item does not reflect "nonrivalry" but the capital-good nature of a book. Nonrivalry of the print medium would require that others could enjoy the book simultaneously. Since reading over the book owner's shoulder is clearly inferior to being the book owner, books and magazines have this quality only in a very limited sense. For a cultural industry in which both content and the medium in which it is fixated are capital goods, currently produced goods compete with previously sold goods.

When the medium is a capital good, the exhaustion principle limits the ability of a copyright holder to realize its value. Once a book is sold, for example, the copyright holder in North America cannot control its subsequent resale or lending to others. Buying a used book or borrowing from a library are substitutes for buying a new book. These alternative ways of obtaining access to a story discipline the price that can be charged for a new book. This discipline depends on the durability of the book and the evolution of the demand for content over time. A badly bound paperback deteriorates rapidly with use, which stimulates new sales rather than its further circulation. The value of content independent of the medium also changes value over time. There would be little demand for last year's sports scores even if newspapers were more durable. Used book stores are ubiquitous while used newspaper stores are rare or nonexistent.

The owners of copyrighted works that sustain their value over time and are contained on a durable medium have lobbied for greater economic control of their works. This has resulted in many countries adopting a rental right for recordings, which suspends the exhaustion principle by preventing the owner from renting the recording without permission from the owner or owners of the record's rental right.[1] In North America books have generally not received a rental right or a public lending right that would control use of copyrighted material by noncommercial libraries.[2]

Paradoxically, scarcity can sometimes be alleviated by making a nonrivalrous good rivalrous. Without some means of excluding users from content, there is no incentive to pay for access and compensate the supplier of the content. For many people, the question "Why pay when it is available for free?" has one answer. Without payment, the content supplier cannot recoup costs and is unlikely to pursue impoverishment by staying in the business.

There are different ways of building fences around content. Among these are private sanctions imposed on copiers. For example, a Mafia boss may protect the content of his novel about the pastoral pleasures of Sicily by putting out contracts on those who copy the content. In the business world, nineteenth-century American publishers reduced copying by rivals through a set of business strategies that included fighting brands, larger initial print runs, and pricing policies (Plant 1934).

Private sanctions are not a very satisfactory instrument for dealing with this problem. Potential authors generally lack the instruments available to crime bosses, and most crime bosses are not talented writers. The structure of today's cultural industries also differs from that of nineteenth-century publishing. Even if that were not the case, both private and business threats of imposing damages can have negative social and economic side effects. Since the eighteenth century a remarkable and controversial legal structure—copyright law—has been developed to provide a contracting skeleton for organizing all of the cultural industries.

---

1. See the 1992 EC Directive on Rental and Lending Rights, in particular, articles 1 and 5 (Council Directive 92/100/EEC of November 19, 1992).

2. The Canadian government created a public lending right in mid-1986, which remunerates some Canadian authors whose books are lent out by Canadian libraries. The plan was created by an administrative decision. It is not part of Canadian copyright law. The amounts distributed have been less than $10 million per year and are financed out of general tax revenue.

A copyright policy that is economically optimal balances at the margin the incentive to create against the social cost generated by pricing that uneconomically limits access to existing copyrighted works. The legal restrictions on the monopoly power of the copyright holder include limiting the duration of the right, exempting some users from having to pay fees, and regulating some licensing fees.

As copyright is costly to enforce, infringement occurs, further limiting the monopoly power of a copyright owner. The fences created by copyright induce piracy. The costs of enforcing vary with different means of distribution and the quality of "burglary" tools. The established players and their industry associations promote more protective copyright laws, more severe penalties for infringement, and better enforcement. The industry associations also provide statistics on the extent of piracy in different countries. These numbers are often cited, but it is inherently difficult to quantify the extent of illegal activity of this type. The associations make significant contributions to the enforcement of copyright laws by discovering and providing evidence of bootlegging activities to the relevant authorities. They also lobby for taxes and prohibitions on the burglary tools as well as the creation of funds from these taxes to be distributed among the creators affected by piracy.

Neighboring rights relate to obligations and rights of broadcasters and other users of recorded music and audiovisual material to provide remuneration to performers and record producers. The state also augments the supply of copyright material by subsidizing production. In some instances, the state may either buy or produce content and make it available at no charge to the audience. Public television is an example.

Effect of Nonrivalry on Distribution

Most means of distribution in the cultural industries have low incremental costs rather than the zero incremental costs implied by pure nonrivalry. As the number of people receiving the content increases, some form of crowding occurs, reducing the value received by both the additional person and those already receiving the content. A movie viewed in a cinema is largely nonrivalrous up to the capacity of the theater, but there may be some reduction in the value of watching as the theater becomes more crowded. A moviegoer prefers the large cowboy with the large hat to be on the screen and not sitting in the row ahead. In addition, not every seat in the cinema offers the same view of the screen. Once the theater is sold out, access to the film ceases to be nonrivalrous.

The theatrical distribution of films involves the coordinated distribution of prints, many of which cross national borders. Increasingly for broadcasting and prospectively for cinematic distribution, film content is transported electronically. Bookstores or magazine shops can be converted to other uses at low cost. In contrast, cinemas have traditionally required more specific capital. This is less true for modern multiplexes, but the showing of 70 mm. films in IMAX theaters, for example, demand large sunk investments. In contrast, the costs of entry and exit to video renting and retailing are low.

Technology has significantly extended the reach of films. The rental and sell-through market for videos provides a viable alternative to the movie house. PPV, movie networks, and conventional television deliver a wide array of films electronically to the home. Video on demand, or near demand, will enhance the importance of electronic delivery.

For free over-the-air broadcasting, the costs of adding an additional listener or viewer within the range of the transmitter is only the cost of a television set. For satellite broadcasting, the incremental cost also includes the cost of a dish and a smart box. Expanding the receiving footprint of a terrestrial broadcaster or a satellite broadcasting service to reach a larger potential audience generates a more substantial incremental cost. Compared to wired systems, fine adjustments in coverage are prohibitively costly. For example, a wired cable system in Detroit, Michigan, or across the border in Windsor, Ontario, can respect the national boundary at a reasonable cost. A Detroit or Windsor television station or a nationally licensed satellite broadcasting system cannot do so.

With cable there is a different cost to add a customer to an existing network compared to expanding the network to accommodate an additional customer. There is both a network scale and a density of custom effect on the costs of servicing a given number of people. New cable systems typically build the lower cost parts of their networks first and then extend them to higher cost areas. For some high-cost areas, wireless solutions are often more economical than the fiber or coaxial links typical of densely populated areas.

Adding a new subscriber to an existing cable network requires a "drop" or connection from the network to the customer's premises. Linking apartment residents to a network is cheaper than providing connections in a rural area. A wired system is less costly to police than a nonwired system. Although a wired cable system does have a problem with illegal drops, the monitoring problem is not severe enough to warrant scrambling all of its channels. With wireless and satellite systems, the problem of illegal access is greater. As digital compression becomes the norm, the costs of effective scrambling will be reduced significantly.

Expanding the network size, once a cable franchise is covered, requires acquiring another franchise contract. When cable systems were one-way, stand-alone, franchise monopolies, the configuration of systems owned by multiple systems operators (MSOs) was not a significant determinant of costs. If the cable system is configured so as to provide two-way services as well as the traditional cable business, geographical contiguity becomes important for costs. As technological change and regulatory decisions induce more competition among systems, a rash of takeovers, mergers, and exchanges of spectrum and other rights are occurring and more can be expected. "Churning," the turnover of subscribers on a network, also generates costs. As a side effect of competition, the churn on any given system will increase.

With media that are not dependent on a communications system, a mix of distributional technologies coexist. For example, magazines have different costs of reaching new customers through sales at newsstands and subscriptions. Similarly, records and books can be distributed to new customers through stores, mail order, record clubs, and (increasingly) Internet services.

Extending the Domain of the Market through Content Differentiation

Once produced, content can be tailored to better satisfy demand in different markets. Differentiation is commercially attractive if it raises the total value of the product across markets by more than the cost. One important dimension of differentiation is language. Successful books are translated. Films and television programs are dubbed or subtitled into other languages to raise their value in different linguistic markets.

Altered or cut versions of a film or television program may be offered to some markets to increase potential box office revenue. In this way, the films are "watered down" to avoid issues that are controversial in the viewing area. Variants of films and programs may differ as to ending, the amount of explicit sex or violence, and the like. A broadcaster, exhibitor, or publisher can choose the version most attractive to its audience or most in line with the type of content with which its brand or imprint is associated.

The Social Process of Consumption and the Informational Setting

As well as declining costs and nonrivalry in some dimensions, cultural products are consumed differently than many other products. Consumption is often social, or jointly enjoyed, and continues over time. Reading a book, viewing a movie, or listening to a song played on the radio are opening events in a process of evaluation. Consumption continues with unconscious and conscious mulling over of images, sounds, and meanings and related conversations with friends and family. This interaction includes inputs from critical reviews and street "gossip." The process is valued in itself.

In describing the social process of consumption, we begin with the act of consuming the cultural product, but what determines why one book or film is chosen rather than another? Cultural products are often chosen by consumers in a different informational setting than most products. The book reader or the filmgoer does not know what he or she is buying in any detail. If a consumer knows what each page of the book or each frame of the movie contains, he or she will have no need to buy the book or the cinema ticket. Access is bought in the hope of being pleasantly surprised.

This uncertainty is characteristic of all the cultural industries and has spawned a number of related practices and strategies in response. Potential quality may be signaled by knowledge of the genre, the reputations of performers and other creators, a positive review, the recommendation of a friend, or the observation that others are consuming the product. A brand name also signals information about the viewing, listening, or reading experience that will be provided. Brands are not limited to commercial organizations. Public broadcasters also nurture reputations for a particular type of programming. In England, the British Broadcasting Corporation (BBC) is known for its high quality but middle of the road broadcasting philosophy. In contrast, Channel 4, an advertising-supported English public channel, has a reputation for providing edgy, in-your-face content that embroils its management in much public controversy. Some of its critics describe it as the pornography channel.

International Cultural Products and the Interpretation of Domestic Market Shares

Low costs of distributing existing content in additional markets and in modifying the content to raise its value in those markets create a strong incentive for marketing a film, television program, book, or record widely. Of course, for some productions the only viable market is local. There is no demand in Los Angeles for a report on road conditions in Ottawa and vice versa. This type of programming has to be supported by the value it creates locally.

The economic incentive to market content internationally is not limited to mass market material. The audience for most specific-interest films or programs is both relatively small *and* international. A documentary filmmaker successfully examining, for example, the ethics of assisted suicide for the terminally ill will face a niche market that is international, not national. If the documentary film is from a small market country and is sold in the open market, the bulk of the revenues from the project are likely to come from abroad. The implications of this for interpreting viewing statistics are not well understood. The cultural industries of a small country operating in an international market can compete effectively, generate interesting and creative jobs, and contribute to the balance of payments while the share of domestically produced product in bookstores and cinemas and on television channels, record shelves, and magazine racks remains small.

To illustrate, consider the following stylized example of the North American market for a particular type of English-language television programming. Suppose that English-speaking Canadian and American viewers have similar demands but that only one of every 15 English-speaking viewers in North America is Canadian. Licensing fees reflect viewership. For concreteness, assume that American licensing rights can be bought at $1,400,000 and Canadian rights at $100,000. Suppose Canada produced one of every 15 of these differentiated but interchangeable shows transmitted on North American television. Canadian broadcasters would pay American producers a total of $1,400,000 for the Canadian rights to the 14 American shows while American broadcasters would pay $1,400,000 for the American rights to the one Canadian show. In Canada, only one out of 15 hours of television would feature the Canadian-made show, but international payments for program licensing fees would be balanced. Assuming that production techniques are the same in both countries and the American labor force is 14 times as large as the English-Canadian labor force, there would be the same proportion of workers employed in program production in Canada as in the United States.

The viewing statistics would show that Canadian television only aired Canadian programming 6.7 percent of the time while American television aired American programs 93.3 percent of the time. In the assumed situation, these figures do not reflect American dominance. Judging the competitiveness of the Canadian industry requires appropriate benchmarks. By assumption, there are no separate Canadian and American shows. Television in both countries is airing 100 percent international programming. Canada and the United States have shares of that market that are coincident with their relative weight in the overall market for international programming. Of course, other factors, such as a preference for home-produced output, differences in income, and disparate production capabilities, will affect actual market shares, but the relative weight in the market remains an important factor to keep in mind when looking at prime time viewing statistics.

The preceding example focuses on the demand side for international cultural products. The international imperative also affects production, particularly in the audiovisual field. A film or television program is produced by a skilled team. These teams form for one project, break apart, and come together, often with changes in composition, for the next project. Their composition is often international. Another international element is location. There is much movement of skilled personnel among countries, as the location of the shoot is affected by subject matter, local costs, exchange rates, and subsidies.

Marketing, Finance, Contract, and Organization

The low probability of success of any particular project creates problems for financing production in the cultural industries. Producers and performers who do not have the required wealth rely on informed downstream firms—publishers, distributors, broadcasters—to commit to the project. To protect their position those who put up the money constrain the degrees of freedom of the creators through vertical contracts or vertical integration. If the distributor's promises are creditworthy, independent producers can use the contracts as collateral with financial institutions. In the absence of such quality collateral, many financial institutions do not lend to film and television projects even if they have completion insurance. Those that do lend develop special divisions and assessment practices to better judge the risks.

In a vertical contract, funding is sometimes exchanged for claims against the income of the project. A distributor may, for example, provide a nonrefundable advance on a contract that stipulates sharing revenue from different sources at specified percentages. "Strings" or constraints on the producer that are mutually advantageous, at least ex ante, such as approval of key personnel, are typically part of such a contract.

In many countries outside of the United States, the government is an important source of finance for the cultural industries through subsidies, favorable tax treatment, and direct production. A political rather than commercial calculus guides investment decisions. This typically requires a balanced allocation of funds between different regions, language groups, or other politically important partitions of the country. The tendency is to spread the subsidies widely and support a more fragmented production sector than a commercial approach would do.

Industry Sectors

We now turn to how each of the cultural industries copes with protecting its investment in content, distributing product, exploiting content in different ways, coping with uncertainty, promoting and marketing, selling internationally, and financing projects. The organizational and contractual responses to these problems are of particular importance in assessing domestic and international policy alternatives.

Film

With film, the costs of production are typically high, involving significant capital and personnel costs. The product is created not by an individual but by a team. Screenwriters, cinematographers, and composers provide the building blocks that are orchestrated by directors and editors. The inputs are coordinated by contracts, which in turn depend on a number of copyrights. The screenplay, the music in the film, and the movie itself all have separate copyright protection. The MPA, which represents the major Hollywood studios, has aggressively lobbied for more restrictive copyright legislation and effective enforcement around the world. It has also boycotted countries that condone widespread film piracy.

Film distribution has altered since the 1950s. Under the pressure of competition from television, B movies and double bills have largely disappeared from theaters. Movies made for cinematic distribution embody more production values than in the past and have become correspondingly more expensive to produce. In the international film industry, the major Hollywood movie studios continue to play a significant but changing role, particularly with respect to finance and distribution. Although they continue to produce some films, many more are now made by independent producers. Some deals between independent producers and a major studio are limited to a particular film. Others involve commitments for a number of films over a specified period of time.

Talent agencies have also emerged as important players in the industry based on the actors, directors, screenwriters, and other personnel that they represent. Frequently, an initial treatment of a film plus a team of key personnel are packaged by an agency and "shopped around" to the studios or other financial and distribution sources. The more expensive talent often help finance and share in the risk of a movie by receiving claims on future revenues or profits as part of their remuneration.

A number of international films are also currently produced in countries other than the United States. These films typically are financed by the state, either directly through subsidies or indirectly through tax shelters, and by distributional contracts for rights in various markets. A major Hollywood distributor occasionally finances a foreign-produced film and acquires in the process world rights to all media. In making these arrangements the domestic producer usually surrenders significant elements of control over the creative process. More frequently, participation in foreign films by American interests is lower key, involving contracts with independent distributors or specialized divisions of the majors, which provide less money with less intrusion in return for a more limited set of rights. These films are generally distributed in North America on the art house circuit.

Commercial success is often illusive for independent producers making feature films for theatrical release, even for firms that are sufficiently large to obtain some insurance from a portfolio effect and have earned a reputation for integrity and know-how. The British independent production company,

Goldcrest, for example, developed and produced a number of David Puttnam's films as well as those of other talented producers or directors. Puttnam was an independent British producer who had a sufficiently solid reputation internationally to later be hired as chairman and chief executive officer of Columbia Pictures.[3] Jake Eberts, the head of Goldcrest at the time, provided the following financial accounting of Puttnam's work for his company, which included many of its most commercially successful ventures:

> David Puttnam's entire output for the company—£33 million worth of investments, spread across eight films and nine television features—was to produce, by the end of August 1987, revenues of £25.5 million. The residual book value at that time was put at £6.7 million and the long-term forecast showed a net deficit to Goldcrest of about £420,000. Puttnam made, amongst other titles, *Chariots of Fire, The Killing Fields, Local Hero* and *The Mission,* all of which he, and Goldcrest can be proud of. None of these films was shoddily produced, and only three can be counted duds: *The Frog Prince, Knights and Emeralds* and *Mr. Love.* If Goldcrest found it impossible to make money out of a portfolio such as that produced by Puttnam, then there was surely something wrong with the business. (Eberts and Ilott 1990, 294)

International film distribution is becoming more competitive, as large regional and international distributors are emerging in Europe and Asia. As mentioned in the first chapter, the ownership of the Hollywood studios is no longer solely American but international. In today's world, a film is distributed through a number of sequential "windows": theaters, PPV, video, subscription movie services, and conventional television. Since the late 1980s, the box office revenue from theaters for Hollywood films has been less than the video revenue. PPV and subscription revenue has also been growing more rapidly than box office revenue. The new satellite broadcasting services have further stimulated the marketing of subscription movie channels and PPV services in the United States.

Despite the declining importance of a theatrical release as a direct revenue source, a successful theatrical run substantially affects the revenue potential of the other windows. The promotional capital expended on generating theatrical momentum for a film and the international "buzz" surrounding a box office

---

3. His attempts to change the way business is done in Hollywood angered insiders and, perhaps more importantly, failed to generate profits. Puttnam was hired in mid-1987 and sacked a little over a year later. In 1995, he was knighted for his contributions to British industry and culture.

blockbuster remains critical to the commercial success of a film, regardless of whether it is oriented to a mass international audience or to art house film buffs.

In cinematic exhibition, theaters compete by offering amenities and location, reducing search costs through multiplexing, and charging better prices. Advertising clips are shown in the cinemas of some countries, producing an additional stream of revenue. Sales of food are a ubiquitous and significant source of revenue to theaters. Once in the movie house, the food counter is a monopoly service.

There are also important constraints imposed on cinemas by traditional relationships, vertical contracts, and/or ownership links with film distributors. Contracts between distributors and the cinemas are negotiated in some jurisdictions. In others, the right to show a movie or a set of movies is auctioned. A number of contracting practices have characterized relations between the distributors and the cinemas historically. These include block booking, blind booking, granting clearances, and pooling. Block booking involves contracting for a set of pictures as a unit. Blind booking is the acquisition of exhibition rights for a film or films that have not yet been produced. A clearance grants a theater an exclusive exhibition right for a period of time in a designated zone, which includes rival theaters. Pooling occurs when two or more independent theaters agree to pool receipts and expenses and share profits or losses. Each could in some circumstances enhance market power. They also have possible efficiency grounds in terms of coping with uncertainty. All four practices are monitored and sometimes prohibited or regulated by antitrust or other regulators. There is no uniformity in the law about these matters across countries or, for that matter, across states in the United States.

It is common for countries to have specific legislation restricting structure and contractual practices, negotiated agreements with foreign distributors about acceptable practices and conduct, or antitrust precedents restricting the degrees of freedom in distributor/exhibitor contracting or ownership links. American antitrust history reflects the political attention paid to this interface in a situation in which foreign ownership has not been an issue. For other countries the relationship is even more politically sensitive because of the presence of foreign interests in distribution, exhibition, or both.

Theatrical distribution is an extremely risky business. In the industry, the rule of thumb is that only one out of 10 films is profitable. In the mid-1980s, United Artists hired Billy Wilder, who earlier in his career had directed *Sunset Boulevard* and many other artistically and commercially successful films, as an executive to provide advice on the production schedule. In the following exchange Wilder explains to writer David Freeman how he used this rule in carrying out his executive duties:

Wilder: "Every script, I tell them the same thing: Don't do it."
Freeman: "Do they listen?"
Wilder: "They do it anyway. Nine times out of ten, the picture flops. Then it's 'We should have listened to Billy.' When there's a hit, they're so happy they forgot what I said." (Dialogue described in Freeman 1993, 72)

The rule of thumb may overstate the degree of uncertainty. The MPEAA provided the following comments on this subject to the U.S. Trade Representative in May 1987:

> Making and distributing movies is a very risky business. There is no formula to accurately predict when a film will be a box office success. Eight out of ten movies made in the United States never make a profit from exhibition in American theaters. Only four in ten movies make a profit from all ancillary and foreign markets.

Whether it is one or four of 10, the uncertainty is very high and has not disappeared with extensive experience.

The phenomenon of products facing the type of informational problem encountered by films and other cultural products is just beginning to be studied in the economics literature of informational cascades (Bikhchandani, Hirshleifer, and Welch 1992; Hirshleifer 1995). In an empirical study, De Vany and Walls (1996) have argued that the success of movies follows Bose-Einstein dynamics, which is consistent with the informational cascades perspectives.

Long before this research agenda was initiated, a number of business practices developed in response to the marketing challenge. One is the dependence on stars—both actors and directors. The role of a star is to prime the informational pump by assuring an audience for a film when it is first released. As the screenwriter William Goldman explains:

> A star may not guarantee you a profit—budgets can grow wildly for reasons totally out of their control—but they will absolutely be a hedge against disaster. A star ensures that, even if the movie is a stiff, the movie will open. (1983, 12)

In order to attract filmgoers to their film, distributors advertise and promote heavily as well as do everything imaginable to create word of mouth support. The most important advertising items are television spots and trailers shown in cinemas in the period immediately preceding the release.[4] In 1990, the Hollywood film *Total Recall* cost an estimated $60 million to produce and another $30 million for promotion and advertising.[5] The trend since 1990 has been to increase the proportion of the budget spent on promotion. It is not uncommon to have promotional budgets that exceed the production costs.

An accompanying decision is which strategy to employ in order to capitalize on the publicity campaign. Films that have famous stars or directors or are part of sequence of successful films lend themselves to a wide opening—the simultaneous release of the film in a large number of cinemas internationally. In contrast, a well-made film that deviates from the conventional template and has skilled but unknown actors is better nurtured by a platforming strategy. The latter was applied, for example, to *Ghandi,* a long film targeting an older audience that does not attend the cinema frequently. Its producer described the process adopted by the North American distributor:

> To get the word of mouth going, Columbia used the summer months to screen the film to hundreds of invited audiences: journalists, religious leaders, students, athletes, politicians—anyone whose favourable response might carry some weight. They then opened it at only four cinemas in New York, Washington, Los Angeles and Toronto. Then, as the good word began to get out, Dickie Attenborough, Ben Kingsley and Martin Sheen did radio chat shows, newspaper and magazine interviews, all the while generating greater interest, as, at the same time, Columbia increased the number of prints and the film began to go wide. This release pattern, known as platforming, was followed in every major territory. (Eberts and Ilott 1990, 136)

Distribution of a film to windows other than the theatrical is a more mechanical process, which rides on the success of the theatrical release. The cross effect on subsequent windows of promotion expenses, incurred in the theatrical release, is internalized if, as is common in the industry, a single

---

4. A trailer involves clips from the movie with some bridging. It typically costs $200,000 to $300,000 and runs for two to three minutes. The style of music video channels has influenced the "grammar" and look of trailers. They begin screening about two months before release and are increasingly accompanied by polling of the audience that sees them. A Gallup-Variety poll showed "that next to television advertising, movie trailers are the best remembered and most influential forms of marketing a motion picture" (*Variety,* November 28–December 4, 1994, 24).

5. *Wall Street Journal,* July 27, 1990, B3.

distributor obtains the rights to all the windows. The timing of the PPV, subscription movie channel, and conventional television windows is also influenced by the incidence of piracy.

Films are dubbed to penetrate other language markets, and their content is modified to increase returns in different cultural markets. The following account describes adjustments made to a prominent film when it was released in Japan:

> When Bernardo Bertolucci's epic, *The Last Emperor,* opened in Japan in 1988 it was missing a key snippet: old newsreel scenes of Japanese soldiers in Nanjing, China, in 1937, gunning down Chinese and dumping their bodies. The movie's distributor, using an expression that often crops up here when debate over anything from politics to high prices seems likely to cause discomfort, explained that "we had better avoid unnecessary confusion in the movie theaters." If Japanese are confused, it may be because the *Rape of Nanjing* is glossed over in the schoolbooks as the *Nanjing Incident.* So is Japan's forty-five year occupation of Korea.[6]

A more modestly budgeted film may not be distributed theatrically but be released directly to video or to television as a movie of the week (MOW). Different promotional strategies are adopted in each case. Movies released directly to video are often genre movies—mystery, horror, or soft pornography—or made for television movies, which receive an initial visibility from the advertising preceding their airing and subsequent word of mouth support. In the video, pay, and nonpay television markets, a recently released film faces more competition from previously released films. Previous years' films are not generally available in the movie houses but are in video stores. Films are a capital asset, and the new technologies have raised the value of existing libraries of older films. The television rights to older films are often marketed in bundles. Some large buyers license rights to complete libraries.

A number of films profit from the value of ancillary merchandising rights. Depending on the story or content, related clothes, records, books, dolls, toys, and other paraphernalia are frequently marketable. Cross-promotions with fast food outlets or other retailers are also common. Another cross effect is related exhibits in theme parks developed in conjunction with entertainment and real estate projects. The informational difficulties in coordinating production, promotion, and distribution and the extreme uncertainty of marketing in the film industry create an incentive for vertical integration, through either ownership or relational contracts.

---

6. *New York Times,* December 2, 1990, E5.

The feature film industry has always marketed widely and absorbed resources from many parts of the world. De Sola Pool (1990, 76) has commented that "No medium has a more multinational history than the motion picture." The prospects of foreign revenues have been factored into decisions about content. The American industry has exploited almost every classic in European literature. When David Selznick made *David Copperfield* in 1934 with, for the time, a large budget of over US$1 million, he expected a huge gross from the British Empire and was not disappointed:

> Of *Copperfield*'s (U.S.) $2.8 million gross 25% came from Commonwealth countries, versus 54% in the United States and Canada and 21% from "other foreign. (Schatz 1988, 169)

Currently, a Hollywood film, will often generate more revenue abroad than in the United States. De Vany and Walls give a reverse twist to the common cry from commentators outside the United States that their nationals are being corrupted by the values embodied in American films:

> There is a certain irony here. Some stars and films earn so much from foreign distribution rights that third world motion picture tastes may play a large role in determining the kind of films seen in U.S. cinemas. (1996, 1510)

The future of film looks no less multinational.

Broadcasting

Television and radio differ from cinematic exhibition in the terms of access, the sources of finance, and scheduling conventions. We restrict our comments in this section to television, but much of what is said also pertains to radio. In the subsection discussing the music industry, we address briefly the interaction of the recording industry with radio.

Television programs are also produced by teams of professionals. Production is a volume business geared to meeting tight deadlines. Content is protected by copyright, but piracy is not as significant an issue as it is for the movie industry. An exception is satellite broadcasting, where pirates use illegal decoders.

For over-the-air television signals, expensive programming content is made available to viewers at no charge. If the signal is delivered by a commercial broadcaster, revenues are generated by selling the audience delivered by the programming to advertisers. The commercial broadcaster cannot exclude viewers but can decide the terms on which it will include advertising messages in its mix of content. In effect the advertisers pay for all the content—the programming and the advertising.

By scrambling the television signal or making it available only over cable, the signal owner creates an artificial scarcity, which allows viewers to be charged for access. The scrambled service has two interdependent sources of revenue—subscribers and advertisers. Viewers pay to receive particular content; advertisers pay to send their messages. The interdependence occurs because the type and incidence of advertising may reduce the value of the programming to a subscriber. A commercial subscription channel will choose a mix of advertisements and programming to maximize total profit from the two sources. In some instances, this decision will result in no advertisements and an exclusive reliance on subscription revenue. In most cases, a mix of advertising and programming will be delivered. At the other end of the spectrum are channels carrying all advertisements and no programming, such as a cable "classified ad" channel.

When fences are built and users charged, there is a tradeoff between paying more for what was previously "free" and obtaining better and more responsive content in the future. In some countries, such as the United Kingdom and Australia, the migration of some premiere sporting events from traditional television to pay or subscription channels has been prohibited by law. The content of television shows can also be delivered by videocassette rather than over-the-air or by a cable system. Viewers do not have to watch at a scheduled time, but they do have to either buy or rent the video.

Public television provides an alternative to commercial television. There are different public broadcasting models operating around the world. The BBC service in England carries no advertisements and is largely financed by a license fee. The American PBS is paid for with a mix of taxpayer money, voluntary support drives aimed at viewers, and quasi advertisements of corporate sponsors. The CBC, the Canadian public broadcaster, receives an annual allocation of funds, obtains additional finance from government funds, and sells advertising.

When only a few channels were available, Steiner (1952) argued that a monopoly public broadcaster would provide more variety than a competitive framework.[7] With the development of cable, satellite broadcasting, and encryption techniques, subscription television has become more important in providing services to smaller viewing audiences with intense demands for particular types of programming. Public broadcasting, which once dominated in Europe, is declining in relative importance.

---

7. Beebe (1977) and Owen and Wildman (1992) elaborate on and provide some qualifications to the Steiner argument.

Broadcasting, satellite television, and wireless cable are dependent on rights to the spectrum. The signals of broadcasters or broadband microwave systems (sometimes called wireless cable) do not check in at customs when crossing borders. Agreements exist between countries to coordinate spectrum rights along the border to avoid interference. Similar agreements allocate orbits or stationary sites for satellites among countries and regulate the spectrum used by each. Border television stations are affected by regulation in their home and contiguous countries. The American stations on the Canadian border, for example, have an association that represents their interests in issues with Canadian regulators.

Vertical integration in broadcasting is extensive. Many public broadcasters were historically integrated but are under current pressure to contract out for more of their programming. The commercial networks are often integrated with production units but also buy programming from independent sources. Some multinational media companies like News Corp. and Time Warner own television production facilities, television stations, traditional networks, cable networks, PPV channels, satellite broadcasting systems, and cable franchises. Smaller media companies typically have less comprehensive international interests. Regulatory safeguards against abuses arising from cross ownership of media interests are common.

In the last 15 years, with the expansion of channel capacity and the rapid growth of commercial television in countries previously served exclusively by public television, the international market in programming and services has grown rapidly. Audiences in many countries reveal a more marked preference for locally produced material in their viewing choices than is the case for film. U.S. exports are greater than those of any other country, but other players like the United Kingdom, France, Mexico, Brazil, Canada, and Australia are significant exporters of programs.

There is a growing trade in rights to soap operas, news, and series as well as in the niche markets for arts, horror, science fiction, cartoons, children's, and minority-language programming. International coproductions, which for the past 30 years have been a popular means of financing films and gaining access to more sources of subsidized funds, have become even more popular for television shows. In each of the participating countries, coproduced television programs frequently qualify as domestic television with respect to viewing quotas.

Dubbed television programs have had a mixed reception in various markets. *The Rich Also Weep*, a Mexican soap opera that was "rather crudely dubbed into Russian." It started its run of 249 40-minute episodes in the "best of times, worst of times" Russia of 1992. Allen (1996, 110) quotes the following account, which he considers only slightly hyperbolic, from the *Moscow Times*, describing the impact on Russian society when the show was aired: "[S]treets became desolate, crowds gathered in stores selling TV sets, tractors stopped in the fields, and guns fell silent on the Azerbaijani-Armenian front."

In contrast, dubbed material has not been successful with television audiences in the United States and English-speaking Canada. Only recently has the CBC, the Canadian public broadcaster which has separate English and French services, begun to dub some French-language programs into English and show them on its English service. John Haslett Cuff, the *Globe and Mail* television critic, labeled these efforts as "little more than a futile token." He ascribed the lack of success to the quality of the dubbing. "Quite understandably, the best writers in any language are not naturally drawn to transcribing the words of others, so viewers are sometimes stuck with crude, workmanlike translations that are often unintentionally hilarious."[8] The audience reaction depends on the variety and quantity of nondubbed offerings. A poor dubbing from the original Spanish transfixes Russia, while a workmanlike dubbing from one of Canada's official languages to the other generates unintended comedy and few viewers.

Uncertainty has spawned a variety of practices in this industry. A producer creates a pilot of a proposed series and shops it around looking for a commitment. Each channel provides saturation promotion for its new series and continuing support for renewed programming. If a recently launched series fails to attract a critical mass of viewers the series will be canceled and replaced. A series that is successful for a number of seasons will amass sufficient episodes for syndication. Advertising contracts frequently share risk by adjusting rates for the ratings actually received when the program airs.

Publishing

Currently and historically, the print media can be divided into three broad categories: newspapers, periodicals, and books. Some common features and differences of the three segments are portrayed in table 2.

The commonality includes the interaction of a series of stages. Authorship provides the content that has to be acquired by a publisher who screens and packages the various items of content and arranges for their printing, essentially a manufacturing process, and then for their distribution to consumers. With minor exceptions, advertising content is carried only by newspapers and periodicals.

Differences occur at all stages. A newspaper publisher may employ journalists and editorial writers or contract with independent writers. Advertising content will typically be provided by agencies except in the case of classified

---

8. *Globe and Mail*, June 17, 1997, A11.

advertising. Printing may take place on the publisher's premises or be contracted out, and the papers may be delivered by the publisher's trucks or independent operators. Ultimately the papers are delivered to homes and offices, placed in street boxes, distributed via newsstands, or made available electronically. All this has to occur each day for a daily newspaper. Other print media face the same choices with more forgiving time constraints.

TABLE 2. Content Providers and Carriers in the Print Media

	Newspapers	Periodicals	Books
Content Providers	Employee journalists and editorial writers Freelance writers Advertisers	Employee and freelance writers Advertisers	Authors
Carriers	Publishers	Publishers	Publishers
	Printers	Printers	Printers
	Home delivery Newsstands Libraries Mail Internet	Wholesalers Newsstands Libraries Mail Internet	Wholesalers Bookstores Libraries Mail Internet

While the same stages apply to periodical and book publishing, the frequency of publication and extent of vertical integration vary. Periodicals tend to be weekly or monthly, and books depend on the timing of contractual arrangements between author and publisher. Book publishers will contract out for printing and distribution through wholesalers and bookstores, while some periodical publishers may own printing facilities if they produce a number of publications but will tend to contract out for distribution services.

The target audience for each type of publisher varies. Newspapers have the broadest appeal, with sections catering to specialized interests: international, national, and local news; sports; business, travel; homes; and a wide variety of leisure time activities. In fact, newspapers try to reach in one publication all the interests targeted by individual special interest periodicals. The sections of a newspaper can provide the reader with a series of periodicals or individual periodicals can be purchased to cater to the specific interests contained in each section of a newspaper. On-line news and other services now compete with both traditional print and broadcasting services, leading to convergence between these media. Competition for advertising takes place among newspapers and periodicals as well as between the print and other media, for example, radio, television, and the Internet.

The links in the vertical chain shown in table 2 involve differing organizational and contractual relationships. Common ownership or control through vertical integration exists where writers are employees and printing plants are owned by publishers, but in all three cases some distribution and most retailing tends to be contracted out. An author who decides to work on a freelance basis has the option of arranging to publish and distribute his or her own book, a process known as vanity publishing. Desktop publishing and Internet distribution facilitate vanity publishing but are not helpful to authors who are unknown and need the quality control and recognition provided by a publisher.

The economic factor common to the three segments is that many of the costs of producing the content are not sensitive to the number of copies sold. Once these upfront costs are incurred, the costs of making additional copies available are typically small in comparison. All three media can be cheaply copied, making copyright protection a problem, especially for material whose value does not diminish with time. Some revenues may be collected up front. Presales occur when a reader subscribes to a newspaper or periodical but seldom in the case of a book unless a book club has managed to attract membership. Consequently the profitability of individual publications is known only some time after the costs have been incurred, and this uncertainty accounts for the contracts signed with the content providers. In the case of authors of books, the contract typically provides a royalty for the author as a percentage of the purchase price of the book, with the royalty increasing with the number of copies sold. For authors having a track record, an advance against future royalties may be made. With the use of word processors, more of the costs of composition are being put on authors who contract to submit manuscripts in a format ready for editing and printing. Newspaper articles are written by salaried employees and by freelancers on a per article basis. Authorship of magazine articles is usually paid by the article, and authors do not share directly in the profits of the publisher's sales. An issue of contention now is whether publishers have the right to distribute articles through new media that were not in existence at the time the authorship was undertaken.

Sources of revenue vary among segments of the print media. Unlike books, which contain no advertising and rely entirely on copy sales, part of the content of newspapers and periodicals is advertising. The amount paid to publishers by advertisers depends on characteristics such as age, income, and gender, of the readership. The amount and orientation of advertising and the quality of content are judiciously managed to maximize the profits from advertising and circulation.

Publishers intensively promote and advertise their own products. For the 12 largest Canadian consumer magazines published in 1991, editorial content represented 14.5 percent of costs while advertising, marketing, and promotion expenses were 21.7 percent of total costs. For all U.S. consumer magazines in the same year, the percentages were 11.2 and 23.5 respectively. The cost of providing content apparently declines relative to advertising, marketing, and promotion costs in the larger market (Canada 1994, 23).

Given its economic nature, the print media tend to flourish in an open environment of content and distribution. While publishers are located in one country, their interest is to increase the readership of their publications. For newspapers and periodicals dealing with topics of local interest, the potential audience is largely local. For academic journals, periodicals for children, and magazines focusing on hobbies, there will be a potential foreign readership, and subscriptions may be taken out by foreign university and other libraries. Books are a different case. Publishers actively promote the foreign sales of their books. Foreign markets are also exploited by translating manuscripts into different languages. Newspaper publishers access foreign news stories through their own reporters or more frequently through wire services, which provide a way for publishers collectively to offer a service that could not economically be provided individually. Without access to foreign sources for content, periodicals such as the *Economist* and *Variety* would have fewer readers. Many of the readers are themselves neither English nor American.

Sound Recordings

Copyright plays a significant role in all the cultural industries, but the pattern of its influence is particularly complicated in the recording industry. For songs or melodies on a recording there are two sets of copyrights, one pertaining to the compositions (the songs or melodies) and another to the record itself. The composition copyright includes a reproduction right, a mechanical right, a public performance right, and a synchronization right. The reproduction right applies to sheet music. The mechanical right is another reproduction right of a song, which allows a record producer to press copies of the record containing the song. Royalties are paid to the composers and their music publishers for each song under copyright contained on each record produced. Synchronization rights result in the payment of royalties for compositions used in films or television programs.

Composers also earn income from the public performance right. When recorded music is broadcast or played by others for commercial reasons, for example, in a tavern or by a background music company, a royalty is collected by performing rights collectives and distributed to the composers and music publishers. Since the authors of compositions on a recording are scattered around the world, the distribution of public performance funds is of international concern. Composers from countries that are members of the WTO are entitled to national treatment in other WTO countries. There are periodic disputes arising from the way this equal access principle is administered.

Piracy is a major problem for the recording industry. Digital audiotapes and CDs have increased the average quality of illegal offerings. New regulatory initiatives are requiring the provision of anti-copying devices in duplicating machines and taxing the copying medium and machines to create funds that will be dispersed to performers and record companies.

The recording industry is divided into a small set of large multinational concerns, which dominate distribution in many countries, and a large set of small local or regional companies, which seek out and nurture new talent or service niches in the market. Like the situation with the Hollywood majors, most of the international concerns are not owned by Americans. Nevertheless, the American operations of these firms are crucial to their international success. Record companies of any significance usually own a music publishing firm. The catalog of prior releases and the library of music copyrights held by the publishing divisions of the major international record companies are significant assets. Another asset is the stable of performing artists under contract to the recording company. These contracts are complex documents that create numerous obligations, including the company's commitment to produce and release a specified number of recordings featuring the artist, to pay for the recording costs (including union fees) to the artist and others involved, and to pay royalties after recouping the recording costs at a prescribed rate. In 1990, a typical artist contract with a Canadian recording company was 50 pages long.[9]

Distribution to specialized record shops is typically organized by the international companies. Rack jobbers are smaller companies, often national, which act as wholesalers to nonspecialty sellers of recorded music such as department stores. "One stops" are wholesalers that stock small retail outlets with a wide assortment of releases from different companies. Specialized retailing is often dominated by chains, some of which are international but under different ownership than the producing and distributing multinationals. The current trend is toward megastores that often sell both books and recorded music. Record clubs, which first appeared in the 1950s, are a significant distribution vehicle. Negative-option selling contracts, whereby the recipient of the recording is assumed to have made a purchase unless he or she informs the club to the contrary, are a controversial aspect of this type of marketing.

---

9. See comments by Richard Hahn of Smith, Lyons, Torrance, Stevenson and Mayer of Toronto in Reynolds (1989, 48).

Like the other cultural industries the recording industry faces much uncertainty in picking winners. The industry spends heavily on promotion, packaging, and advertising. A large part of the promotion of different releases is provided by radio and in the past decade by music video channels on cable television. The relationship of the industry with the radio industry and the music video channels is symbiotic.

Consider the radio relationship. Playing recorded music provides attractive content for radio stations, which in turn attracts advertising revenue. At the same time the playing of a recording on the air accompanied by a discussion of the artists and identification of the record company advertises the products of the record companies. Together the two industries create more value than the sum of the stand-alone revenues that would be generated by radio without recorded music and recorded music without radio. What has been difficult to arrange is a process for orchestrating payments between the two that creates incentives for realizing the potential wealth from their joint efforts. In a number of countries a levy is imposed on broadcasters and the resulting fund is divided among performers and record companies. The resulting public performance right for performers and record companies is similar to the public performance right for composers, but unlike the latter it is governed internationally by the Rome Convention, which requires reciprocity rather than national treatment. This causes friction with nonmembers of Rome such as the United States. An emerging dispute on this matter between the United States and Canada is discussed in chapter 14.

International trade in musical recordings is significant. Recordings still face significant tariffs in some countries. Where tariffs or transportation costs are a factor, the international flows are in rights to reproduce masters rather than recordings. Recording masters are shipped and tapes or discs produced under license in the consuming countries. The multinationals, which include large Canadian, Japanese, and European companies, either produce and distribute through subsidiaries or license items from their catalogs to firms in the foreign markets.

Conclusion

After providing this overview of the economic characteristics and general organizational responses to them of the cultural industries, we turn our attention in the next three chapters to describing the structure of these industries and the policies affecting them in Canada. Although specific to Canada, the chapters provide generic information about the industry structure and policy problems in smaller economies that have adopted inward-looking policies to the cultural industries. Our thesis is that, having reached the present state of development, the Canadian cultural industries are facing challenges driven by an interaction between technology and the trade policy response of other countries. Meeting these challenges requires rethinking and reorienting domestic policy and promoting an international agreement in which the reduction of protection would be exchanged for ensured access in foreign markets with safeguards tailored to the political sensitivity of these industries.

CHAPTER 7

Canadian Film and Television Production

In this chapter we examine the production of films and television programming in Canada. The fastest growing firms in the Canadian cultural industries are the private producers of audiovisual products. This expansion is fueled by export sales and subsidies. We describe and assess the subsidies of federal and provincial granting agencies and those offered through tax programs. The public sector in Canada produces television programming through the CBC and provincial government educational television broadcasters. The NFB is a public producer of feature films, documentaries, and animated films. These public agencies have been important in the development of a production capability in Canada, but there is some uncertainty as to what their role in the future will be.

Private Film and Television Production in Canada

Canada has never been a significant producer of feature films. Gerald Pratley, who has written about film in Canada over the past five decades, commented in 1955 that

> there is little point in considering a quota for full-length films when none are available—and there are as yet no facilities for making them. (1988, 95)

This state of affairs persisted until two events occurred: television and video developed as significant media; and the federal government began to subsidize the industry significantly, directly in 1967 and indirectly through tax policy in the mid-1970s. In the eight years before the Canadian Film Development Corporation (CFDC) began to provide film financing in 1967, feature film production varied between one and seven and averaged 4.5 per year. By 1979, the annual output had risen to 87. From this period to date, support has been maintained, but the details of the subsidy and tax programs have changed.

The number of feature films made annually has fallen in the 1990s from that achieved in the 1980s. There were 38 features made in 1995, and the distribution revenue for theatrical features received by Canadian producers was C$42 million in that year. The reduction in the number of features has been accompanied by a rapid rise in the value of private television production. Table 3 records the sources of production revenues for the film, video, and audiovisual industries as reported by Statistics Canada for the 1990–91 to 1995–96 period by customer type.

TABLE 3. Film, Video, and Audiovisual Production, Canada

Production Revenue (by client type) ($millions)	1990–91	1991–92	1992–93	1993–94	1994–95	1995–96
Distributors:						
Theatrical Features	17.0	8.5	3.7	3.7	42.0	
Other Placements	12.3	74.2	63.6	55.9	78.3	
Conventional TV	146.1	138.0	200.3	236.8	290.2	
Pay Television	32.5	33.9	7.3	23.4	18.0	
Non-theatrical:						
Advertising	131.9	137.0	147.3	146.0	142.8	
Government	38.0	45.0	45.8	70.3	35.8	
Educational	5.0	3.5	2.1	3.2	2.2	
Industry	95.1	78.1	54.1	68.4	75.2	
Sub-total	270.0	263.6	249.2	288.0	256.1	
For other Production Companies	89.3	50.2	42.1	87.4	90.1	
Other	14.0	13.3	20.3	38.7	22.5	
Total	581.2	581.8	586.4	733.9	797.4	867.7
Exports	80.6	82.8	132.0	148.8	163.1	320.7

Source: Statistics Canada 87F0010XPE.
Note: The information is based on a survey designed to cover all firms in the industry. The revenue figure includes sales of assets. The aggregate figures for 1995–96 are from Statistics Canada, The Daily of March 27, 1998.

As the table reveals, the audiovisual export market doubled in the five-year period from 1990–91 to 1994–95 and then doubled again in the next year. Although there are disputes about the total value of exports, there is general agreement about the rising trend.[1] Programs and films for television have dominated the international sales. In commenting on the 1992–93 exports,

1. Although the figures in the table are from Statistics Canada, only the figures up to 1992–93 have been published. Figures for the more recent years were provided by the agency.

Statistics Canada noted that made-for-television productions represented 85 percent of the C$132 million in exports.[2]

Another significant international linkage is the production of films and programs by foreign companies in Canada. This occurs through the location of a shoot at a Canadian site in which some Canadian personnel and production services are hired or through subcontracting the production to a Canadian company, which acts as line producer for the foreign principal. Exchange rates, union rules and labor relations in different countries, availability of the range of supportive services that are or might be required, time zone compatibility, and the attractiveness of the scenery influence location decisions. British Columbia (in the same time zone as Los Angeles), Ontario, and Quebec have hosted an increasing number of foreign, particularly American, projects. Table 4 breaks down the number of projects in different categories that were foreign or domestic and the relative values of the total production of domestic versus foreign content in Ontario for the 1994 to 1996 period.

TABLE 4. Productions Shot in Ontario, 1994–96

	1994	1995	1996
Feature Films			
Canadian	23	26	21
Foreign	11	8	12
Total	34	34	33
TV Series			
Canadian	28	17	27
Foreign	3	0	1
Total	31	17	28
TV Movies, Mini-Series, Specials, Pilots, Docudramas			
Canadian	35	35	27
Foreign	22	27	37
Total	57	62	64
Production Dollars Left in Ontario (C$ millions)			
Canadian	$359.3	$338.9	$277.4
Foreign	$141.7	$156.6	$252.8
Total	$501.0	$495.5	$530.2

Source: Ontario Film Development Corporation (OFDC).

Note: The production dollars left in Ontario reflect production expenditures in Ontario, and do not always reflect the total budgets of the projects. The production dollars figures include television commercials, corporate video or music video production, but do not always capture all in-house broadcast production.

2. Statistics Canada, Cat. 87–204, 1992–93, 13.

Company Profiles

Since many of the leading companies in the production industry are public, audited information about their financial and commercial operations is available. In 1996, the top five firms in the industry by revenue were Alliance, Atlantis, Coscient, Cinar, and Nelvana.[3] All of these firms stress television program production, although Alliance, the largest of the firms, has maintained a small but consistent presence in the feature film industry. Alliance and Atlantis focus their television programming on the English-language market but also service other markets. Both companies are important producers of television series and made-for-television movies. Alliance has a joint venture with the Harlequin division of Torstar, a large Canadian newspaper and book publisher, to produce a series of movies based on the romance books published by Harlequin. The Montreal-based firms, Cinar and Coscient, produce series, children's, and other programming for both English- and French-language markets. Cinar, Nelvana, and Coscient (through its subsidiary, Cactus Animation) are important producers of animation programs and series.

Most of these firms are vertically integrated into distribution, broadcasting, musical publishing, and a variety of postproduction services. Alliance also provides financial services designed to take advantage of its knowledge of the industry and of Canadian and international tax laws. These companies have acquired rights to international programming, either directly or indirectly through takeovers, to augment their libraries. Each of the five has its origins in a small operation reflecting the creative efforts of a pioneering core of people. This core group has typically maintained managerial control as the range of activities and volume within each division has expanded. All of these companies are listed on at least one Canadian stock exchange. Alliance and Cinar have also listed their shares on the American NASDAQ exchange. They have been successful in raising additional equity through new issues of shares. The capital structure typically includes voting shares, which are closely held and lightly traded, and nonvoting shares. Nonvoting shares protect the control exercised by insiders but reduce the attractiveness of the investments to outsiders, who receive a lower return if control is sold. They are a pervasive feature of the capitalization of public firms in the Canadian cultural industries.

These five Canadian firms have grown rapidly, mostly due to internal expansion but also through the acquisition of other companies, often foreign, and their libraries. Their expansion has been supported both by production subsidies

---

3. These were the top five companies for 1996 in an annual survey carried out by *Playback* (April 21, 1997), 28.

and foreign revenue. The total revenue of Alliance, including grants, was C$269 million in 1996. It was C$109 million in 1994.[4]

International Alliances, Investments, Project Finance, and Markets

Each of these companies aggressively markets abroad. Typically they have offices in other countries and are linked by contract, strategic alliances, and ownership with foreign companies. A sample of these foreign branches and relationships with other countries illustrates the variety of their international involvement:

1. Atlantis has a foreign offices in Santa Monica, Amsterdam, Australia, and Barbados and acts as the distributor in Canada for a large part of the Columbia Broadcasting System program portfolio. In 1993, the Interpublic Group of Companies, a world-scale organization of advertising agencies, bought slightly less of Atlantis than the 20 percent allowed foreign investors at that time. E. W. Scripps Company, owner of Home and Garden Television in the United States, has a minority interest in and contractual links with Atlantis, which delivers a cable service with a similar format and the same name in Canada. Atlantis has won a number of awards in international competition, including an Oscar, two Emmys, and 24 CableACE Awards.

2. By 1996, Alliance had sold 12 of its drama series, representing a total of 575 episodes, to U.S. over-the-air and cable networks.[5] In its press releases, Alliance describes itself as an international, integrated, entertainment company with headquarters in Toronto and offices in Montreal, Vancouver, Los Angeles, Paris, and Shannon. An Alliance film, *The Sweet Hereafter,* won Le Grand Prix, the International Film Critics Prize for Best Film, the Ecumenical Jury Prize for Best Film at the 1997 Cannes Film Festival, and was nominated for an Oscar.

3. Coscient has strategic alliances to coproduce with Ellipse, a subsidiary of the French service Canal Plus; Expand Group, a major private production firm in France; Columbia-Tristar (to distribute videos in Canada); Dreamworks (to distribute films theatrically in Quebec); and firms like Triumph (Sony Entertainment) for U.S. distribution and Saban International for foreign distribution of films produced by its subsidiary, Allegro Films. Typical of the shifting international arrangements that are put together for a project is Coscient's 1998 coproduction with foreign partners Canal Plus, FR 2, and FR

---

4. In chapter 3, we noted the inadequacy of published statistics in this area. It is interesting to note that the total of foreign sales reported by these five companies in their 1995 annual reports exceeds by C$94 million the 1994–95 export figure for audiovisual producers as reported by Statistics Canada and listed in table 3.

5. Alliance Annual Report, 1996, 4.

3 in France and ACC Entertainment in Germany of *Babel,* a feature film by French director Gérard Pullicino, which will be shot in Montreal. The film is to be distributed by France's UGC International and Coscient's subsidiary, Motion International.

4. Cinar has been extremely successful in developing, producing, and distributing quality children's and educational programming throughout the world. In late 1996, Cinar acquired the FilmFair library and animation studios from the U.K.-based Caspian Group PLC and in 1997 and 1998 bought two educational publishers from the United States, Carson-Dellosa Publishing Company, Inc,. and HighReach. Each of its projects has an international flavor. On September 3, 1997, Cinar announced that Time-Life had bought the U.S. and Japanese video distribution rights for *The Adventures of Paddington Bear,* described as a Cinar/Protcra coproduction, in association with Canal J, ITV, TF1, and FilmFair, with the participation of TeleToon, a newly licensed Canadian cartoon specialty channel in which Cinar has an interest. With the public television station WGBH Boston, Cinar produces *Arthur,* which in early 1998 was PBS's most popular show for children and a winner of a Daytime Emmy Award for Best Children's Animated Program in 1997.

5. Like Cinar, Nelvana has a large library of animated children's programming and animated features, which it licenses throughout the world. A recent acquisition by the company in the United States was Windlight Studios, a small 3-D animator. An eclectic and shifting mix of international partners is involved in individual projects. In the fall of 1997, Nelvana, in coproduction with the U.K.'s Channel 4, initiated production of a 13-episode primetime, adult animation series, *Bob and Margaret.* This series is based on an Academy Award–winning short, *Bob's Birthday,* coproduced by Channel 4 and Canada's NFB.

The management philosophy of these companies is clearly not inward looking. The following statements taken from their annual reports reflect a commitment to and reliance on the international market:

1.   Our goal is to build a Canadian-based filmed entertainment company with a global platform. (Alliance Annual Report, 1996, 2)
2.   Atlantis is significantly an export company. In 1995, approximately 86% of our program license revenue came from outside Canada. (Atlantis Annual Report, 1995, 5)
3.   [I]nternational sales now account for over 30 percent of our total sales, and the value of the programs designed for foreign viewers represents over half of our production. (Coscient Annual Report, 1995, 3)

4. International production revenues continued to account for over half of total production revenues. (Cinar Annual Report, 1996, 20)
5. The continuous international demand for Nelvana's programs generates steady and growing revenue from broadcasters in over 145 countries. (Nelvana Annual Report, 1995, 3)

To illustrate the importance of international sales we present in fig. 1 a breakdown of the sources of revenue for Cinar over the most recent six years for which data are available. We chose Cinar because of its clear and detailed financial reporting and because it illustrates the importance of foreign markets, particularly the American market, for companies with a strong French-language as well as an English-language capability. In 1996, American and foreign non-U.S. sales represented 30 and 20 percent of total revenue and 66 percent of total revenue excluding subsidies.[6] The Cinar figures also reveal the importance of grants and the rapid growth in sales in the 1990s.

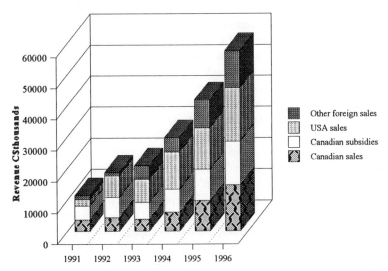

Source: Cinar Annual Reports.
Notes: Subsidies include tax credits, Telefilm investments (some recoupable), and net benefits of limited partnerships.

Fig. 1. CINAR Films Inc. revenue sources, 1991–96

---

6. Cinar Annual Report, 1996, 21.

All of these companies have grown very rapidly by expanding production and acquiring foreign and domestic firms. In July 1998, the two largest firms, Alliance and Atlantis, announced that they would merge. The CEO of the merged entity, Michael MacMillan of Atlantis, stated that:

> Alliance and Atlantis provide an excellent strategic and operational fit. With strong core businesses in television programming, feature motion pictures and cable channels, Alliance Atlantis will be better positioned to compete in the global market. A strengthened home base will enhance our international competitiveness and increase the distribution of our products in international markets. (Press release, July 20, 1998)

Alliance and Atlantis were of a sufficient size before the merger to dominate the Canadian production of high-budget television MOWs. As a rule, MOWs are licensed by both a Canadian and a foreign broadcaster.

The CFTPA's submission to DCH and Industry Canada[7] provides the financing percentages for fourteen actual but unidentified productions by member companies, covering a range of miniseries, MOWs, and dramatic series. Generally, the more expensive the production the greater is the dependence on foreign, usually American, licensing for finance.

To illustrate we present the financing percentages for the four MOW cases in table 5. Three of the four were presold abroad. In the remaining case, public funding agencies picked up the slack.

The contribution of international sales to the commercial success of the relatively large, by Canadian standards, production companies is clear, but small Canadian companies making quality products also rely on international markets to finance and show their products. An excellent example is Rhombus Media Inc. of Toronto, which, over the past 15 years, has earned a reputation for the quality of its television programs and films featuring music, dance, and drama. Much of this work has been done with coproduction partners and has been sold around the world. One film on Arnold Schoenberg involved 12 coproducers. The output of Rhombus relating to music varies from stories inspired by the works or lives of relatively unknown Canadian and European composers, such as John Weinzweig and Hans Eisler, to the more famous, such as Dmitry Shostakovitch and Kurt Weill. The interweaving of music and dance or other visual comple-ments sells well in foreign as well as domestic markets. For example, the film on Weinzweig, who is not a household word even in his native Toronto, has sold in the world market.

---

7. "Policy Discussion Respecting DTH Satellite Distribution Undertakings," appendix 2.

TABLE 5. Financing Percentages in Canadian Movies of the Week

Financing Source	$250,000 to $750,000/hr (Case 14)	over $750,000/hr (Case 10)	over $1.5M/hr (Case 11)	over $1.5M/hr (Case 12)
	Cost per MOW (2–hr)			
Canadian Broadcaster Licence Fee[a]	15	16	4	4
Canadian Broadcaster Equity	5	10	15	
Foreign Broadcaster Licence Fee		30	57	68
Public Funding Agencies	77	10		12
Producer	3[c]	34[b]	24[b]	9[b]

Source: The Canadian Film and Television Producers Association's (CFTPA) submission to Heritage Canada and Industry Canada, "Policy Discussion Respecting Direct to Home Satellite Distribution Undertakings," Appendix 2.
[a] In some cases there was more than one Canadian broadcaster with a license. The figure is the total of all Canadian broadcast licenses.
[b] Included in the producer financing are funds raised through the Capital Cost Allowance, and certain provincial incentives directed to production companies, as well as corporate investment.
[c] In this case, the producer's share is 1 percent and deferrals of fees is 2 percent.

In 1998, Rhombus produced and released *Red Violin*, a feature film, with dialogue in five languages: English, Italian, German, French, and Mandarin. The director and cowriter of *Red Violin* is Françoise Girard, who directed Rhombus's *32 Short Films about Glenn Gould*. The financing of this film illustrates how foreign markets can be tapped by a small firm without significant sacrifices of creative freedom. After the success of the Gould film, Rhombus circulated the script of *Red Violin* to major U.S. film companies. It received offers of complete finance but with conditions that meant sacrificing or sharing key decisions and abandoning the multilingual aspect of the film. Instead of signing a single contract with these stipulations, much effort was expended in negotiating a coproduction with Italy and a production agreement with England's Channel 4. With this base, a presale of American rights was negotiated with no significant conditions attached to complete the financing. Rhombus has maintained some unsold foreign markets for the *Red Violin*, which represent its lottery tickets on the commercial success of the film.

Like the more traditional commercial companies, niche companies depend significantly on federal and provincial subsidies and tax incentives to finance their operations. Rhombus is not exceptional in that regard.[8]

---

8. Information on Rhombus is drawn in part from a videotape of a *Banff Television Festival* session "The Art of Rhombus," June 12, 1997, 11:30–12:30 PM.

Subsidies and Tax Incentives

Telefilm Canada

Subsidies for television and film production come from a number of different sources. The federal government began subsidized production through a specialized agency, the CFDC, in 1967. Since that date, the CFDC has become Telefilm Canada. With the change in name, the mandate was also expanded to support television as well as film. In 1997–98, Telefilm committed C$79.9 million to television programming production, C$32.8 million to feature film production, and C$12.2 million to distribution. The agency finances smaller programs for versioning, marketing, closed captioning, and industry and professional development.

The total commitments of Telefilm Canada in 1997–98 were C$165.3 million. In the early 1990s, annual spending was at about the same nominal level. The agency is financed by a parliamentary grant and revenues from past investments. Recoupments from past investments have totalled C$128 million in the period since 1983. Telefilm Canada operates under a number of political constraints. Among the most important is establishing a "balance" between supporting English-language and French-language projects and spreading its support across the regions of Canada. Telefilm has a memorandum of understanding that calls for 37 percent of its funds to support French-speaking projects. The realized percentage was 48 in 1994–95 and averaged 38.5 in the prior five-year period.[9] In 1997–98 it was 36.

Telefilm Canada supports participation by Canadian filmmakers in foreign film festivals and markets and explicitly encourages exports and coproductions. In drawing up an action plan to deal with recent budgetary cutbacks, the agency stated:

> Telefilm Canada's main objective in its activities abroad is to position and promote Canadian productions in foreign markets and to foster the development of partnerships between its Canadian clientele and foreign companies, and, through financial assistance to companies, to complement the efforts made by the private sector to *increase exports* of Canadian productions.[10]

An awareness of the international effect of subsidized funding has existed since the direct funding program began:

---

9. Telefilm Annual Report, 1994–95, 45.
10. Telefilm Annual Report, 1995–96, 6: emphasis in the original.

The Chairman of the CFDC recently noted that on films for which the CFDC advanced money in 1978 and 1979, about 75% of the "producers' return" had come from outside Canada. The Corporation's Executive Director also estimated recently that approximately 10% of the films on American screens, in 1981, will be Canadian. (Bird, Bucovetsky et al. 1981, 54)[11]

Telefilm has maintained foreign offices for a number of years. Part of the recent action plan was to close the London and Los Angeles offices.

Cable Production Fund

In 1993, a CRTC decision augmented the direct funding of Telefilm. The federal regulator of broadcasting had earlier granted increases in cable rates to finance system improvements. These rate increases were scheduled to be rolled back to their former level after five years. In response to a suggestion from the cable industry, the CRTC offered the eligible cable companies the alternative of rolling back the rates or donating half of the amount to be refunded to support Canadian programming and keeping the other half. To no one's surprise, the cable companies enthusiastically supported the alternative. The Cable Production Fund (CPF), variably estimated to have generated between C$250 million (CPF fact sheet) and C$300 million over its first five years, began operations in 1994.[12]

The CPF was given explicit instructions by the CRTC concerning its allocations including target proportions with respect to language and genre.[13] A fee from a Canadian broadcaster at least equal to a specified percentage of the budget is a condition of eligibility. The subsidy is called a Fee Program because it is viewed as a means of topping up the license set by the market to a more "just" level.

In September of 1996, the federal government reorganized the administration and expanded government support of subsidized funding. C$50 million granted to Telefilm's Broadcast Fund and C$50 million from the CPF plus an additional $100 million grant from the government were combined in a new fund the Canada Television and Cable Production Fund (CTCPF).[14] In 1998, the government committed itself to this level of support to 2001 and renamed the

---

11. The granting agency has taken a more commercial orientation than the NFB, a public institution that is discussed below. See Magder (1993, 112–28) for more detail.

12. CRTC Public Notice 1994–10, 1, Ottawa, February 10, 1994.

13. CRTC Public Notice 1994–10, which is updated in Public Notice 1995–89, Ottawa, June 2, 1995.

14. Canadian Heritage news release, September 9, 1996.

fund the Canadian Television Fund (CTF). The CTF also collects levies from new distribution undertakings, in particular the recently launched Canadian direct-to-home (DTH) satellite broadcasters. There are two parts to the program. Telefilm administers the Equity Investment Program, which assesses proposals, negotiates changes, and if approved provides funding.[15] Another board, administered by the broadcasters, allocates the Fee Program on a first-come first-served basis to all who have a licensing contract with a broadcaster. If a broadcaster applies to both, the support of the Equity Investment Program must be obtained before money can be obtained from the Licence Fee Program.

In late April 1998, this system created what front page newspaper stories headlined as "Chaos in the Culture Industry."[16] The demand for the Fee Program portion was three times the available funds. A line of applicants formed and grew daily. Some hired young employees to claim a position in line. The money ran out with no funds allocated to a number of premiere shows. The government made another $20 million available, ostensibly as an advance against future budgets. One editorial concluded:

> Thanks to the tortuously tangled system that has been developed to put public money in the hands of TV enterprise, we're now seeing queuing for cultural funds in the same way that people in the old Communist countries used to line up for food. Is this any way to run a TV industry?[17]

Ten days later the chaos had spread to the allocation of funds to French-language filmmakers.[18] Having discovered the dissipating effects of what economists refer to as the common property right problem, the fund hurriedly revised its administrative process and abandoned the first-come first-served allocations for the Licence Fee Program. Under the new scheme the fund will support only the number one priority project of each Broadcaster Ownership Group.[19]

---

15. Telefilm receives rights on future revenues conditional on the fulfillment of other claims with priority.

16. *Globe and Mail*, April 25, 1998, A1, A8.

17. *Globe and Mail*, May 2, 1998, D4.

18. The *Globe and Mail* (May 12, 1998, A12) begins its story on this development: "Like wartime civilians stampeding for diminishing stocks of bread, Quebec filmmakers queuing for reduced federal production money have inadvertently pitched Telefilm Canada into yet more turmoil."

19. See letter to its constituents from CTCPF executive director Garry Toth, dated August 4, 1998.

The embarrassing confusion also highlighted the recurring tension between the support of two types of Canadian programming—the industrially viable and nonviable. The projects that required both Telefilm funding and Licence Fee Program support were those most likely to be crowded out of the latter. Telefilm approval was necessary for eligibility for the license fee, and the problems arose because of delays in granting Telefilm approval, which in turn were caused in part by an increase in applications. Those that were not sufficiently Canadian to qualify for Telefilm support but were eligible for the license fee—programs such as *Psi Factor: Chronicles of the Paranormal* and *La Femme Nikita*—were able to line up early and in general received Licence Fee funds. The emergency funds were necessary to support costly and critically acclaimed series—*Traders* and *Due South*—which required Telefilm and Licence Fee support. These programs are "international fare" but also are either set in Canada or contain visible Canadian symbols. The lack of such identifiers appears to be a significant factor. The cochair of the Canadian Independent Film Caucus, which represents documentary filmmakers, Barri Gordon, asked "What is Canadian about *Psi Factor?*"[20] Of course, if continued support requires a paranormal Mountie he or she is likely to be supplied.

Other Policy-Induced Funding Sources

In addition to the CTCPF, there are a number of smaller funds, most of which were created to gain CRTC approval of the transfers of ownership of broadcasting and cable licenses. When approving license transfers, the CRTC routinely imposes what amounts to a takeover tax by exacting some contribution to achieving its Canadian-content goals. The acquiring company, anticipating that the CRTC will impose a commitment of some kind, frequently "volunteers" a commitment conditional on receiving approval. A common form of tribute is a fund. If the CRTC accepts the package, it expresses its delight at this expression of solidarity with its goals. Otherwise, it rejects the suggested package and imposes an alternative contribution.[21] The Shaw Children's Programming

---

20. Quoted in Etan Vlessing, "Canadian Dis-content," *Television Business International,* September 1998, 48.

21. To illustrate the process and amounts involved, the Shaw Fund was established with a C$10 million allocation as part of Shaw Cablesystems Ltd.'s successful efforts to gain approval of its purchase of a Toronto cable system. Shaw later committed C$17.5 million to establish the Conway Fund, named for the founder of the cable company CUC Broadcasting Ltd., which it also acquired. Both funds are administered by the Shaw Children's Programming Initiative, which uses the Shaw Fund to support programming for preschoolers and the Conway Fund to support programming for children aged eight to 12. The Shaw Children's Programming Initiative's interests reflect those of the donor,

Initiative, the Rogers Telefund, and the Maclean Hunter Television Fund have been created in this way.[22] In mid-1998 the Canadian government also announced the introduction of a new $30 million Telefilm Multimedia Fund. The press release notes that the fund has been established for five years to support the development, production, and marketing of high-quality, original, interactive, Canadian multimedia works—in both official languages—intended for the general public.

There has been very little political agitation by consumers or their associations concerning the suspension of the sunset clause on cable rate increases or from shareholders of the companies paying the discretionary levies on takeovers. The rising level of subsidies has also not generated any significant opposition at a time when other activities are being cut back because of budgetary pressure. The CRTC regulates both broadcasting and telecommunications. In telecommunications, public interest groups such as the Consumers Association of Canada (CAC) are compensated for the costs of intervention while in broadcasting they are not. The executive director of the CAC informed us that they intervene less in the broadcasting hearings for this reason.

Provincial Funding

Most of the provinces also provide subsidized funds to audiovisual projects. In some of the provinces, the support is modest. Each province has its own method for determining eligibility, but all emphasize employment of provincial residents For example, the Manitoba Film & Sound Development Corporation provides support for drama, children's programs, documentaries, animation, and variety. A successful applicant receives 20 percent of eligible expenses or $400,000, whichever is larger. Eligibility is determined by a Manitoba content point system, which varies across program type.[23]

---

which, besides being a MSO in the cable industry, also owns the Canadian children and youth specialty channel YTV.

22. When the Maclean Hunter Fund was established, the CRTC said no to the company's offer to contribute C$8 million to Telefilm and instead required a capital contribution of C$29 million to establish an independently administered fund. Maclean Hunter was later taken over by Rogers, but the fund remained separate as a result of this earlier decision.

23. For drama and variety, there are 24 production positions listed, with the most prominent receiving two points and others, from the line producer to the props master, receiving one point. Two points are granted if the remaining production crew is 50 percent Manitoba residents, and a further two points are earned if 50 percent of postproduction costs are met in the province. If the screenplay is based on a Manitoba literary work, it scores one point. Nineteen points make the project Manitoba content.

Federal and Provincial Tax Shelters and Production
Service Partnerships

The federal and provincial governments have also provided tax incentives for audiovisual projects. A tax shelter program generated varying, but generally significant, investor interest between 1974 and 1995.[24] Only films were eligible for tax shelters between 1974 and 1980; both television programs and films were supported from 1981 to the mid-1990s. A point system based on the nationality of key personnel and the proportion of expenditures made in Canada determined which projects qualified for special tax treatment.

In Canada, the rules governing shelters changed frequently and were sometimes unclear even to practitioners. From 1974 to 1987, almost 500 projects, a mix of feature films, short films, and television programs, were certified. From a political perspective, a disproportionate number of these projects originated in the two largest provinces, Ontario and Quebec. Another political liability of the policy was the large proportion of Quebec projects that were in the English language. In 1987, the CCA for qualifying projects was reduced from 100 to 30 percent and the upper personal income tax rates were lowered. There was an immediate decline in shelter activity, and members of the legal and financial communities introduced new shelter arrangements. In the early 1990s, the number of financings of Canadian content audiovisual projects responded positively to the new instruments.

The amount of subsidy generated to the audiovisual producer in any particular tax year by tax shelters, and the cost in foregone tax, are difficult to calculate. Poddar and English (1994, 30) estimate that, in the early 1990s, the tax shelter investor typically paid 17.7 percent of a representative project's budget and realized a total tax saving equal to 24.5 percent of its budget. Of the 17.7 percent of the budget made available by the tax shelter investor, the promoters received over half, or 9 percent of the budget, leaving 8.7 percent available to the producer. In other words, for every dollar of tax credit claimed, only 35 cents filtered through to the producer. The authors estimate the revenue cost to governments in Canada of the tax shelters for the period 1990 to 1993 (Poddar and English 1994, table 12). These estimates are reproduced here in the

---

24. Under most tax laws, expenses eligible for deduction cannot be transferred from one taxpayer to another. A film tax shelter, for example, allows net losses of the film to be transferred to those who purchase units in the shelter. The legal structure of the film tax shelter is described in Bacal (1988). For a discussion of the economic aspects of the tax shelters, see Bird et al. (1981) and Acheson and Maule (1991b, 1994a).

second column of table 6. The third column of the table provides an estimate of the subsidy received by producers equal to 35 percent of the revenue cost.[25]

TABLE 6. Estimated Government Revenue Costs and the Amount
Received by Producers from the Canadian Tax Shelters

Year	Estimated Government Revenue Costs of Canadian Film Tax Shelters (Millions of C$)	Estimated Subsidy Equivalent Received by Producers (Millions of C$)
1990	80	28
1991	95	33
1992	85	30
1993	100	35

Source: Poddar and English (1994).

A further "innovation" to support the film production industry through the tax system was the Production Service Partnership, which transferred tax benefits generated by the production in Canada of non-Canadian film and television projects.[26] The traditional tax shelters and new vehicles were sold to a set of wealthy buyers, with the marketing hype typical of such schemes, as is illustrated by the following report in the *New York Times:*

> According to Martin Johnson of Alliance Equicap Corporation, a Vancouver company that sells tax shelters, including the one for

25. The Poddar and English (1994) study is the only serious attempt to quantify the cost to the treasuries and the subsidy equivalent of the tax shelter program. There are considerable difficulties in estimating these elements and a number of places where a researcher could make alternative assumptions. The above estimates of the revenue cost to the government assume that no taxes are collected on the incomes supported by the issue costs of the limited partnership and that subsequent income inclusions are either delayed sufficiently to warrant ignoring them or do not occur. Estimates are made based on including the issue costs as fully taxable incremental income. Neither of these assumptions affect the estimate of how much is passed on to producers. If the producers also act as the designers and marketers of the shelter instruments, their share of the transfer rises.

26. This scheme took advantage of the general characteristics of tax policy by exploiting leverage, the delaying of tax through the timing of expenses and claims on income, and certain privileges given to partnerships. They did not depend on special tax treatment for the activity. This initiative could not then be contained solely in the audiovisual sector. It was viewed as threatening to the Canadian tax system.

"Johnny Mnemonic," the numbers for a typical investor break down as follows: For each US$1,000, the investor puts up US$220 in cash. The US$780 balance is borrowed by the film's producers from a bank. The investor is entitled to reduce his or her taxes by US$440 or double the cash invested. And because the loan is secured only by pre-sale of the videocassette and television rights, the investor is not liable for repayment, even if the film flops. Thus, even when a film is a commercial dud, the investor pockets US$220, and if the film makes enough money to pay back the loans, the investor may make even more.[27]

Production service financings grew from C$100 million in 1993 to C$450 million in 1994 (Poddar and English 1994, 77). The Department of Finance reports C$800 million of foreign film production in Canada during 1996.[28]

A series of 1997 policy decisions by the Finance Department ended both the traditional tax shelters for the production of Canadian films and television programs and the tax-based vehicles for subsidizing foreign productions in Canada.

Federal and Provincial Tax Credit Programs

A production tax credit (PTC) program was introduced in 1996 to replace the tax shelter on Canadian audiovisual products. The credit is 25 percent of qualified labor expenditures with a ceiling on eligible expenditures of 48 percent of the project's budget. Given that labor expenditure generally exceeds 48 percent of the budget, the usual result is a subsidy of 12 percent of the budget. This level of support is more generous than under the tax shelter regime. The PTC is simpler than the tax shelter devices and is expected to be more efficient in transferring dollars to the targeted activity.

The trend in the provinces is also away from tax shelters to tax credits. The federal initiative was influenced by the decision of Quebec to shift its tax support to a refundable tax credit in 1990. Nova Scotia and Ontario have also introduced tax credit programs, and British Columbia has announced that it will follow suit. These programs have a similar structure to the federal program described above, but they differ in detail.

Public Television Broadcasting and Program Production

In television, the CBC produces as well as broadcasts. Much of its programming is generated in-house, although the amounts contracted to independent Canadian

---

27. *New York Times,* May 21, 1995, 11.
28. Canada, Department of Finance Release 97–063, July 30, 1997.

producers have recently risen. CBC production is divided into two parts, the English-language service and the French-Speaking Radio Canada. These have generally been two solitudes, although there is some talk and a little action toward more cooperative exploitation of programming.

Outsourcing has risen in part because the direct budget of the CBC has been progressively reduced in real terms since the mid-1980s. By contracting out the public broadcaster could access the CPF and its predecessors. The guideline is that one half of production funds are allocated to the public broadcaster. The contracting out to private producers has been most prominent with respect to drama, a costly area of programming. The English-language CBC has had very little success with in-house production of sitcoms and dramatic series.

The export potential of the CBC is mostly in news, public affairs, comedy, and documentary programming. CBC Newsworld International, which predominantly carries in-house production, is available on the U.S. DirecTV service. Another service, TRIO, which also appears on the U.S. DirecTV satellite service, has access to a large library of CBC and Canadian private television programs. Reflecting one of a number of contradictions in the Canadian regulatory system, TRIO is not licensed to provide service in Canada.[29]

In earlier times, CBC television imported a number of American dramatic series, but in the past ten years the public broadcaster has been under pressure from the CRTC to Canadianize its schedule. It is an oddity of Canadian broadcasting that a government regulator monitors and hectors the government's broadcaster. In 1993–94, the percentage of foreign programs appearing in prime time was 13.9, down from 24 in 1985–86. More foreign programming is shown in the rest of the schedule. The television format in which many other countries—Mexico, Brazil, and Australia—have succeeded in "telling their stories" is the soap opera or telenovela. In contrast, the CBC has depended on American programming in this genre. It presented its first daytime Canadian soap opera in the 1997–98 season. Overall the CBC's percentage of Canadian content was 65 percent in 1995–96. This is not dramatically above the level required of the Canadian commercial channels.

Like public broadcasters in other countries, the CBC has also become more active in seeking coproductions with foreign partners. Some exports to third parties may result from these initiatives. In the past, the CBC has infrequently bought programs off the shelf from its public service counterparts in other countries. A Canadian viewer typically sees more BBC material on the American PBS and A&E or on Canadian specialty channels than on the CBC.

---

29. In the American DirecTV promotional material, Newsworld International is billed as "The renowned CBC suppliers of international coverage devoted to hard-hitting news and comprehensive current affairs features" and TRIO as "A family-oriented entertainment service from Canada which features drama, arts, and journalism."

It is difficult for outsiders to assess the degree of current financial stringency. As Raboy comments:

> As anyone who has ever tried to read a CBC financial statement can attest, budgetary sleight-of-hand appears to be one of the corporation's most valued administrative qualities. (1996, 190)

In 1997–98, the corporation spent C$546 million dollars on its television operations. After subtracting the costs of the radio service from the parliamentary grant to cover operating expenses of C$760 million, C$560 million was available for the television service from that source. In the same year, C$383 million in revenue was raised from advertising and net income from program sales. C$28 million was available from the surplus on its two specialty services, Newsworld and RDI. As the direct parliamentary grant for operating expenditures has fallen, from C$985 million in 1990–91 to a level of C$760 million, support from other government or quasi-government sources and increased advertising revenue have compensated.

The operating expenses of the CBC for television, radio, and other services of the CBC provide a better indicator of its budgetary situation than its direct grant. They have risen slightly from C$1.39 billion in 1990–91 to C$1.41 billion in 1997–98. The CBC also receives significant capital grants and has recently built a state of the art production center in Toronto. The capital grant was C$89.2 million in 1990–91 and C$105.7 million in 1997–98.

Advertising has become a more important financing source for the CBC. In 1995–96, advertising revenue covered 50 percent of the English-language and 40 percent of the French-language service's expenditures.[30] Advertising is the only source of revenue that the management of the CBC can directly influence. The private broadcasters have been critical of what they consider to be aggressive pursuit of advertising dollars by a highly subsidized competitor. Supporters of a distinct role for public television also express concern that dependence on advertising revenue generates programming that is similar to what is available on commercial television.[31] Between 1985–86 and 1993–94, public affairs shrank from 24.8 to 14.8 percent of programming while sports, mostly advertising-intensive professional sports, expanded from 18.1 to 25 percent of programming.[32]

---

30. Canada (1996d, 37).

31. See Acheson and Maule (1990). A constructive step would be to cap advertising so that it does not affect decisions at the margin.

32. Canada Federal (1996, 68).

A comparison of the importance of advertising revenue to the CBC and the commercial Canadian channels for 1995 to 1997 is shown in fig. 2.[33] Advertising by the CBC adds to other sources of tension between it and its private affiliates, which typically have other broadcasting holdings.[34] In contrast to television, the radio division of the CBC has not accepted advertising since 1974 and depends exclusively on public funding.

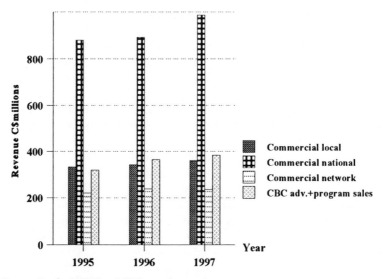

Source: Cansim M1800 and CBC annual reports.
Note: As the CBC's fiscal year ends on March 31, its revenue, for say 1997, refers to the year ending March 31, 1998.

Fig. 2. Public and commercial television advertising revenue

33. The CBC figure is for advertising plus program sales. The 1994–95 Annual Report breaks this figure down into advertising C$305,508 and program sales C$13,598. We assume that the figure is predominately advertising in the three year period.

34. For example, in CRTC hearings about the structure of the Canadian broadcasting system, Craig Broadcasting, which owns stations in Manitoba, commented:

CKX-TV is a CBC affiliate station and has been since it went on the air in 1955. At the present time we have no contract with the CBC and negotiations for a new network contract are not proceeding very fast. One main problem is the CBC's newly adopted sales policy. Instead of selling national advertising as they have done for many years, they are now selling regional advertising. This is affecting not only our national TV sales but local TV sales as well. We urge the CRTC to give direction to the CBC as to their new regional sales policy. It is affecting affiliate sales and ultimately could have severe impact on our ability to provide local programming. (Brief to the CRTC, Structural Hearing, Ottawa, March 1, 1993)

The Mandate Review Committee, which assessed the CBC as well as the NFB and Telefilm, suggested curtailing advertising revenue, cutting back sports programming, and funding the CBC by means of a communications distribution tax (Cana da 1996d). The committee recommended that the CBC's specialty news channel, Newsworld, not charge subscription fees to cable companies. This approach differs from that of the BBC, which has a 50 percent share of a joint venture with the American service provider Flextech to provide up to eight pay or subscription-supported channels for cable, satellite, and new digital-terrestrial television transmitters.[35] There is almost no discussion of export sales by the CBC in the Mandate Review Committee's report.

Public Filmmaking in Canada

In his history of Canadian filmmaking, Peter Morris comments that "[a]mong the most significant defining characteristics of film in Canada is the manner in which governments have had a persistent involvement in film production" (1978, 127). There have been intermittent forays into the activity by the provinces, and since 1918 a continuous involvement of the federal government in producing films. After World War I, the Exhibits and Publicity Bureau of Canada had a mandate to produce low-key advertising films "to promote the image of Canadian industries, and natural resources in general, not films which would sell specific products" (132). With a change of title to the Canadian Government Motion Picture Bureau and many films about the timber industry later, the bureau faded and was replaced by the NFB in 1939.

The NFB, under the leadership of a Scot, John Grierson, "led the country through the war with its progressive film propaganda of education, inspiration, and promise of a better tomorrow" (Evans 1990, 6). After the war the NFB concentrated on nonentertainment films and public interest series, which were distributed through community centers, municipal libraries, schools, cinemas, and television. It developed an excellent animation group and experimented with new documentary approaches. In the 1970s it branched out into feature film production, directly and through coproductions with private companies. Currently, the plan is for the board to abandon feature film production.

The NFB has experienced considerable difficulty in reconciling French- and English-language film interests. Sporadically, but for significant periods in the 1950s and early 1960s, the NFB's films were banned by the provincial government censor in Quebec. Eventually, after a period of dominance by the English-language stream, two distinct production streams were developed along language lines. The French-language documentaries and feature films spoke to

---

35. See *Economist*, March 15, 1997, 61.

the rapid changes that were occurring in Quebec society. They sparked both controversy and viewer interest in Quebec. The 1971 feature *Mon Oncle Antoine,* directed by Claude Jutra, is often cited as one of the best Canadian films ever made. The irony is that Jutra was a separatist, as were many of his artistic colleagues, and that he compared his NFB experience and subsequent stints directing commercial English-language feature and made-for-television films to working for "a friendly foreign country."[36] The alienation and resentment about the history of relations between English-speaking and French-speaking Canadians harbored by the latter are clearly evident in *Mon Oncle Antoine.* As a general rule, when the NFB made dramatic or documentary films that received critical acclaim, those who favored the spin championed the agency but others, who were attacked and considered the treatments to be manipulative, opposed it.[37]

The NFB's output is a portfolio of contrasts: a long list of workmanlike documentaries sponsored by government departments; documentaries funded by the board itself, some of which were studied in their neutrality while others were controversial advocacy pieces; a small number of influential English and French feature films; and a body of experimental animated and other short pieces. Unless it was receiving an award for an innovative cartoon with no discernible political content, the agency has either been invisible to the bulk of the population or embroiled in political controversy.

The NFB has been relatively centralized in its administration and remains largely dependent on federal government funds. Between fiscal 1992–93 and 1994–95, the budgetary grant averaged C\$82.8 million per year with little variation from year to year. Over the same three years, average earned revenue, of which television licensing fees were the largest component, was C\$9.8 million per annum. These sources gave the agency an average C\$92.6 million to spend each year.

---

36. Knelman (1988, 229).

37. Evans's chronicle of the NFB is filled with examples. The following reaction to a 1980 French-language docudrama feature is one illustration:

Yet public goodwill could be lost if a single film drew the ire of influential persons or bodies, as occurred in French Production's feature *Cordelia,* directed by Jean Beaudin. This was the true story of the 1897 trial of a woman and her lover, who were tried and executed for the murder of her husband. Superior Court Justice Jules Deschênes attacked the Film Board publicly in a thirty-page document, accusing the filmmakers of unfairly tarnishing justice. He was outraged that the scenario ignored the evidence and the three trials that had found them guilty. Deschênes's attack demonstrated the pitfalls of incomplete research and a questionable use of artistic license; in a cavalier response, the unheeding filmmakers insisted on their right to criticize the weakness of Canadian institutions. (1990, 264)

The NFB is under pressure to do more contracting out. The Mandate Review Committee recommended that the NFB "must move to a system under which creative functions are performed to a far greater extent by outside filmmakers, rather than by long-term or permanent Board staff."[38] If all of the Mandate Review Committee's recommendations are adopted, which is less likely than the appointment of yet another committee, the NFB will be transformed from a government producer/distributor to a project initiator, selector, and subsidizer for "more complex productions that focus on Canadian themes and are designed primarily for domestic audiences, rather than for export audiences."[39] It is unlikely that the contracting out will be open to foreign producers. Ironically, the NFB's reputation in experimental animation has been enhanced considerably by foreigners whose professional careers began in other countries.

The NFB has nurtured the development of professional skills. A number of talented directors, cinematographers, animators, and producers received training at the NFB before attaining commercial and sometimes critical success in the private sector. At one time, there were few training alternatives in Canada, but that is no longer true. Recently, cooperatives, supported largely by provincial funding agencies—the Liaison of Independent Filmmakers of Toronto, the Winnipeg Film Group, and the Atlantic Filmmakers' Cooperative—have arguably provided more decentralized, less bureaucratic, and more politically insulated spawning grounds for an impressive number of Canada's younger filmmakers.

Conclusion

Both the large firms and the niche players of the dynamic private production sector are dependent on foreign sales and domestic subsidies for sustaining their production schedules. The maze of subsidy and tax programs mobilize significant and growing financial support for film and television program production.

The CBC is an important public producer of television programs, but the dependence on advertising revenue at the margin significantly compromises its ability to produce programming that differs from what is available on the private channels. At least in Canada, public television has not been an imaginative producer of drama. What has been successful in this genre has often been produced for the CBC by private companies. Despite its increasing reliance on advertising, the corporation continues to receive a significant public appropriation. As in other countries, the need for rethinking the role of the public

---

38. Canada Federal (1996, 170).
39. Canada Federal (1996, 167).

broadcaster has been recognized, but no consensus has emerged as to what its continuing role in production will be. The government film producer, the NFB, has had even more trouble than the CBC in finding a credible rationale in the current environment.

In the next chapter, we examine the organization of film and program distribution as well as cinematic exhibition and broadcasting in Canada and the complicated set of policies governing their evolution.

CHAPTER 8

Canadian Film Distribution and Exhibition and Television Broadcasting

Production, distribution, and exhibition or broadcasting of audiovisual material are interwoven activities. We begin by exploring the organization and policy environment of distribution and cinematic exhibition. A discussion of the broadcasting industry, concentrating on television, follows. Broadcasting policy features several instruments affecting international trade of which the most important are a system of national content quotas for Canadian programming plus carriage priority rules for Canadian broadcasting signals on cable. The Canadian quota system contains both rules and discretionary elements.

Film, Video, and Television Program Distribution and Film Exhibition

The Canadian Industry

The Canadian audiovisual distribution system has a small number of multinational firms that are focused on distributing international product and a larger number of smaller, mainly Canadian-owned firms. Most of the smaller distributors concentrate on one of the language divisions of the Canadian market. The largest of the Canadian distributors, Alliance Releasing, now a division of Alliance Atlantis Communications, has become a significant player in Canadian theatrical distribution and also distributes in other countries. Coscient and Alliance Releasing distribute both English- and French-language films. Coscient is the largest of the French-language television distributors and Alliance Atlantic the largest in the English-language market.

Table 7 provides a breakdown by market of distribution revenue in Canada for the most recent year for which data are available, 1994–95, and as a point of comparison for 1990–91. The largest source of distribution revenue in Canada is supplying programs to conventional and pay television broadcasters. The second is the share of box office revenue accruing to feature film distributors, while the third is the revenue from the distribution of home videos. Videocassettes are sold to large retailers and corner stores by wholesalers. The wholesaling of videocassettes is a narrow margin, large volume business.

TABLE 7. Revenue from Film, Video, and Audiovisual Productions and Video Wholesaling

Primary Market	1990–91		1994–95	
	Revenue (C$millions)	Foreign Controlled Share (%)	Revenue (C$millions)	Foreign Controlled Shared (%)
Theatrical	193.4	84.0	239.0	75.6
Pay TV	33.5	na	56.4	na
Conventional TV	329.5	na	305.4	na
Home video	74.9	na	132.9	na
Sub-total: home entertainment*	437.8	47.7	494.7	29.4
Non-theatrical	24.3	9.8	20.3	2.2
Videocassette wholesale	495.4	32.6	717.0	32.2

Source: From information provided by Fax dated August 20, 1997, from Statistics Canada, Culture Statistics Program.
* Sum of pay TV, conventional TV and home video.

Table 7 also documents the shares of the various categories provided by foreign-owned suppliers. Foreign firms have their largest presence in theatrical film distribution and their smallest in nontheatrical distribution to advertising, government, educational, and industrial clients. The share of foreign ownership has declined for feature films and home entertainment.

A frequently cited measure of Canada's cultural dependence is the number of American films shown in Canada. A premise of Canadian cultural policy is that this phenomenon reflects the dominance of the Hollywood majors in film distribution. The foreign management of these concerns is not in touch with Canadian sensibilities and the Canadian films that play to those sensibilities. Few people have more knowledge of what the Canadian film industry is capable of producing than the new owners of Universal. If the premise were believed by those that cite it as justification for policies designed to Canadianize distribution, one would have expected positive recognition of the acquisition by Canadian interests of Universal. Instead, there has been silence from the DCH, the spiritual and financial sponsor of these policies in the Canadian government. When we asked those in charge of cultural statistics at Statistics Canada whether Universal's distributional activities will be recognized as Canadian when a more current version of the statistics reported in table 7 is released, we were told that the matter is under study. The one part of the government that was clearly delighted by the takeover was the Department of National Revenue, which quickly recognized Universal as a Canadian corporation for tax purposes.

Government-sponsored studies of the cultural industries frequently justify transferring economic activities from foreigners to Canadians on the basis of a cross-subsidy rationale. The hypothesis is that if the distribution of foreign product is restricted to Canadian-owned distributors they will spend the resulting profits on developing and distributing Canadian productions. A rationale for this behavior might be better knowledge than a foreign concern has of what is available nationally. With film distribution, the majors have been operating in Canada for a long time and are well informed concerning its potential. The belief that Canadian firms will voluntarily dissipate profits to pursue governmental goals has no persuasive economic rationale nor empirical support. It nevertheless has considerable valence in film policy circles and is also appealed to with regard to book publishing policy, discussed in the next chapter.

Another Statistics Canada figure that is often cited in the cultural debate is the proportion of distribution revenue received from foreign rather than Canadian films. This figure does not appear in table 7, as it was not included in the updated information provided by Statistics Canada, but our understanding is that it currently ranges between 94 and 95 percent.[1] The Canadian-content percentage is higher in video than in cinematic distribution. In 1992–93 the Canadian content ratio was 23.0 percent in video or home entertainment market distribution compared to the 5 to 6 percent in theatrical distribution. The video rental business is unregulated, so this difference in availability is commercially driven, reflecting a different mix of product than that which appears in cinemas. The Canadian licensed movie channels also provide air time to most Canadian films as a condition of license. In an earlier study, we examined a sample of 40 Canadian tax shelter films. Although most of the films were unknown even to film study scholars and professionals in the industry, a significant number were available in local video stores and most had appeared on the licensed movie channels (Acheson and Maule 1991b).

Distribution is a risky business, even with a large portfolio of films. The share of the U.S.-Canadian market captured by any single major distributor varies considerably from year to year.[2] For small distribution firms with only a few filmic "lottery tickets" to market each year, the experience is even more variable. This uncertainty is reflected in the Canadian bankruptcy figures. The number of Canadian, mostly small, distribution firms going bankrupt over the

---

1. In chapter 6, we presented our views on interpreting this ratio.

2. See Globerman (1987, table 10, 44), constructed from data published in Audley (1983).

period 1990–96 was 34 per year.[3] As a point of comparison, the average number of firms operating theaters that went bankrupt in the same period was two.

Canadian theaters are supplied by two national chains, regional chains, and independents. In 1995–96, the chains owned 54 percent of the movie houses, including drive-ins, and generated 80 percent of ticket sales.[4] Famous Players, founded in 1920, is the oldest of the two national chains. It has 477 screens in 108 theaters and is wholly owned by Viacom, the U.S. parent of Paramount. The other national chain, Cineplex-Odeon, has 682 screens in 132 Canadian locations and 861 screens in 183 U.S. locations.[5] A Canadian family, the Bronfmans, controls Cineplex-Odeon through the share holdings of Universal and those of the Charles Rosner Bronfman Trust.[6] A merger between Cineplex-Odeon and Sony's Loews Theaters, announced at the end of September 1997, has received regulatory approval in Canada and the United States. It has created one of the largest cinematic chains in North America.[7]

Distribution and Cinematic Exhibition Policy

A Negotiated Relationship with the Hollywood Majors

Film distribution policy has a long history dating back to a major antitrust investigation and court case in the 1930s. After World War II, the Canadian government and the Hollywood majors entered into a repeated sequence of confrontations followed by temporary reconciliations. The reconciliations have typically involved commitments by the majors to make more Canadian films available to cinemas. In return the majors have enjoyed, at least for brief periods, a special status in the Canadian market. The competition policy authorities have sporadically become involved in these interactions with respect to concerns about the contracting process between the distributors and exhibitors. More recently, the Canadian agency monitoring foreign investment and the CRTC have played

---

3. Data provided to the authors by the Office of the Supervisor of Bankruptcies, by fax.

4. Statistics Canada, October 2, 1997.

5. As of December 31, 1996. See Cineplex Annual Report, 1996, 45.

6. There were links between Alliance and Cineplex-Odeon. The president and executive vice-president of Cineplex-Odeon were both on the board of directors of Alliance, the largest of the Canadian distributors.

7. Sony Retail Entertainment owns 49.9 percent of the new company, Loews Cineplex Entertainment Corporation. Universal Studios owns 26.7 percent, and the Charles Rosner Bronfman Family Trust owns 9.6 percent. (*Globe and Mail,* October 1, 1997, B1, B14). Investment Canada approved the merger on December 18, 1997 (see Industry Canada news release for this date).

a role in maintaining pressure on foreign distributors while protecting Canadian distributors.

Proprietary Rights

In 1988, Investment Canada issued a directive forbidding any distributor that was not Canadian from distributing a film in Canada for which it did not own proprietary rights. Proprietary exhibition rights are deemed to exist when a foreign distributor provides major financing for a film or owns its worldwide distribution rights.[8] An immediate dispute was avoided, as the Hollywood majors were exempted from the Investment Canada directive. By 1996, the Investment Canada directive and the resulting grandfathering of the Hollywood majors generated a dispute with the EC. Polygram, a European media multinational with growing interests in audiovisual distribution, was denied inclusion among those foreign firms exempted from the 1988 directive. The EU began the process of registering a formal complaint in the WTO, claiming that Canada had breached its commitment to MFN in the GATS. While Canada was in preliminary discussions with the EC about the complaint, Seagram, the Canadian owner of Universal Studios, one of the grandfathered majors, bought Polygram. The complaint was then shelved.

In a December 20, 1995, decision, the CRTC extended the carveout for Canadian distributors of films with nonproprietary rights to cover the distribution of films to new satellite PPV and movie services. In contrast to the earlier decision concerning theatrical distribution, the CRTC did not exempt the Hollywood majors. A more detailed discussion of contentious issues arising with the majors from film distribution policy and of the Polygram case appear in chapters 16 and 17.

Subsidy Policies

To be eligible for production subsidies from Telefilm and the provincial granting agencies an applicant must have negotiated a distribution contract with a Canadian distributor. The new tax credit policies, unlike the tax shelter program that they replace, also require a Canadian distributor for eligibility. This indirect protection for distribution by means of ties with the production subsidy programs is augmented by direct financial support to Canadian distributors from another Telefilm program. From its Distribution Fund, Telefilm creates lines of credit for Canadian distributors that help them finance distribution contracts with film producers.

---

8. Since there are no public cases testing the terms used in the 1988 Investment Canada directive, what world rights and majority financing mean in practice is not clear.

When this program was initiated in 1988–89, Telefilm supported Canadian distributors in buying the Canadian rights of both Canadian and foreign films. The intensified bidding for Canadian rights of foreign (mostly non-American) films resulted in a rise in the prices of those rights. Currently, the support is targeted at subsidizing the guarantees for Canadian films, but marketing costs are supported regardless of the nationality of the film being distributed in Canada. The average annual amount provided to the Distribution Fund in the first five years of the 1990s was more than C$15 million.

Broadcasting Policy

Broadcasting policy also impacts the distribution of films. The CRTC's 1995 decision limiting the distribution in Canada of films with nonproprietary rights to Canadian distributors was discussed above. In mid-1997, three bilingual, one French, and one English video-on-demand services were licensed. The bilingual and English services must maintain in their inventory at all times a minimum ratio of Canadian to non-Canadian feature films of 1:20. The French service ratio is 1:12. The traditional video rental outlets with which these services compete are not regulated as part of the broadcasting system.

Television and Cable Policy

Public Television

The development of a Canadian television system differed from that of the earlier experience with radio. In the latter, a national public broadcaster was superimposed on a private system, which according to Nolan (1989) was more varied and innovative than commonly acknowledged. In television, the opposite sequence occurred. When the rapid postwar development of American television generated a forest of tall outside aerials in Canadian communities close to the border, the Canadian government's response was to support the development of a national public broadcaster. CBC television began service in 1952. Four years later, there were eight CBC stations and 22 private television stations that "operated in partnership with the CBC in helping to distribute national . . . television services."[9] Canada's first national microwave system, completed in 1958, was the technological skeleton on which this set of CBC-owned and privately affiliated stations provided a national television network.

The CBC was national Canadian television during the 1950s. In 1968, the CBC was explicitly given a legislative mandate to support national unity and

---

9. See "Broadcasting in Canada" (*Canada Year Book, 1956,* 887–89, reprinted in Bird 1989 as document 27).

Canadian identity. Unfortunately its television service has had difficulty finding its own identity. The CBC's viewership and influence have declined since the introduction of an independent private television system.

Commercial Broadcasting and In-house Production

In 1960, a complicated governance structure for television was established to encourage the development of a private broadcasting system. The CBC had "leavened Canada's cultural diet from a position to the left of political center" (Raboy 1990, 138). When a Conservative government was elected in 1958, there was some pressure from within its ranks to establish a more balanced diet of ideas. Populist support for pluralistic television was more concerned with gaining access to a wider set of entertainment sources than with the orientation of public affairs coverage.

The private system has grown rapidly since its introduction and currently attracts considerably more viewers than its public rival. CTV, the national private English-language network, is the most viewed national network in English Canada. The network was originally comprised of a loose alliance of member companies, each of which typically owned a number of stations. By mid-1997, Baton Broadcasting Incorporated had completed a number of transactions that gave it control of decision making at CTV. There are also English- and French-language regional networks. CanWest Global is the largest of the English-language regional networks and primarily serves Ontario. It has aspired to put together an English-language national network. It awaits CRTC approval of acquisitions that give it the necessary coverage. There are two French-language regional commercial networks, TVA and Television Quatre Saisons. Both are based in Quebec. TVA is the larger of the two. Independent stations, which serve a local market but can also have a national presence through retransmission on cable systems, complete the portfolio of over-the-air television stations.

Specialty and Pay Channels

Canadian specialty and pay channels are not available over the air but are distributed to Canadian viewers through what the Canadian Broadcast Act refers to as distribution undertakings—cable, wireless cable systems, and DTH satellite systems. Despite the greater penetration of cable in Canada than in the United States, the development of Canadian specialty channels lagged behind that of cable networks in the United States. In 1984, a sports channel, The Sports Network and a music video service, MuchMusic, were launched. In 1987, six more specialty channels were licensed.[10] A larger set was launched in 1995 and a still more expansive set approved in 1996.[11] This acceleration continues. A call for applications in 1997 elicited over 70 applications.

The CBC has participated in the specialty channel expansion. The CBC was granted a license to provide a specialty news channel, Newsworld, in 1987, and this service began broadcasting on July 31, 1989. Each cable company with sufficient capacity had to carry the channel. The fee to be paid by the cable company to the service was not negotiated but imposed by the CRTC.[12] In 1991, this fee varied between C$.32 and C$.30 per subscriber. In the same year, the Cable News Network (CNN), which had been on the air for a number of years and had 50 million subscribers in the United States, charged cable companies US$.25 per subscriber.[13] In 1995, Réseau de l'information (RDI), a CBC French-language specialty news channel, began cablecasting.

In 1982, the CRTC licensed two national and four regional pay services. Some failed and others experienced financial difficulties. On reorganization, the pay movie channels survived. The pay movie services are split into three monopolies: western Canada (English language) controlled by Allarcom, eastern

---

10. Among these channels are Le Réseau des Sports and MusiquePlus, the French-language sports and video channels; YTV, a youth and children's network; Newsworld, a 24-hour news service from the CBC; Vision, a religious, ethical, and family channel; and the Weather Channel.

11. The 1995 group (licensed in 1994) included: Discovery Channel, Showcase, Life (lifestyle), New Country Music (country music videos), Women's Television Network (programming from a woman's perspective), and Bravo! (performing and visual arts). The group licensed in 1996 included: six entertainment services—The Comedy Network, Teletoon (cartoon), MuchMore Music, Musimax, Space: The Imagination Station, and Star-TV; two sports networks—CTV Regional Sports and Sportscope; three news channels—CTV N1 (headline news), ROBTV (business news), and Le Canal Nouvelles (French news); three educational services—History & Entertainment, Treehouse TV, and Canadian Learning Television; five lifestyle networks—Home & Garden TV, Outdoor Life, Prime TV, Talk TV, and Le Canal Vie; and two ethnic channels—Odyssey (Greek) and South Asian TV.

12. Startup services in the United States, even with owners having broadcast experience and deep pockets, often have to pay or transfer an ownership interest to cable companies to gain access to a critical mass of cable services. When the National Broadcasting Company (NBC) and Cablevision launched CNBC, a business and consumer news channel, they offered $3 per subscriber as an enticement to systems to sign a long-term affiliation agreement. "If the offer attracts enough subs, it could vault CNBC from the 16 million to the 25–30 million sub level, making it more attractive to advertisers" (Paul Kagan, Association of Cable TV Programming, June 30, 1990, 2).

13. CNN was also carried on Canadian cable at the time of the licensing of "Newsworld." Their interaction is discussed in more detail in chapter 11 on the CMT case, which involved delisting the American alternative when a Canadian service was licensed.

Canada (English language) controlled by First Choice, and French-language movie services controlled by First Choice: TVEC Inc.[14] The Family Channel was licensed in 1987 to provide a pay family entertainment service. It broadcasts much of the programming available on the American Disney Channel.[15] The specialty services, along with pay television, have filled a range of audience needs. Some are broad based but most target a clearly defined market niche.

The Commercial Broadcasters

The firms in the private broadcasting sector typically have the following characteristics:

1. They are either closely held corporations, often controlled by a single family, or subsidiaries of media conglomerates.
2. If public, their ownership includes nonvoting or limited voting as well as the traditional voting common shares.
3. Some recent entrants have developed broadcasting services from a base in production.
4. The larger companies have a web of media holdings—traditional television stations (some associated with different networks), specialty channels and/or pay interests, satellite services, production facilities, publishing entities—or are subsidiaries of even larger media conglomerates.
5. Some Canadian broadcasters are exporting broadcasting expertise through direct investments in foreign broadcasting systems.

As the private television industry matured, some family firms exited and sold their holdings to others. In the process, the expanding firms acquired a disparate mix of channels. The requirement of approval by the CRTC of ownership changes and the practice of exacting a variable "tax" on transfers of ownership have made the reconfiguration of station groupings costly. As a result, commercial rationalization of the private broadcast system has slowed. A

---

14. In the hearings before the CRTC decision, the director of investigation and research under the Combines Act favored the competitive status quo. He viewed the proposed restructuring of the English service into two distinct East-West regional services as "a solution of last resort" that would lower the level of competition well before circumstances justified such action (see CRTC Decision 84–654, Ottawa, August 16, 1984).

15. In its application for a license, the Family Channel indicated that it would provide Canadian content for a minimum of 25 percent of its schedule, combined with up to 60 percent from the Disney Channel and the rest from other international sources (see CRTC Decision 87–905, Ottawa, December 1, 1987).

number of potentially anticompetitive groupings persist or have been created as a side effect of efforts to rationalize. For example, Baton, which has finally consolidated a controlling position in CTV, is also the largest provider of affiliated stations to the CBC, CTV's rival in national and network advertising. In a number of smaller locations, Baton owns both the CTV and the CBC affiliate.[16] As the last step in obtaining control of CTV, Baton concluded deals to take over the CTV stations and network holdings of Electrohome and CHUM. As a result, rival stations in important television markets came under the control of the same owner.[17]

The Canadian television services have expanded internationally through a combination of investment and transfer of formats, acquisition of a position in foreign networks, and licensing their services to cable or satellite broadcasters in other countries. The scope and commercial returns for selling broadcasting formats "off the shelf" internationally is limited. This expertise can best be commercially exploited through a transfer of format and operating knowledge accompanied by investment. CHUM Ltd. of Toronto owns CITY TV, an independent Toronto station, which has developed a distinct format for presenting local news, information, and entertainment. CITY has exported this format to Helsinki, Buenos Aires, Madrid, and Cape Town. CHUM has a 26 percent interest in Canal Joven in Argentina and a partnership with Rainbow Programming Holdings Inc. to distribute its musical video programming on American cable systems.[18] MuchMusic, CHUM's music video channel, is also carried by the American satellite broadcasting service, DirecTV.

CanWest Global acquired a 15 percent interest in New Zealand's TV3 in 1991, and in the next year acquired an interest in Australia's Network Ten. In 1996, the Australian and New Zealand investments generated slightly more operating profit before amortization for CanWest than for its Canadian television system.[19] In late 1998, the TV3 network in which CanWest Global has a 45 percent interest began service in Ireland. The company also has an approxi-

---

16. In its submission to hearings on the structure of the broadcasting system held by the CRTC in 1993, Baton reported: "Eleven of its stations are affiliated with the CTV Television Network in Toronto, Ottawa, Pembroke, Sudbury, Timmins, North Bay, Sault Ste. Marie, Saskatoon, Regina, Yorkton and Prince Albert. Six television licenses are affiliated with the CBC English Television Network in Sudbury, Timmins, North Bay, Sault Ste. Marie, Yorkton and Prince Albert" (Baton Broadcasting Inc., CRTC notice of public hearing 1992–13, scheduled for hearing, Ottawa, March 1, 1993).

17. For details of these complicated transactions and the regulatory rationale for approval, see CRTC Decision 97–527, Ottawa, August 28, 1997.

18. This service has four million subscribers in the United States. CHUM estimates that 10 million are needed to attract significant advertising interest.

19. CanWest Annual Report, 1996, 3.

mately 29.9 percent interest in Ulster Television, a commercial television franchise in Northern Ireland.

The large values generated by the development of Canadian television broadcasting have accrued largely to a number of closely held firms that gained original stewardship of the valuable spectrum and licensing rights granted by the Canadian government. This original advantage has been reinforced by subsequent allocations of, for example, specialty channel licenses favoring companies with broadcasting experience. At first, the private concerns succeeded in obtaining market share at the expense of the public broadcaster. They chafed at content controls and regulatory restrictions. As the CBC's market share receded the competitive boundary with American broadcasters became more important to the commercial broadcasters. Along this boundary the regulator is seen as an asset, not a liability. As Raboy (1996, 180) notes in the 1995 Information Highway hearings, the Canadian Association of Broadcasters (CAB), which represents the private broadcasters, "presented itself as the champion of Canadian content, which, if memory serves correctly, it had at one time eschewed." We now describe the complex set of constraints that the CAB has come to see in a different light.

Canadian Content Regulation

For Canadian broadcasting the roots of content provisions lay in the 1932 decision to regulate radio broadcasting. In these regulations and the many manifestations that have followed, the definition of *Canadian* has often appeared arbitrary and more consistent with industrial than "loftier" objectives. In the first paragraph following the announcement of a 40 percent limit on imports of foreign programming, the original regulations provided this exemption:

> A program of foreign origin which advertises goods manufactured in Canada, and names the address in this country where such goods are produced and distributed, shall be deemed a Canadian program.[20]

Canadian content provisions have been part of the governance structure of the current mixed private and public television broadcasting system since its inception. In December of 1959, the Board of Broadcast Governors (BBG), introduced a system of program quotas beginning with a requirement of at least 45 percent Canadian content with a provision that this would rise to 55 percent. These regulations classified as Canadian all news and commentaries on news televised on a Canadian station, regardless of content or whether it was bought

---

20. CRTC, Rules and Regulations, PC535, April 15, 1993; reprinted as document 18 of Bird (1989, 130).

from a foreign source, as well as special events of general interest to Canadians occurring outside of Canada. After introducing the content controls, the BBG initiated a policy of rewarding its licensees for increasing Canadian content by making the minutes allowed for commercial messages depend on achievements in Canadianizing the viewing schedule.

In 1984, the CRTC, the BBG's successor as broadcasting regulator, adopted the point system, originally developed by the Canadian Film and Videotape Certification Office of the Department of Communications for the tax shelter program, to determine what was a Canadian television program. According to this system, the "nationality" of a program depends on a weighted sum of the citizenship of those performing key functions in program production and the percentage of expenditures on services provided by Canadians. For the citizenship requirements, the producer must be Canadian and six points must be earned by the nationality of other key positions.[21] At least 75 percent of what is paid to personnel other than those in key positions earning points, or for postproduction work, must be paid to Canadians, and at least 75 percent of processing and final preparation costs must be spent in Canada.[22] Variations of this system currently apply to other categories of programming such as animation, children's programming, and variety shows, with the point allocation tailored to the program's personnel requirements and production processes.

There has been a tendency to add more and more distinctions to the Canadian content system. One extension is the introduction of degrees of Canadian content. The movie channels, for example, were granted a 150 percent Canadian content credit for original Canadian dramas. Foreign programs that are dubbed into either English or French are awarded 25 percent Canadian content. Since most of the dubbing is into French, the French-language percentages of Canadian content are not directly comparable to the English-language ones as indicators of content differences.

Official coproductions have always qualified as Canadian content. In 1984, the CRTC recognized coventures, which are a vehicle for joint ventures with American firms, as 100 percent Canadian, even if producer functions on the project are shared by the partners, as long as "the Canadian production company has no less than an equal measure of decision-making responsibility with other coventure partners on all creative elements of the production and administers the Canadian portion of the budget."[23] A coventure must meet the same points criteria and expenditure requirements as a domestic production, but, as is typical

---

21. The original television weights are as follows: director, 2; writer, 2; leading performer, 1; second leading performer, 1, head of Art Department, 1; director of photography, 1; music composer, 1; and editor, 1. The budget requirements are also complicated.

22. See CRTC Public Notice 1984–94, Ottawa, April 15, 1984.

23. CRTC Public Notice 1984–94, Ottawa, April 15, 1984.

in this area, there are exceptions.[24] In 1987, the CRTC formalized a policy, which it had followed for the previous three years, of giving Canadian content status to twinning projects. Twinning represents parallel rather than cooperative production. Both of the twinned projects receive status as domestic content.

Additional content terms are also applied to established broadcasters when licenses are renewed or on new broadcasters when they are given the right to transmit. Requirements depend on what programming genre is perceived at the time to be inadequately Canadian and the economic condition of the applicant. To illustrate the detail—the extent of the micromanagement involved—consider the following stipulation, which was one of many, placed on CTV:

> With regard to international news services, the Commission notes that CTV maintains foreign bureaux in Washington, London, Beijing and Jerusalem. While the Commission is aware of the high cost of maintaining foreign correspondents, it also considers that Canadian broadcasters should maintain their existing foreign correspondents and where possible reduce their dependence on foreign news services in order to provide viewers with a Canadian perspective on important international issues. The Commission therefore strongly expects CTV to retain all of its existing news bureaux and where possible to expand its team of foreign correspondents during the coming license term.[25]

Requirements of the regional Global Network, imposed in the same year, illustrate the extent of the overall requirement and its dispersion over categories of programming that the CRTC deems to be inadequately Canadian. Global was instructed to supply 200 hours per year of first-run Canadian drama, music, and dance, and children's and documentary programs over its base Canadian content requirement.

Requirements are also relaxed when a licensee experiences financial difficulties. One example is First Choice and the Super Channel, which were licensed in the early 1980s to provide English-language pay movie channels. The two companies ran into financial problems and were reorganized as regional monopolies with First Choice operating in Central and Eastern Canada and the Super Channel in the west. In approving the new arrangements, the CRTC stipulated 30 percent Canadian content during the broadcast day and prime time, with the percentage to rise to 50 percent after December 31, 1986. Unfortu-

---

24. For example, a coventure with a commonwealth or French-language country need only attain five points and a minimum expenditure requirement of 50 percent, rather than 75 percent, to qualify as Canadian.

25. CRTC Decision 87–200, Ottawa, March 24, 1987.

nately, these services and the French-language movie channel, Super Écran, continued to struggle financially. In 1986, the CRTC approved their application to have their Canadian content requirement lowered to 20 percent outside of prime time.

Lifting the veil on licensing and Canadian content reveals a complex continuous auction of the right to broadcast with payments adjusted to circumstance. The means of payment is Canadian content commitments. This discretionary regime system provides some insurance against outside shocks for the broadcasters but also has some unfortunate incentive effects. The system taxes commercial success and subsidises both bad luck and incompetence. It also encourages successful broadcasters to present a negative picture of their economic viability.

The content provisions raise the license fee for an international program that qualifies as Canadian. In this regard, Cinar notes in a recent prospectus: "Broadcasters generally pay a premium for Canadian-content productions."[26] The extent of the premium varies with the type of programming. For the more expensive MOWs, the Canadian broadcaster pays a license fee that is at least twice what it would pay for a foreign MOW with a similar potential to attract viewers.

The broadcasters also gain by producing international product rather than material that would only have a market in Canada because any foreign revenue reduces their costs of meeting the content provision. Similarly a Canadian producer has an incentive to produce international product and earn the premium in the Canadian market plus whatever can be earned in license fees abroad. The content program has subsidized, at the expense of the Canadian broadcasters, the replacement of foreign programs with domestic ones that are similar in style and treatment. Other anomalies occur. For example, if the Rhombus film based on the life of Glenn Gould, mentioned in the previous chapter, had been made by an American company, it would have been considered non-Canadian in content and penalized for broadcast in Canada.[27]

Those supporting content policies argue that expanding the "shelf space" for Canadian product will ultimately lead to significantly more consumption of a product that they continue to claim is distinctive. These policies have now been in place for 25 years, but Canadians' desire for international quality programming in drama, news, and sports has arguably increased, not decreased. Programs classified as Canadian that are of this standard are successful in drawing audiences both here and abroad. Those that are not are given shelf space but are not watched. There is little evidence that Canadians have been

---

26. Cinar Prospectus, September 3, 1993, 21.
27. We analyze the content provisions in more detail in Acheson and Maule (1990).

conditioned into a higher state of being by a number of largely unwatched shows taking up air space.

Canadian Viewing Patterns

Figure 3 presents the viewing shares in Canada of services originating in Canada: traditional public broadcasters,[28] conventional broadcasters,[29] and Canadian pay and specialty services.[30] The figure also includes viewing shares of two service categories originating in the United States: conventional private television[31] and U.S. pay, specialty channels and PBS. The data cover the period 1984 to 1998.[32]

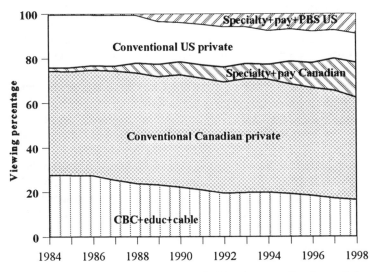

Source: *TV Basics 1998* and earlier editions. The Television Bureau of Canada supplied 1998 figures by fax.
Notes: See footnotes appended to discussion of fig. 3 in the text.

Fig. 3. Canadian viewing shares by service and origin

---

28. CBC, provincial educational television, and the cable community channels.
29. CTV, Global, TVA, Télévision Quatre Saisons, and independents.
30. Including CBC's Newsworld.
31. ABC, NBC, CBS, Fox, affiliates of other networks, and independents.
32. The data, originally collected by BBM, measures the share of TV viewing of different services for all persons two years or older. In figure 3, the share of VCR viewing and of "others" (unidentified stations) are excluded. The remaining shares are the percentage of total hours of watching excluding VCR and others.

In this period, the share of the CBC, educational and community channels declined significantly from 27.6 to 16.5 percent, and conventional Canadian private television's share fell slightly from 46.9 to 45.8 percent. The share of Canadian subscription and pay television rose from 1.4 to 15.8 percent. The private Canadian services—conventional, subscription, and pay— increased their joint share from 46.9 to 61.6 percent of the market. Conventional American television stations declined in popularity with their market share falling from 23.7 to 13.2 percent of viewers, but this was partially offset by a rise in the share of American pay and specialty services from 0.4 to 8.7 percent.[33] The total share of American stations fell from 24.1 in 1984 to 21.5 percent in 1990 and rose fractionally in the next 8 years. Canadian viewers shifted to pay and subscription services from conventional networks regardless of whether the services originated in the United States or at home. Within the Canadian services, the share of public television declined significantly. Both of these trends diminish the amount of Canadian content associated with watching Canadian rather than U.S. services as public television generally has the highest and the Canadian specialty and pay channels the lowest levels of Canadian content.

Canadian producers favor a retention of Canadian content and unconstrained access to the American market. From the evidence presented in chapter 7, the large and niche Canadian producers of internationally attractive product would be net losers if the content policies were continued but access to foreign markets denied. There are also indirect production effects of a culture of protection that deter creativity and commercial innovation. Unless they have a high "existence value" for programming that they do not watch, consumers clearly lose by the policy.[34] Some of the major consumer groups have argued against aspects of content policy. In renewing the license of the CTV network in 1987, the CRTC noted that:

> The CAC made a strong appeal for the removal of Canadian content requirements as they apply to private broadcasters. The CAC believes that consumers would benefit from increased choice in television programming if private broadcasters were free to respond to the demands of the market and the CBC alone was required to produce and broadcast Canadian programming.[35]

---

33. A small part of this increase is due to a reclassification by BBM of 6 U.S. superstations in the Fall of 1991 that reduced our "Conventional private US" category and increased our "Specialty+pay+PBS US" category.

34. Existence value is generated when a person values the knowledge that the good exists. See Krutilla (1967).

35. CRTC Decision 87–200, Ottawa, March 24, 1997.

Cable and Other Distribution Undertakings

Canada is a highly cabled country. 72.6 percent of the approximately 8 million subscribers in 1997 received discretionary services as well as basic and total revenues from basic and discretionary services were $1,968 million and $775.5 million respectively.[36] By 1995, 27 percent of cable subscribers could access 70 channels or more.[37] The noncabled households are largely in rural areas that either depend on over-the-air signals or use satellite dishes. Three percent of households are authorized to receive television by satellite and use the large television receive-only dishes that can be switched to different satellites (Jeffrey 1996, 204). Since September 1997, two licensed Canadian DBS (direct broadcasting satellite) services, ExpressVu and Star Choice, have offered programming to viewers using a smaller, 60 cm. dish. In addition, there are an estimated 200,000 to 300,000 gray market subscribers to American digital satellite broadcasting services. On land, new wireless broadband systems have begun to be introduced.

Although the difference has diminished over time, Canada has had higher cable penetration rates than the United States. Because the Canadian population is concentrated in a thin band north of the U.S. border, American television can be received by many Canadians over the air. A driving force for the rapid cabling of Canada was an increase in the number and variety of American stations received. As is true in the United States, a handful of Canadian MSOs service a large number of subscribers and a large number of small systems service a relatively small number of subscribers. Among the important MSOs are Rogers, Vidéotron, Shaw, and Cogeco. Recently, the MSOs have been reconfiguring their holdings into concentrated groupings through takeovers or trades to better position themselves for pending competition with telephone systems. The MSOs typically have vertical links to conventional broadcasters, specialty channels, and pay services as well as interests in other media and telecommunications.

The two Canadian satellite services currently in operation are ExpressVu and Star Choice. ExpressVu is controlled by Bell Canada Enterprises (BCE), a holding company that inter alia owns or controls key players in the Canadian telephone industry, including Telesat, Canada's provider of satellite communications services. Star Choice is owned by Shaw Communications Inc., a large MSO with specialty channel interests. The Canadian services currently provide a smaller choice of packages than DirecTV and other American satellite broadcasting services. Both Canadian services plan to expand their offerings.

---

36. Cansim matrix 1819-1829.
37. CBC Annual Report, 1995–96, 13.

The saga of the interaction between Canadian broadcasting policy and the spillover of American satellite broadcasters is addressed in chapter 12.

The 3 + 1 Policy

The CRTC has traded off providing cable subscribers with access to American television against requiring cable systems to carry Canadian content. This balancing act included an early concession. In 1979, the CRTC allowed Canadian cable franchises, wherever they were located, to import the signals of NBC, CBS, ABC, and PBS and place them on the basic cable tier. This ruling is known as the 3 + 1 policy. In 1994, the policy was altered to allow any three of the above American commercial networks plus Fox to be the "3" in the 3 + 1 formula. The American network that is excluded from basic service can be carried on a discretionary tier.[38]

The Linkage Rules

The CRTC has established a set of priorities that govern a cable company's decisions to place channels in different tiers that can be marketed to subscribers. Most cable companies are required to carry the Canadian specialty channels licensed before 1993 as part of the basic service unless the originator opts to have it put on a discretionary tier. The other Canadian specialty channels are carried on a discretionary tier unless the cable company and the service operator agree on terms to include it on basic.

A set of linkage rules governs the access of foreign services appearing on two lists, sections A and B of part II of Eligible Satellite Services. Some of the more popular American services in the A category are CNN's services (Cable News Network and Headline News), the Nashville Network, the A&E Network, and the Learning Channel. The B group contains a number of American superstations and some cablecasters such as American Movie Classics. Until 1995, a cable company could combine Canadian specialty services with non-Canadian services from schedule A in a ratio of one to two in a discretionary tier. Currently, the ratio is one to one. If a Canadian pay channel is included in a discretionary tier, the cable operator can then include five foreign channels drawn from section A or B. A ceiling of five is placed on the total number of foreign services on any discretionary tier.

The criteria for distinguishing between A and B schedules are not clear. Black Entertainment Television, for example, once on the B list, was recently moved to the A list. Historically, a non-Canadian service on any of the eligibility lists had no security of tenure and could be removed by a decision of the CRTC.

---

38. CRTC Public Notice 1994–107, Ottawa, August 29, 1994.

The removal of an American cable network, CMT, from this list triggered a trade dispute discussed in chapter 11. The resolution of this case has strengthened the status of channels on the eligibility lists, however, the criteria for inclusion remain unclear and the opaque process continues to be an irritant to those excluded.

Simultaneous Substitution

Simultaneous substitution occurs when a program appears on a Canadian channel at the same time an American station is carrying it. The policy requires that the cable company replace the American signal with the domestic one on its service. If, for example, the program appears on both a CTV and a NBC station, the CTV signal will appear on its own cable channel and on the NBC station's channel position. The policy makes the right to broadcast the program in its area more valuable to CTV because its advertising content reaches a wider audience. Correspondingly, the value of the right of NBC to broadcast the program in the United States declines, as its advertising reach is reduced when its signal does not reach the Canadian viewer. A program that is licensed to both NBC and a Canadian broadcaster is likely to be American. Its owner will receive a higher price in selling to CTV and a lower one from NBC and not be significantly affected. In contrast, the economic positions of the American border stations and the Canadian broadcaster are affected, and they have respectively protested and championed the policy.

Simultaneous substitution was part of a four-pronged cable policy announced by the CRTC in 1971. Another prong was to pass legislation making advertising on an American station ineligible for tax deduction by a Canadian company. In licensing the new era of satellite broadcasting undertakings at the end of 1995, the CRTC imposed simultaneous substitution with some add-ons. The DTH licensees are required to delete the programming service of an out of market station when the identical program is broadcast on both stations within the same broadcast week. The commission will accept alternatives when this policy is unfeasible or prohibitively costly. The CRTC held hearings in 1997 to consider advanced substitution, which encompasses a number of possible initiatives. In the public notice of the hearings, the CRTC noted that the CAB estimated that advanced substitution could result in up to C$35 million annually in additional advertising revenues for Canadian television stations.[39]

Measures to make the property rights in programming more secure result in less uncertainty and more efficient contracting. In that sense, the Canadian initiatives are beneficial and have their counterparts in a number of countries, including the United States. A more problematic aspect of the policy is the

---

39. CRTC Public Notice 1997–7, Ottawa, January 10, 1997.

protection of domestic advertising markets for domestic media. In this regard, the income tax provisions are the more troublesome of the measures for Canadian consumers.

Ownership

Subsection 22(a) of the Broadcasting Act prohibits the CRTC from granting a license if it is not in accordance with a direction to the commission by the governor-in-council. The current instructions are that at least 80 percent of the shares must be owned by Canadian citizens. This has recently been amended to provide more scope for foreign investment. The 80 percent rule is maintained, but non-Canadians can own up to one-third of a Canadian holding company and it will still be considered Canadian. This means that a foreign company can create a holding company of this type with Canadian partners. This holding company can then own 80 percent of the broadcasting concern with the foreign corporation holding 20 percent in its own right. As a result the foreign company holds a 44 percent interest in the broadcasting entity. An unfortunate aspect of this method of relaxing the constraint is that the holding company cannot be publicly traded. Any purchase by a foreigner of a listed share would prevent the company from qualifying as Canadian. The consequences for Canada's equity markets could be significant.

The 20 percent limit on foreign ownership was imposed on broadcasting in the United States before being imported into Canada.[40] The American cable industry does not have foreign ownership restrictions while the Canadian does. Because of Canada's experience in the cable business, a number of Canadian companies successfully sought and obtained cable franchises in the United States. Rogers financed part of its expansion to become the largest MSO in Canada from a profitable sale of its American cable interests. Our reading is that the support for foreign direct investment restrictions on broadcasting, particularly on cable, is eroding.

Conclusion

The relation between distributors and cinemas involves contracts and ownership linkages that create wicked problems for competition policy in sorting out efficiency effects from the enhancement of potential market power. Distribution of international product requires a coordinated international system. Traditionally multinationals have provided an international distribution service. Patching together a set of regional and national distributors is an alternative, but to date

---

40. For a history of ownership restrictions on broadcasting in Canada, see Kowall (1992).

it has not had the same degree of success. Canadian distribution and exhibition policy for films has focused on carving out rights for the Canadian market and reserving them for Canadian distributors. This favors the participation by Canadian distributors in the second alternative. At the same time Canadian private interests have bought a Hollywood studio with interests that are not coincident with the direction of Canadian distribution policy. Whatever the internal effect, distribution and cinematic exhibition policy are generating a number of trade disputes.

Broadcasting has an extremely complex regulatory structure that is based on promoting import substitution wherever possible. At the same time, forestalling a viewers' revolt requires the government to allow access to a wide variety of international products. Content quotas are a prominent component of this system and a target of American commercial diplomacy. They depend on measures of national content that are at odds with the rhetorical stories that protect them politically. In Canada, they have succeeded in generating a substitution of Canadian international product for foreign at a significant cost to the Canadian taxpayer. Further, many less visible components of broadcasting and cable policy are protective of Canadian producers. The broadcasters have an interest in exploiting their skill and experience in other markets and are vulnerable to protective policies abroad. This vulnerability is currently not as great as that of the Canadian producers of international programming discussed in the previous chapter.

CHAPTER 9

Canadian Publishing, Sound Recording, and Radio

Book publishing is the greybeard of the cultural industries. In contrast, sound recording and radio are twentieth-century industries. In this chapter, radio is only discussed in terms of its relationship to the recording industry. Sound recording and publishing rely on copyright law as a legal basis on which a web of contracts create value. Many developments in both, but particularly in sound recording, are conditioned by the piracy problem. Some of the policies designed to either cope with or compensate for the effects of sound recording piracy have international implications.

Foreign sales are important sources of revenue for both the multinational record company and the small quality press dealing with content that has a thin but international market. The magazine sector is similar to the other cultural industries in facing vigorous foreign competition within Canada, but it is an exception in lacking any component that has been able to attract custom abroad. All the cultural industries share the challenges of identifying attractive content, nurturing the development of projects, producing a marketable product, promoting, distributing and selling. Despite that similarity, the historical differences in the economic characteristics of their product and technology have generated distinct policy settings and degrees of success.

The Print Media

Newspapers

The total daily circulation of the 105 general interest newspapers in Canada, as of March 1998, is about 4.6 million copies for a population of 30 million persons according to the Canadian Newspaper Association. The top 20 newspapers account for nearly 70 percent of the total circulation and the largest, the *Toronto Star*, distributes about 450,000 copies daily. The majority of daily newspapers are owned by firms that have a chain of newspapers. The dominant firms, with the number of newspapers owned in parentheses, are Hollinger International (58), Sun Media Corp. (15), Thomson Newspapers (eight), Quebecor (four), and

Power Corp (four). Hollinger, controlled by Conrad Black, owns nine of the top 20 newspapers, followed by Sun Media with four, and Thomson and Quebecor with two each.[1]

The international interests of these major players extend beyond daily newspapers and involve substantial sales in foreign markets. Torstar, owner of the *Toronto Star,* earned 37 percent of its operating revenue from book publishing in 1997 compared to 46 percent from newspapers. Its book-publishing subsidiary, Harlequin Enterprises Ltd., published in 23 languages and sold 165 million books in more than 100 international markets. Over 95 percent of revenues from book publishing came from outside Canada, and a major portion of foreign revenues were realized in the United States. Harlequin has contracted with Alliance Communications to produce programs for television based on its romance novels. A new business for Torstar is the production of educational material for children with the acquisition of a number of firms in the United States. It is also experimenting with electronic publishing.[2]

Thomson describes itself as being in the specialized information and publishing business. As well as 68 daily newspapers in North America, numerous nondailies, and more than 250 advertising-based supplemental publications, Thomson services the needs of professionals, providing legal, tax, accounting, regulatory, and human resource services using a variety of print and electronic formats. Earnings in 1997 were 70 percent from information and publishing activities other than newspapers, 17 percent from newspapers, and 13 percent from the travel group. By region, most of these earnings occurred in the United States and 95 percent outside of Canada; the same was true for the geographic distribution of sales and assets. Thomson combines newspaper with periodical publication in traditional and new formats to service world markets. While the first Lord Thomson traveled to the United Kingdom to publish newspapers, his son is developing international markets from a Canadian base for a variety of information products and services.

For 1997, Hollinger Inc. reported worldwide ownership of 117 daily newspapers and 320 nondaily periodicals, including magazines. Non-Canadian markets accounted for around 50 percent of Hollinger's sales and profits. These were split approximately evenly between the United States and the United Kingdom.[3] In 1996, Hollinger divested itself of its minority interest in John

---

1. See <http://www.cna-acj.ca/english/>. Subsequent to March 1998, Quebecor purchased a number of Sun Media daily newspapers and Hollinger introduced the *National Post.* These changes are not reflected in the data.

2. See *Quill & Quire,* October 1997, 1; and Torstar Annual Report, 1997. A selection of the material found in Torstar's annual report plus additional information can be found on Torstar's web page at <http://www.torstar.com/corporate/index.html>.

3. Hollinger Inc. Annual Report, 1997, 77.

Fairfax Holdings Ltd. in Australia after promises by various Australian politicians that Hollinger would be allowed to increase its ownership position were not fulfilled. The company reported:

> Much though we regret leaving that great company, we are sure that our shareholders' best interest would not be served by any further effort to navigate the parochial quagmire of Australian politics. The proceeds will be better applied in jurisdictions where foreigners are not treated with official bad faith and insurmountable suspicion.[4]

In the policy arena, corporate concentration has been a repeated concern in the newspaper industry. A case of monopoly via merger was brought and lost, on appeal to the Supreme Court, by the Canadian government against K. C. Irving's ownership of English-language newspapers in the province of New Brunswick.[5] One issue was the extent of editorial autonomy exercised by each of the Irving-owned papers. Corporate concentration was again the issue in a competition case involving Southam and Thomson newspapers, and again the case was lost by the government. These actions led to a Royal Commission on Newspapers,[6] which inquired into concentrated newspaper ownership. Similar questions were raised at the time of Hollinger's recent acquisition of several dailies. The concern has been with concentrated and cross-media ownership by Canadians leading to a diminished number of independent voices providing news and editorial comment.

The antitrust activity reflects the economics of the newspaper industry, which requires a large market to justify more than one supplier, but the intensity of activity in Canada is probably increased by the restrictions imposed on potential competition from foreign newspaper interests. Foreign ownership was effectively limited in 1965 when the income tax act was revised so that Canadians were unable to deduct advertising expenditures in newspapers unless they were 75 percent or more Canadian owned. Canadian newspapers are vulnerable to competition from new media. Cable television has offered effective competition for real estate advertisements through specialized channels providing information about houses and properties for sale. The Internet promises to both augment the reach of newspapers and offer a competitive venue for information and advertisements. Traditional newspaper owners like Thomson in Canada and Pearson in the United Kingdom are protecting their

4. Hollinger Inc. Annual Report, 1996, 6–7.
5. *R. v. K. C. Irving Ltd.* (1976), 25 CPR (20) 223.
6. Canada (1981).

interests by diversifying into the provision of information through electronic platforms.

In commenting on other aspects of cultural policy, newspaper editorials have often been supportive of the aims of the Canadian Broadcasting Act, which permit the CRTC to impose content quotas and levy fees for the production of Canadian programming through its licensing procedures in order to promote Canadian content. If the same restrictions were imposed on Canadian newspapers, there would undoubtedly be strong protests concerning freedom of the press. Another irony is the fact that newspapers are permitted to use material from foreign sources and package it with local advertising, a procedure that is disallowed in the periodical industry, where it is called a split-run. For example, the *Globe and Mail* reprints in its business section pages from the *Wall Street Journal*. Use of foreign news services is another source of foreign content in Canadian-owned newspapers. Like a split-run, newspapers use content published elsewhere.

Periodicals

Data describing the Canadian periodical market are reported by Statistics Canada, industry associations, and in *Canadian Advertising Rates and Data* for purposes of advertising.[7]

A total of 1,440 magazines, 60 percent English language, 22 percent French language, and 18 percent other (some of which are bilingual French and English). are classified by type of magazine and source of revenue for 1991:

1. 167 general consumer magazines like *Maclean's* and *L'Actualité*
2. 407 special interest consumer magazines such as *Hockey News* and *Coup de Pouce*
3. 383 business or trade magazines such as *Canadian Architect* and *L'Automobile*
4. 64 farm magazines
5. 191 religious magazines
6. 228 scholarly magazines

---

7. We use the results of a detailed study of the industry undertaken for the Task Force on the Magazine Industry (Cebryk 1994). In it there is a useful discussion of the problems associated with collecting and evaluating the various sources of information. Figures for 1996–97, not directly comparable with the Cebryk study, reported a total of 1,552 publications with advertising revenue as 62 percent of total revenue. Advertising revenues rose C$55 million from 1994–95 (Statistics Canada, *The Daily*, September 14, 1998).

Overall revenue sources were 22 percent from subscription sales, 7 percent from newsstand sales, 64 percent from advertising, and 7 percent from other, including membership fees and subsidies. While many different combinations of revenue sources occur, the following are illustrative of tendencies. Many business and some consumer magazines derive 90 percent or more of their revenue from advertising and are referred to as controlled circulation magazines as they are typically delivered free to readers. Revenue is more evenly spread between advertising and circulation revenue for many consumer magazines, while for scholarly magazines receipt of advertising revenue is often less than 10 percent of their total revenue and government grants may be received. Business and trade magazines will often obtain revenue from membership fees as well as advertising. For all 574 consumer magazines in Canada, advertising revenue accounts for 56.1 percent of the total and circulation revenue for 39.8 percent.

Frequent reference is made to two dimensions of the magazine market, the number of copies circulated and the revenue from paid circulation (subscription and newsstand). In 1959, Canadian magazines accounted for 23.3 percent of the copies circulated, rising to 67.6 percent in 1992, the balance being copies of foreign magazines. This 67.6 percent of copies translated into 25.5 percent of circulation revenues, with the remaining 74.5 percent going to foreign publications. In the English-language segment of the market, 81.4 percent of the copies sold on newsstands were foreign, almost all American. This last figure is usually quoted to argue that Canadian magazines have little shelf space, but it presents only a partial assessment of the market. It measures only one means of distribution, namely, newsstands, and deals only with those consumer magazines that are distributed on newsstands. The 67.6 percent Canadian share of total circulation presents a different picture, one that implies a more vibrant industry.[8]

A brief comparison with the American market reveals an estimated 11,000 to 15,000 periodicals in 1991, in comparison with the 1,440 Canadian figure. Eighty-four American periodicals have circulations in excess of 1 million copies per issue in the United States and include *Time* and *Reader's Digest*. Only one Canadian periodical exceeds the 1 million figure; that, too, is *Reader's Digest*, with 1.3 million copies. The thirteenth largest is the Canadian edition of *Time*, with 354,000 copies (Cebryk et al. 1994, EI-1). It might seem surprising that these two would be considered as both American and Canadian periodicals, but the vagaries of the policy process have resulted in this circumstance, which continues to this day.

Canadian periodical policy has a long and tortuous history, dating back to the 1951 Massey Royal Commission and with antecedents to the turn of the

---

8. The task force fails to mention that Canadian authors, such as Mavis Gallant and Alice Munro publish their work in foreign magazines like the *New Yorker*.

century. Central to the policy has been the split-run issue and related policies. Split-runs occur nationally when substantially the same content with a different set of advertisements is sold in different regions of the countries. Canadian policy has been aimed at preventing American publications from putting out Canadian editions with little change in content but with Canadian advertisements. The policies to deter or prevent split-runs have involved prohibitive tariffs and taxation policies such as not permitting advertising expenditures of Canadian companies in American publications from qualifying as deductions for corporate tax purposes.

Over the years, in the process of attempting to support the Canadian periodical industry, measures have included postal and publication subsidies, a tariff prohibition, and provisions of the Income Tax Act aimed at channeling advertising revenues to Canadian publications. The outcome has been the industry described in the data presented above, the inclusion of *Reader's Digest* and *Time* as part of the Canadian industry, and a continuing series of disputes with the United States, the latest culminating in a challenge to Canadian periodical policies that has been upheld by the WTO. The most recent policy, introduced in October 1998, is a prohibition on foreign periodical publishers selling advertising aimed at the Canadian market.

Canada's major policy objective has been to channel advertising revenues to Canadian periodicals in the belief that they would publish and promote Canadian content. No point systems were created to measure "Canadian" content, as was devised for television programs, the assumption being that a given level of Canadian ownership would ensure that the publication had the desired content. The policy brought the government into conflict with two major American publishers, Time and Reader's Digest, beginning in the 1960s. After a bruising battle between the Canadian government and these two firms in the 1970s, an accommodation was reached so that both remained in Canada, publishing so-called Canadian editions. For 15 years the issue remained dormant, although there was always the fear that some American publication would adopt the format used by Time Canada to conform with the government's stated policy. In 1990, Time, now Time Warner, announced its intention to publish a split-run edition of *Sports Illustrated*. The outcome of this action and the associated policies are described in detail in chapter 10.

At the center of the split-run policy in the 1970s was the desire to promote a weekly Canadian newsmagazine. The original target was support for *Maclean's* magazine. It was believed that without some handicap imposed on Time, *Maclean's* would not survive. It had been published for a number of years but had never managed to be profitable. There was also an ideological concern that *Time* had more of a right-wing focus than suited the Liberal government of the time. So, whereas the policy was clothed in Canadian nationalist rhetoric, there was a more political agenda simultaneously at work. The irony has been that despite the twists and turns of policy both *Time* and *Reader's Digest* maintain major circulations in Canada as general interest magazines.

Aside from a postal subsidy that has shrunk from over C$200 million to less than C$50 million in 1998, the only other federal subsidy is a C$2 million fund administered by the Canada Council available for magazines that devote themselves to poetry, literature, and the visual and performing arts. Some provincial governments also provide small amounts of funding; the Ontario Arts Council budget for magazines was C$500,000 in 1996–97. A loan program, the Cultural Industries Development Fund (CIDF), with a pool of C$33 million administered by the Federal Business Development Bank, provides loans of C$20,000 and up to Canadian producers of books, films, magazines, new media applications, and music recording. In 1994–95, almost C$1 million was assigned to consumer magazines. The Canadian Magazine Publishers Association (CMPA) has also lobbied without success for the removal of the goods and services tax on reading material on the grounds that it is a tax on the promotion of literacy.[9]

While the subsidy policies can be listed in terms of their wording and intent, their actual administration involves greater complexity, as discretion is used to classify magazines in terms of their eligibility for support and their degree of Canadian ownership. Only insiders know how decisions are reached, and the end result does not appear to provide the transparency that is required in the GATS.

Canadian policy initiatives have been focused on preserving the home market for domestic producers rather than contemplating the possibility of servicing export markets. While alluding to this possibility, a recent task force report (Canada 1994, 60) dismisses it without recognizing that at least one Canadian publisher, Harrowsmith, was doing just that. In addition, a large number of trade magazines exist, some published by firms such as Maclean Hunter (now owned by Rogers Communications), which cater to industries such as trucking, plumbing, and wood products. These target audiences much larger than Canada and would benefit from being encouraged to produce split-runs for the U.S. market.

Among the larger Canadian periodical publishers are Rogers Communications, Quebecor, and Telemedia.[10] All have interests in other industries. In 1997,

9. Details of these policies are contained in the Annual Report of the Canadian Magazine Publishers Association, 1994–95 (130 Spadina Ave., Toronto), and in issues of the *CMPA Newsletter*. The association has about 320 members with a combined per issue circulation of 10 million copies and an annualized circulation of over 165 million.

10. Details extracted from the 1997 annual reports for Rogers Communications Inc. and Quebecor Inc. Telemedia has been a private company since 1985. It publishes five French-language and seven English-language periodicals (information supplied by Telemedia, March 29, 1999).

77 percent of Rogers' revenues came from wireless communications (mainly cellular services) and cable television operations, while 9 percent came from nine consumer and 40 business magazines, with the remainder from broadcasting, telecom, and new media. Previously the periodicals were owned by Maclean Hunter, which Rogers acquired in 1994.

Quebecor, in 1997, obtained 93 percent of its revenues from printing and forest products operations and the remainder from newspaper, periodical, and book publishing and a multimedia subsidiary. The company owns 57 mainly French-language regional newspapers and 11 magazines. Two of the four daily newspapers are published in English. Quebecor has provided printing services to Rogers for its periodical publications and to Torstar for the production of Harlequin Books. It also has a contract with Time Warner to publish regional editions of *Time, Sports Illustrated,* and *People,* in total over one million copies per week. Because of its printing operations, Quebecor has a major interest in maintaining open markets. It now owns printing plants in the United States, the United Kingdom, France, Germany, Spain, Mexico, Chile, Argentina, Peru, and India as well as in Canada; printing accounts for 60 percent of total revenues and 63 percent of operating income.

Both Rogers and Quebecor are experimenting with new or multimedia applications for the production and distribution of informational, educational, and entertainment materials in a manner that will break down the traditional boundaries between the print and audiovisual media. These initiatives will challenge the application of existing trade and intellectual property policy frameworks. Publishing an electronic version of a periodical raises issues concerning copyright, advertising, taxation, and the applicability of broadcasting regulations that have significant international consequences.[11]

Books

From an author's viewpoint, preparing a manuscript is a risky business. It requires a larger commitment of time to write a book than an article or news story, and the financial returns may be further away, unknown, and perhaps few. The publisher tries to transfer this risk onto the author through the terms of the royalty agreement, while the bookstore tries to do the same with the publisher by negotiating a returns policy whereby any unsold books can be returned for a refund. This can be serious in the case of chain bookstores buying in large quantities from small publishers where the possibility exists that a large unsold shipment will be returned to the publisher. Under these terms, the accounts

---

11. Presentation by Blair Mackenzie, general counsel, Southam Inc., "Impact of Regulations on the Marketplace: A Publishing Perspective," October 19, 1995.

receivable of the publisher may be difficult to confirm. For periodical and paperback publications, returns are dealt with by retailers taking the publications on consignment. Unsold magazines are returned and destroyed; paperbacks have their covers removed and returned, while the remaining content is destroyed.

All of the cultural industries distribute differentiated products. Each has developed categories for classifying output. These aid in gathering descriptive statistics but also hide many distinctions. In book publishing, frequently encountered categories are text, trade, mass market paperback, and reference as well as fiction and nonfiction. Book-publishing policy circles have added adjectives such as foreign and Canadian, import and export, and own and agency titles. The latter dominate the trade categories in terms of statistical series. The available numbers reveal the following profile of the Canadian industry.[12]

1. The Canadian industry consists of 366 firms, 20 of which are foreign owned. The industry generated about C$1.7 billion in revenue from domestic sales and exports in 1994–95, which translates into about C$3.0 billion of Canadian retail sales.[13]

2. Three types of books are published and/or distributed: those published in Canada for which the author contracted with the Canadian publisher, those published elsewhere whose rights to Canadian publication have been acquired by a Canadian firm, and those that are imported by Canadian publishers and distributors that act as agents to sell the books in Canada. The first two categories are referred to as "own" books and the last as "agency" titles, where the Canadian firm provides a wholesaling function and sometimes contracts for printing on behalf of foreign publishers.

3. Agency sales amounted to over half of Canadian domestic sales, and half of the agency sales were made by the 20 foreign-owned firms, many of which are subsidiaries of foreign multinational firms, which are prominent as trade and textbook or educational publishers.

---

12. Data were obtained from the Association of Canadian Publishers (ACP) (1997) and interviews with Canadian government officials. They are based on the 1994–95 survey of book publishers.

13. Statistics Canada reports value added for book publishing to be about one-tenth that for magazines and periodical publishing although wages and salaries are slightly less (Cansim Matrix 5500 and 5502).

4. Over 80 percent of the titles published by Canadian authors are put out by Canadian publishers.

5. Imports other than agency sales enter the country by mail, but there is no reliable record of their value.

6. Books exported as merchandise items totaled C$122.7 million in 1994–95, to which can be added C$247.0 million, mainly from the sale of rights abroad where the foreign publisher obtains the right to publish the book, but also from sales abroad by subsidiaries of Canadian companies. Revenue from exports accounts for over 20 percent of total revenues.[14] Different sources of data on exports all agree that export revenues are becoming a more important source of total revenues.[15]

Most of these numbers are subject to qualification, and Rowland Lorimer (1996, 5), a close observer of the industry, cautions the reader about the reliability of official statistics. From these figures, the following picture emerges. Most of the Canadian-authored books sold in Canada each year are published by Canadian publishers. Of the foreign books imported for sale on an agency basis, about half are sold by a relatively large number of Canadian firms and half by a small number of foreign firms. The principal imports are associated with agency sales. Exports, which account for about 20 percent of total industry revenue, are made mainly by Canadian as opposed to foreign publishers and thus account for a larger percentage of the revenues of Canadian publishers.

14. The export figure is another example of the questionable reliability of official data. One Canadian company, Torstar, alone generated revenues in 1995 of C$485 million from book publishing, over 90 percent of which came from foreign sources, a figure that exceeds total industry exports and other foreign income as reported by Statistics Canada. In a verbal communication with Statistics Canada, we were told that "other foreign sales" includes some items that appear in the balance of payment statistics and some that are not included. The breakdown is not available, so accurate figures for book exports cannot be quoted. The preliminary published export figures for 1996–97, using these dubious categories, are C$121.5 million for book exports and C$284.2 million for other foreign sales (figures provided by fax on October 20, 1998, by Statistics Canada).

15. Preliminary figures for Statistics Canada's survey of book publishers and exclusive agents for 1996–97 were published on the Statistics Canada web site on July 9, 1998. While the latest survey is not directly comparable with the 1994–95 survey because of increased coverage of smaller firms, total revenues appear to have increased from C$1.7 to C$1.9 billion. Exports of C$119 million and other foreign sales of C$284 million combine to make foreign markets account for over 20 percent of total revenue (details provided by telephone from Statistics Canada, October 9, 1998).

Over the years, book-publishing policy has followed three approaches: to provide funding to Canadian authors and publishers, to restrict the number of foreign-owned publishers in Canada, and to channel the revenues from imported books to Canadian publishers. Some funding is also available from provincial governments.

Subsidy Programs

Direct funding for the publication of Canadian books involves three separate programs, the Book Publishing Industry Development Program (BPIDP) administered by the DCH with funding of about C$20 million; the Block Grant Program of the Canada Council of the Arts, with about C$7 million; and the Aid to Scholarly Publishing Program of the Social Sciences and Humanities Federation of Canada, with C$1 million. Although each program has a differently worded mandate, they have a common aim to assist in the financing of Canadian-authored works published by Canadian publishers. The BPIDP has three components; aid to publishers, aid to industry and associations, and international marketing assistance. The last provides assistance in the sale of foreign rights by Canadian publishers and general export marketing assistance.

In addition, Canadian publishers that have had difficulty obtaining bank credit for working capital purposes can apply to the CIDF, a revolving loan fund set up by the Business Development Bank under a memorandum of understanding with the DCH.[16] About one-third of lending has been to book and magazine publishers. The ACP has also raised the possibility of introducing a refundable investment tax credit measure similar to that available for Canadian film production as well as general tax incentives to attract equity investment.

A brief survey of the general and supplementary eligibility criteria for funding under the BPIDP supports the view that the administrative process is anything but simple and transparent. The policy does not conform to standards of national treatment. Whether the resulting subsidy is countervailable depends on its impact on exports and injury to foreign industries. The policy supports Canadian-owned book publishers that have a track record[17] as well as the

---

16. There are some parallels here to the procedure used by the DCH in funding postal rates for magazines, which has been considered an ineligible subsidy to domestic producers under the WTO.

17. The regulations require that the principal activity of the firm must be book publishing, that the firm must be owned and controlled by Canadians with a minimum of 75 percent ownership, and that the company headquarters and 75 percent of the employees must be based in Canada.

Canadian printing industry.[18] Publishers must be above a certain minimum size[19] and must not be a front for a vanity press.[20]

A formula is then calculated so that all eligible applicants in a given year receive a portion of the funds available. If a firm enters the race it will receive some sort of prize, unlike those contests that operate on a first-come first-served basis in a given year until the money runs out.[21] Listing these conditions for one program is undertaken not just to bore the reader but to point out how each of the conditions leads in turn to further interpretations so that attaining transparency and consistency of application over time is difficult. The process has other costly effects. Firms must spend time conforming to a complicated application process and will be encouraged to structure their operations so as to become eligible candidates for funding. Administration costs also fall on government departments. Whether the package of policies is ever evaluated to determine its effectiveness is doubtful.

Ownership and Copyright

The ownership structure of the industry is frozen in the sense that no new foreign publishers can be established in Canada. Foreign takeovers of firms now controlled by Canadians are not permitted, and Investment Canada guidelines state that all acquisitions, such as when a foreign-owned firm is to be sold to another foreign-owned firm (an indirect acquisition), should be examined to ensure that they are of net benefit to the Canadian-controlled segment of the industry. At the wholesale and retail levels, Investment Canada guidelines block the expansion of foreign firms into Canada.

---

18. To qualify a firm must have printed a minimum of 50 percent of its eligible titles in Canada.

19. The firm must have been in business as a book publisher for at least 36 months. In the last three years it must have published a minimum of 15 Canadian-authored trade titles or 10 Canadian-authored educational or scholarly titles. It must also have attained net eligible sales of C$200,000 in the most recent financial year and have maintained a minimum-level sales to inventory ratio with the ratio, varying with the type of book. It is not eligible if it had net sales from book-publishing activities exceeding C$15 million in the previous financial year and if its average profit margin for the last three financial years was equal to or greater than 12 percent (the method for calculating the profit margin is provided).

20. There is a limit on the income that the firm can earn from the sale of vanity titles, from nonauthored books such as directories and catalogs, and from books written exclusively by its shareholders or owners. The details of all of the requirements are available at <http://www.pch.gc.ca/culture/cult_ind/bpidip-padie/english.htm.>.

21. As was described in chapter 7, the first-come first-served process was used by Telefilm Canada in funding television programs in April 1998 but has since been altered.

The Copyright Act has now been amended to bar parallel imports if there is an exclusive Canadian or regional distributor of the book. Parallel imports are copies of a book legitimately published under license in a market other than the one they are entering. This measure requires that booksellers acquire from Canadian rights holders those books for which they hold exclusive agency rights. No longer is it lawful for retailers to buy around the Canadian rights holder and acquire the book directly from sources abroad. The purpose of the policy is to encourage use of the earnings from agency sales to support the future publication of works by Canadian authors, even though there is no requirement that the funds be used in this way.

Policy Dilemmas

The cumulative effect of the interaction between existing policies and changing technologies poses a number of dilemmas for domestic policies and international agreements. Existing rules are such that foreign publishers and booksellers can stay if they already operate in Canada, profits earned from imported books are supposed to be channeled to Canadian publications, and subsidies are available to Canadian authors and Canadian-controlled publishers. The cross-subsidy thesis sustains ownership policy and the parallel import ban, which presumes that Canadian publishers and booksellers are more likely to publish and distribute the works of Canadians. Those arguing this case point out that over 80 percent of the books authored by Canadians are published by Canadian publishers without referring to the accompanying fact that only Canadian publishers are entitled to claim subsidies for these publications. The argument for Canadian ownership of book retailing is based on the assumption that profit-driven booksellers will select books on the basis of nationality rather than expected sales. We questioned the logic and empirical content of this argument in the previous chapter. A more telling problem with these policies for the government is that their administration clearly fails to offer foreigners national treatment. That being the case they are vulnerable to challenge under the WTO if the items traded, namely books, are deemed to be goods. Further discussion of this issue is found in chapter 13.

The international success of Harlequin Books as a Canadian publisher reveals a dilemma of cultural policy. As publisher of popular romance novels, Harlequin does not satisfy the aims of policymakers to promote highbrow writing that may lack commercial appeal. Policy measures try to be a silver bullet targeted at a particular type of product that is unlikely to have broad audience appeal. Their success depends on how creativity occurs and whether the government can promote it.

While developments in information technology assist creators in their research and writing, it is also having a major impact on distribution. A firm such as Amazon.com provides an Internet source for locating and ordering books. Some consumers will bypass the traditional bookstore to place their orders, thereby reducing the distribution role of the bookstore and allowing individual consumers to buy around both the Canadian bookstore and the agency publisher. Amazon.com offers 2.5 million book titles compared to 175,000 in the branch of a large physical store like Barnes and Noble and several thousand copies in a neighborhood store.[22]

Services offered by libraries are also changing. They have always provided a distribution channel for books, periodicals, and newspapers. Increasingly sound recordings and videotapes are made available, and connections can also be made to electronic data bases. Traditionally public libraries have offered their services free to users with funding provided by government. Not only do readers not need to purchase hard copies, but libraries are usually equipped with photocopying machines. Under the revised Copyright Act, a library can provide photocopying machines on its premises and patrons can use them to make copies of material for personal research if the library has reached an agreement to provide compensation with a reprographic collective representing the rights of authors and publishers. In essence, part of the revenue from on-site photocopying is paid to the collective, which then redistributes funds to its members.

A user charge may also apply for access to an electronic data base, which may be located within or outside the country, another example of services trade that may escape the official records. Since 1986 a public lending right has been in existence in Canada, which is paid by libraries via a collective to authors for the use of their books.[23] This is the print equivalent to performing rights contained in copyright legislation (see chapter 14). As the services of public libraries change so do funding mechanisms, but government support still provides the mainstay for funding.

Because of their government funding, the purchasing practices of libraries could be directed to purchase national content in the same way that public broadcasters or publicly regulated private broadcasters are directed to carry national content. This has not happened, but surveys have been undertaken on the purchasing policies of libraries to determine the extent to which they acquire

---

22. *Economist,* August 16, 1997, 47. Aside from Amazon.com, other firms have entered or are reported to be entering the Internet bookselling business. These include Barnes and Noble, Borders, Chapters, and Bertelsmann (*Globe and Mail,* September 28, 1998, B1).

23. Details of public lending right systems in 15 countries are discussed in Parker (1977) and in papers presented by G. Hoover and J. Larivière at the PLR's Tenth Anniversary Conference, Ottawa, November 1996. Further details are available from the Public Lending Right Commission, Ottawa (fax: 613–566–4418).

Canadian books. As a 1984 study commented on the difficulty, "we all know what we mean by a Canadian book until we try to be precise."[24] The evidence suggests that Canadian-authored books account for about 14 percent of cataloged library collections, but the message is mixed as to whether this results from a policy to target Canadian books regardless of readers' demands or because it satisfies readers' demands. In general the pursuit of national content policies found in the broadcast media through use of a point system does not occur in the print media, but subsidies and policies targetting split-runs do assist in promoting such content.

Sound Recording and Radio

The Canadian recording industry has been growing quickly. Between 1989–90 and 1993–94 total sales grew from C$454.3 million to C$738.0 million. The 13 percent annual rate of growth was comparable to that experienced in the United States between these two dates. The Canadian industry is small and less of a relative presence in the Canadian economy than it is in the American. In 1997, the retail value of sales in the United States was US$11.91 billion and in Canada was C$1.35 billion (US$.98 billion).[25]

In 1993–94 sales of recordings with Canadian content in Canada were just under 13 percent of total Canadian sales. In the same year, there were 719 new releases of Canadian content out of a total of 6,367 or 11.2 percent of the total.[26] Canadian-content releases therefore experienced higher than average sales in that year.

In the record industry, trade flows typically occur in masters rather than recordings. The compact discs and tapes sold in Canada are mainly manufactured within the country. This feature of the industry was once thought to be an artifact of the tariff, but it has persisted with the recent removal of the tariff with the United States under the CUSFTA. The removal of the tariffs represent an opportunity as well as a threat to manufacturers. There are two large Canadian manufacturing firms, Cinram and Disque Améric, and a newly built plant owned by Sony. Cinram has operations in the United States, and 35 percent of its revenue in 1993 was generated from American sales. Disque Améric manufac-

24. "Development of Options for Action in Key Sectors of Canadian Book Distribution," report of a study undertaken for the Department of Communications, Ottawa, August 1984 (mimeo).

25.From International Federation of the Phonographic Industry web site: file world_sales3.html dated March 23, 1999.

26. The Canadian statistics in this paragraph are from Statistics Canada, *The Daily,* March 22, 1995. The American statistics are from the Recording Industry Association of America (RIAA), 1996 statistical overview.

tures for most of the Quebec-based and other independents, contracts with majors, and exports. Ernst & Young (1995, 16) report that 38 and 12 percent of Disque Améric's 1993 revenue were generated from sales to the United States and Latin America respectively.

The industry has some similarities to and differences in structure from the other cultural industries. Like the film industry, distribution in Canada is dominated by major multinationals—Polygram, MCA, Warner, EMI, Sony Music, and BMG. Only one of these companies, Warner, is American controlled. EMI, Sony, and BMG are respectively, English, Japanese, and German owned. MCA is Canadian owned. Polygram, which was Dutch, is also now Canadian, as it has been acquired by MCA's parent, Seagram. As a result of this consolidation, the largest record company in the world is Canadian. In the first quarter of 1995, MCA and Polygram had shares of the Canadian market equal to 19.1 and 19.8 percent respectively.[27] Surprisingly, those who consider the nationality of ownership to be a significant determinant of behavior have not rejoiced at this shift from dominated to dominant. Together the recording majors had a market share of 90.6 percent. Their dominance is even greater if the measure is control of titles, since all have significant back catalogs. The same is true if the measure is contractual control of established international and regional talent. The majors are also important manufacturers in Canada.

The retailing sector is dominated by large chains of which one is Canadian and the others are multinationals. Unlike the film industry the multinational chains are typically not integrated with the large distribution companies. There is an integrated presence, but it is not in traditional retailing. Compact discs, like books, lend themselves to Internet selling. A number of Internet retailers operate in North America. Record clubs, such as Sony's Columbia House, connect the customer directly with the large distributors. Their sales are reported to rival those of the large retail chains. Distributors deal directly with the large retail chains and supply a hierarchy of middlemen—wholesalers that service the nonspecialized retail outlets, rack jobbers that distribute to the department stores and general discount houses, and "one stops" that service smaller retail outlets.

A number of small Canadian record producers have an extensive knowledge of their local musical scene and a portfolio of contracts with emerging, or sometimes receding, talent. The larger Canadian companies also produce content for foreign independents under license. A WWW self-portrait of one the largest and most successful of these companies conveys a sense of their role:

Attic Music Group is Canada's largest integrated music company. In twenty-three years of business, Attic has received over ninety gold,

---

27. The market shares cited in this paragraph are originally from the *Record*, a Canadian trade magazine (see Straw 1996, 110, table 4–4).

platinum and multi-platinum awards from the U.S., Canada, U.K., Holland and Japan. Attic has ten full time professionals in marketing and promotion and has the full support of its distributor, MCA. The 1996 awards include Platinum for Weird Al Yankovic's "Bad hair Day", Gold for Seven Mary Three's "American Standard", Gold for The Irish Rovers', "It Was A Night Like This" and gold for the compilation "In Between Dances." As well as a select roster of top Canadian artists, Attic is the Canadian licensee/distributor for some of the best foreign independents including Scotti Bros (U.S.A.), Roadrunner (Netherlands), Mammoth (U.S.A.), Metal Blade (U.S.A.), First Night (U.K.), Edel (Germany), Edel/America (U.S.A.) and more.[28]

The Quebec music industry has a reputation for artistic and organizational creativity. Quebec-owned companies have developed a national capacity for distributing French-language music (Grenier 1996, 313), whereas the English-language producers like Attic rely more heavily on the majors for distribution.

The music industry is less dominated by large productions and more heterogeneous than the film industry. As a result, the majors are prominent players in the non-mass-music genres as well as popular music. Their organizations have been more decentralized than the film studios, and they are becoming increasingly effective at competing with the small firms in discovering and developing talent linked to regional or niche music. Straw (1996, 96) recently commented that "since no musical style, apparently, was too marginal or underground for major multinational firms, the fate of small, Canadian-owned firms that had long nurtured those styles seemed uncertain." Nevertheless, the majors remain more mass market oriented than the small companies. According to Statistics Canada the foreign-controlled companies accounted for less than a third of new releases with Canadian content in 1993–94, but these releases accounted for 55 percent of the sale of Canadian content records.

The masters of a significant number of the Canadian recordings released by the majors are produced by Canadian companies. The comparative advantage of the majors is to nurture a success through promotion and market successes internationally. Like film, record production is risky. The Task Force on the Future of the Canadian Music Industry (Canada 1996c, viii) reports that "[r]isks are high in originating master tapes since only one in ten is financially successful."

It is generally acknowledged that the multinationals have promoted and nurtured the careers of an array of Canadian recording stars who have achieved international success. A few artists sell well in Canada but not abroad. These are the exception. The correlation between success in the two markets is generally

---

28. Attic profile on <http:www.cirpa.ca> as of October 24, 1997.

high. What is less evident than the association of national and international acclaim for stars is the international orientation of the activities of smaller companies. They do not just represent a "farm system" for the major distributors. The Attic self-portrait reveals a number of international linkages. Straw confirms that this trend is general:

> As major firms construct a global audience from national niches, small independent firms that had hitherto dominated these niches in their own countries find their room to manoeuvre shrinking. To survive they, too, must move into international markets, licensing their own products in other territories, selling publishing and other rights on a country-by-country basis, and picking up the inventory of other small national labels for distribution. (1996, 104)

Subsidy Programs

In 1982, a fund, the Foundation to Assist Canadian Talent on Records (FACTOR), was initiated by the radio interests of CHUM, Moffat Communications, and Rogers Broadcasting. Since that time, the support base of the fund has expanded to include contributions from 12 Canadian broadcasters. There is a similar initiative covering the French segment of the industry called Music-Action. FACTOR and MusicAction also administer much of the DCH's Sound Recording Development Program, introduced in 1986. The budget of that program began at C$5 million. It is approximately C$9.5 million in 1997–98. The larger provinces also have modest funds supporting the recording industry.

FACTOR and MusicAction provide assistance for producing the works of recording artists and songwriters, creating videos, and financing promotional tours. FACTOR claims to have had a significant effect on international as well as domestic sales when it reports that "FACTOR-supported recordings have generated over $230,722,000 in world wide sales."[29]

The CRTC had traditionally "asked" private broadcasters at license renewal time to support Canadian talent either financially or by other means. Radio stations were generally excused from such obligations if they were incurring losses. In 1996, the CRTC introduced an explicit fee structure, which was expected to generate C$1.8 million to parties working with Canadian talent such as FACTOR and MusicAction.[30] This shift reduced the support provided by radio broadcasters to the recording industry from C$7 million to the C$1.8 million figure. Consequently, the Task Force on the Future of the Canadian Music

---

29. FACTOR web site.
30. CRTC Public Notice 1995–196, Ottawa, November 17, 1995.

Industry (Canada 1996c, 117) expressed "its profound disagreement" with the initiative. In 1998, the CRTC introduced a Canadian talent development tax of 6 percent of the value of the transaction when a radio station changes hands (with discretionary relief if the station being purchased is unprofitable). The payments are made to a new Canadian music marketing and promotion fund to support cooperative broadcaster/music industry activities and initiatives, FACTOR, MusicAction, and other eligible Canadian talent development initiatives.[31]

In summary, the Canadian recording industry does not have a tax credit program and the direct subsidies are low relative to the revenue of the industry. Like the feature film industry, it faces great risk in developing successful releases. Consequently, the recording industry is promotional intensive. Unlike the film industry, it does not have to pay for saturation radio advertising. Its messages are carried "for free" or at a price far below the going advertising rates as content in radio programming. The government initiative that most generously supports the Canadian industry is the Canadian content requirement for music played on the radio.

Radio and the Recording Industry

The CRTC imposes Canadian content quotas for music played on Canadian radio stations. Canadian content is determined by scoring at least two points according to the "MAPL" criteria. A point can be earned in each of the following categories: M = music composed by a Canadian, A = music or lyrics performed principally by a Canadian artist, P = live performance recorded wholly in Canada and broadcast live in Canada, and L = lyrics written by a Canadian. Some flexibility is granted to accommodate team production, performance, or composition when the team is multinational. There is the usual set of puzzling exceptions.[32]

---

31. CRTC Public Notice 1998–41, Ottawa, April 30, 1998: "the Commission has amended the benefits test for commercial radio to require, as a general rule, a minimum direct financial contribution to Canadian talent development representing 6 percent of the value of transactions involving transfers of ownership and control. Consistent with the Commission's existing benefits policy, the Commission will not impose benefits requirements in the case of transactions involving unprofitable undertakings."

32. A recording does not need two points to qualify as Canadian if it is an instrumental performance of a musical composition written or composed entirely by a Canadian. A second example occurs when either the composer or the lyricist collaborates with a non-Canadian. A point is assigned if a recognized performing rights society rules that the contribution of the Canadian was at least 50 percent.

The CRTC micromanaged FM radio while providing a loose rein to AM. The regulation retarded the development of FM radio in Canada compared to the United States. It cushioned the fall in asset values of AM stations that would otherwise have taken place as listeners migrated to the FM band. From 1975 to 1991, FM stations were required to maintain the mix of programming to which they had committed to when licensed. The stations maintained logs of their actual programming, which were monitored by the CRTC. In the 1990s, the CRTC adopted a more flexible system for regulating FM stations. Content categories were simplified and reduced in number. The CRTC reduced the formats (configurations of content categories) that it recognized from 14 to two, and general "talk" requirements were relaxed to a minimum commitment of 15 percent per broadcast week. The stations were required to meet four guidelines with respect to playing music:

1. use of "hits" limited to 50 percent of all popular music played in a broadcasting week
2. non-Canadian selections not repeated more than 18 times in a broadcasting week
3. commitments of time devoted to playing instrumental music
4. 850 different selections at least per week

The hit requirement was discriminatory, as it excluded Canadian songs for a year after they appeared on a Top 40 chart.

These specifications confined to the AM band the saturation play of songs, which is a standard strategy for nurturing a hit by feeding an informational cascade. This imposed a restriction on the multinational record companies, which supply many of the "Top 40" hits, but the incidence fell more heavily on the owners of the FM stations. A number of companies with radio holdings provided "insurance" against technological and regulatory developments by owning both an AM and a FM station in the same market. These Canadian content constraints had a brief life, as the maximum repeat ceiling and minimum number of distinct selections requirements were withdrawn.[33] For FM stations, the CRTC committed to removing the 15 percent spoken word restriction and relaxing a long-standing restriction on advertising time.[34]

The Canadian content requirement for AM radio was 30 percent for popular music and 7 percent for traditional and other music until recently. FM policy made more distinctions. In 1990, Canadian content was set at 30 percent for

---

33. CRTC Public Notice 1992–72, Ottawa, November 2, 1992; CRTC Public Notice 1993–38, Ottawa, April 19, 1993; CRTC Public Notice 1993–113, Ottawa, July 28, 1993.

34. CRTC Public Notice 1993–38, Ottawa, April 19, 1993. AM advertising time had not been restricted.

popular and country music, 20 percent for stations that broadcast up to 49 percent instrumental music, 15 percent for those broadcasting 50 percent or more instrumental music, 10 percent for special interest music stations such as classical[35] and jazz, and 7 percent for ethnic stations. If the station plays music for which the CRTC deems the Canadian supply of recorded music to be less "thick," a lower ratio is accepted. Canadian content requirements for television musical video channels is 30 percent. The newly licensed pay audio services have a 15 percent Canadian content requirement.

The content regulations have been extended to address issues of language. For popular music, French-language stations are required to devote a minimum of 65 percent of air time to recordings in the French language.[36] Stations restricted by this requirement were reportedly losing market share to English-speaking stations in Ottawa-Hull and Montreal, especially among young listeners. One of the responses adopted by these stations was to meet the commitment by shortening French-language vocal music selections. After hearings in which these matters were discussed, the CRTC decided not to reduce the 65 percent requirement and to change its regulations to prevent the shortening of the French musical selections.

In 1998, the CRTC raised the base rate of Canadian content from 30 to 35 percent.[37] The increase was opposed by the CAB, which argued that the supply of Canadian music cannot support the tighter constraints. The CAB has proposed that the limit be set at two times the percentage of Canadian records sold to total records sold in Canada. By this rule, the rate would be significantly less than the new CRTC target. The CRTC has not adopted such a policy. As in any discretionary import substitution program, requirements will be adjusted as availability changes. The Task Force on the Future of the Canadian Music Industry (Canada 1996c, xii) has advocated 40 percent.

Neighboring Rights and Blank Tape Levies

In the 1920s, Canadian radio stations were not allowed to play recorded music because of the political influence of performers (Nolan 1989). Since then, the

---

35. The commission allowed a program playing only music composed before 1956 to meet a 2 percent Canadian content requirement (CRTC Public Notice 1993–95, Ottawa, June 28, 1993).

36. CRTC Public Notice 1993–173, Ottawa, December 8, 1993. In 1998, the CRTC announced that it will seek a proposed amendment to the regulations requiring that a minimum of 55 percent of the popular vocal music selections broadcast between 6:00 AM and 6:00 PM, Monday through Friday, be in the French language (CRTC Public Notice 1998–41, Ottawa, April 30, 1998).

37. CRTC Public Notice 1998–41, Ottawa, April 30, 1998.

radio and recording industries have developed a symbiotic relationship in which the activities of each raise the value of the other. They are drawn to cooperate to make the pie larger, but they contest to alter the share that accrues to each. Recently, Canada introduced a public performing right for performers and record producers. Not surprisingly, this policy change was sought by the record companies and opposed by the radio stations because it involves taxing the former to create a fund that is divided among the performers and record producers.

The legislation that amended the Copyright Act to create the neighboring right regime also introduced a levy on blank audio tapes sold in Canada. The revenue from the tax is placed in a fund, which is divided among collectives representing composers, lyricists, performers, and producers of sound recordings. The amount of the levy is determined by the Copyright Board. Both the neighboring right initiative and the blank tape levy compensate for lost revenue due to piracy. The distribution of these funds has international implications. The content that is copied or played on the radio is not limited to that which is classified as Canadian. The performers and record companies responsible for the large percentage of American music played on Canadian radio will not receive anything from the fund. Similarly, illegal copying in Canada is not limited to Canadian content recordings, but the compensation for copying is limited to Canadian producers and performers or those from countries offering materially similar programs that include Canadians. The United States has argued that distribution should be based on national treatment rather than on reciprocity. The dispute over the current Canadian neighboring right initiative and blank tape levy is addressed in chapter 14.

Piracy may become a more acute problem as the development of MP3 files and players allows copyrighted music to be posted on and downloaded from the Internet. If these threats are countered by the creation of larger compensating funds, the distribution issue will become even more disruptive of trade relations in the future.

Conclusion

The print and recording industries are producers and merchants of content. In these sectors there are no public producers or distributors of significance, but there is a pervasive public policy presence. The common policies are production subsidies that benefit domestic producers and distributors. Foreign ownership of Canadian newspapers is effectively ruled out by tax law and frozen for Canadian book publishing by investment policy. The distribution policies differ. Foreign firms cannot sell books in Canada but can sell records. The recording industry has a unique relationship with radio broadcasting. As a result, broadcasting content policies are the most significant support program for the recording industry.

There are no entry constraints for Canadians in the record and publishing industries. As a result a changing set of small companies provides a vehicle for experimentation absent in the highly regulated broadcasting sphere. In the recording industry, Canada has opted to create funds financed by levies on broadcasters and consumers of blank tape to be distributed among composers, performers, and record companies. What the ultimate effect of these will be on the contractual and organizational nexus in the industries is moot.

Policy measures taken in the cultural industries frequently have an impact on other countries. Those highlighted in this chapter include the cross-subsidy arrangements whereby profits from the sale of imported books are intended to fund Canadian-authored works; restrictions on foreign ownership on the grounds that nationality of ownership affects the type of material published and distributed; and defining content on the basis of nationality for purposes of subsidies or establishing air time quotas. A number of these policies have elicited diplomatic responses. The Canadian foreign ownership and control restrictions in the print media have initiated a dispute. The conflict is over the denial of entry into book retailing by an American firm, Borders, on the grounds that its contractual relationship with the majority Canadian investor gave it control of the enterprise.[38] Foreign trade in books and contracting between foreign publishers and Canadians will also be affected by Canada's banning of parallel imports of books under revisions of its Copyright Act. The new Copyright Act also introduced neighboring rights and the blank tape levy.[39] This chapter provides background for assessing those conflicts, along with others in broadcasting and film, in part III.

---

38. This case is discussed in detail in chapter 13.
39. This case is discussed in detail in chapter 14.

Part III

The Cases

The following cases represent a series of actual and potential disputes between Canada and the United States involving both the production and distribution of cultural content. Each case is unique except for the common cultural thread. Each contains a wealth of detail, which in one sense is mind numbing but in our view necessary to appreciate the complexities that will have to be addressed when negotiations occur to develop an international governance structure. By providing background and historical context for each dispute, our aim is to enhance understanding of the present circumstances.

To date, the debate has often been framed in simplistic terms, suggesting that culture can be removed from the negotiating table and each country can act as it pleases. The cases clearly show that this is not the case. In a number of instances, the current international system does constrain the degrees of freedom for domestic cultural policy. Countries like Canada that have tried to insulate their policies from trade agreements have only partially succeeded in doing so. Where Canadian diplomacy was successful in insulating cultural policies from the jurisdiction of the formal system, disputes have still arisen that have had to be dealt with through informal processes. One reason for looking at the cases is to assess the efficacy of the alternative resolution processes. A second reason is to throw light on the following question. In the next round of trade negotiations, should countries like Canada be seeking to extend the domain of the formal constraint system or to roll it back? A third reason is to assess the need to give domestic policies a different orientation. Our conclusion is that domestic policy ought to be realigned. Countries like Canada cannot afford to limit the access of their readers, listeners, and viewers to international content nor to deny their creative industries the opportunity to sell abroad. A domestic realignment to a more open policy posture will strengthen the case for integrating the cultural industries into the existing international governance structure of trade and investment.

CHAPTER 10

Sports Illustrated

The case involving *Sports Illustrated,* a magazine published by Time Warner, is the 1990s sequel of a 1960s dispute involving *Time,* another Time Warner magazine, and *Reader's Digest.* In both instances, the central issue has been competition in Canada for advertising revenues between Canadian-owned and split-run editions of foreign magazines or periodical publications. Owners of Canadian periodicals and their industry advocate, the CMPA, have argued vigorously that without appropriate protective policies they would be unable to compete against the foreign split-runs. The trade issue arises due to a series of Canadian policies designed to keep foreign split-runs out, which in their most recent dress were the subject of WTO dispute panel and Appellate Body rulings (World Trade Organization 1997a, 1997b). These decisions determined that a tariff, excise tax, and postal subsidy arrangement protecting the Canadian magazine industry was not consistent with Canada's international trade obligations.

Federal and provincial governments of all political stripes in Canada have supported the industry's appeal for protection but not always the individual policies. The argument advanced is the familiar nationalist one tailored to the conditions of this industry—that without protection Canadian periodicals could not survive, that these periodicals are necessary to assure that Canadian writers are read and that Canadian readers have the opportunity to select their works, that national unity/identity is promoted by Canadian periodicals, that over 80 percent of the English-language periodicals distributed via newsstands in Canada are foreign (mainly American), and that split-run editions of American magazines involve unfair competition due to the dumping of the editorial content into the Canadian market.

Before examining the *Sports Illustrated* case in detail, we briefly define a split-run and discuss the market for advertising aimed at Canadians, which is at the heart of the conflict. As in all of the cases, the history of the issue has shaped the current interaction. As this is particularly true of *Sports Illustrated,* we provide a guided tour through the historical tangle.

What Is a Split-Run?

Magazines consist of two types of content, advertising and nonadvertising or editorial content (articles, photographs, artwork). Revenues accrue to publishers from the sale of space to advertisers and the sale of the magazine to readers at newsstands or through subscriptions. A split-run is a commercial technique used in the magazine industry to combine common editorial content with advertising tailored to particular markets.

The term *split* refers to the separation of the editorial and advertising content. Thus, the American edition of *Sports Illustrated* sold in Canada via newsstands has the same editorial and advertising content as the copy sold in the United States and is not a split-run. It becomes a split-run when the edition sold in Canada has substantially the same editorial content but different advertising content, which targets audiences in Canada.

At times, split-runs are referred to as regional editions of magazines, as they target either different countries and language groups or different regions within countries. In effect, split-runs reflect product differentiation by periodical publishers, a marketing strategy widely used in this and related industries. Newspapers, for example, employ regional editions with different news and advertising content as a way of targeting different foreign and local or subnational markets, while cable television services such as Discovery and CMT employ a similar split-run type format adapted to their means of delivery. Book publishers produce different language versions of books or different editions of the same book with each edition tailored to a national market. Thus, there are American, Canadian, and U.K. editions of introductory textbooks in economics. With book publishing, the regional editions do not contain advertising.

Historical Context of the Split-Run Issue

An early reference to Canadian periodicals was made in 1871 in a letter by Goldwin Smith, editor of the *Canadian Monthly Magazine,* requesting material from a German publisher for translation into English and use in this publication. Smith's concern was the shortage of suitable material for his Canadian magazine and the threat of intellectual annexation by the United States (Eggleston 1951, 51). During the 1920s, references can be found in parliamentary debates to the subject of periodicals. These address both the undesirable content of periodicals crossing the border from the United States and the pressure from foreign competition (Litvak and Maule 1974, 14–28).

In 1951, the Royal Commission on National Development in the Arts, Letters and Sciences (Massey Report), while recognizing the contribution made by magazines to the development of national understanding, also reported that it was "impressed by the fact that the Canadian periodicals neither desired nor requested any protective measures apart from an adjustment of the tariff rates on paper imported from the United States for publishing purposes" (Canada 1951, 64). In subsequent years, pressure for domestic measures of support built, and as a result of lobbying a 20 percent tax on all advertising in split-runs of foreign periodicals in Canada was proposed and implemented by a Liberal government on January 1, 1957. Following the election of a Conservative government under Prime Minister Diefenbaker, the tax was repealed in June 1958. Two years later, the Diefenbaker government established a Royal Commission on Publications, chaired by Grattan O'Leary, to make recommendations regarding the industry, which at this time was perceived to be in a constant crisis situation (Canada 1961).

Reporting in 1961, O'Leary noted the existence of 76 American magazines offering split-run editions, six of which had regional editions in Canada (Canada 1961, 36) and made two substantive recommendations in support of Canadian publishers that continue to the present. First, Canadian advertisers should not be allowed to deduct expenditures for tax purposes for advertising directed at the Canadian market and placed in a foreign periodical; and, second, foreign periodicals containing advertising directed at the Canadian market should be prevented from entering Canada. The two measures recognized that the advertising could be placed in split-runs printed in Canada or those printed abroad and imported. Both recommendations were aimed at diverting advertising revenue to Canadian periodicals.

The two proposals were implemented. An amendment was made to section 19 of the Income Tax Act to address the tax deductibility of advertising expenditures (similar provisions apply to newspaper advertising), and Tariff Item 9958 was introduced to block the importation of foreign periodicals with advertising aimed at the Canadian market, in effect to prevent the inflow of split-runs. The two largest split-runs and the ones with the most political influence, *Time* and *Reader's Digest,* were exempted from the legislation. They continued to publish in their existing formats for the Canadian market.

Almost a decade after O'Leary reported, an inquiry was undertaken by a committee of the Canadian Senate chaired by Senator Keith Davey (Canada 1970). The committee found that 70 percent of all magazines distributed in Canada came from the United States and that *Time* and *Reader's Digest* had increased their share of Canadian periodical advertising revenue from 43 percent in 1958 to 56 percent in 1969. It concluded that it had been a mistake to exempt these two periodicals (Dubinsky 1996, 43).

Subsequent to the Davey report, in 1976, a Liberal government introduced Bill C-58 to amend section 19 of the Income Tax Act and eliminate the grandfathering provision granted to *Time* and *Reader's Digest* regarding tax deductibility. In order to continue to sell advertising for a Canadian edition, the new legislation required *Time* and *Reader's Digest* to become at least 75 percent Canadian owned. In addition, their Canadian editions had to contain content not substantially the same (at least 80 percent different) as the issue of a periodical that was printed, edited, or published outside Canada, that is, their American editions. No changes were made to the tariff item. These amendments induced significant private responses by the two American magazines.

Reader's Digest Becomes Canadian

Reader's Digest responded by creating a foundation in Canada that permitted its publication to qualify for 75 percent Canadian ownership, and since it was a digest of previously published works it was allowed to avoid the "different material" provision. The Canadian edition of *Reader's Digest* was published by the new foundation, which was controlled by Canadian directors whose equity had been provided by a subsidiary of *Reader's Digest* in the United States from which editorial services were contracted. A veil of Canadian ownership was provided and approved by the Canadian tax authorities, but there is little doubt that the American parent company made the critical editorial and commercial decisions (Litvak and Maule 1980, 80–82). The end result has been that *Reader's Digest* is not a split-run in the traditional sense. It has a licensing agreement with the American parent company in order to use the trademark names and logo, and publishes some material from previously published sources, including Canadian and foreign magazine articles and some original material.[1] Ironically, *Reader's Digest*, as a result of these measures, became and remains the largest circulation "Canadian" magazine.[2]

The *Time* Puzzle

Time, on the other hand, closed its Canadian editorial office in 1976, but continued to sell advertising in Canada by reducing the rate charged to Canadian advertisers so that on an after-tax basis the cost per thousand for advertising was competitive with advertising placed in a Canadian periodical. It transferred

---

1. Details of the corporate arrangement are set out in Hearings of the Standing Committee on Canadian Heritage, Wednesday, November 18, 1998, at 16:35 to 16:45 hours.

2. *Reader's Digest* had a paid circulation in Canada of 1.2 million copies per year in 1992, 30 percent more than *Chatelaine,* which ranked second (Cebryk 1994, El–1).

editorial copy on microfilm from the United States to Canada, where the Canadian edition was printed and distributed.[3]

This is where the story becomes puzzling and somewhat opaque. Since Tariff Item 9958 was still in effect in 1976, the customs authorities could have stopped the film carrying the editorial content from crossing the border since it was a physical tangible item. This did not happen. In 1993, when *Sports Illustrated* transmitted its copy electronically across the border, it was argued by the members of the task force named to investigate the problem and government officials that *Sports Illustrated* had found a loophole in the Canadian policy. By relying on electronic transmission it had circumvented the customs tariff. A prohibitive excise tax was proposed by the task force and legislated into existence in 1995 as a means of closing the loophole.

The puzzle is that from 1976 on, *Time* had circumvented the same tariff by shipping editorial content into Canada in a tangible format on microfilm. If the definition in the tariff item classified the editorial content on film as subject to the tariff, the government could have prevented entry. Either it chose not to do so, or the legislation did not cover content imported separately from advertising. In either case a loophole has existed since this tariff item was introduced. The puzzle, given the widespread opinion that many split-runs would enter without a barrier at the border, is that only *Time* took advantage of the loophole contrary to the spirit of Bill C–58. Later we speculate on why subsequent governments, Liberal and Conservative, turned a blind eye to enforcing this policy.

Time's Success as a Mystery Split-Run

An examination of Time Canada's financial performance after the passage of Bill C–58 shows that at first advertising levels fell but within two years they had been restored to their previous levels. Revenues for Time Canada increased from C$14.2 million in 1978 to C$35.8 million in 1989. Thereafter, it becomes impossible to follow the data, as disclosure has been suppressed. From 1990 to the present, the financial information has been filed by Time Canada with the Corporations and Labor Unions Returns Act but has been classified as confidential by the Canadian authorities at the request of the company. Why the government, which was publicly hostile to split-runs, would prevent the publication of information that would help Canadian competitors of *Time* is a part of the mystery. The ruling did have the side effect that it is also unavailable

---

3. From 1976 to 1988 the editorial material was transmitted on microfilm and since 1988 in digital files via telephone lines, which is faster and more efficient. At first *Time* was printed at Ronalds Printing in Montreal. Ronalds was acquired by Quebecor, and printing now takes place at Quebecor's plant in Richmond Hill, Ontario (information supplied by Nita_Acker@time.inc.com, February 1998).

to those wishing to analyze the impact of government policy. From the data that are available, we conclude that Time Canada remained a profitable operation, and may have become more profitable, after it closed its Canadian editorial offices in 1976 and continued publishing a split-run edition with less Canadian content. Its profitability in recent years and the determining factors are hidden in the absence of financial disclosure by this wholly owned subsidiary company.

Events Leading to the 1997 WTO Decision

The next chapter in the story begins in 1990. It becomes quite complex and at times opaque, but it is necessary to recount it in order to show the thrusts and parries made in handling trade disputes. On August 15, 1990, Time Canada Ltd., a company owned by Time Warner Inc., was advised by Investment Canada that its proposal to publish a Canadian edition of *Sports Illustrated* was consistent with section 15 of the Investment Canada Act (United States 1996a, 7). An existing foreign firm can expand an existing business in Canada without getting approval, but approval is required to establish a new business. The issue was whether Sports Illustrated Canada would be a new business or not; Investment Canada decided that it would be the expansion of an existing business, as Time Canada already published a magazine in Canada.

Subsequently, the government of Canada changed the rules for future cases, but not for *Sports Illustrated*. In a communications news release of July 19, 1993 (reprinted in Canada 1994, 92), the government revised the Related Business Guidelines under the Investment Canada Act. The revisions made new policy by altering regulatory procedures in this one sector. In the future, an investment in a magazine by a non-Canadian publisher already operating in Canada would be an investment to establish a new business and not the expansion of an existing business. An investment to establish a new business in the cultural industries requires approval of Investment Canada. Approval may be denied on the basis that the investment threatens the cultural objectives of the government.

With the 1990 Investment Canada opinion in hand, on January 11, 1993, Time Warner announced its plans to publish a split-run edition of *Sports Illustrated* in Canada. Most of the editorial content would be drawn from editions of *Sports Illustrated* sold outside of Canada. Some would be written specifically for the Canadian edition. The advertising would be targeted at the Canadian market (United States 1996a, 8). Editorial content would be transmitted electronically across the border for printing in Canada. Realizing that Tariff Item 9958 could not stop this transfer, as no physical object was involved, the Canadian government responded on March 23, 1993, by establishing a Task Force on the Magazine Industry with a mandate "to recommend ways in which the current measures [supporting the Canadian magazine industry] could be brought up-to-date" (Canada 1994, iii). Despite the inapplicability of the tariff measures, section 19 of the Income Tax Act would still apply, but the advertising rate could be set at a level competitive with the after-tax rate for advertisements in Canadian periodicals, a procedure used by Time Canada after the passage of Bill C–58.

On May 31, 1993, J. Patrick O'Callaghan and Roger Tassé, the cochairs of the task force (which also had seven advisers) sent a letter to the honorable Perrin Beatty, minister of communications, confirming the threat to the "health of the Canadian magazine industry" brought about by the ability to bypass the effect of Tariff Item 9958 through the use of new technology (Canada 1994, 86). The government responded in a news release on July 19, 1993, reaffirming "its commitment to the long-standing policy objective of protecting the economic foundations of the Canadian periodical industry."

The final report of the task force, issued in March 1994, noted how the actions of Time Warner regarding *Sports Illustrated* might be followed by other foreign publishers to the detriment of Canadian periodicals as a result of the loss of advertising revenues. The report estimated that there were 53 potential U.S. entrants with consumer magazines and 70 with business and trade magazines and that the majority would actually enter the Canadian market (Canada 1994, 50–52). None of these had copied the *Time* format to publish an edition in Canada after 1976 and up until 1993.

The task force made 11 recommendations (Canada 1994, 63–76). The principal proposal was for an 80 percent tax to be imposed on a per issue basis on the value of the advertising content of magazines distributed in Canada that contain advertisements "primarily directed at Canadians and editorial content which is substantially the same as the editorial content of one or more issues of one or more periodicals that contain advertisements that, taken as a whole, are not primarily directed at Canadians" (Canada 1994, 64).

The content guideline for a split-run would be similar to that in section 19 of the Income Tax Act—a magazine would be substantially the same if it was more than 20 percent the same, and the task force noted that the difference should be "significant and not merely cosmetic or trifling." The task force asserted that the measure was consistent with Canada's obligations under CUSFTA, NAFTA, and GATT (Canada 1994, 66).

In December 1994, the government announced its intention to implement the excise tax recommendation,[4] and on September 25, 1995, it formally introduced Bill C–103, the excise tax bill, in the House of Commons.[5] The bill

---

4. News release, Canadian Heritage, December 22, 1994, 1.

5. *Commons Debates,* September 25, 1995, 14790–1.

became law on December 15, 1995.[6] The 80 percent tax would be levied on the total gross fees collected by the publisher for all advertisements in the Canadian edition of split-run magazines. A responsible person resident in Canada who would likely be the publisher, distributor, or wholesaler would be responsible for collecting and paying the tax. The tax would be nondiscriminatory in that it applied to Canadian as well as foreign-owned magazines, but it did discriminate between domestic Canadian and foreign split-run periodicals.

Section 39 provided an exemption for *Time* and *Reader's Digest,* but not for *Sports Illustrated,* contrary to the task force recommendations. The task force had proposed to continue the exemption for all three for the number of issues published in the 12 months preceding the creation of the task force in March 1993. This would have exempted seven issues in the case of Sports Illustrated. The CMPA, representing Canadian periodicals, objected, and the government decided not to exempt any issues of *Sports Illustrated.* It ceased publication on December 12, 1995, having published six issues in 1993, 12 in 1994, and 12 in 1995 (United States 1996a, 1, 12; United States 1996b, 18). Along with other foreign publications that are not split-runs, the American edition of *Sports Illustrated* continues to be distributed in Canada via newsstands and the mail.

According to newspaper reports,[7] Time Warner contemplated two challenges to the tax. First, it considered that the legislation violated guarantees of free speech contained in the Canadian Charter of Rights and Freedoms and, second, that the tax had an improper purpose, namely, to drive a firm out of business rather than raise revenues. The tax had been set at a level to prevent the entry of further split-runs so as to retain advertising revenues in Canada, and therefore no revenues would be collected if the measure achieved its stated objective. The constitutionality of the tax was discussed in the parliamentary hearings, as was the possibility of amending the Tariff Code to apply to intangible as well as tangible items.

In the end, Time Warner decided to use the dispute resolution process of the WTO to adjudicate the issue raised by the tax, but in so doing it asked that two other measures be included: Tariff Item 9958 and the postal subsidy available to Canadian periodicals. On March 11, 1996, following Time Warner's complaint to the USTR, the U.S. government requested consultations with Canada pursuant to article 4 of the Understanding on Rules and Procedures Governing the Settlement of Disputes and article XXIII of GATT 1994 regarding the three measures. The request was circulated to WTO members on March 14, 1996. Consultations between Canada and the United States were held on April 10. They failed to settle the dispute. The United States requested the establishment of a panel to evaluate the complaint on June 19, 1996 (United States 1996a,

---

6. Bill C–103, 42–43–44 *Elizabeth II,* chap. 46, December 15, 1995, exhibit D.
7. *Globe and Mail,* March 12, 1996, A2.

1–2). The ruling was handed down on March 14, 1997. Both sides appealed different parts of the ruling. The decision of the Appellate Body was issued on June 30, 1997, giving Canada until October 1998 to respond to the decision. Canada repealed or amended the offending measures but introduced new legislation (Bill C-55), discussed below, which awaits, as of April 1999, final approval and implementation.

The WTO Decision

The United States asked the WTO panel to find that three Canadian policies affecting periodicals were inconsistent with its GATT obligations: the quantitative restrictions embedded in Tariff Code 9958; part V.1 of the Excise Tax Act, which levied a prohibitive tax on advertising in split-run editions; and the lower postal rates for Canadian periodicals charged by Canada Post. Subsequent to a decision of the Appellate Body following the panels's decision, the position taken by the United States was supported on all the issues. The panels's decision will be examined first followed by that of the Appellate Body.[8]

Panel Decision

The panel decision deals with three issues: the import restrictions, the excise tax, and the postal subsidy. We address each separately.

Import Restrictions

Article XI of GATT 1994 prohibits quantitative restrictions on imports, which the United States claimed was the effect of Tariff Code 9958 on foreign split-runs. Canada responded that the tariff item is justified under article XX(d), which permits measures necessary to secure compliance with laws and regulations providing these are not inconsistent with the agreement. It was argued that the measure was necessary to secure the attainment of the objectives of section 19 of the Income Tax Act, which disallowed the tax deductibility of advertising in foreign periodicals. The two measures were seen to be an integral part of a package of measures with a single objective, namely, to divert advertising expenditures to Canadian periodicals.

   The panel decided that the tariff code is not necessary to secure compliance with section 19 and that, while both measures have the same objective, the

---

8. This section is based on World Trade Organization (1997a, 1997b).

promotion of Canadian periodicals, they are not a single indivisible package. Thus, the tariff code item was found to be inconsistent with Canada's GATT obligations.

Two aspects of this decision are of interest. Since the tariff item dealt with a good, the physical shipment of periodicals, it could have been challenged many years earlier but was not. Second, the United States did not list section 19 in its complaint as being inconsistent with Canada's GATT obligations, perhaps because it wanted to separate it from the tariff item in view of the counterargument likely to be made under article XX(d). It may raise the question of section 19 at a later date.

Excise Tax

Canada's principal argument regarding the excise tax was that it applied to a traded service, advertising, and not to a traded good, periodicals. Advertising is a service subject to treatment under the trade in services provisions of the GATS, whereas periodicals fall under the trade in goods provisions of GATT 1994. Canada has made no commitment regarding trade in advertising under the GATS; thus it argued that it has not contravened any obligations. The United States countered that not only does GATS not take primacy over GATT 1994 but article III of GATT 1994 prohibits the possibility of discrimination by services attached to goods such as distribution and transportation.

The panel decided that article III of GATT 1994 does apply to the excise tax, which affects trade in periodicals. It did not agree with Canada that because of the existence of both instruments, GATT 1994 and GATS, both of which may apply to the tax measure, "it is necessary to interpret the scope of application of each such as to avoid overlap." Rather it referred to article II:2, which states that "The agreements and associated legal instruments included in Annexes 1, 2 and 3 . . . are integral parts of this Agreement, binding on all Members" (World Trade Organization 1997a, 70). Thus, members cannot cherry pick and select only those parts of the agreement that suit their interests.

Once it was decided that article III applied, the panel found that the tax discriminated between like products, namely, foreign split-run and domestic non-split-run periodicals. Canada argued that these types of magazines were not like products, as they would contain different editorial content. However, the panel referred to the example provided in the Canadian testimony regarding *Harrowsmith Country Life,* whose Canadian edition and foreign American edition contained much of the same editorial content (World Trade Organization 1997a, 73–74). Finally, the panel decided that the tax, although levied on advertising, applied indirectly to periodicals, placing it in contravention of article III.

Postal Subsidy

Two issues were examined with respect to postal rates: first, whether the postal rates applied to imported periodicals were higher than those applied to domestic periodicals in violation of article III:4; and, second, whether the funding that provides for the lower rates is allowable as a subsidy under article III:8.

Canada did not contest that lower postal rates applied to the delivery of domestic magazines but argued that Canada Post is a Crown corporation with a legal personality distinct from the Canadian government. The rates it charges are not controlled by the government and do not qualify as "regulations" or "requirements" within the meaning of article III:4. The United States countered, and the panel agreed, that while Canada Post has a mandate to operate on a "commercial" basis it does so under governmental instructions that can be regarded as regulations or requirements within the meaning of article III:4 and are therefore inconsistent with this article.

Only on the issue of whether the funded rate scheme, whereby the DCH provided funds to Canada Post to provide the lower postal rates, was an allowable subsidy under article III:8 did the panel agree with Canada. Article III:8 permits "the payment of subsidies exclusively to domestic producers." The United States argued that the funds were paid to Canada Post and not directly to the domestic periodical publishers. However, the panel decided that the subsidy is directed to the Canadian publishers and that its transfer through Canada Post is merely a mechanism to channel the resources. Canada Post does not retain any of the funds for its own benefit.

Appellate Body Decision

The United States appealed the ruling that the postal rate scheme involved a permissible subsidy, and Canada appealed the excise tax ruling. The Appellate Body agreed with the U.S. position on the subsidy issue and reversed and modified the ruling with respect to the excise tax. In essence, the U.S. position was upheld on all the issues. Regarding the subsidy, the appellate ruling was that it was not permissible because it was not paid directly to the periodical publishers.

Regarding the excise tax, two issues were examined on appeal. The Appellate Body ruled that the tax affected both a service and a good but that because a good was clearly affected the absence of a GATS commitment did not overrule the GATT obligations. Canada then argued that if GATT did apply the tax was permissible because it did not treat "like" products, namely, imported and domestic products, differently, as required in an interpretation of the wording of article III.2, sentence 1. A comparison of imported and domestic periodicals made by the panel was considered by the Appellate Body to be invalid, causing this part of the panel decision to be reversed in Canada's favor, but the appeal decision went on to modify the finding, ending up with a ruling that supported the United States.

The Appellate Body referred to the second sentence of article III.2 which had not been part of the panel decision and states that: "Moreover, no contracting party shall otherwise apply internal taxes or other internal charges to imported products in a manner contrary to the principles set forth in paragraph 1." It then ruled that imported and domestic products were treated differently as a result of the excise tax and so the tax was inconsistent with GATT 1994.[9]

The final outcome of the dispute was that the tariff item is inconsistent with GATT 1994, as it is a quantitative restriction applying to a good not a service; the excise tax is inconsistent because it applies to a good as well as a service and does not provide national treatment; the postal rate structure is inconsistent because it does not provide national treatment; and the funding of the postal rate scheme is not an allowable subsidy because the payments are not made directly from government revenues to the publishers.

Issues for the future arising out of this case involve the treatment of services when combined with goods, the interpretation of "like" products when the likeness has to do with both editorial and advertising content, the interpretation of wording in an appeal ruling that was not part of the original panel decision, and the determination of when a support scheme constitutes an allowable subsidy to domestic producers.

The Foreign Publishers Advertising Services Act, Bill C-55

In response to the WTO ruling, Canadian policymakers searched for some replacement magazine policy that could resist a challenge under either the WTO or NAFTA. Alternatively, the government could maintain the policies and accept retaliation. As October 30, 1998, approached, the deadline for compliance with the WTO ruling, the government announced that it was preparing to implement measures in accordance with the decision. At the same time it

---

9. It did not help Canada's case that the measures were introduced with the purpose of switching advertising from Canadian to foreign split-run magazines, thereby suggesting that the two types of magazines competed with each other.

reported that it was preparing new legislation aimed at advertising, which would prevent the entry of further split-run magazines into the Canadian market.[10]

The draft legislation was introduced as Bill C–55 on October 8, 1998, entitled the Foreign Publishers Advertising Services Act, and received second reading in the House of Commons on October 22, 1998.[11] This time the legislation targeted the foreign publisher, not those placing advertising in foreign publications. The choice was deliberate since there was resistance from Canadian advertising interests and an unwillingness to impose on them directly the prohibitions and fines proposed for foreign publishers.

The key provision in Bill C–55 is the prohibition set out in paragraph 3(1): "No foreign publisher shall supply advertising services directed at the Canadian market to a Canadian advertiser or a person acting on their behalf." Two avenues are open to enforce this prohibition in the event of a suspected breach of the law. The minister may require a foreign publisher to cease the offending action and can follow this with a court order. Failure to comply would lead to a contempt of court charge (paras. 7 and 8). Alternatively, the person or corporation can face prosecution. On summary conviction, the maximum fine is C\$20,000 for a first offense and C\$50,000 for a subsequent offense; on conviction on indictment, the maximum fine for a corporation is C\$250,000 and for an individual C\$100,000 (para. 10).[12]

Additional fines (para. 12) can be levied if the person convicted acquired monetary benefits from the prohibited actions. This fine can be equal to the court's finding of the amount of monetary benefit earned, but no guidance is given as to the types of benefit to be assessed. The minister may initiate an investigation and designate an investigator. That person may receive search and investigatory powers with a warrant issued under section 487 of the Criminal Code. Enforcement of the legislation involves criminal law procedures.

The draft legislation seeks to prevent publishers of foreign split-run magazines from selling advertising space to Canadian advertisers when the advertisement is aimed at the Canadian market. As with the previous excise tax, exemptions are provided for those foreign publishers in Canada that have lawfully been supplying advertising services in the year previous to the introduction of the act (para. 21). This would include *Time*, the *New England*

---

10. Backgrounder (2) to news release "New Advertising Services Measure to Promote Canadian Culture," issued jointly by the DCH and the Department of Foreign Affairs and International Trade, Toronto, July 29, 1998.

11. Bill C–55, An Act Respecting Advertising Services Supplied by Foreign Periodical Publishers, 46–47 *Elizabeth II*, 1997–98, House of Commons of Canada.

12. The prosecution chooses whether to proceed as a summary conviction or an indictable offense.

Journal of Medicine and licensed editions of *Elle Quebec.* There may be more but the DCH is unaware of how many split-runs exist.[13]

In December, after committee hearings, Bill C-55 was passed to the House of Commons for third reading which, if it occurs, is not expected until after March 1999. The United States through its embassy in Ottawa and the USTR engaged in active political lobbying to have the legislation either amended or withdrawn. In order to buy time for negotiations to take place, the Canadian government has proposed an amendment which states that if the legislation is enacted it will not be put into effect unless the government decides to activate it. This can only be a temporary measure as the existence of the act has a chilling effect on potential investors even if it is not activated.

Implications

Domestic Policy Enforcement

The Canadian policy objectives, using the Income Tax Act and the Tariff Code Domestic was in general successfully achieved except in the case of *Reader's Digest* and *Time* from 1976 and until Time Warner decided to publish a Canadian edition of *Sports Illustrated* in 1993. In administering this policy, compromises were made. First, a Revenue Canada ruling allowed a foundation created by *Reader's Digest* to be considered 75 percent Canadian owned and in control of the company publishing the Canadian edition, when it appears that commercial control rested with *Reader's Digest* in the United States. The issue of the locus of control has arisen again in the cases of CMT (see chap. 11) and book distribution involving Borders Books and Chapters (see chap. 13) and appears not to have been treated consistently across these cases.

Second, there was a failure to enforce Tariff Item 9958 against Time Canada in the period after 1976 and the passage of Bill C–58, when its grandfathered status was ended.[14] In fact, as noted, it continued to produce a Canadian edition

---

13. Another issue posed by the legislation is how jurisdiction would be obtained when the foreign publisher had no assets in Canada, and where this may involve an extraterritorial application of a law. The legislation applies to periodicals that are printed publications and so exempts magazines distributed electronically. Unlike the repealed excise tax, the prohibition applies only to foreign and not to Canadian publishers selling advertising in split-run magazines. Other possible split-run titles are *Ming Pao,* a Chinese language periodical, and the *World Journal Mail.*

14. The Appellate Body decision refers to Canada's argument that Time Canada has been grandfathered as a split-run. This is incorrect as far as the tariff item is concerned. Time Canada operates as a split-run but does so because its importation of editorial content has not been challenged (World Trade Organization 1997b, 6, n. 10).

of *Time* with less Canadian editorial content, using material shipped by microfilm into Canada and with advertising sold in Canada at a rate competitive with advertising sold by Canadian magazines. If the Tariff Code applied to the import of editorial content, the government could have prevented the cross-border transfer of the microfilm containing *Time's* editorial content. We have been unable to obtain an explanation of why this did not happen and why Canadian publishing interests did not complain, since *Time* was drawing advertising revenues that might have gone to competing publications. We can therefore only speculate on the failure to respond. First, the Canadian government had gone through a bruising round of negotiations involving *Time* and *Reader's Digest* over Bill C–58, and it did not want to pursue the matter further by drawing attention to related cultural policies that were viewed as protectionist. Moreover, as *Time* then printed its Canadian edition in Canada, it was contributing jobs to the Canadian economy. Prolonging the dispute may also have been seen as harming Canada's image as a host country for foreign investment. Time, through its worldwide publications, would have been in a good position to portray Canada in a negative way. Finally, the Canadian government may have known that what came to pass in 1997 could have happened earlier, namely, that protectionist periodical policies can be found contrary to the GATT when trade in magazines is seen as a good not a service. The silence on the part of the Canadian industry, especially Maclean Hunter, may have been due to its unwillingness to prolong the dispute after having achieved most of its objectives in Bill C–58, that is, reduced competition for its weekly newsmagazine *Maclean's*.

International Regimes

The principal changes in the international trade regimes came with the inclusion of a cultural exemption in the CUSFTA, which was carried over into the NAFTA, and with the passage of the GATS as part of the WTO. Canada felt it had achieved two outcomes, the removal of the cultural industries from the provisions of the two regional agreements and the ability to shelter them, at least for a while, from the obligations of the WTO. Along with other countries, Canada made no commitments under GATS for the cultural industries and advertising. This situation changed when the United States challenged the 80 percent excise tax on periodicals as a good under GATT 1994 and not as a service under GATS.

In the case of the 1997 WTO decision, the United States has chosen to argue that by introducing Bill C-55, Canada has not complied with the WTO ruling, since the measure simply replaces one of the withdrawn measures. Canada argues that Bill C-55 is a new and different measure, and one aimed at a service for which it has made no GATS commitment.[15]

The United States could have chosen to respond to Canadian magazine policy under NAFTA. In that forum, because of the Canadian cultural exemption, the complaint would have been a chapter 20 dispute concerning the general applicability of the agreement to cultural trade with Canada. The United States did not choose this route, perhaps because it did not want to test the meaning of the cultural exemption. Canada and the United States are on record as having conflicting views of its meaning, and it appears that neither side wants to test their respective views. By placing the dispute before the WTO, the United States was able to test its views on cultural policies in a forum where, if it won, it could use the precedent as a lever to alter similar policies of both Canada and other countries such as France and Australia. It had lost the battle to include culture in the WTO, and here would be a chance to either win the war or at least win a partial victory.

The panel's ruling that GATT 1994 applies to the excise tax, despite Canada's commitments under GATS, in effect means that when a service is tied to a good a measure that restricts the provision of the service cannot be applied if it also restricts the provision of the good. The tax on advertising services was found to restrict trade in periodical goods and has been disallowed. It remains to be seen how the prohibitions in Bill C–55 will be resolved.[16] More generally, the ruling raises the issue of whether GATS or GATT 1994 has primacy when there is a conflict (United States 1996b, 24).

The Canadian Industry

The dispute highlights the DCH view of what is in the best interests of the Canadian periodical industry. We identify DCH as the chief spokesperson for what has been the intent of successive Canadian government periodical policies because that department has been the strongest proponent of the policy of cultural nationalism. The policy has been inward looking by trying to restrict the inflow of split-runs that would draw advertising revenue from Canadian

---

15. The United States had the following alternatives: 1. accept the Canadian actions; 2. challenge Bill C-55 either as a failure to implement the WTO decision or as a new measure—the former would take less time than the latter; 3. initiate a complaint under NAFTA; or 4. invoke a section 301 complaint.

16. Other examples that would likely be disallowed would be a tax on the leasing of foreign made construction equipment and a tax on restaurant meals served using imported food and drink. In effect, whenever a service is connected to a good and the service measure imposes a competitive disadvantage against an imported good it would be disallowed.

periodicals. It has not tried to restrict the inflow of foreign editions of magazines that are available for purchase on newsstands or through the mail. It has pursued this policy through a combination of tax and tariff policy, ownership rules, subsidies for publishers, and preferential postal rates. The excise tax would have gone one step further by eliminating the possibility of Canadian publishers supplying foreign markets with split-runs. In the absence of the excise tax, Bill C–55 attempts to provide a replacement measure that is WTO acceptable.

The focus of public debate has been on the general consumer periodicals sold via newsstands since this is where the foreign periodicals dominate. Overall, the picture is of an industry in which Canadian publishers account for by far the largest share of magazines sold overall but not those magazines sold via newsstands. The question is which ones will survive in the absence of protective measures. The CMPA, with support from the task force, argued that elimination of the excise tax would be disastrous for the industry, and that is certainly the view of those who would face increased competition from split-runs. However not all magazines are equally vulnerable. There are approximately 1500 magazines published in Canada. Each targets a particular audience in a particular way using different combinations of advertising and circulation revenue. At one extreme, a controlled circulation magazine depends entirely on advertising revenue, while at the other, a scholarly magazine may depend solely on circulation revenue.

Magazines such as *Quebec Home and School News,* and *Lethbridge Living,* are unlikely to compete for advertising with general consumer periodicals that might consider publishing a split-run in Canada. Others such as *Sky News* (on astronomy), *Synchronicity* (on holistic living), and *Pacific Yachting* (on sailing on the west cost of North America) appear to cater to generic interests rather than those directly connected with some aspect of Canadian identity and could possibly face competition from new split-runs. At the same time these magazines could appeal to foreign readers. *Hockey News* is an example of a Canadian periodical with over 60 percent of its circulation in the United States.

Publishers of trade magazines are another market segment. They attract advertising from the United States and their editorial content for matters such as mining, trucking and air conditioning could be of interest to audiences in the United States. The *Northern Miner* for example has 20 percent of its circulation in the United States.

The split-run of *Sports Illustrated* is an example of a magazine for which there is no direct competitor for its editorial content in Canada. It competes for readers with the American edition of *Sports Illustrated* and with the sports sections of other publications, such as newspapers, as well as with televised sports channels. For advertisers, however, it has a much broader range of competitors. We examined the May 15, 1995, issue of *Sports Illustrated* Canada and found messages from 26 advertisers displayed on 24 pages of advertising in a 78-page edition. Ten full pages are devoted to advertisements for automobiles or automotive products.[17] Presumably some of these advertisements could have appeared in Canadian magazines had a Canadian edition of *Sports Illustrated* not been published, suggesting that short-run rents and income in parts, but not all, of the Canadian magazine industry will most likely fall with the introduction of new split-runs.

There was another, more harmful aspect of the excise tax that is not present in Bill C–55. By applying to Canadian as well as foreign-owned split-runs, the excise tax would have confined Canadian publishers to the small domestic market and prevented them from servicing foreign markets using a split-run format. They could have still supplied foreign markets with the Canadian edition and Canadian advertisements but this is less lucrative than the publishing arrangements adopted by *Time* and *Sports Illustrated*. In the absence of the tax, would there have been any Canadian split-runs? We already know that there was one and that it ceased publication because of the tax. The case of *Harrowsmith Country Life* is documented in Canada's submission to the WTO, where it is noted that the passage of the excise tax legislation caused the magazine to stop publishing its American edition (Canada 1996a, 9–10, fn. 23).

Canada made the excise tax nondiscriminatory in order to conform to the national treatment standards of GATT (although if it thought that GATS applied it did not need to provide national treatment), and in so doing it ended the life of at least one Canadian split-run. In our view it seems shortsighted to design a policy that kills off one successful Canadian split-run and prevents the possibility of others being developed or, what is the same thing, confining Canadian publishers to producing only domestic editions of their magazines when foreign split-runs might be a profitable alternative. The magazine industry is the one Canadian cultural industry that has experienced little success in international markets. We believe that one of the reasons for this is the way it frames its opportunities. Foreign markets are viewed as breeding grounds for competitors in the Canadian market rather than as opportunities for Canadian writers and publishers. In the magazine sector the culture of protection is so entrenched that creativity is largely restricted to developing new arguments for the protection of culture.

---

17. The list of advertisers with full or partial pages includes Toyota, General Tire, Joop (eau de toilette), Participation, American Express, Heart and Stroke Foundation, Pontiac, GM Smart Lease, Preferred Stock Cologne, Motomaster, Adidas, Johnson and Johnson, B. F. Goodrich, International Trucks, Compaq, Chevrolet, Spruce Meadows, Lumina Van, Crown Scalp Stimulator, Better Hearing Institute, Mizuno Golf Company, Honda, Strength Shoe, Foster Parents Plan, and Stihl.

The counterargument is that there are no other Canadian publications likely to become split-runs. This implies the ability to predict the future for an industry experiencing substantial change and is contrary to conditions found in the Canadian film and television production industry. While Bill C–55 does not penalize Canadian firms that produce split-runs, the underlying rationale of Canadian policy remains misdirected in its concentration on domestic market protection rather than encouraging firms to expand by accessing foreign markets.

Finally, we note that in attempting to eliminate split-runs by means of an excise tax imposed on publishers and distributors in Canada and now by introducing new measures to penalize foreign publishers, policymakers may be building walls around a wasting asset. New technologies such as the Internet are being used by periodical publishers to promote and distribute their product directly to consumers, thereby bypassing the entities on which the tax was levied or for which prohibitions apply. The Internet may also provide an advertising medium that will compete with magazines and other carriers. There is little likelihood that Canadian policy can provide protection for this source of competition.

Conclusion

There is no conclusion to this saga. As we write, the response by the United States awaits the final form of Bill C–55.[18] Canada has crafted its most recent legislation so that it addresses the sale of advertising services and argues that it is exempt because no commitments affecting these services have been made under GATS. It also argues that failure to respect the provisions of GATS when a service is tied to a good will undermine the working of GATS. Much is made of the WTO panel report, which states that "the ability of any WTO member to take measures to protect its cultural identity was not an issue in the present case."

Further rounds of the same unproductive engagement appear inevitable unless technological developments force a rethinking of the position. An odd feature of Canadian cultural policy is that protective measures are passionately supported but there is little effort expended to determine whether the results are in line with the expectations of supporters. The Canadian magazine industry is by all reports in as precarious a state in 1999 as it was 40 years earlier. *Reader's Digest* and *Time* are still extremely successful in the Canadian market. The

---

18. In the debate on Bill C–55, it is noted that the USTR has indicated that it intends to "react vigorously" if Canada does not amend its new policy (See Canadian parliamentary web site for transcript of the House of Commons proceedings, October 23, 1998, at 1535 hours).

industry lacks the dynamism of its counterparts in television program production and music. The horse appears to us to be dead, but the Canadian policymakers refuse to dismount.

On the trade diplomacy side, the complex set of actions and responses over the past four decades illustrate the convolutions of policy designed to protect a content-dependent activity in a world in which the distribution of content internationally has become relatively cheap. It also reveals how time consuming and costly it can be to proceed with a trade dispute. Countries can impose considerable costs on each other by initiating the process and can act strategically to tie up the time of officials. Obviously, larger countries have more to gain from this type of behavior. The *Sports Illustrated* case illustrates use of both the informal and formal processes, the lack of transparency of domestic policies, the inadequacy of official data to describe events, opportunistic use of data by interested parties, and the impact of changing technology. All represent issues that will have to be addressed in the future governance structure for the cultural industries.

CHAPTER 11

Country Music Television

Protection of Canadian-owned cable television services was the central issue in the dispute involving CMT. In 1994, the CRTC announced the removal of the CMT channel from a list of American services that can be carried by Canadian cable companies and its replacement with a Canadian-owned service, the New Country Network (NCN). By the summer of 1996, CMT was back in service as the minority investor in a split-run type format for cable that for magazine publishers was considered by the Canadian government to be unacceptable. One year later, the CRTC announced that "it will not be disposed to remove a non-Canadian service from the lists, even should it license, in the future, a Canadian service in a competitive format."[1] In effect, it removed the policy that led directly to the dispute with CMT, but it did not remove its powers to screen access by foreign cable television services to Canada.

Few viewers watching CMT on cable are aware that this signal has been the focus of a protracted trade dispute between Canada and the United States. They watch the music videos, often unaware of and probably uninterested in the nationality of the composers and performers, which is the concern of Canadian policymakers. Aside from their immediate entertainment value, these videos act as advertising for artists and music companies in the same way that music played on the radio provides a promotional service. CMT could be considered an advertising channel.

In the interests of Canadian culture, successive governments have enacted legislation that empowers the regulator, the CRTC, to determine the menu of domestic and foreign television signals from which Canadian viewers can choose and to influence the rates they pay. That power stems from the Broadcasting Act, first enacted in 1932, with the most recent version passed in 1991.

Through this act, the CRTC licenses broadcast, cable, and satellite broadcasting services. As a condition of license, Canadian content is promoted. Viewers have a choice of signals, country music and other, which depends on whether they receive only off-air signals, cable signals (which include the off-air

---

1. CRTC Public Notice 1997–96, Ottawa, July 22, 1997.

signals), or satellite signals, provided either legally or through the gray market. Their choice is further expanded through the use of VCRs and compact disc players. Over time, the ability of the CRTC's policy to promote Canadian content has declined as audiences make choices from an increasing array of legal and gray market signals that the CRTC does not influence.

CMT was listed originally as an eligible foreign service in 1984, along with 17 other foreign services, including A&E, CNN, and the Nashville Network.[2] The authorized non-Canadian list grew after 1984. Seventeen additions and a revised complete list were published in July 1997.[3] Between 1984 and 1996, the CRTC also licensed 43 Canadian specialty services, six Canadian pay television services, and five PPV services for distribution on cable and/or DTH satellite systems.[4] On October 3, 1997, the commission announced that it was reviewing applications for another 70 new Canadian specialty services. In mid-1998, the CRTC reversed its decision to add more Canadian specialty licenses and continued a moratorium on listing more American specialty and pay channels as eligible for carriage. The commission cited the "emerging competitive environment" and the delays in expanding cable capacity to carry digital signals as among the factors influencing its decision.[5] The attraction of a specialty service to advertisers is that even though the audience may be small it is relatively homogeneous as to income, age, and taste.[6]

Television offerings are beginning to resemble a magazine store, with the difference being that no publisher has to apply to a government agency for permission to be stocked by the retailer and the store is not required to carry Canadian content. A combination of digital compression technology, expanded distribution capacity, and the growing gray market penetration by foreign satellite services has forced the CRTC to approve additional services.

The CMT dispute arose because the government screens and approves the television offerings to Canadians. Again, we ask the reader to be patient with the arcane details, for they are necessary to show how governments become mired in their own regulations by refusing to recognize that conditions have changed, by being unwilling to listen to consumer preferences, and by resisting the loss of bureaucratic powers. This case is one involving an informal dispute resolution process, as was noted in chapter 4. It reveals inconsistent behavior and some of the contradictions of domestic policy.

---

2. CRTC press release, Ottawa, April 2, 1984, appendix A.
3. CRTC news release, Ottawa, July 22, 1997, appendix A.
4. CRTC Fact Sheet, Ottawa, October 9, 1996, 1.
5. CRTC Public Notice 1998–79, Ottawa, July 30, 1998.
6. In 1995, NCN had a 0.5 percent share (percentage of time spent watching a particular signal by cable households) and a 27 percent reach (percentage of cable subscribers who tune in at least once a week).

Development of the Dispute

In 1983, Canada undertook to license specialty television channels and in so doing made provision for a linkage policy that would permit cable services to offer specified American specialty channels in discretionary tiers or clusters of offerings with Canadian pay and specialty channels. If a Canadian service received a license and no American service covering the same area appeared on the approved list for linkage, no competitive American service would subsequently be added to the list. In addition, if an American or other foreign service was authorized and subsequently a competing Canadian service asked to be licensed, the foreign service would be removed. The CRTC's position at this point was not ambiguous: "[S]hould the Commission license, in the future, a Canadian service in a format competitive to an authorized non-Canadian service, the latter *will be* replaced by the Canadian service."[7]

On November 30, 1987, the commission altered its policy regarding the termination of a foreign service. If in the future a Canadian service was licensed, "the non-Canadian service *could be* terminated."[8] In 1994, the CRTC held hearings to consider applications for further specialty channels, one of which was NCN's request for a country and western channel and the removal from the eligibility list of the competing American-owned CMT channel. The request was granted and the changeover occurred on January 1, 1995. At the time, CMT was owned by Westinghouse and Gaylord Entertainment and NCN by Canadian cable and media interests. CMT had been on the CRTC eligibility list as an authorized non-Canadian service for 10 years and had built up a substantial audience for that category of service.

CMT responded first by appealing the regulatory decision to the Canadian Federal Court of Appeal on the grounds that the principles of natural justice had been violated because CMT was not permitted to participate in the oral hearing that preceded the CRTC decision. It lost on the grounds that its views had been expressed when it made a written submission stating its opposition to removal.[9] Later it was refused the right to make a further appeal to the Supreme Court of Canada.

With this avenue closed, CMT turned to the U.S. government for assistance by filing a 301 petition on December 23, 1994, with the USTR complaining of its unfair treatment in Canada. CMT noted that its removal had been requested on economic rather than cultural grounds and that it had been supportive of Canadian country music artists by distributing their works in Canada, the United

---

7. CRTC Public Notice 1984–81, 13, Ottawa, April 2, 1984, italics added.

8. CRTC Decision 1987–260, 85, Ottawa, March 31, 1987, italics added.

9. The appeal was heard on November 22, 1994, and the judgment delivered on December 20, 1994.

States, Europe, Asia, and Latin America through its operations in these parts of the world. As it had been barred from reception in Canada, CMT proposed to blacklist the distribution of Canadian music videos on its other services.

The petition, and the later written comments submitted to the USTR, provide a lengthy discussion of the grounds for 301 action, namely, the reasons why Canada's actions are "unreasonable or discriminatory" and "unjustifiable" and why damages should be assessed and retaliation undertaken. In these submissions, note is taken of the NAFTA cultural exemption, but stress is placed on the right to retaliate, which was recorded in testimony before congressional committees at the time NAFTA was approved. The complaint also argued that the action is a violation of chapter 11 on investment and chapter 12 on services in NAFTA. On investment, Canada is accused of violating the letter and the spirit of articles 1102 on national treatment, 1105 on fair and equitable treatment, 1106 on performance requirements, and 1110 on improper expropriation. On services, failure to provide national treatment was noted. In contrast, Johnson (1998, 271) argues that the CRTC's decision to delete CMT affected the provision of a service not covered by CUSFTA in the absence of a cultural exemption. In his opinion, the CRTC action was not open to retaliation under CUSFTA or by extension NAFTA. The final submissions to the USTR were filed by CMT jointly with Court TV, EMI, the National Cable Television Association, the Nashville Network, the Travel Channel, the Weather Channel, and United Video.[10]

Section 301 of the U.S. Trade Act of 1974, as amended by the Omnibus Trade Act of 1988,[11] allows the government, firms, or citizens to file a petition with the USTR alleging illegal or unfair actions by governments. If the USTR decides to initiate an investigation, it "must publish a summary of the petition, provide opportunity for public hearing, and request consultation with the foreign government or instrumentality concerned. If the case involves a trade agreement and no mutually acceptable resolution is obtained, the U.S. must involve the dispute resolution procedures of the agreement" (Jackson 1991, 105).

The USTR responded to the petition on behalf of CMT that Canada had behaved in an "unreasonable and discriminatory" manner and on February 6, 1995, called for comment within 30 days. A decision of the USTR would be due on June 21, 1995. In the intervening period a number of actions took place in an attempt to influence the outcome.

First, a letter was sent to the Canadian minister of trade in which the USTR set out its timetable but also requested a review of Canadian cable policy, in effect trying to determine whether other cases similar to that of CMT might arise

---

10. These arguments are made in the submissions to the USTR by Dewey Balantine on behalf of CMT.

11. Title III, Trade Act of 1974, 19 U.S.C. 2411, Supp. 1993.

in the future. Meanwhile, the Canadian government argued that delisting was the decision of a regulatory tribunal, which it did not control, and that the decision was in conformity with a published policy.

Second, a letter was sent by Michael Kantor, the USTR, to Reed Hundt, chair of the Federal Communications Commission (FCC), requesting information about "FCC current policies and procedures that involve the following: i) identifiable Canadian ownership interests; ii) control by Canadian interests; and/or, iii) international facilities that specifically interconnect with Canadian-owned or authorized facilities." The intent was to make Canada and vulnerable Canadian interests aware that the CRTC's action could adversely influence FCC decisions affecting Canadian firms. The FCC is the American agency with similar responsibilities to those of the CRTC. It could deliver a tit for Canada's tat.

While the investigation was under way, a news report[12] stated that American officials were drawing up a list of Canadian telecommunications and cultural industry firms operating in the United States for possible retaliation. These included Teleglobe Inc., Cineplex-Odeon Corp., and Much Music, a rock music video channel available by satellite through DirecTV to viewers in the United States. Mention was also made of American imports of Canadian maple syrup, bacon, fur coats, and sound recordings. Retaliation was clearly contemplated within and outside the cultural sector. In a previous dispute arising from Canadian regulatory actions affecting American border broadcasters, retaliation targeted the tourist business in Canada. Convention expenses were disallowed as a deductible item for tax purposes when Americans attended conventions in Canada.

As these steps were being taken, a parallel set of actions was occurring that would lead to a resolution of the dispute. CMT and NCN were reported to be negotiating a private business arrangement that would allow CMT to maintain some presence in Canada. While it appeared to be a private initiative, we have been informed, though we have no way of documenting it, that the two governments encouraged the parties to resolve the dispute and even suggested to them what type of commercial arrangement might be acceptable.[13] On June 21, 1995, the date for the USTR to report, the two companies announced the formation of a business partnership with CMT, acquiring a minority share and announcing that it would no longer blacklist Canadian music videos, thereby giving wider circulation to Canadian artists.

---

12. *Wall Street Journal,* May 19, 1995, B12.

13. The final paragraph of the March 6, 1995, submission by CMT to the USTR states: "We do not believe that the Canadian Government lacks the capacity to reach an accommodation meeting the needs and interests of all parties. . . . We do believe, however, that in order to reach that outcome, forceful U.S. Government action is needed."

Difficulties arose in the formation of the partnership, leading the owners of CMT to lobby the USTR again to bring pressure on Canada to resolve the issue. Threats of retaliation were repeated, but a final resolution was achieved by the two parties in March 1996.

What was the partnership arrangement? NCN was originally owned by two Canadian media companies, Rawlco (51 percent) and Maclean Hunter (49 percent). Subsequently, Maclean Hunter was bought by cable operator Rogers Communications, which then sold 29 percent of NCN to Shaw Cablesystems, a cable firm that also bought Rawlco's 51 percent share, ending up with 80 percent of NCN. In the announcement made by NCN,[14] the plan was for CMT to own the remaining 20 percent of the equity. In the final ownership configuration after Rogers disposed of its interests, Shaw ended up with 90 percent, and CMT with 10 percent of the holding company "whereby Shaw will assume effective control of the holding company and thereby the licensee."[15] The name of the licencee reverted from NCN to CMT despite the majority Canadian ownership. In 1995, CMT was owned by Westinghouse and Gaylord Communications. In 1997, Westinghouse bought Gaylord Entertainment Co.'s interest in CMT and the Nashville Network for US$1.5 billion.[16]

Between March and November 1996, the CRTC was involved in approving the new ownership configuration of NCN/CMT. It first issued a notice of public hearing on May 10, 1996, to consider the reorganization of the licensee by the Canadian investors and on July 29, 1996,[17] approved the ownership configuration of the holding company and a wholly owned subsidiary, which holds the license. Since the level of foreign ownership of the holding company and the licensee do not exceed the permissible limits, the CRTC would only become involved if questions were raised about the possibility of the foreign investor, despite its minority ownership position, having effective control of the licensee in some manner. No questions were asked.

As noted above, an important footnote to this dispute is the July 1997 announcement by the CRTC that it will no longer consider removing a foreign specialty service if a competing Canadian service applies for a license. It also stated that it will not authorize non-Canadian services that are either totally or partially competitive with existing Canadian pay or specialty services and it will consider removing existing non-Canadian services if they change their format so as to become competitive with a Canadian pay or specialty service.[18]

---

14. NCN press release, June 22, 1995.

15. CRTC Public Notice 1996–148, Ottawa, November 15, 1996.

16. Westinghouse owns the CBS television network as well as eight country music radio stations and broadcasts the annual Country Music Awards (*Globe and Mail*, February 11, 1997, B12).

17. CRTC Decision 96–287, Ottawa, July 29, 1996.

18. CRTC Public Notice 1997–96, paras. 29, 30, Ottawa, July 22, 1997.

While the CRTC has altered some of its ownership restrictions, it still controls market access by ruling on the listing of new services. For example, in July 1997, it refused authorization requests from the Popcorn Channel, Prime Time 24, Bloomberg Information Television, Newsworld International, and several religious services. Bloomberg was refused on the grounds that it would be competitive with a new Canadian business news service, ROBTV. CNBC, which had previously been permitted to provide a business news service on a limited basis because it competed with existing services, was now permitted to provide a full service. It is not clear why Bloomberg and CNBC were treated differently. In a different genre, Playboy TV was permitted to be distributed to a subscriber at the subscriber's specific request but not as part of a package of signals. Ironically, Playboy became the one foreign specialty service that the viewer can pick and pay for on an individual basis. No such choice is offered to devotees of the Golf Channel.

Neither NCN nor CMT used the dispute resolution procedures of NAFTA or of the WTO. They went head to head at the political level, using the Canadian courts, section 301 and the USTR, the CRTC, the FCC, private sanctions through video boycotts, threats of adverse consequences in activities undertaken by Westinghouse in Canada, lobbying by other American specialty television interests, and diplomatic and private dispute settlement procedures. While the last led to the final outcome, it was conditioned by pressure from the two governments in the context of what had taken place in the other arenas and what issues were pending.

In the absence of a formal dispute resolution mechanism for the cultural industries and an unwillingness to test the NAFTA cultural exemption, governments use whatever leverage is available to further their interests. This includes actions by diplomatic representatives. James Blanchard, the American ambassador to Canada, appeared on CBC radio, January 26, 1995, in an interview with Peter Gzowski on the popular show *Morningside*. The ambassador appeared sensitive to Canadian concerns, stating: "I would not fault a single Canadian for wanting to protect and preserve, and frankly, promote and spread that culture," but he reminded the audience that Americans viewed the CRTC action as confiscating the investment of Westinghouse, which is a major employer in other Canadian sectors. The ambassador noted that Westinghouse "has been a good corporate citizen, and they get scared when something is just pulled away. Particularly when we feel there's as much or more Canadian content with our [CMT] station."[19] Probably no American ambassador before

---

19. The timing of the dispute coincided with an automotive trade dispute between the United States and Japan. It suited the American administration to show that it was being tough on a number of trade fronts and not just targeting one country.

had expressed publicly such sensitivity to Canadian cultural interests, but the threat of possible adverse repercussions was clearly stated.

In the absence of a private settlement, it is not clear what sequence of political actions would have occurred. Both countries had obligations under the NAFTA and the WTO. If NAFTA had been invoked by one of the parties, the nature of the complaint would have determined the procedure used to resolve the dispute.[20] The petition on behalf of CMT claimed that delisting was contrary to the services and investment provisions of NAFTA. Canada would likely have claimed that the cultural exemption provisions applied. Under article 2005 of NAFTA, the complainant can choose whether to use the WTO or NAFTA if both agreements apply.

If the WTO had been invoked, it could have led to a dispute panel process and possible appeal similar to the *Sports Illustrated* case for split-run periodicals (chap. 9). In the event of a political resolution, outside of a formal agreement the first step is crucial in determining the sequence. In this case, the Canadian courts and section 301 plus the USTR following the CRTC decision created the atmosphere that conditioned the private resolution. Linking the formal and informal processes is the knowledge that if a private settlement is not reached the dispute may be dealt with under NAFTA or the WTO. This may encourage the parties to reach a private settlement, in which case the informal process may be both initiated and disciplined by the formal process.

Use of section 301 provides a means of drawing more players into the dispute. The 301 process asks interested parties to make submissions to the USTR stating their positions. The Washington law firm of Dewey Ballantine made the petition to the USTR on behalf of CMT (December 23, 1994), but there were written submissions both from parties that felt they might be affected by a similar CRTC ruling and from those, like Time Warner, that used the occasion to raise awareness of the emerging split-run periodical issue. As of March 6, 1995, there were 13 entries in the public file (301–98) on CMT held by the USTR. These included the petition and several sets of written comments from Dewey Ballantine on behalf of CMT as well as written submissions from or on behalf of the National Cable Television Association, Time Warner Inc., International Family Entertainment, Word Inc., the Recording Industry Association of America, CNBC, the Weather Channel, C-Span, and the International Intellectual Property Alliance. Interested parties in the United States used the incident to argue that Canada was engaging in a new wave of restrictive cultural policies that would harm their interests.

---

20. NAFTA's chapter 19 deals with dispute settlement matters related to antidumping and countervailing duties, and chapter 20 deals with disputes involving the interpretation and application of the agreement.

On the Canadian side, warning signals went up in other industries, which realized that if retaliation occurred subsequent to the outcome of a 301 action they could become the victims of a cultural dispute in which they had no part. The United States would likely retaliate in areas that would hurt Canadian interests, and these might well be unrelated to the cultural industries. Thus, Teleglobe Inc. or Northern Telecom, for example, might have been drawn into the dispute. Even if the United States had no case under NAFTA or the WTO, trade relations between the two countries might have been adversely affected.

Government's Role in the Process

The American government can hide behind the 301 process and argue that individuals initiate complaints to which it is forced to respond given the legislation. If persons choose to use available quasi-judicial processes, the government claims it has no options short of amending the law. The 301 process is a stick used to bludgeon the weak (Jackson 1991, 107).

On its behalf, the Canadian government claimed that the CRTC was an independent regulatory agency over which it had no control as long as it stayed within its mandate and that court procedures were available to assess its behavior under Canadian law. Here it was on shaky ground since it had recently used its power to intervene under the Broadcasting Act to instruct the CRTC to alter its decision regarding the licensing of DTH satellite services (see chap. 12), and in a related area it had ordered the commission to alter a decision regarding telephone rates. Some in Canada had criticized it for interfering in the regulatory process in these cases.

CMT was the first American service to appear on Canadian cable systems and the first to have its eligibility terminated. Seven years before the CMT decision, the issue of a newly licensed Canadian service facing an established American counterpart had arisen, but the outcome was different. When the CBC's news channel, Newsworld, was licensed in 1987, two CNN news services were already operating in Canada. The CRTC licensing decision for Newsworld notes that the CBC did not ask for the removal of these services from the eligibility list.[21] The CRTC also comments that, in the Newsworld application, the CBC had drawn attention to the "active partnership" that it had enjoyed with CNN for a number of years and to the reaffirmation of both CNN and the CBC of "their intention to maintain this relationship." Although the precise nature of

---

21. Why the CRTC would expect the CBC to make that request is unclear, since at the time of the hearings on the Newsworld application the earlier policy requiring mandatory exclusion of an American station offering a competitive format was in place. The new discretionary policy was announced after the preparation of the applications and the public hearings on them.

this partnership between the CBC and CNN is not public information, it involves the exchange of news programming. Canada is one of the few countries in which CNN has no bureau. Presumably, the services provided by the CBC have relieved CNN of the need to invest in such facilities in Canada. At the license renewal hearings for Newsworld, the CRTC reiterated that it was not asking for the American service to be delisted. If it had done so, there would likely have been a public outcry, and this is another reason why the CBC kept silent.

The case of CMT illustrates the difficulty of identifying services that are in a format competitive with a Canadian service. The commission decided that CMT would be removed but permitted the American-owned Nashville Network (TNN) to continue operations in Canada. TNN plays country videos but not to the extent that they are delivered by CMT and NCN. At the time, TNN and CMT had partial common ownership. TNN was wholly owned by Gaylord Entertainment Co., while CMT was owned 70 percent by Gaylord and 30 percent by Westinghouse. Of the two services, TNN is the more expensive, with programming originating with the network, while CMT generally uses videos supplied by record companies.[22] One of the concerns of the American owners was that TNN would face a similar fate at the hands of the CRTC in a subsequent round of licensing Canadian specialty channels. A comparison of similar cases suggests that the commission uses the wisdom of Solomon to differentiate between remarkably similar cases and to make convenient rather than consistent decisions.

Determining what is and is not a competing service becomes a devilish problem as more services are approved. The 70 new applicants propose services in categories like news, entertainment, biography, comedy, and lifestyle, which inevitably overlap with existing services. Especially for news services, the commission has been willing to license or authorize competing services, thereby muddying its own criteria for approval. The cases of CBC, CNN, ROBTV, BBC, and CNBC attest to this confusion. Another contradictory consequence of the CRTC's decision was that the American cable network, CNBC, was picked up by Canadian cable before the new Canadian business channel, ROBTV.

Consistency across Industries

While a regulatory commission's internal consistency is one issue, a government's policy consistency across similar industries is another. The CMT outcome resulted in the formation of a split-run type arrangement for cable services that successive Canadian governments had resisted for over three decades for magazine publishing. The similarities are as follows. The split-run

---

22. A report noted that TNN had five million subscribers in Canada, as opposed to less than two million for CMT (*Inside U.S. Trade,* January 13, 1995, 21).

of a foreign magazine in Canada contains the same editorial content but different advertising than the edition of the same magazine sold abroad. In the case of the new CMT, with 10 percent foreign and 90 percent Canadian ownership, there will be a large portion of foreign content provided by CMT, mixed with Canadian content, and there will be advertising aimed at the Canadian market. The license issued in 1994 requires 30 percent Canadian content in the first year, rising to 40 percent in year six and beyond. We can anticipate a format similar to the way CMT operates in other countries. For example in Brazil, CMT has a partnership with Televisao Abril in which it transmits a Spanish signal by PanAmSat 3 to all of Latin America. Televisao Abril takes down the signal and customizes it by adding Portuguese titles and up to four hours of Brazilian country music. The signal is then uplinked to a satellite for delivery to cable operators and DTH viewers, thus providing a split-run type arrangement.[23]

Not only is there inconsistent treatment between cultural industries, but the American owners of CMT have ended up being recognized as a licensed Canadian specialty channel as opposed to an authorized foreign specialty service. Having gained a preferred position, CMT can also be expected to support the Canadian policy that excludes the authorization of further foreign specialty services competitive with their country music format. Like *Reader's Digest,* with its special ruling, CMT has become an insider benefiting from protectionist Canadian policies. Other foreign allies may include BRAVO and the Discovery Channel, which have their formats licensed in Canada; Barnes and Noble, which has a minority position in a Canadian book retailer (see chap. 3); and those foreign book publishers that operate in Canada and do not face the Investment Canada barriers for new foreign entrants. Splitting the opposition is the strategy used by the Canadian government to create a category of most favored foreign companies to provide support for protectionist policies.

The Issue of Control

Foreign ownership regulations have been used as a way to achieve cultural objectives, with the idea that ownership will make a difference as to what is delivered by broadcasters and cablecasters. The premise is that if Canadians own the carriers they will use Canadian content. One question has become how to insure that the minority owner does not call the shots in the partnership. The policy has been amended to state that if minority foreign ownership occurs up to the permitted level the regulator may look behind the veil of ownership to determine where effective control over commercial decision making lies. The issue has arisen in the case of Investment Canada's rulings about foreign investment by Borders Books in book distribution in Canada, and it is implicit

---

23. See *Broadcasting and Cable International,* June 1996, 12.

in the tax ruling that permits *Reader's Digest* to publish a Canadian edition in Canada. The issue also arises in the case of CMT. Having become a minority investor in a licensed specialty service, CMT will likely be able to introduce its format for the operation of the service. Its name is being used, as opposed to that of the majority Canadian partner, NCN, and it has access to more country music titles because of its worldwide operation. There are probably too few Canadian titles to run a successful country music specialty service. Thus, a reasonable presumption is that CMT will call the shots. Whether this constitutes effective control over commercial decision making is questionable.

The CRTC has powers to examine the details of "effective control," but the partners, knowing this, can probably achieve their objectives in a manner that satisfies the regulator. The relevant regulations are published, instructing the CRTC to determine whether effective control is exercised by Canadian or non-Canadians, where control may arise through personal, financial, or contractual arrangements.[24] At the time of license issuance, renewal, or amendment, opportunities exist for outsiders to intervene in response to material filed. This would be the procedure used to raise concerns about foreign control. In licensing the Discovery Channel, the CRTC issued the license subject to revision of the partnership arrangement, which originally gave the minority foreign partner veto power over the appointment of the general manager. The revision was made, completing the requirements for the license.[25]

The process of reviewing control as well as ownership is an example of new regulations having to be added to existing regulations in order to close all possible loopholes. The situation is further complicated by the fact that the level of permitted minority foreign ownership has recently been increased for broadcasting in order to attract more investment into Canadian cable operations. Canada is signaling that it wants more foreign investment in the cultural sector, providing that foreigners do not control operations and where it is already known that lower levels of permitted foreign investment create problems for determining effective control—perhaps a case of wanting it both ways.

Help to Canadian Artists

The purpose of the policy is to assist Canadian country music artists. Cable systems can do this by financing and distributing their music. Did the delisting achieve this? To answer this question requires establishing a counterfactual

---

24. In dealing with foreign ownership, the CRTC is bound by direction to the CRTC [ineligibility of non-Canadians] *Canada Gazette,* pt. II, vol. 130, no. 9, SOR/96–192, April 1996. Transfer of ownership of a specialty service is set out in Specialty Services Regulations, 1990, as amended, June 21, 1993, *Canada Gazette,* pt. II, vol. 127, no. 14, July 14, 1993, 3092.

25. CRTC Decision 94–283, Ottawa, June 6, 1994, 2.

situation. Would Canadian artists have been better off with NCN 100 percent Canadian owned, or (like CMT) with 90 percent Canadian and 10 percent American ownership, or with two channels, NCN and CMT, separately owned?

With 100 percent Canadian ownership, Canadian artists would probably have been blacklisted by CMT in other parts of the world, which would not have been helpful. In its original license application NCN indicated the support it was prepared to give to Canadian artists. This included an initial payment of C$300,000 in the first year for the production of Canadian country music videos as well as an annual contribution of C$1.8 million in the first year, rising to C$2.3 million in the sixth year, to encourage Canadian production. This fund would require NCN to pay Canadian artists who "produce broadcast-quality music videos C$150 per play for each video, subject to a minimum of C$4,500 [and] to a maximum of C$15,000."[26]

These conditions remain with the licensee, which now has input from its minority American partner, giving it more financial muscle. As well, the Canadian blacklisted artists were reinstated and probably are more widely distributed now than if they had been distributed by NCN. CMT's worldwide network of outlets provides a better international platform for exposure than having the work restricted to the Canadian market. The downside is that there is only one country music outlet where there could have been two, NCN and CMT. Canadian artists would probably have been better served by having competition for their services.

Conclusion

The CMT case followed its own peculiar path through the cultural policy jungle, a path that would have been difficult to map. It ignored signs leading to NAFTA and WTO dispute resolution procedures; it picked up supporters from other industries, government agencies, and diplomatic representatives; it did battle with the Canadian courts and at times with the Canadian regulator; and it reached its destination as a different but relatively unscathed television service now protected by those with whom it had battled on its journey. No one will ever replicate CMT's trek because in the process it changed the signposts for those who follow. The narrative reveals how complex the process of dispute resolution in the cultural industries can be when there are no guiding rules. It provides the ingredients for a challenging new computer game.

Highlighted by the facts is the informal dispute resolution process. No rules apply. Transparency is absent, and the regulatory process is politicized. A wide range of public and private sector players are drawn into the dispute, and the costs of interacting with the process may be higher than when there is a formal

---

26. CRTC Decision 94–284, Ottawa, June 6, 1994, 3.

rules-based system with tight deadlines, as occurs with NAFTA and the WTO. The outcome may lead to precedents and actions that are contrary to the interests of both protagonists. In this case the CRTC changed its delisting policy and CMT ended up with 10 percent of a Canadian service as opposed to 100 percent of an American service operating in Canada. Sidelined in the informal process is the public interest in terms of country music artists and viewers, none of whom is well represented. A possible benefit of the informal process is lower costs of reaching a settlement if the process is disciplined by the knowledge that a formal process such as NAFTA or the WTO might be used.

CHAPTER 12

Satellite Broadcasting

In 1957, the Soviet Union launched the world's first satellite. Sputnik I carried only a radio transmitter and a thermometer. On earth the political temperature rose as a new dimension of technological competition was introduced into the cold war. Although being first in space was an important symbolic "victory" for the Soviets, the communications potential of satellites was of more lasting and universal significance.

The direct events leading to the recent dispute over digital satellite broadcasting between Canada and the United States began in 1993. As background we first discuss the circumstances that gave rise to the use of satellites for broadcast purposes.

Satellites, International Communications, and Broadcasting

Sputnik I's crude radio signal foreshadowed a revolutionary change in global communications. Exploitation of this potential began almost immediately. The idiosyncrasies of the costs of production and exclusion as well as the nature and reach of satellite communications services shaped the organizations, international legal framework, and regulatory institutions, which developed in response to the opportunity. A satellite provides services over the full extent of its terrestrial reach, which is unlikely to conform to national boundaries. Up to the capacity of the satellite's transponders, the incremental costs of providing services are low. Capital costs for a satellite and its launch are high. Among the many uncertainties involved are: whether the launch will be successful, whether the satellite will operate properly, and whether events in space such as solar storms will adversely affect performance. These hazards result in high insurance costs.

International and regional cooperatives were particularly important during the early years of satellite communications development. Within a few years of the launch of Sputnik, 11 countries formed Intelsat, an international not-for-profit cooperative with a mandate to develop and operate a global communications system. Today Intelsat has over 140 countries as members and provides a variety of mainly wholesale communications services from 20 satellites. Each member country nominates investing entities, which provide funds according to their anticipated usage of the system. Each investing entity is charged for using the system and realizes a prescribed rate of return on capital (12.7 percent in 1996). As of April 24, 1998, the "ownership" share of Canada's investing entity, Teleglobe Canada, was 2.05 percent (versus 2.87 percent in 1988) while that of the United States' investing entity, Comsat, was 17.99 percent.

The growth of Intelsat's circuit capacity was 35.5 percent per year between 1965 and 1982. By the latter year, satellites were providing a similar capacity for communications across the Atlantic as did submarine cable. Since 1982, fiber optics have made submarine routes more competitive. Technological change continues to reduce the costs of international communications transmitted over either submarine or satellite links. Intelsat I, launched in 1965, provided 240 telephone circuits and one television channel. An Intelsat VIII satellite, launched in 1998, carries 22,500 two-way telephone circuits and three television signals. This change understates the economic impact of technical improvements. Current satellites have powerful transponders that require less elaborate earth facilities and have longer expected lives. A transponder's effective capacity can also be significantly boosted by digitizing and compressing signals.

Intelsat's dominance of international telecommunications services has eroded as a number of competitive sources have emerged. Eutelsat, Arabsat, and Asiasat are regional consortia that provide their members with linking satellite services. The Russian government offers an alternative satellite carrier for international business. Private interests have launched successful satellite service providers, such as Astra, which services European countries, and PanAmSat, which has expanded from a Latin American orientation to an international one. As a result of a 1997 merger with Galaxy Satellite Services, PanAmSat is controlled by a wholly owned subsidiary of General Motors. It delivers its global services from 17 satellites. As the industry matures, private suppliers have been growing rapidly and cooperatives like Intelsat have initiated plans to convert to shareholder-owned corporations. Competition among American, European, Chinese, and Russian interests has reduced the price of launching satellites. More recently, different consortia have either initiated or announced ambitious projects to develop global wireless systems.[1]

In Canada, domestic and cross-border communications have been provided by Telesat, which is a monopoly provider of domestic satellite communications

---

1. The Motorola-led Iridium project has launched 66 low-orbit satellites to create an international wireless network. M-star is a proposed Motorola-led system offering high bandwidth over a 72-satellite system. Celestri is a third Motorola system which will cost US$12.9 billion and have 63 satellites orbiting 900 miles above the earth and one or more fixed-position satellites orbiting at 22,300 miles. Loral Corp. with Qualcomm is building a 32-satellite digital telecommunications system called Globalstar. Teledesic plans a US$9 billion high-speed satellite system involving 288 satellites carrying Internet services and telephony.

services. In 1972, Telesat was the first commercial company to launch a geostationary orbit (GSO) communications satellite. Telesat was no ordinary commercial company at the time, as the Canadian government was its largest shareholder. In 1993, various telecommunications interests and Spar Aerospace bought the government's share of Telesat, which was then 53 percent. BCE, which owns or controls both major telephone service providers and Nortel, a large telecommunications hardware manufacturer, currently owns Telesat. As part of the WTO agreement on trade in telecommunications services of February 15, 1997, the Canadian government agreed to end Telesat's monopoly of Canada–Canada and Canada–United States fixed satellite services on March 1, 2000.

Broadcasting and Satellites

In the United States, the 1975 decision by HBO to distribute its movie service to cable companies on satellite transformed it from a small regional cablecaster into one of the dominant producers and distributors of film and special events in the United States and the world. A little over a year later, in December 1976, a local Atlanta station, WTBS, became a "superstation" by making its signal available to cable companies from satellite. Turner Broadcasting later launched its news channel, CNN, which depended on satellite transmission for its international success. More generally, the development of specialized pay or packaged cable networks, typically mixing advertising revenue with subscriptions, has been accelerated by satellite transmission. In the United States these services have been more profitable than traditional broadcasting services and have steadily increased their market shares. Cable was relatively well developed in Canada and the United States when satellite communications developed. The incidence of cable in Europe is more varied, and its development has generally lagged behind the North American pace. Belgium and the Netherlands have cable penetration rates of over 90 percent. The United Kingdom has very low penetration rates, while Germany and France have moderate rates. Cable households are increasing rapidly from a low base in the larger European countries.

In Europe, satellite transmission to cable companies has become a key factor in the expansion of the Luxembourg broadcasting firm Compagnie Luxem-bourgeoise de Télédiffusion. Its stations are important participants in the television markets of Belgium, France, Germany, and the Netherlands. In France, the pay movie channel, Canal Plus, began service in 1984 and quickly became the most successful of Europe's pay television broadcasters. Its signal is distributed by a ground network augmented by satellite transmission. Like HBO in the United States, Canal Plus is an important source of financing for films in Europe.

Through alliances with local companies, it has extended its service to Germany, Belgium, and Spain.

Satellites complemented cable systems by providing economical transport of diverse services to their head ends. Traditional television networks transport programs to member stations by satellite. At both a domestic and an international level, cable networks, superstations, and pay services supply their signals to subscribing cable systems by satellite. Transporting video signals at the "wholesale" level represents a significant part of the rising demand for both national and international communications services. In 1996, carriage of video represented 26 percent of the operating revenue of Intelsat.

Satellites also offered the prospect of direct competition with cable by delivering signals directly to the home. During the past two decades, many DTH broadcasting services have been announced and a more modest number launched in Europe, Asia, and North America. DTH broadcasting and video face less competition in countries that are lightly cabled. One of the earliest commercial success stories in Europe was England's BskyB, which emerged from the ashes of fierce competition between British Satellite Broadcasting and the Sky Channel. Sky had pioneered DTH service in the United Kingdom in 1989, offering four services: 24-hour news, general entertainment, sports, and a movie channel. BskyB, which, like Sky, uses a low-powered satellite transmitting an analogue signal, became profitable shortly after the merger. The S Astra system based in Luxembourg has also experienced significant DTH success.

The program capacity of the early direct broadcasting systems was limited, and the equipment was bulky and expensive. The development of more powerful satellites, better digital compression techniques, and the ability to capture the signal with a small dish transformed DTH services into more effective competitors of established cable systems. The American services DirecTV and United States Satellite Broadcasting (USSB) initiated such services. DirecTV is a subsidiary of General Motors. Its service was launched in the spring of 1994, tested for a few months, and then marketed to the public. By May 1995, over a million subscriptions had been sold. The service carries over 40 cable channels, a number of special interest pay channels available in packages or à la carte, a varied set of PPV sports channels, about 50 channels of PPV movie and special events offerings, and 30 audio channels of commercial-free music. A subscriber must purchase and install an 18-inch antenna and an intelligent decoder. The decoder can unscramble only the services subscribed to by the customer, selectively block programs that do not have copyright clearance in the customer's area, and facilitate billing and payment. The picture and sound provided by satellite digital television compare favorably with those of cable, although quality can be affected by weather conditions and the intensity of solar storms.

International Constraints

The provision of satellite services has spawned the development of an evolving set of international rights, protocols, and obligations. The International Telecommunications Union (ITU), an agency of the United Nations, manages the international regulatory structure for the spectrum required to uplink and downlink communications.[2] It is also responsible for an evolving structure of rights governing the location of satellites in space. The ITU has focused on allocations of slots for GSO satellites and on developing processes to limit interference among the signals of neighboring satellites. The ITU's decisions are implemented by national governments.

Satellites provide both broadcasting and point-to-point telecommunications services. For the latter, links between countries are voluntarily agreed upon and jointly managed. In contrast, broadcasting spillovers are not always welcomed by the recipient country. International agreements typically recognize both the right of national sovereignty and the right of citizens to a free flow of information, but they offer little guidance for reconciling conflicts between these goals.

Many countries receive spillovers of over-the-air television and radio signals that they have not approved or licensed. Families in towns along the border of the United States with Mexico or Canada can readily tune in radio and television stations from the other country. Intertwined with the imprecise but politically sensitive cultural issues raised by these spillovers is the impact of foreign competition on the advertising markets of the border stations.

Spillovers of broadcasting signals typically occur in both directions. How they are viewed by each country is problematic. A small country may welcome the opportunity to export broadcast services. In the interwar years, Luxembourg, for example, exported commercial radio services to many listeners in England, Germany, and France, despite the efforts of incumbent national broadcasters to curb this unlicensed competition. As described in chapter 8, Canadian policy-makers have viewed the spillover of American television signals as a negative factor. On the other hand, the success of cable in Canada reveals the willingness of Canadian viewers to pay for receiving American television signals. Canada's policy has been a schizophrenic mixture of protective measures and actions facilitating the spillovers.

With respect to satellite broadcasting, officials of the governments of Canada and the United States exchanged letters in 1972 and 1982.[3] Both exchanges dealt

---

2. See Smith (1990, chap. 9).

3. The 1972 exchange was between Minister K. B. Williamson and F. G. Nixon of Canada's Department of Communications and Bert W. Rein of the U.S. Bureau for Economic and Business Affairs of the State Department. In 1982, the correspondence was between Francis Fox and Alan Gotlieb (ambassador to the United States) on the Canadian side and Robert Hormats of the U.S. Department of State.

with telecommunications in detail. The 1982 letters permitted authorized U.S. satellite communications companies and Telesat to negotiate agreements with each other to carry telecommunications traffic. This right was not extended to satellite broadcasting.[4]

Canadian Policy and the Satellite Broadcasting Spillover

Satellite broadcasting spillovers occur over a very wide area. A geostationary satellite may be configured so as to have line of sight communication with about one-third of the world.[5] A typical North American GSO satellite covers Canada and the continental United States, with more narrowly focused beams serving Hawaii and Alaska. DTH broadcast signals delivered to an American audience can be received by most Canadians and vice versa. The pressure has come on the Canadian side of the border because of the earlier appearance of American services. In response to the competitive threat, Canadian cable companies and putative Canadian DTH services have insisted that the American DTH suppliers conform to the Canadian regulations imposed on them. On the other side, American services contend that they have been willing to meet culturally motivated restrictions only to find that other regulations and the interpretation of content regulations have been unfairly marshaled to keep them from serving the Canadian market.

Low-Power DTH and the Regulation of the Canadian Broadcasting System

Before the launching of the American digital DTH services, the CRTC singled out cable as the backbone of the television distribution system and perceived other modes of distribution, including satellite, as playing a supplementary role. Local microwave systems, other wireless technologies, and satellite delivery could be employed in situations in which cable was uneconomic. With respect to satellite delivery, the CRTC allowed any Canadian licensee to deliver its service directly to the home within its service territory. Services taking advantage of this opportunity sought permission to combine their licensed service with American channels.

---

4. As Ambassador Gotlieb wrote: "These principles shall not derogate from the authority of our respective governments and regulatory authorities to authorize and regulate the reception and distribution in their own country of radio and television programming services originating in the other country and carried on a fixed satellite service" (letter to Robert Hormats, August 24, 1982).

5. The actual coverage depends on the power of the transponders and their focus.

First Choice, the movie channel provider in eastern Canada, was permitted to market a DTH package of its service, plus the American services CNN and Headline News, to subscribers in its franchise area. Weak sales led First Choice to propose adding three more U.S. cable television networks to the package. The CRTC approved the request despite the fact that these three channels had *not* previously been listed as eligible for carriage by cable in Canada.[6]

Another licensee, Canadian Satellite Communications, Inc. (Cancom), held an exclusive national right to provide third-party transportation of satellite television signals to the head end of Canadian cable companies. Cancom was also given permission to broadcast a package of encrypted services directly to the home. In order to make the service profitable, the CRTC approved a package of services that was judiciously balanced by "nationality." For example, the package of services which Cancom was permitted to carry in 1983, was the "3 + 1" bundle of American services (ABC, CBS, NBC, and PBS) and a set of four Canadian channels. As the company's brief to a 1993 special hearing of the CRTC on the structure of the broadcasting system states:

The 3 + 1 signals were attractive to cable subscribers in remote and under served areas who knew that cable subscribers in urban areas received similar signals as a matter of course. They thus made a more complete Cancom package and allowed the service to be financially viable.

These examples illustrate how the CRTC judiciously adjusted obligations and privileges, often in the form of permitting carriage of American signals, in an effort to maintain the viability of the licensees involved in the first generation of DTH services.

As we described in chapter 8, broadcast and cable licensees with sufficient market power to generate excessive profits have been "taxed" by the CRTC to support the objectives of broadcast policy.[7] As an implicit quid pro quo, the CRTC has protected struggling elements of the system by shifting economic rents to them from other players. The CRTC managed this intricate system with considerable technical and political skill. Unfortunately, the system had a number of negative effects. It focused managerial efforts on protecting rents and gaming

6. Authorization occurred in two letters from the CRTC to First Choice dated October 11, 1989, and April 2, 1990 (Whitehead 1994, 8).

7. The anticipation of such levies creates a temptation, probably not resisted by all companies, to disguise profits by clever accounting and to shift them to related companies that are not subject to broadcasting regulation. The regulator responds to these defensive tactics by tightening loopholes and surveillance.

for new rights or privileges from the regulator. This orientation is in our opinion partly to blame for Canada lagging the United States in the development of cable networks. An inward-looking business culture deterred early experimentation with new specialty channel formats at home and the export of the successful cases to the United States. Instead Canada delayed and protected existing broadcasting interests. When the specialty channels were licensed in the 1980s, there were few innovative services and many Canadian clones of formats that had been successful in the United States.

More recently, technological convergence, increased system capacities, new media combinations, and the emergence of alternative ways of delivering content have created new profit opportunities and had an uneven impact on established players. The balancing of privileges and obligations has required increasingly frequent adjustments. In some instances, the government found it too costly to integrate a new way of delivering programming into the regulatory system. In others, it banned services that it could not integrate and then turned a Nelsonian eye to the emergence of a gray or black market.

Video is an example of the former strategy. The majority of Canadian homes have access to one or more video recorders, and video stores are a ubiquitous neighborhood feature. There are no Canadian content requirements in these stores. Video rental outlets vary in their coverage. Some have offerings that are dominated by Hollywood films. Others carry a wide array of art house videos. There are no solemn hearings on the structure of the video rental business nor a flow of decisions about where stores will be located and the like.

The government's response to the first generation of satellite dishes and illegal decoders illustrates the latter strategy. Cancom and the two regional pay movie services repeatedly encouraged the federal authorities to enforce vigorously prohibitions against the use of illegal decoders in receiving unlicensed American services. Either because of the difficulty of enforcement or because of a lack of political will to do so, the licensees failed to receive the support they were seeking. There were an estimated 400,000 to 500,000 backyard dish owners in 1993, the year before DirecTV. In that year one of the two services offering a DTH package, Cancom, had some 31,000 subscribers for its DTH service. The dominant suppliers of signals to these dishes were presumably American signals.

Both video and unlicensed satellite services have enjoyed an advantage in competing against legal broadcasting and cable because they do not bear the costs of cultural protection. The costs of picking up and returning a video and the cumbersome hardware associated with this vintage of DTH service have limited the damage done to the fiscal base of the protected system. The new generation of DTH services has posed a potentially more significant threat to the Canadian broadcasting system.

In 1993, the CRTC acknowledged that the new DTH services could not be restricted to filling gaps in the cable system and were potential competitors of cable. The entry path for DTH competition is more abrupt than that of telephone system or wireless cable competition. The day before the successful launch of a Hughes satellite, competition from digital broadcasting satellites was an abstraction. The countdown to the launch of commercial services and the stocking of dishes and decoders in American stores began the following day. Within months the signals from USSB and DirecTV were available to almost every Canadian cable customer and gray market competition had begun.

This chapter addresses the difficulties that the CRTC and the government had in folding the new generation of DTH services into the Canadian broadcasting system. This case is important for the strain it put on commercial relations with the United States and for its influence on the course of broadcast regulation in Canada.

Canadian Policy and the New DTH Services

The plot of the satellite broadcasting case takes many twists and turns. The issues between Canada and the United States were not addressed in either NAFTA or the WTO agreement but were mediated through the informal system of resolution. As of late 1998, the dispute has entered a quiet period, but we do not consider the current situation to be sustainable. To help the reader through the labyrinthine path of this dispute, we provide a chronology of events in table 8.

The CRTC held "structural hearings" in the year of the countdown to the launch of the Hughes DTH satellite. Interveners gave evidence on a number of topics, including satellite broadcasting. The commission subsequently reported that "Canadian parties at the hearing stress the urgent need to develop a Canadian DTH alternative because of the imminent threat posed by DirecTV and other foreign satellite services to the Canadian broadcasting system."[8] Officers of DirecTV also gave testimony. They claimed that DirecTV did not require CRTC approval to market its planned service in Canada. No legal opinion to that effect was presented. Mr. McKee, the general manager for Canada, reported that DirecTV would carry one or two Canadian channels and feature Canadian cultural events, such as plays from the Stratford Festival, on its PPV service. The commission was not persuaded by the DirecTV jurisdictional argument nor mollified by the cultural tribute offered.

---

8. CRTC Public Notice 1993–74, Ottawa, June 3, 1993.

TABLE 8. Chronology of Events: Canadian Satellite Broadcasting Policy

Year	Event
1993	• CBC and Power Broadcasting announce agreement to supply programming services to DirecTV. • CRTC Structural Hearing Report: Canadian satellite broadcasting will be an important part of "the overall response by the Canadian broadcasting system to non-Canadian DBS services." • CRTC pay audio licensing decisions reversed by Cabinet—use of Canadian satellites an issue.
1994	• Agreement in principle among Canadian telephone, cable, satellite distributors and pay-specialty channel providers to market a single DTH service (the "grand alliance"). • DirecTV and USSB begin to market services in the United States. • CRTC Decision exempts DTH undertakings from licensing requirements if certain conditions, including use of Canadian satellite facilities, are met. • DirecTV and Power Broadcasting form Power DirecTV. • Cable companies exit the Canadian "grand alliance."
1995	• Report of the Policy Review Panel (Canada 1995b). • Government directives filed with CRTC and Parliamentary Committees. • DirecTV protests to FCC Tee-Comm's application to provide a DTH service, AlphaStar, in the United States. • After hearings, House of Commons and Senate Committees file reports. • Modified directives issued which call for licensing of DTH and PPV undertakings by November 1, 1995, and require Canadian satellite use only for Canadian broadcasting services. • ExpressVu announces a delay in its September launch date. • CRTC licences ExpressVu and Power DirecTV as distribution undertakings, four English-language and one French-language PPV\DTH service. • CRTC imposes protective film distribution requirements on PPV.
1996	• Power DirecTV refuses to initiate service under licence conditions . • Mexico and the United States sign a satellite agreement. • Tele-Communications Inc. (TCI) and TelQuest announce agreement with Telesat to launch four DTH satellites. FCC dismisses application as Canadian government has not licensed slots. • Tee-Comm leaves ExpressVu Inc. and licenses AlphaStar in Canada. • Court cases initiated regarding gray market.
1997	• AlphaStar, Star Choice, ExpressVu initiate licensed service. • AlphaStar goes out of business. • 300,000 gray market subscribers to American services estimated. • Conflicting decisions but momentum shifts against gray-market providers by year end. • Canadian government licenses slot to Telesat for a Canadian built satellite.
1998	• Star Choice and ExpressVu each have over 100,000 subscribers by August 1998. • In the United States DirecTV adds 183,000 subscribers in December, 1998 to reach a total of 4.46 million subscribers. • DirecTV announces merger with USSB in December 1998 and with Primestar in the next month. When mergers completed will have over 7 million subscribers.

In its report, the CRTC asserted "its jurisdiction over foreign DTH distributors, where certain elements exist, when these distributors operate in whole or in part in Canada."[9] The commission argued that a DTH distribution undertaking could only operate in Canada with its approval. A DTH distribution undertaking might have no physical presence in the country, but if it billed Canadian subscribers it could be considered to do business in Canada. Of course, enforcing sanctions against an American service conducting guerrilla marketing in Canada would be costly regardless of the strength of the legal position (Whitehead 1994).

In its "Structural Decision," the commission also threatened the American services that had access to the Canadian system. The CRTC stated that it would consider cancelling the eligibility for cable distribution of any American service with that status if it appeared on an unauthorized satellite broadcasting service distributed in Canada. The fairness and effectiveness of this threatened action were questionable. It would punish the American services carried by an unauthorized DTH service that are least likely to attract gray market subscribers—services that are also available through Canadian cable services.

Nor was the threat credible. Although the proposal was put forward by the Canadian Association of Small Cable Operators, the large cable franchises would probably not have welcomed competing against a new rival without being able to offer, for example, A&E, the Learning Channel, CMT, TNN, Black Entertainment Television (BET), WTBS, and the CNN pair of channels. The American government responded vigorously to the CRTC's removal of CMT from the eligibility list (see chap. 11). An even stronger response would presumably occur to the removal from the eligibility list of services appearing on DirecTV.

Subsequent events are consistent with the threat lacking credibility. Despite DirecTV's estimated 300,000 Canadian gray market subscribers, the CRTC has not made ineligible any of the services vulnerable to the threat. To the contrary, after DirecTV's gray market success, the commission added an unprecedented number of new U.S. channels to the eligibility list, many of which were also being carried by DirecTV. Presumably the greater set of American choices included in the packages offered by Canadian cable companies made them more effective competitors to the gray market satellite services.

Between the structural hearings and the CRTC's "structural decision," a partnership between the CBC and Power Broadcasting Inc. of Canada agreed to supply DirecTV's American service with two channels—an international version of the CBC's specialty channel, Newsworld, and TRIO, a channel based on the public broadcaster's current programming augmented by a library of CBC and private television programming. DirecTV also contracted with CHUM, a

---

9. CRTC Public Notice 1993–74, Ottawa, June 3, 1993.

Canadian private broadcaster, to carry MuchMusic, a music video channel, which is a staple of Canadian cable systems. Many of the key parties in the Canadian broadcasting system considered these contracts by the public broadcaster and an important private broadcaster to be similar to trading with the enemy.[10] Ironically, the TRIO channel is not available in Canada, although some of the same programming appears on the CBC. For Canadians to be able to watch TRIO's presentation of these "Canadian stories" they would have to either travel to the United States or become clandestine Canadian subscribers of DirecTV.

Having staked its claim to jurisdiction, the CRTC became a catalyst in bringing into existence a Canadian alternative. The commission chair attended the annual convention of the cable industry and publicly rallied support for a Canadian response. By May 1994, an alliance of telephone, hardware, and broadcasting interests—BCE, Cancom, Tee-Comm Electronics Inc., Astral Communications Inc., Allarcom Pay Television Limited, and Labatt Communications Inc.—formed DTH Canada Ltd. for the purpose of bringing digital satellite broadcasting to Canadian homes. Three large cable companies—Rogers, Shaw, and CFCF—developed a competing plan. On May 17, 1994, an improbable agreement in principle among all these interests was reached to establish a single marketing agency.

Within a short period of time, this grand marketing alliance began unraveling. The noncable members were only willing to invest if DTH competed head-to-head with cable, as DirecTV was doing in the United States. Not surprisingly, the cable companies wanted the service to be marketed as a complement rather than a substitute for cable systems.

In the fall of 1993, Tee-Comm and Telesat made separate submissions to the CRTC, recommending that Canadian DTH distribution undertakings be exempted from holding a license. The CRTC decided to issue a call for comments on this proposal at a meeting in December 1993. In the next month, a delegation of the commission's senior officers visited executives of DirecTV and Hughes in Colorado. The American management was informed that DirecTV would require a license to operate in Canada, and only corporations with 80 percent Canadian ownership could obtain one.[11] The CRTC also told

---

10. A spokesperson for the Canadian Cable Television Association responded to the news of the CBC initiative by stating:

The CBC is an agent of the government and responsible to parliament. It has made this deal well in advance of the publication of the CRTC's findings on the restructuring of the Canadian broadcasting industry, which seems to say the government has given its blessing to an "open-skies" broadcasting policy. (*Toronto Star*, May 28, 1993, W4)

11. Meeting between the chairman and broadcasting vice chairman of the CRTC and executives of Hughes Industry in Boulder, Colorado, on January 21, 1994.

their American hosts that "the Commission's policy position with respect to DTH is to encourage the use of Canadian satellite facilities."[12]

The CRTC issued a call for comments on the exemption proposal with a deadline of April 15, 1994. In the meantime, DirecTV and Power Broadcasting Corporation began negotiating the formation of a partnership, Power DirecTV, which met the requirement of 80 percent Canadian ownership. The CRTC did not postpone the hearings to allow the new partnership to testify. In its decision, the commission exempted DTH services from licensing requirements if they met specified conditions.[13] A DTH service that did not meet the conditions for exemption could apply for a license and make a case for why its business plan should be allowed to deviate from the CRTC's template.

That a DTH service must deliver all of its programming from a Canadian satellite was one of the controversial conditions imposed by the CRTC. This stipulation prevented the realization of economies from delivering at least some of the programming on a continental rather than a national basis. George Addy, the director of investigation and research of the Competition Policy Bureau, later testified that this "would cost hundreds of millions of dollars in additional costs over the average twelve year life of a satellite."[14] The satellite condition in the CRTC's licensing exemption regime differed from the satellite policy that the commission applied at that time for delivery of services to cable companies. The cable policy allowed American signals to be transported to Canadian cable companies on American satellites while Canadian signals were required to be transported on Canadian satellites.

Power DirecTV considered the CRTC's conditions to be an opportunistic policy designed to handicap it in competing with other providers. Either it would have to comply with the condition and pay unnecessary transportation costs—to bring back to earth its signal and then upload it to a Canadian satellite for delivery—or it would be mired down in a lengthy licensing procedure to obtain relief from the condition.

Power DirecTV's business plan also failed to meet another license exemption condition—that the DTH service provide PPV services only through Viewers' Choice in eastern Canada and Home Theatre in western Canada. Power DirecTV's business plan included the delivery of its own PPV service,

12. CRTC Fact Sheet G7–09–95 (undated). The CRTC interprets but does not make satellite policy.

13. CRTC Public Notice 1994–111, Ottawa, August 30, 1994.

14. Comments of the director of investigation and research on DTH and PPV proposed directions to the CRTC and the Senate Standing Committee on Transport and Communications, Ottawa, June 7, 1995, 4.

which it would modify to conform to CRTC content requirements[15] through programming of the Canadian black box and would deliver by means of the American satellite.

If these conditions kept Power DirecTV out, who, if anyone, qualified? The grand alliance had dissolved under the weight of pressure from the Bureau of Competition Policy and the divergent interests of the participants. The cable interests regrouped to develop a defensive satellite service to augment their cable offerings. From this a satellite initiative emerged, controlled and managed by Shaw, a large Canadian cable company. Its proposed service, originally called HomeStar, was not ready to launch. The telephone, broadcasting, satellite broadcasting, and hardware firms—BCE, Western International Communications Ltd., Cancom, and Tee-Comm—had coalesced in a partnership, ExpressVu, which promised a service by September 1995. Its business plan conformed with the conditions of the exemption order.

The Canadian partners in Power DirecTV launched an effective lobbying campaign to reverse the exemption order. Although the government's public response was initially neutral, within two weeks of the exemption decision it announced a review of satellite broadcasting policy.[16] The resulting panel's report recommended that the government issue two directives to the CRTC, as permitted under the Broadcasting Act.[17] These directives would order the regulator to adopt open licensing of DTH satellite distribution undertakings, separate and open licensing of PPV service providers, common ownership possibilities for DTH systems and PPV services, transport of Canadian programming services by Canadian satellites, a tax of 5 percent on gross revenue of both distribution systems and PPV services to finance Canadian programming, the licensing of at least one French-language PPV service, carriage by a licensed DTH service of at least one French-language PPV service, and similar content requirements for DTH and cable systems.

Within three weeks of receiving the panel's report, the government issued directives in line with the spirit, but not every detail,[18] of the recommendations and presented them to parliamentary committees. After hearings in which almost

15. A new, slightly larger aerial would be required in Canada with two horns to receive signals from two satellites, one carrying PPV and other services from the DirecTV satellite and the other receiving Canadian services from the Canadian satellite.

16. Gordon Ritchie, Robert Rabinovitch, and Roger Tassé were appointed as commissioners to examine satellite broadcasting policy.

17. The act permits directives on matters of policy but not on the detail of decisions. Before implementation a draft directive has to be considered by committees of each house of Parliament, which must report within 40 days of receiving the directive.

18. For example, the final directive requires that distribution and PPV undertakings make significant financial contributions to the production of Canadian programming, with the CRTC determining the contribution as a percentage of gross annual revenues.

identical testimony by the various parties was presented to each committee, a brief House of Commons committee and more fulsome Senate committee report agreed with the thrust of the directives while adding some general and specific suggestions.[19] New binding orders were then delivered to the CRTC. ExpressVu was allowed to begin its service under the terms of the licensing exemption order but would have to apply for a license.

On December 20, 1995, the commission licensed ExpressVu and Power DirecTV as distribution undertakings. Four English- and one French-language DTH-PPV programming services were also licensed. HomeStar's application was refused. The commission required the DTH distribution undertakings to maintain a predominance of Canadian programming in their services. PPV services could be marketed on their own, that is, being bundled with other services. The commission decided not to regulate DTH rates on the grounds that competition among the two services, cable, and wireless cable would be sufficiently robust to discipline market power. All DTH distribution undertakings were to be taxed 5 percent of their gross revenue to support a fund to finance Canadian productions.

Competition from the Canadian Services and the Gray Markets

The anticipated competition from the licensed Canadian DTH distribution undertakings was glacially slow to develop. Power DirecTV decided not to launch because the conditions of the license were too onerous. Its president, Joel Bell, argued that the licensing conditions discriminated against DTH compared to the regulatory treatment of cable.[20]

During the dispute that followed the CRTC's license exemption decision, ExpressVu argued that any revisions in policy should not cause a delay in its planned launch. The government agreed but did require ExpressVu to obtain a license when the CRTC held hearings for that purpose. ExpressVu experienced technical and satellite difficulties and was not able to launch by its announced target date of September 1995. Two Septembers later ExpressVu was launched using the DISH technology of Echostar, an American DTH service. In the meantime, BCE had increased its share of ExpressVu and had become sole owner by 1998.

---

19. It was of concern to both committees that the order be broad enough to establish new policy rather than be a reversal of an individual decision made within a policy framework that is unchanged. The Senate report (Canada 1995a, 40) recommended that the CRTC be denied the right to refuse to license a DTH distribution or PPV service because in its opinion the applicant is not economically viable.

20. See *Globe and Mail*, February 2, 1996, A1 and March 5, 1996, A10.

Like TRIO, Newsworld, and MuchMusic, Tee-Comm went continental and launched its AlphaStar service in the United States on July 1, 1996. Tee-Comm then applied for and received a license to launch its service in Canada.[21] The CRTC allowed AlphaStar to deliver its Canadian services using American satellites until it could arrange to obtain space on Canadian satellites. By the end of May 1997, AlphaStar was out of business and Tee-Comm was in receivership. At the time of its bankruptcy, there were an estimated 7,000 subscribers in Canada and 60,000 in the United States.[22]

Shaw reapplied for a DTH license for its HomeStar service. The CRTC granted the application but required HomeStar to be operated as a separate subsidiary.[23] Shaw bought 50 percent of another licensed service, Star Choice, and merged it with HomeStar.

Until recently, DirecTV and other American DTH services provided more effective competition to Canadian cable systems than the Canadian DTH services. In this activity, *gray* describes a market in which customers decode signals with the authorization of the lawful distributor but receive them in an area where the programming service is not permitted to be sold. This would be the case if Canadians subscribed to DirecTV using an American billing address. *Black,* in contrast, describes a market in which subscriptions are sold without the authorization of the service, for example, the use of smart cards in a decoder to obtain access to a service without paying for it. Despite the uncertainty as to whether those who retailed and subscribed to American services in the gray market were acting illegally or not, the estimated number of subscribers at the time of the Senate and House of Commons hearings was between 30,000 and 70,000. By late April 1997, journalists were using the figure of 300,000. This figure has retained currency in the newspapers into 1998.

The key to the legal cases brought against gray market participants was the Radiocommunication Act.[24] In particular, the justices differed in their interpretation of section 9(1)(c), which states:

No person shall decode an encrypted subscription programming signal or encrypted network feed otherwise than under and in accordance with an authorization from the lawful distributor of the signal or feed.[25]

---

21. CRTC Decision 97–87, Ottawa, February 27, 1997.

22. *Globe and Mail,* August 7, 1997, B1, B6.

23. CRTC Decision 97–38, Ottawa, January 31, 1997.

24. *Statutes of Canada,* 1989, chap. 17.

25. For a judicial paraphrase of this section, see Justice Gibson's decision in the Federal Court of Canada, Trial Division, *ExpressVu Inc. et al. v. NII Norsat International Inc. et al.,* July 23, 1997.

Section 10(1)(b) makes anyone who "manufactures, imports, distributes, leases, offers for sale, sells, installs, modifies, operates or possesses any equipment or advice, or any component . . . for the purpose of contravening" section 9(1)(c) guilty of an offense punishable by fine or jail sentence or both. The justices have generally agreed that section 9(1)(c) prevents anyone from using or selling a decoder for a DTH service that was licensed in Canada without the permission of the licensee. Their disagreement concerns whether or not section 9(1)(c) prevents the selling of decoders for encrypted American signals, as in this case there is no "person in Canada who has the lawful right to . . . authorize its decoding."

Judge Kiebec of the Queen's Bench of Saskatchewan argued that the section only applies to signals "lawfully intended for reception by the public in Canada and the public must also be entitled to lawfully subscribe for it in Canada" and that "mere production of 'pirate' or 'grey market' programming signals is insufficient to constitute an offence."[26] In contrast, Judge J. N. LeGrandeur ruled that the section "must be interpreted to prohibit the decoding of encrypted subscription programming signals unless there is a lawful distributor for the signal in Canada who has so authorized the decoding. If there is no lawful distributor, the signal cannot be decoded."[27]

Under another section of the Radiocommunication Act, a licensee that is damaged by anyone guilty under sections 9(1)(c) and 10(1)(b) can bring suit. Judge Gibson of the Federal Court of Canada agreed with Judge LeGrandeur's conclusion in an important case in which ExpressVu and others sought damages from a number of distributors and retailers marketing equipment for receiving American DTH services.[28] After the judge made a summary ruling that the defendants were liable for damages, a deal was struck in which the defendant agreed not to sell gray market dishes and the plaintiffs waived their damage claims. Following this successful action, more ambitious suits were threatened. The consortium indicated that it would expand the suits to include distributors and retailers of the large C-band dishes and sports bars, which were showing programming from the unlicensed American services to their patrons. The potential political backlash from expanding the campaign is large. No one, as yet, has sued an individual subscriber, although it is our understanding that such subscribers are likely acting illegally under the LeGrandeur ruling.

---

26. In the Queen's Bench, Judicial Centre of Saskatoon, about an Application for an Order Restoring to the Possession of Ronald Ereiser and Kerrobert Satellite and Cellular Certain Articles Seized Pursuant to Two Search Warrants (June 24, 1996).

27. In the Provincial Court of Alberta, Criminal Division, Judicial District of Lethbridge, *Her Majesty the Queen v. Quality Electronics (Taber) Ltd., Ernest Knibb and Donna Knibb* (February 21, 1997).

28. See note 25.

Star Choice and ExpressVu both offer favorable terms to new subscribers who hand in their American service hardware. These pricing packages have become more and more generous. For Star Choice:

> It now gives away $800 worth of programming for anyone who returns a DirecTV or Echostar dish. Put another way, turn in a U.S. dish and get free Canadian satellite service for up to two years. The company's previous amnesty was a combination of a $250 rebate on hardware and $150 of free programming for a total of $400.

For ExpressVu:

> When someone buys a $599 ExpressVu dish and box, they get $599 worth of free programming when they hand over the U.S. product. For Express-Vu's higher-end $749 receiver, they get $749 of free programming in exchange for the DirecTV or Echostar dish.[29]

The competitive disadvantage for the Canadian services is that they offer fewer channel alternatives in general and do not have the saturation coverage of sports and movies offered by the growing set of American services and subscription packages. Their advantage is their carriage of Canadian channels, their clear legality, and the availability of service support.

Two International Subplots

The Market for Satellite Services

An important subplot to the satellite broadcasting dispute concerns gaming for position in the international market for satellite services. Canada has taken various measures to protect the broadcast transport services provided by Telesat. At the same time, Telesat has vigorously sought the right to market satellite broadcasting services to American broadcasters.

Satellite policy is the responsibility of the government of Canada.[30] The CRTC interprets that policy with respect to broadcasting subject to the right of appeal to the Cabinet by affected parties. The CRTC's requirement in its exemption order that all services be transported by Canadian satellite was not an isolated policy initiative. In mid-1993, the CRTC granted licenses to two

---

29. Both quotations are from the *Globe and Mail,* December 17, 1997, B7.

30. See letter from the deputy ministers of Industry Canada and Heritage Canada, dated June 14, 1995, to the CRTC.

separate pay audio services, DMX (Canada) Ltd. and Cogeco Radio-Télévision Inc.[31] Each service proposed to deliver music programming (advertising free) to cable systems. A supplier of an American pay audio service, International Cablecasting Industries Inc. (ICI), owned 20 percent of DMX. Digital Cable Radio, ICI's competitor in the United States, had contracted to supply Cogeco. Both services packaged some Canadian channels with channels provided from the United States. For example, DMX planned to deliver three channels of digital audio programming produced in Canada, and 30 channels produced in the United States by ICI. The CRTC licensed both services, but the decisions were overturned on appeal to Cabinet because the use of American satellites did not conform to Canadian policy.

The CRTC's treatment of satellite carriage in the DTH dispute generated a response in the American regulatory arena. Tee-Comm had contracted with AT&T for satellite services to deliver its AlphaStar service in the United States. DirecTV requested the American broadcasting regulator, the FCC, to deny AlphaStar the right to provide the DTH service. The request was based on two arguments. One was that delivering a DTH signal using a Canadian uplink was illegal. The second was couched in terms of "fundamental fairness." DirecTV maintained that allowing AlphaStar to operate in the United States if DirecTV could not provide a service in Canada was unfair. Tee-Comm and AT&T responded to both allegations. They claimed that all uplinking services could and would, if necessary, originate in the United States.[32] With regard to the fairness issue, they told the FCC that "procedures in Canada are changing and may permit the market entry that DirecTV is seeking."[33] When the Canadian directives to the CRTC established rules for licensing consistent with Power DirecTV's business plan, DirecTV withdrew its petition and the FCC dismissed it without prejudice.

On May 9, 1996, the satellite dispute resurfaced when Tele-Communications Inc. (TCI), the largest cable company in the United States, and TelQuest Ventures contracted with Telesat Canada Ltd. to launch four direct broadcasting satellites. In the first agreement, Telesat was to purchase two satellites from TCI, which would be launched in late 1996 and 1997. TCI would lease a portion of the capacity for 12 years. The TelQuest contract called for two satellites to be launched in 1997 and 1998. Larry Boisvert, Telesat's president and CEO, declared:

31. CRTC Decisions 93–235, and 93–236, Ottawa, June 25, 1993.

32. See "DirecTV attempts to block AlphaStar U.S. DTH bid at FCC," *Satellite News,* May 22, 1995.

33. FCC order DA 95–1995, Washington, DC, September 18, 1995.

The future of the satellite business is international, and this is another step on Telesat's path to becoming a provider of satellite facilities right across North America.[34]

The attraction to the American partners was six fixed-orbit satellite positions held unused by the Canadian government since 1983. The FCC had earlier completed an auction of two DTH American satellite slots for which TCI and TelQuest were unsuccessful bidders. As an indication of the value of the Canadian rights, the winner of the slot at 110 degrees, MCI Telecom, paid $682,500,000 and the winner of the slot at 148 degrees, Echostar, paid $52,295,000. The problem for the American partners was that Telesat only had an agreement in principle from the Department of Industry for two of the slots.

The FCC was asked to approve the agreement. The winners in the American auction and other American DTH suppliers opposed the request. They argued that there is a sufficient number of U.S. licensed DTH satellites to serve the U.S. market and noted that Canada "severely restricts the manner in which U.S. programming may be provided to and U.S. satellites may be used to provide service in Canada."[35] In a joint letter to the FCC, the USTR, Department of State, Department of Commerce, and Department of Justice elaborated on that theme. The executive branch intervenors expressed concern "that Canada's content restrictions serve to discriminate against U.S. and other foreign programmers and service providers by mandating a minimum amount of Canadian content in television, cable, and DTH broadcasting" and "that Canada maintains restrictions over the use of non-Canadian satellites for the distribution of telephony and broadcasting services to Canada and would therefore not permit a U.S. licensed satellite to provide DTH service to Canada."

On the Canadian side, Telesat claimed that the cultural policy and satellite service trade should not be linked. This was a rather ingenuous argument for an old war horse of the Canadian regulatory battles. Almost no request is made in that forum without linking the two. In a press release entitled "Straight Talk from Telesat" the company posed a question, gave its answer, and drew a moral:

Question: Why should the U.S. let Canadian orbital slots be used, when Canada restricts U.S. television content—an unfair trading practice?
Answer: When the vast majority of TV programs and movies Canadians watch comes from the U.S., it's pretty hard to argue that there are

---

34. Telesat press release, July 2, 1996.

35. Federal Communications Commission, Report and Order, TelQuest Ventures, L.L.C. and Western Telecommunications, Inc. Adopted: July 15, 1996. Released: July 15, 1996.

any serious barriers to the entry of U.S. content and culture into Canada!

Moral: Confusing content and facilities is a specious "apples and oranges" argument used by interests who seek to restrict U.S. DBS competition, and to protect their share of this lucrative market.[36]

The FCC dismissed the request because it was premature, as Canada had not licensed the rights in question. The commission noted, perhaps with relief, that it therefore did not need to address what it termed to be "substantive issues" raised by the industry intervenors and the executive branch letter.

Although Telesat tried to resurrect the deal with TCI, the Industry Department refused to approve the submission because the proposed arrangements to buy the satellite and the Canadian DTH leases were not firm. Later the Canadian government approved a project for one of the slots involving a satellite built by Lockheed Martin Aerospace. The design has experienced problems, and the launch has consequently been postponed. The main lessees are ExpressVu and Electronic Digital Delivery, a joint venture between Cancom's parent company, which has subsequently been taken over by Shaw, and Emc3 IHBV of the Netherlands.

Contrast the Canadian-U.S. situation on satellite broadcasting with the agreement reached on that subject between the United States and Mexico.[37] Under the latter, the satellites of each country will be able to provide service to the other country if they conform with the laws of that country. According to Richardson (1998, 43): "(T)he United States and Mexico agreed to limit content regulations to a few of the channels that were provided through DTH satellite systems "

The Film Rights Subplot

The 1995 CRTC conditions of licensing for the DTH distribution undertakings also picked at an old scab in American-Canadian relations—film distribution policy. The CRTC imposed a set of terms on the contracts between PPV distribution undertakings on the one hand and the distribution undertaking on the other. It required that the satellite broadcasting service, the PPV service, and the program supplier share revenue equally. The CRTC explicitly noted that this

---

36. Telesat press release, Ottawa, July 12, 1996. Note that DBS in the quotation stands for direct broadcasting satellite.

37. Agreement between the Government of the United States of America and the Government of the United Mexican States concerning the Transmission and Reception of Signals from Satellites for the Provision of Satellite Services to Users in the United States of America and the United Mexican States of April 28, 1996.

arrangement would reduce the amount that would have to be paid for the rights to programming, which were owned by foreigners, and thereby free funds to subsidize Canadian production:

> At the hearing, certain parties argued that competition among PPV services could produce a situation in which licensees would be required to pay a greater portion of their revenues to foreign rights holders than is currently the case in the cable PPV market.
>
> The Commission considers that the "1/3 split" serves to promote market stability by ensuring that no licensee is unduly pressured to accept escalating program costs. Because contributions to Canadian production funds are to be based on the gross revenues collected by Canadian DTH distributors and on those earned by licensees of DTH PPV programming undertakings, a predictable 1/3 split will also serve to maximize the levels of contributions to Canadian production funds.[38]

The commission also required PPV television programming undertakings to purchase nonproprietary exhibition rights from Canadian distributors for films. In this context, proprietary exhibition rights exist when a foreign distributor has financed more than 50 percent of a film or owns worldwide rights. As the commission noted, this decision extended an existing Investment Canada policy defining proprietary rights for distribution of films to cinemas. The commission failed to note that the Investment Canada policy covered new distributors and had grandfathered the American majors. The CRTC initiative applies to all non-Canadian film distributors. This decision rekindled an ongoing dispute between Canada and the United States concerning film distribution and exhibition. We examine the subsequent events, which include a suspension of these requirements in March of 1998, in chapter 17.[39]

Conclusion

In response to the arrival of the second generation of DTH broadcasting services, the CRTC moved quickly to assert jurisdiction over the regulation of satellite broadcasting and to integrate the new technology into Canadian policy. The resulting process generated conflicts with the United States and was marked by the precedented but still uncommon action of the government overruling the CRTC. The case illustrates the operation of the informal resolution process, as the case was not appealed to any formal international agreement. In the dispute, the Canadian regulator, the CRTC, and its American counterpart, the FCC, were

---

38. CRTC Decision 95–906, Ottawa, December 20, 1995, 5.
39. CRTC Decision 98–76, Ottawa, March 13, 1998.

pressured or volunteered to support the stance of their governments in the dispute. The leading American service, DirecTV, partnered with a Canadian company, Power Broadcasting, to offer a "Canadianized" version of its service. While the Canadian policy authorities were developing a policy framework, gray market subscriptions of American services increased rapidly.

Two licensed Canadian services currently offer digital DTH services. Another service, operating under probation, has gone bankrupt and ceased transmitting. Power DirecTV was eventually granted a license but chose not to operate under the conditions imposed. Since its decision, some of these constraints have been suspended.

The policy that eventually emerged represents a break from the past in providing considerable freedom of entry to DTH service.[40] Unfortunately, with satellite broadcasting the decision to license only Canadian entities and think exclusively in terms of the Canadian market reduces the probability of any of the licensed services achieving economic viability. The two surviving Canadian services have had limited success. Star Choice reported attracting 105,000 subscribers by the end of August 1998 and losing C$42 million dollars during the fiscal year ending on that date. ExpressVu's subscription at that date was slightly less. Star Choice reported spending $23 million subsidizing DTH equipment to subscribers ($220 per subscriber).[41] One U.S. service, DirecTV, reported adding 183,000 subscribers, a comparable number to the total subscriber base of the Canadian services, during December 1998. Its total subscriber base at the end of 1998 was 4.46 million. There are significant economies of scale in DTH services and there has been considerable consolidation in the larger U.S. market. DirecTV's parent, Hughes Electronics Ltd., announced buying USSB in December of 1998 and Primestar one month later. When these takeovers are completed the company estimates that it will have over 7 million subscribers and will be in a position to deliver more than 370 channels.[42]

The role of Canadian DTH in offering effective competition for traditional cable systems is in flux. That a major supplier of Canadian telephone service, BCE, owns ExpressVu may retard its development of wired alternatives to cable systems. On the other hand, BCE's learning from its ExpressVu service is transferable to terrestrial digital broadband wireless systems in which BCE has an interest. It is possible that a marriage between terrestrial wireless and satellite

---

40. One might argue that the original license exemption initiative contemplated freedom of entry but that the qualifying terms were such that no one was in a position to comply.

41. *Globe and Mail,* October 17, 1998, B4.

42. DirecTV information from <http://www.directv.com>.

DTH may offer a more attractive competitive alternative to wired systems.[43] That Shaw, a leading cable company, owns Star Choice, may reduce the vigor of its competition with cable. Its satellite service may increasingly complement cable by playing a transport role for new digital specialty services. In the interim, given high fixed and low incremental costs, competition between the two DTH services is likely to be vigorous. If only one can be profitable, a war of attrition is likely. If broadband wireless systems and upgrading of traditional cable systems intensify the competition among terrestrial distribution systems, no state of the art Canadian DTH provider may survive without subsidies.

The satellite case reveals that the American government is increasingly linking changes to Canada's cultural policy with assessments of any Canadian initiatives to gain access to the American market. If the reciprocity approach is applied to trade in television programming, American and Canadian viewers will be harmed, but the bulk of the damage will be felt by Canadian producers, professionals, and technical personnel, who are increasingly exporting to the American market. When applied to inherently international activities like satellite broadcasting, reciprocal protection will generally hurt the producers and consumers of the smaller country more than those of the larger.

It has been argued that important rights holders in the United States, in particular, the professional sports organizations and the major studios, support the separation of a Canadian and U.S. market (Buchan 1998). The majors have traditionally opposed the separation of the markets in principle. A threatened programming embargo by the majors contributed to the suspension of the CRTC's contractual stipulations on film rentals and the nonproprietary right regulations imposed on DTHs PPV undertakings. Not surprisingly, their opposition diminishes when the distinction does not result in discrimination against them and disappears when it favors them (see chap. 17).

Negotiating a satellite service treaty between Canada and the United States makes economic sense. The Mexican broadcasting industry looks at the Hispanic part of the U.S. market and sees an opportunity. The Canadian broadcasting industry looks at the English-language American market and sees a threat. An economically sensible accord on satellite broadcasting can accommodate separating the broadcasting markets to meet legitimate cultural imperatives.

---

43. Both ExpressVu and the new digital broadband wireless systems have complained that the CRTC's postponement of licensing new digital specialty services has penalized them in their competition with cable. They argue that they could immediately incorporate the new services while many cable systems currently lack the capacity to do so (*Globe and Mail*, March 31, 1999, B7).

CHAPTER 13

Borders Books

Book distribution is part of a vertically related chain of activities. Retail booksellers act as intermediaries between authors and publishers on one side and readers on the other. Publishers view them as gatekeepers for their products and readers as supermarkets or boutiques where their choices are made. Each bookseller faces competition from others in the same area, from distant suppliers that can be reached by mail or wire services, and from libraries, where reading material can be borrowed or rented.

Canadian cultural policy has targeted all segments of this vertically related chain of author, publisher, wholesaler, retail bookseller, library, and reader. By providing grants to authors and subsidies to selected publishers, the work of Canadian authors and the operations of Canadian-owned publishers are promoted. Copyright law reinforces the control of Canadian publishers, which are granted exclusive rights to distribute foreign books in Canada or parts of Canada, by blocking imports of the same books published in other countries. Restrictions on foreign ownership of publishers and booksellers have been imposed, and a content-type system exists wherein provincial governments require the purchase of Canadian books for use in school systems.[1] No attempt has been made to impose on bookstores and libraries the comprehensive content policies that apply to radio and television broadcasting. It would be impractical to do so and would elicit strong public resistance. Two payment schemes assist authors. A public lending right program compensates some Canadian authors for the use of their books held in libraries, and as a result of recent amendments to the Copyright Act, CanCopy, a collective, signs contracts with government departments, schools, universities, photocopy shops, and libraries, for royalties accruing to publishers and authors as compensation for the photocopying of their works.[2] Canada also has a public lending right that is not part of copyright. It is funded by the government under the administrative oversight of the Canada

---

1. According to *Ontario Circular 14,* "Whenever possible, learning materials must be written by a Canadian citizen or citizens or a permanent resident or residents of Canada, and must be produced or manufactured in Canada" (http://onteris.oise.utoronto. ca/c14e/c14kits1.html). Quebec has a similar policy with a list of approved publishers and publications.

2. See *Quill & Quire,* December 1996, 8.

Council. With total funding in excess of C$8 million, including administration, in 1997–98, more than 11,000 registered Canadian authors shared payments averaging C$720 per author (Acheson and Maule 1998b).

The stated rationale for these policies is that in the absence of government intervention the market for Canadian authors would be undersupplied and Canadian readers would be deprived of the opportunity to read their work. In a broader context, national unity and identity would suffer.

The main characters in the dispute addressed in this chapter are two American-owned booksellers (Borders Group Inc. and Barnes and Noble Inc.), two groups of Canadian investors (the partners associated with Borders and Chapters Inc., which is associated with Barnes and Noble), and Investment Canada, an agency within the federal department of Industry Canada. In supporting roles were the Bureau of Competition Policy; associations representing Canadian booksellers, publishers, and writers; and the umbrella arts organization, the Canadian Conference of the Arts. The drama played itself out in the interaction between these players against a background of rising tension in cultural trade relations between Canada and the United States.

In 1995, Borders Books attempted to undertake book distribution in Canada. As a successful book retailer in the United States, Borders proposed to take a minority equity position in a Canadian book-retailing operation with three Canadian partners. After review, Investment Canada banned the proposed partnership because it contravened the government's foreign ownership guidelines related to the cultural industries. Subsequently, another large American bookseller, Barnes and Noble, took a minority equity position in Chapters Inc., a competing Canadian bookstore operator.

The case, which did not evolve into a formal dispute between the two countries, is of interest for a number of reasons: it shows how restrictions on foreign investment may also restrict trade and shield consumers from the benefits of increased competition; it illustrates how limits on foreign ownership are inadequate and now have to be accompanied by an examination into how effective control may be exercised by an investor holding a minority of the shares of a company; and it highlights the ways in which Canadian publishers, acting as agents for foreign publishers, benefit from the sale of imported titles. Comparing Investment Canada's treatment of the determination of whether the American partner had control or not for the Borders and Barnes and Noble initiatives reveals an opaque policy process that cannot be effectively monitored. There are no effective safeguards against "control" determinations creating a privileged set of outside participants, who, with their Canadian partners, are protected in Canada from competition from other foreign and Canadian combinations. The case is also informative on a basic premise of Canadian policy, that foreign ownership restrictions promote Canadian culture.

Borders Canada

In February 1996, Borders Inc. announced the formation of a partnership in which it would take a minority equity position with three Canadian investors: Heather Reisman; Edward Borins, owner of several bookstores in Toronto; and Second Cup Ltd., a Toronto-based retailer of coffee. In the United States, Borders operates book superstores, which typically have about 50,000 square feet of space, in contrast to traditional bookstores, which might have 2,000 to 10,000 square feet. By 1996, in addition to several thousand traditional bookstores, there were an estimated 680 superstores operating in the United States versus none in Canada, which was serviced by about 700 traditional bookstores. At the time of Borders' announcement, traditional book retailing in Canada was due for a change, which would increase competition and affect the livelihood of those in the traditional sector.[3]

The response to the Borders Canada proposal, led by Canadian booksellers and publishers, was immediate. The former feared the loss of business. The latter were concerned that their titles would not be adequately stocked and that lower retail prices would result in lower wholesale prices. Canadian publishers earn over half their revenues from agency sales arising from their acquisition of Canadian rights to books published outside the country. Their concerns included a fear that Borders in Canada would be supplied by foreign sources rather than the Canadian rights holders.[4] A concurrent change was the increasing ease with which consumers could bypass bookstores entirely by ordering directly from wholesalers or publishers anywhere in the world. The service provided by Amazon.com on the Internet is one example. It is an adaptation of the procedure by which a consumer using an 800 number and a credit card can order a book by telephone and have it delivered by a postal or courier service. One difference is that through the use of web pages the reader can search a large data base of titles before placing an order.

In sum, at the time Borders made its announcement the scene was set for change, and indeed Chapters Inc., Canada's largest book retailing operation, made a move at the same time to open a chain of superstores in partnership with Barnes and Noble as a minority investor. A part of Chapters superstore entry strategy was to question whether the investment by Borders conformed with Investment Canada policy and to suggest that Chapters would better represent Canadian cultural interests. In general, Chapters had the support of Canadian authors even though some of them depended on sales in foreign markets and

3. In 1995, Borders' revenues from superstores were equivalent to about 20 percent of total Canadian retail book sales and those of Barnes and Noble were over half of total Canadian retail book sales (Chapters 1996, 9).

4. Subsequent revisions to the Copyright Act prevent buying around the Canadian rights holders except in the case of individual copies for personal use.

would have been hurt by any retaliation against the Canadian policy that restricted the entry of Borders.[5] Other authors favored the entry of both firms so as to provide an alternative outlet if one superstore refused to handle their works.[6] The final act of this drama is that Borders has not entered the Canadian market; Barnes and Noble has entered into a partnership with Chapters and has about 50 superstores open by the end of 1998 in addition to 280 mall stores; Indigo Books and Music (formerly Now Books and Music), owned by some of the Canadian investors who were previously partners of Borders, has eight stores open by the end of 1998. The largest has 42,000 square feet of space compared with about 20,000 square feet in its other stores.[7]

In order to understand how and why foreign investments by Borders and Barnes and Noble were treated differently, it is necessary to outline the evolution of Investment Canada's rules and procedures.

Ownership Restrictions

In 1973, the Canadian government established the Foreign Investment Review Agency to screen inward investment into Canada. The agency's name was changed in 1985 to Investment Canada. Its mandate was altered to attract foreign investment to Canada while it retained responsibility for reviewing certain types of investment. Among these are investments in "cultural businesses" which are defined to include the print and broadcast media, films and sound recordings, and investments in a business activity related to "Canada's cultural heritage or national identity."[8] Section 20 of the Investment Canada Act

---

5. According to *Quill & Quire,* April 1997, 175,000 copies of Margaret Atwood's *Alias Grace* were shipped to the United States, 84,000 to the United Kingdom, and 60,000 to Germany.

6. Graydon Watters is a Canadian author who favored the increased competition that Borders would bring (*Globe and Mail,* February 10, 1996, B1, B8).

7. *Quill & Quire,* September 1998, 5; and material supplied by Indigo.

8. According to section 14 of the Investment Canada Act, a cultural business is one that carries on any of the following activities:

1. the publication, distribution, or sale of books, magazines, periodicals, or newspapers, in print or machine-readable form, other than the sole activity of printing or typesetting of books, magazines, periodicals, or newspapers
2. the production, distribution, sale, or exhibition of film or video recordings
3. the production, distribution, sale, or exhibition of audio or video music recordings
4. the production, distribution, or sale of music in print or machine-readable form
5. radio communication in which the transmissions are intended for direct reception by the general public; any radio, television, or cable television broadcasting undertakings; and any satellite programming and broadcast network services.

Section 15 of the Investment Canada Act relates to "Canada's cultural heritage or national identity."

lists the factors to be taken into account in determining whether an investment under review will be considered of "net benefit" to Canada and permitted, including whether the investment is compatible with Canada's national and provincial policies (sec. 20e). An initial test of control is set out in section 26.

In 1985, this general policy was customized for the publishing industry with the announcement by the government of the "Baie Comeau Policy," to be implemented by Investment Canada with the objective of placing the control of publishing in Canada in Canadian hands. Foreigners would be restricted from purchasing Canadian-owned businesses and establishing new firms, and the policy would require that every foreign direct or indirect acquisition of a foreign-owned company in Canada had to end up with Canadian investors having a controlling interest. In the case of an indirect acquisition, the foreign company had to divest itself of its majority interest in the Canadian firm within two years of purchase.[9]

After the government had found it impossible to locate Canadian investors for the Ginn Canada Publishing Company, which had been acquired by American-owned Paramount Corp. in an indirect acquisition, the "Baie Comeau Policy" was amended in 1992 for book publishing and distribution. The amendment still prohibits foreigners from starting a new business in Canada without yielding majority control to Canadian investors, but it strengthens the prohibition by requiring Investment Canada to determine whether de jure control by Canadians provides de facto control or "control in fact." This was the issue at stake in the Borders case.

In cases of an indirect acquisition of existing foreign-owned companies, the revised policy permits foreign control if the investor gives to Investment Canada satisfactory undertakings that are of net benefit to Canada and the Canadian-controlled sector of the book industry.[10] Direct acquisitions of existing foreign-

---

9. The value of the Canadian publishing subsidiaries to the acquiring companies were reduced by the policy. This reduction was aggravated by the immediate need to make sales in a thin market. The inclusion of the clause in the CUSFTA assuring American companies that had to divest themselves of Canadian assets because of foreign-ownership restrictions in the cultural industries of fair market value reflected the concern of the American negotiators with this aspect of Canadian cultural policy.

10. The Canadian policy statement gives a number of examples of what is meant by a "contribution to culture": (1) a commitment to the development of Canadian authors, such as undertaking joint ventures with Canadian-controlled publishers that would introduce the partners' Canadian authors to new markets both domestically and abroad; (2) a commitment to support the infrastructure of the book distribution system, for example, through distributing titles via a Canadian-controlled publisher or agent, through maintaining a fully integrated warehousing and order fulfillment operation in Canada for both frontlist and backlist titles, and through active participation in industry cooperative ordering/distribution/marketing endeavors; (3) accessibility of the company's Canadian marketing and distribution infrastructure (or international network) to interested and

owned companies are permitted if Canadians have first been given a full and fair opportunity to bid on the company. Foreign acquisitions of Canadian-controlled firms are permitted when the business is in clear financial distress and there are no Canadian purchasers.

In the matter of Borders, the proposal was for a new bookselling operation in Canada since the three Canadian partners did not operate an existing enterprise, although one partner had been an owner of several bookstores in Toronto. The partnership arrangement was submitted to Investment Canada to determine whether the proposed entity would be considered Canadian controlled for purposes of the Investment Canada Act. If it was deemed to be Canadian, the Investment Canada Act and the ownership restrictions of the book policy would not apply. Since Borders only intended to take a minority position in the undertaking, the issue was whether the foreign investor would have de facto as opposed to de jure control of the arrangement. This is where the process becomes difficult to follow since there is no official record of what material was submitted to Investment Canada, nor a written document containing reasons for the decision that de facto control would reside with Borders. According to section 36 of the Investment Canada Act, all information submitted in connection with an inquiry is privileged and not available to the public.

In the event that effective control becomes an issue, as it was in the Borders case, the parties involved may supply supporting information and request a written opinion from the minister responsible for the Investment Canada Act (sec. 37.2). The opinion is binding on Investment Canada as long as the facts submitted are accurate and do not change (sec. 37.3). Neither the supporting information nor the written opinion is publicly available. In fact, it is not publicly recorded that any firm has made a request for a written opinion unless the firm involved makes this known or the information is leaked. There is an opportunity for third-party intervention but only if third parties learn on their own of the request being made. In an industry in which everyone knows everyone else, this may not be a problem, but the process is hardly an open one.

The guidelines (administrative procedures) of the act provide for the unsolicited representations of third parties concerning applications for review or requests for opinions. Where the representations could have an adverse bearing on the determination of net benefit, the substance of the representations are communicated to the potential investors, who are given an opportunity to respond. The source of the representations is not divulged to the investors. The investors are not obliged to reply to the representations and may rely on the

---

compatible Canadian-controlled publishers on a contractual basis; and (4) a commitment to education and research through financial and professional assistance to institutions offering programs in publishing studies (Communications Canada Fact Sheet FS–92–3808E, 2–3).

merits of their original filings. Third-party intervenors are typically related or interested parties such as competitors, Canadian businesses that may be dealing with the investors, concerned associations, and labor unions.

How Is Control Determined?

The decision made by the National Transportation Agency in conjunction with the proposed acquisition of a foreign interest in Canadian Airlines International Ltd.[11] constitutes an important precedent for the application of section 28. According to these guidelines, the issues to be addressed in determining de facto control include among others the nature and extent of the non-Canadian interest in the corporation's capital stock, the cost of the investment compared to the perceived value of the acquired interest, conditions for loans and equipment leasing, non-Canadian representation on the board of directors; and agreements or arrangements that might give non-Canadian shareholders an undue degree of influence.

Knowledge of who some of the intervenors were became available to the authors as a result of a conference paper that contained a copy of the December 20, 1995, letter by the president of the ACP to the minister of industry identifying the issues that should be examined in determining de facto control in the case of Borders Canada.[12] The ACP notes that it joins the Canadian Booksellers' Association, the Writer's Union of Canada, the Canadian Conference of the Arts, and Chapters Inc. in seeking a review. None of these submissions is available from the organizations nor from Investment Canada.

After reference to the Canadian Airlines decision, the ACP provided a lengthy checklist of issues to be examined to determine whether a corporation is in fact controlled by Canadians. Somewhat ironically, at the end the ACP proposed that the minister "hold some form of public process into this investment" despite the public unavailability of submissions by intervenors.

A second intervention with the name of the intervenor disguised was made available to the authors by Investment Canada. While covering much of the same ground as the ACP, this intervenor dealt much more directly with the proposed arrangement. In measuring the actual investment by the foreign partner, which cannot exceed 49 percent of total investment, the intervenor proposed that, in addition to the up-front monetary investment, the following items be added, which in their view would mean that the actual investment would exceed 50 percent of the total investment in Borders Canada:

---

11. National Transportation Agency Decision 297–A–1993, May 27, 1993.

12. See Clarke & Salzman, 1996. The ACP letter is attached as appendix A. The paper notes that "little is known about the analysis used by Industry Canada" in determining de facto control.

- Borders Canada start-up costs to include Borders' executive time in visiting Canada to meet with publishers, government officials, and real estate developers
- The value of the Borders trademark and brand name, estimated at US$259.3 million
- The value of Borders proprietary software
- Use of Borders mainframe computer in the United States
- Purchase of the Borders data base
- Design cost of the superstores
- Management expertise
- Music industry expertise
- Lease covenants for which Borders provides a guarantee in Canada
- Guarantees by Borders of operating lines of credit in Canada
- Borders' storage of nonreturnable inventory

The list of topics suggests that the intervenors wanted Investment Canada to go on a fishing trip to discover as much about the partnership as possible and to interpret information in a way that would show that Borders Inc. has a substantial investment in and de facto control of the partnership arrangement.

The end result of the inquiry, as reported in the press,[13] was that as a result of the analysis performed by Investment Canada Borders withdrew and the Canadian partnership was dissolved. Since that time, one of the partners, Heather Reisman, has formed a company called Indigo Books and Music, which began opening superstores in 1997, starting with one in Burlington, Ontario. The bookstore operation owned by another Canadian partner, Edward Borins, has gone into receivership.

Chapters Inc.

As the Borders partnership dissolved, another entrant, Chapters Inc., consisting of an American minority investor and Canadian majority investors, was forming. Its proposal was vetted by the Bureau of Competition Policy of Industry Canada. The role of Investment Canada is less clear in this case. The only announcement that Investment Canada was involved is found in the prospectus published in connection with a public offering of shares by Chapters stating that "Barnes and Noble received written advice from Industry Canada confirming that the transaction was neither reviewable nor notifiable" (Chapters 1996, 17).

The antecedents to Chapters date from 1933, when Coles was established as a book retailer in Canada. In 1950, SmithBooks, a subsidiary of W. H. Smith Plc., opened stores in Canada, later acquired Classic Books, and in 1995 merged

---

13. *Toronto Star*, February 9, 1996, A1, A24.

with Coles to form Chapters Inc. and become the largest book retailer in Canada and the third largest in North America.[14] On September 26, 1996, Barnes and Noble, the largest bookseller in the United States, acquired a 20 percent interest in Chapters, as is recorded in table 9.

The merger of Coles and SmithBooks to form Chapters was referred to the Bureau of Competition Policy to determine whether there were grounds for the director to apply to the Competition Tribunal for a remedial order pursuant to section 92 of the Competition Act. After assessing the information, the decision of the director not to challenge the merger was reported in a six-page press release. Despite finding that the merger would remove a "vigorous and effective competitor," the director concluded that this was offset by the extent of the remaining competition and ease of entry once certain restrictive covenants were removed. The covenants had restricted entry by competing bookstores to certain prime locations occupied by the merged firm. The director also decided to monitor the competitive impact of the transaction for a three-year period, which ended on April 10, 1998.[15]

TABLE 9. Chronology of Chapters Inc., 1933-96

1933	Coles established as book retailer.
1950	SmithBooks opens stores in Canada as a subsidiary of W.H.Smith Plc.
1985	SmithBooks acquires Classics Bookshops International.
1994	Canadian General Capital Ltd., and a private company controlled by certain directors and officers of Chapters Inc., acquire SmithBooks.
1995	Coles and SmithBooks are amalgamated to form Chapters Inc.
1996	Barnes and Noble purchase a 20% interest in Chapters Inc., later reduced to 12.9%.

As of November 26, 1996, Chapters Inc. operates 362 stores, 11 of which are superstores and 351 traditional bookstores under the names of Coles, SmithBooks, Classic Bookstores and the Book Company.

Source: Chapters Inc., Prospectus of Initial Public Offering, November 22, 1996.

The director's decision also referred to the provisions of the Investment Canada Act related to foreign investment in book retailing and noted that it would monitor this aspect of the transaction as well. Details of information provided to Investment Canada, of possible third-party interventions, and the

---

14. SmithBooks was originally British owned. It was required by the Foreign Investment Review Agency, forerunner to Investment Canada, to sell 50 percent of its voting interest to Canadians. It chose to sell 100 percent and was Canadian by the time it merged with Coles.

15. Proposed Merger of SmithBooks and Coles Book Stores Limited, Bureau of Competition Policy, Industry Canada, March 21, 1995. Discussed in the Annual Report of the Director of Investigation and Research, Competition Act, for the year ended March 31, 1995, 27.

advice given are not in the public domain. From the Chapters prospectus, it is known that Barnes and Noble is entitled to appoint two observers to attend meetings of the company's board of directors, can maintain a 20 percent share if further shares are issued, and has an ex-employee, Curtis L. Gray, in the position of executive vice president and chief operating officer of Chapters.[16]

Implications

The Borders case highlights the way in which domestic controls on foreign investment affect not only competition in Canada but trade between Canada and other countries, with consequences for both Canadian booksellers and Canadian publishers, authors, and readers. The last are seldom part of the debate over policy changes, the assumption being that what is in the interest of publishers, authors, and booksellers is also in the interest of readers. Such is not necessarily the case. A second lesson from the case is that what appears to be a simple policy to administer, restricting the level of foreign ownership, involves a more complex procedure and one that is nontransparent by design.

The issue addressed by the case is the differential treatment applied by Investment Canada to the minority investment proposed by Borders and the actual investment made by Barnes and Noble in Chapters Inc. From the available documentation and news reporting, it appears that Borders' involvement would have led to a degree of de facto foreign control that was unacceptable. A major reason was identified as the use of Borders' inventory control and book-ordering system, which implied that despite its minority equity position Borders would exercise management control.[17] Meanwhile, involvement by Barnes and Noble was considered to be a passive investment that did not confer de facto control. Making this distinction requires the exercise of difficult judgments about facts and timing.

Barnes and Noble learned from the treatment given to Borders and may have been able to structure its involvement so as to conform to Investment Canada's requirements. An industry observer noted: "I am not sure what passive means because anyone who knows Barnes and Noble knows that the word passive does not apply."[18] The executive vice president and chief operating officer of Chapters is both a former senior manager at Barnes and Noble and the highest paid member of the management team, although he ranks in title below the president and chief executive officer. The vice president of merchandising and marketing is also a former Barnes and Noble manager, and Barnes and Noble can appoint two individuals to attend meetings of the board of directors

---

16. In 1998, Barnes and Noble held 17.4 percent of the outstanding shares.

17. *Globe and Mail*, February 9, 1996, B1, B6.

18. *Quill & Quire*, August 1996, 5.

as observers (Chapters 1996, 15, 22–24). The ability to gain a foothold in the Canadian market as an insider gives Barnes and Noble a significant advantage over its rival, Borders, especially if ownership restrictions are relaxed in the future. The benefit to Chapters is access to management expertise.[19]

Does ownership make a difference? Canadian policy toward bookstores has been based on the assumption that domestic ownership will enhance the distribution of Canadian-authored books. It parallels the policy that Canadian ownership of publishers will promote the publication of Canadian-authored material. Both assume that the nationality of ownership makes a difference to the way in which profit-oriented firms behave and that Canadian-owned firms will plough back earnings into the publication and distribution of Canadian authors. In support of this view, it is frequently pointed out that Canadian-owned publishers publish most Canadian-authored books. This ignores the accompanying fact that it is only Canadian-owned publishers that are eligible for the grants that subsidize Canadian-authored books. Thus, Canadian-owned publishers have a much stronger inducement to publish Canadian novelists, poets, and playwrights than do foreign-owned publishers.[20]

The notion that nationality of ownership makes a difference is contrary to that found in related areas. Canadian ownership of movie theaters has not increased the distribution of Canadian films. In television, Canadian ownership of broadcasters, cablecasters and satellite distributors is recognized as an insufficient measure to assure distribution of Canadian programming, since the ownership restrictions have to be accompanied by Canadian content regulations to assure the distribution of the desired type of national programming, as discussed in chapter 8.

The objective of commercially operated firms, regardless of nationality, is to produce and distribute goods and services that will earn a return on investment. In the case of bookstores, the works of Margaret Atwood and Michael Ondaatje will meet this objective, as will those of Martin Amis and John Grisham. No bookstore, Canadian or foreign owned, will have as strong an incentive to carry and promote the works of lesser known authors, and to suggest that Canadian-owned bookstores are more likely to carry the works of Canadian writers is to argue against these incentives. What can be said is that any bookstore operating in Canada, regardless of the nationality of ownership, will have an incentive to display and distribute Canadian-authored works. Readers

---

19. *Quill & Quire,* November 1996, 1.

20. Bert Archer, the book editor of the Canadian trade magazine *Quill & Quire,* pointed out that the fall 1996 offering of Canadian-authored books showed that while the well-known Canadian authors were split between Canadian- and foreign-owned or branch plant publishers in Canada all but one of the new Canadian authors were being published by a branch plant publisher. Archer no longer works for *Quill & Quire* (*Financial Post,* September 7, 1996, 19).

entering a general bookstore in Canada are likely to expect and want a selection of Canadian topics, including works by Canadian authors, and it will be in the interest of the store to stock such material, but this is true regardless of the nationality of the bookstore owners. In fact, it is possible that a foreign-owned store will do a better job than a Canadian-owned store in stocking Canadian authors. Requiring bookstores to be Canadian owned may in fact deprive readers of the benefits that come from increased competition without increasing the distribution of Canadian-authored material.

The emerging emphasis on control as opposed to ownership is recognition that control can be exercised by a variety of contractual arrangements other than ownership. The issue then becomes how to develop criteria to assess effective control. While precedents have been set by the National Transportation Agency's decision re Canadian Airlines International, the criteria used by Investment Canada are only transparent via the guidelines issued by the agency. Details of actual decisions are not published but tend to become known. In the present case, there appears to have been a second-mover advantage that may have allowed Barnes and Noble to gain a foothold in the market:

> Given the federal government's Borders decision, Barnes and Noble appears to have out-maneuvered its U.S. competitor by moving into Canada via a minority stake in Chapters. "They read the Borders decision correctly," says Stoddart, who favors Canadian-U.S. alliances within the framework of a national ownership policy.[21]

Readers will receive fewer benefits from competition at the bookseller level than would have occurred with the presence of Borders, although the entry of Indigo Books and Music will alter that somewhat. The desirability of more competition is illustrated by the conflict that has existed between traditional Canadian bookstores and Canadian publishers over the poor service provided by publishers, especially over agency titles from Europe and the United States. There has always existed pressure to buy around the Canadian publishers for agency titles in order to provide bookstores and their customers with better service. Recent amendments to the Copyright Act require bookstores to buy, under normal circumstances, from those holding exclusive rights to distribute foreign-published books in Canada or a part of Canada, thereby preventing bookstores and readers from getting the service and prices that would exist if foreign competition were allowed. In recognition of the fact that service for and prices of agency titles may be unacceptable, the DCH is undertaking negotiations with Canadian publishers and bookstores to establish guidelines for when bookstores should have the right to buy around the Canadian publishers. For

---

21. *Quill & Quire*, August 1996, 1 and 5.

example, if a book is not available from the Canadian source within a certain time period, or if the price is significantly above its price from a foreign source, then the bookseller would have the right to buy around the Canadian source. Birth is being given to a new set of guidelines to accompany the amendments to the Copyright Act. The act restricts trade in books and encourages trade in rights. The guidelines encourage trade in books when those owning the rights cannot deliver the service. Some organization has to monitor and mediate the disputes that arise.[22]

The type of situation to which the guidelines would apply occurred in 1996, when Canbook, a warehouse/distribution joint venture of Penguin and McClelland and Stewart, failed to supply Canadian bookstores for the crucial end of year sales period. Due to a failure of a computer system, booksellers were "struggling to sort through months of blocked shipments, lost purchase orders and incomprehensible invoices."[23]

The final outcome has resulted in less competition in the Canadian market than there might otherwise have been. The beneficiaries are existing bookstores at the expense of readers and those Canadian authors who might have received better distribution of their works.

Conclusion

Restrictions on foreign ownership and administration of the Copyright Act are the main measures used to promote Canadian authorship through their influence on retail book distribution. As international trade in books increases and new ways are found to deliver content directly from authors to readers, domestic policy regimes will become stretched in attempting to deal with both the changes and international trade obligations. While Amazon.com has achieved a first-mover advantage in electronic ordering systems, Chapters, in a joint venture with the *Globe and Mail*, owned by Thomson, launched its Internet book retailing operation in October 1998. Bertelsmann has acquired a 50 percent interest in a similar U.S. operation set up by Barnes and Noble, and there are numerous other bookstores with web sites that facilitate ordering.

Organizational changes are occurring in the college bookstore market, where firms are signing management contracts with universities and colleges to run stores selling books, stationery, and clothing. Chapters operates the McGill

---

22. Officials of Heritage Canada and industry representatives reached agreement on the guidelines at the end of 1997. The proposed regulatory text was published as the Book Importation Regulations in the *Canada Gazette*, Part 1, January 30, 1998, 252–59. The regulations provide different conditions for books imported from each of the United States, Europe, and other countries. Used textbooks can be imported and are not subject to the regulations.

23. *Quill & Quire*, November 1996, 1.

University Bookstore, while the American-owned Follett Corporation has a management contract for bookstores in several Canadian universities and colleges. Throughout North America, Follett, in 1998, managed over 500 college bookstores with a total of 3.5 million square feet of space through which were sold 18 million books and 1.5 million items of clothing.[24] As long as investment is not involved, the approval of Investment Canada is not required for this type of arrangement. Arguably, Follett exercises as much control, with no investment, over the decisions of the Canadian bookstores it manages as would have been exercised by Borders. The former is not vetted, while the latter is not allowed.

As far as trade disciplines are concerned, books traded as hard copies are undoubtedly goods. Unlike newspapers and periodicals, there is no accompanying advertising service and so the obligations of the GATT will apply regarding market access and subsidies. Attempts have been made to provide electronic copies of books and hand-held electronic readers are being offered for sale.[25] If this becomes commercially attractive, the book trade will become subject to the GATS. Reference material is already available on-line, as are reports from official and other organizations that are not concerned about payment.

---

24. Information from <http://www.fsc.follett.com/index-js.html>, October 1998.
25. *Quill & Quire,* April 1998, 1.

CHAPTER 14

Neighboring Rights

Lack of conformity of copyright laws and their enforcement together with increasing trade in copyrighted material, has led to a series of trade irritants between countries. In this chapter we examine frictions that have arisen with regard to the treatment of neighboring rights, blank tape levies, and parallel imports. As with the other cases, the discussion is prefaced with a background description of the evolution of the relevant regimes.

Copyright provides a legal framework for contracting in the cultural industries. Before the advent of copyright and the development of industries that compete to disseminate information commercially, knowledge was a protected source of power. Julius Caesar chronicled how those selected to become Druid priests "studied for up to twenty years to memorize certain verses, which they were forbidden to write down, all to help the memory and *for the purpose of keeping this material from the public*" (Wincor 1962, 27, emphasis is in the original). The Druid priests could write Greek. To memorize rather than record was a choice.

The invention of the printing press made it economically feasible to disseminate information widely. At first, this power was channeled through crown monopolies. In England, the Stationers' Company was chartered in 1556 to control books, which were "spreading great and detectable heresies against the [Roman] Catholic doctrine of the holy Mother Church" (Prescott 1989, 453). The monopoly was maintained in Elizabeth's time to shelter rather than oppose these heresies. By the early eighteenth century, the Stationers' Company had lost its prerogative. To protect their position, the members supported the Statute of Anne, the first legislation establishing copyright privileges:

No longer having rights as publishers, they came up with the notion that *authors* should be protected and have copyright. This was not public spiritedness on their part. If copyright was a property right, it could then be assigned to the publishers, thereby giving them indirectly what they no longer had directly". (Hammond 1991, 101)

From its origins, copyright has had a commercial and international dimension. The English publishers were concerned about the competition from

Scottish and Dutch printers who were underselling them in their home market. Copyright has proven to be an elastic legal framework and has accommodated the contracting imperatives of subsequent cultural industries—photography, film, recording, radio, and television. Throughout this evolution, its structure has adapted to the international imperatives of the new copyright-based industries.

Over the past two centuries, the United States has vacillated in its commitment to international copyright protection. Knopf notes that "from 1790 until 1891, the USA simply denied copyright protection to all foreign works and authors, and retained until 1986, 'a manufacturing clause' that denied copyright protection to most English language works of U.S. residents printed abroad, with the notable exception of Canada" (1989, 249). In this period, the "Americans adopted the convenient view that the progress of their useful arts could best be promoted through unrestricted access to everybody else's" (Lardner 1987, 65).

The withdrawal of the manufacturing clause from American law coincided with a number of other internationally oriented intellectual property initiatives. The United States finally joined the Berne Convention on March 1, 1989. Five years later, the inclusion of copyright in the WTO agreement extended Berne principles to a wider set of countries and established a more effective mechanism for enforcing international copyright obligations. This initiative received strong support from the United States. The American government and private groups with the support of the government have also taken a number of bilateral actions against countries that have either weak copyright laws or sufficiently protective laws that they fail to enforce. The governments of other industrialized countries have generally supported the United States. The international trend toward more protective copyright laws—most obviously, longer duration and more stringent antipiracy laws—has been offset, at least in part, by the less obvious effect of competition among copyrighted cultural products resulting from trade liberalization.

From an economic perspective, copyright law balances two competing forces. The law allows a period of monopoly as an incentive to produce content and constrains this power by "regulating" the monopoly power and limiting its duration. The temporary monopoly in a magazine article, book, television program, or film granted by intellectual property laws is curbed by the presence of closer substitutes from abroad. For example, Margaret Atwood, a Canadian novelist and poet, enjoys increased protection from illegal copying of her works and better access to bookstores in other countries as a result of the WTO agreement. At the same time, her books share shelf space in Canadian bookstores with a growing number of books by the world's best authors. When exported, her works help discipline the market power of local authors in foreign markets as well as generating income for her and pleasure for her international readers. In Canada, her publishers have to take into account the increased intensity of foreign competition when pricing her book.

Countries with cultural industries that are running a sectoral balance of payments surplus typically support a different balancing point than those in the opposite situation. Small countries with underdeveloped cultural sectors face a more difficult tradeoff than large ones. The immediate balance of payments effects of being solely a consumer of imported copyrighted material are proportionate to size. Protection in response to these circumstances is more costly and does less to develop a national competence the smaller is the domestic market.

These generalizations hide internal differences of opinion about the desirable level of protection. National creators and producers in countries like India are frequently hawks with respect to copyright protection and antipiracy measures (Gadbaw and Kenny 1988). Their stance is similar to that of their counterparts in developed countries, but their influence is less. In general, user groups oppose and producer associations support more protective policies. There is a subtle interplay within and among other pressure groups. For example, the educational establishment typically supports strong protection for the expression of new ideas but lobbies for exceptions to be granted for educational use.

If the world were one country, copyright law would invite many disputes among parties with opposing interests. With many countries, disputes are more visible. They are also more severe because they become intertwined with other strategic interests and the international institutions of reconciliation are less well developed than national ones.

There are a number of sometimes contradictory principles—MFN, national treatment, reciprocity, and transparency—reflected in current international trade and copyright agreements. The Berne agreement combines elements of national treatment and the establishment of minimal standards for coverage, duration, and the structure of copyright. With respect to structure, Berne requires, inter alia, that the obtaining of copyright will not depend on formalities and that basic moral rights must be recognized. In principle, the minimal standards apply to the treatment of foreigners and a country can provide nationals with less or more protection, that is, national treatment does not apply.[1] On balance, the minimum standards have resulted in convergence along the affected dimensions of national copyright laws.

---

1. "It is a common assumption that Berne sets minimal standards of protection for *all* authors. It does not. Rather, it sets minimal standards that each member country must grant to nationals of other countries. If those standards are met, there is no need to grant the same protection to domestic authors and copyright owners. Berne cares not how shabbily each member country's copyright law treats its own nationals, as long as nationals of other Berne countries are accorded the minimal Berne standard of protection" (Koenigsberg 1991, 70).

NAFTA and the 1994 GATT agreement imposed some structural requirements on the national copyright laws of member states. The 1994 GATT Agreement included an Agreement on TRIPs. TRIPs requires each member country to grant treatment to citizens of other countries that is no less favorable than what is accorded to its nationals with regard to the availability, acquisition, scope, maintenance, and enforcement of intellectual property rights. Among the structural requirements imposed were copyright protection for computer programs; adopting rental rights for computer programs, videos, and records;[2] and extending the duration of copyright in records to 50 years. The scope for discrimination among members was reduced by requiring MFN treatment.

TRIPs also placed an unprecedented emphasis on enforcement processes. It goes beyond the boilerplate admonition that enforcement of copyright be fair and equitable to impose specific civil and criminal penalties for different transgressions. The attainment of minimum standards of enforcement can be difficult to measure and enforce because members' legal systems differ. To mitigate this problem, TRIPs obliges members to make their adjudication and enforcement systems transparent to other members.

Although national copyright laws are more uniform in content and enforcement than at any time in history, there is still considerable diversity. Diversity increases just beyond the borders of traditional copyright policy. In particular, TRIPs did not address a series of initiatives that have been recently undertaken by a number of countries: a public peforming right for performers and record companies, a retransmission right, the distribution of funds collected by levies designed to compensate performers and copyright holders for piracy, and measures to control parallel imports. Most of these are included in the World Intellectual Property Organization's (WIPO) definition of neighboring rights:

> Rights granted in an increasing number of countries to protect the interests of performers, producers of "phonograms" and broadcasting organizations in relation to their activities in connection with the public use of authors' works, all kinds of artists' presentations or the communication to the public of events, information, and any sounds or images. The most important categories are: the right of performers to prevent fixation and direct broadcasting or communication to the public of their performance without their consent; the right of producers of phonograms to authorize or prohibit reproduction of their phonograms and

---

2. With cinematographic works and records, a country could continue to decline to grant a rental right if commercial rental is not giving rise to the material impairment of the exclusive rights of reproduction of right holders. A country that does not have a rental right but has a record rental business must have a system of equitable remuneration of right holders with respect to these rentals.

the import and distribution of unauthorized duplicates thereof; the right of broadcasting organizations to authorize or prohibit rebroadcasting, fixation and reproduction of their broadcasts. (WIPO Glossary, 164, undated)

National antipiracy measures and the process for determining the remuneration payable by users of recorded music to performers and producers have the potential to generate international frictions. In the absence of international constraints, countries have usually limited access to the funds collected from commercial users of music to national performers and record companies and those of a small set of other countries. Piracy circumvents the process of rewarding creators for their efforts. As well as increasing efforts to enforce antipiracy laws, a number of countries have taxed the "burglary tools"—blank tapes, recording machines, photocopying machines, and the like—and distributed the funds to those damaged by piracy. The taxes have a direct deterrent effect on piracy. Both the tax and the distribution of the collected funds can be structured so as to discriminate against foreigners.

Parallel imports occur when reproductions made under license in one jurisdiction are imported into another. If the licensed party in another country sells directly in a country not covered by the contract, it is in breach of its licensing contract. The damaged licensee can take action under contract law. Parallel import measures are introduced to stop third parties that are not licensees in either country from buying in one and selling in the other. If copyright licensing restrictions are "exhausted" by sales in the exporting country, the third-party exporter is not in violation of any contract. A parallel import restriction bars these "gray market" imports and prevents the arbitraging of differences in price between the different national markets.

A country may be constrained in introducing neighboring rights and parallel import restrictions by international convention or regional agreements. The Rome convention (see chap. 4) governs neighboring rights and requires reciprocity for member countries that grant a comparable level of protection. The EU does not permit members to impose restrictions against parallel imports from other member countries. NAFTA did not address the issue. There are no international guidelines governing how antipiracy levy funds are to be distributed nor how parallel imports are to be treated at the border.

Canada has recently amended its copyright legislation with respect to all three of these areas. The amendments introduced neighboring rights, a blank tape levy, and a ban on parallel import of books under some circumstances. The USTR considers all three of these programs to be potential trade irritants.

Neighboring Rights

Retransmission Right

American negotiators of CUSFTA considered the commercial recognition of copyright in the retransmission of television signals on cable to be of significant importance. They were successful in persuading Canada to adopt a nondiscriminatory process for remunerating program copyright holders for value generated from retransmission of distant television signals on Canadian cable systems. Following the signing of CUSFTA, the Copyright Board held hearings and developed a royalty structure charging larger cable systems 70 cents per month per subscriber and smaller systems reduced amounts.[3] A pool of C$51 million dollars resulted, which was shared among collectives representing different program owners according to a formula reflecting viewership adjusted for the ratio of Canadian distant signals to American.[4]

The collective representing the U.S. motion picture and television production industry received 57 percent of the available funds. American border broadcasters and major league baseball received about 6.5 percent in total. The three collectives that represented other major American programming interests—NBC, ABC, CBS, PBS, and other major leagues sports—also included Canadian members. Estimates of the share of the pool paid to American program owners ranges up to 85 percent (Grant 1991, 3). Canadian program producers share in a differently structured American distant signal copyright scheme that predates CUSFTA.

The distinction between local and distant signals causes anomalies with the potential for creating future frictions between the two countries. In the United States, a local station can either insist on carriage by the cable franchise in its area or not allow carriage unless a fee can be negotiated with the cable company. In Canada, local Canadian stations must be carried on the basic service. A number of American stations can also be carried on basic. Some American stations that are local to an American cable company are also local to Canadian cable systems. Owners of programs aired on an American television channel that is local to a Canadian cable company have no claim on the Canadian distant signal royalty pool. The anomaly of, for example, a Buffalo cable company having to pay for a signal from a local station that its Fort Erie counterpart receives for "free" is likely to generate some political heat.

Along some dimensions, the distant signal retransmission scheme resembles another neighboring right—the public performance rightorming right for performers and record companies. The symbiotic relationship between programs

---

3. Copyright Board of Canada (1990).

4. The board did not consider the distinction between Canadian and American signals used in its calculations to be discriminating according to nationality.

carried on distant television signals and cable companies that retransmit them is similar, but not identical, to that between recorded songs and the radio stations that air them. In both cases the linking of the activities creates more joint wealth. Without unscrambled over-the-air television channels to retransmit, cable would be less valuable to its subscribers. Over-the-air stations that gain more viewers from retransmission by distant cable franchises than they lose from competition by distant stations retransmitted by their local cable franchise earn more advertising revenue.[5] Even when this is not the case, the joint wealth of the cable companies and television stations almost always rises. Similarly, radio stations are more valuable because of the existence of record companies and vice versa. The value of each of the entwined services to the other depends on the details of the relationship, with, for example, a talk radio station experiencing little benefit from recorded music. There is considerable evidence that new superstations or cable networks and companies representing recording artists without an established track record are willing to pay (sometimes called payola) for carriage on cable or radio respectively. The reverse is true for established recording artists and specialty channels.

With current policy there are mandated payments in one direction. The resulting rigidity may be softened by the parties adopting compensating arrangements. Granting a right to retransmission as a basis of negotiated access provides a more flexible means of coordination than compulsory contracting. The flexibility may be accompanied by rising bargaining costs.

In this vein, the EU has shelved an earlier proposal to adopt a compulsory licensing scheme for cross-border retransmission.[6] Instead a process developed incorporating negotiated settlements between the cable operator and collectives representing relevant rights owners (Dreier 1991, 45). At the same time as the Canadian scheme was being introduced, agreements covering retransmission were negotiated in Belgium, the Netherlands, Germany, and other countries.

The Canadian distant signal and the public performance right for performers' and record companies' royalty systems both involve collectives representing a broad group of rights holders. Both are compulsory licensing schemes. Combining these elements creates two levels at which discretion can be exercised—the determination of contract terms and the allocation of obligations and claims within the collective. The collective may also exercise discretion in spending funds on behalf of its members. These areas of discretion create

---

5. An empirical analysis by Liebowitz (1980) found that retransmission had not decreased the revenues of the broadcasters.

6. The EC commission was responding to decisions by the European Court of Justice (Cotidel I and Cotidel II), which ruled that material delivered in nonmaterial form, such as satellite transmission, was not subject to the same exhaustion principles that operate if delivery were in tangible form. This meant that retransmission could not occur without authorization (Orf 1990). See also chapter 4.

monitoring challenges for the memberships of the collectives. The Canadian collectives are large. Sometimes one collective represents all rights holders.

A Public Performance Right for Performers and Record Companies

A stylized flow of funds among songwriters, music publishers, performers, the recording industry, broadcasters, and other users of a public performance right is depicted in fig. 4. The flows are shown before and after the introduction of a public performance royalty scheme. In both cases, the record companies earn revenue from the sale of compact discs and cassettes and pay performers according to the terms of their contracts. Songwriters and music publishers are paid a mechanical royalty by the record companies using their compositions. Canada has abandoned the compulsory mechanical right contracting that is currently law in the United States. In Canada, record companies acquire a blanket right to include a copyrighted song in a record from the repertoire of the Canadian Musical Reproduction Rights Agency (CMRRA), a collective that negotiates a contracting framework, including royalty rate provisions for mechanical rights. The collective monitors the contract, but the record companies make payments directly to the music publisher, who pays the composer according to the terms of his or her contract.

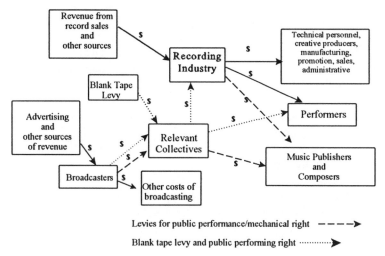

Levies for public performance/mechanical right   — — — —▶

Blank tape levy and public performing right   ··········▶

Note: ₁he public performance right also requires payment by users other than broadcasters. These are not shown in this diagram.

Fig. 4. Public performance right and blank tape levy

Songwriters have another source of revenue from recorded music. The broadcasters and other commercial users of recorded music pay a royalty set by the Copyright Board of Canada for the public performance right to the songs played over the air.[7] These payments are made directly to a collective to which all the copyrights have been assigned for this purpose. The collective then passes on the funds, after deducting its costs, to the members who have made the assignments. Some discretion is exercised on the division of the pool of funds among the different compositions played. This discretion is the root of domestic and international agitation about discrimination.

Composers of songs typically assign their songs to a music publisher. The publisher pays a stipulated percentage, for example, 50 percent, of the royalties it receives to the composers. A successful songwriter may set up his or her own music-publishing firm, but most deal with established music publishers. Many of these are owned by record companies. In Canada and many other countries, the fund from public performance right royalties, after the administrative and other costs of the collective are deducted, is paid directly by the relevant collective to the music publishers and the composers on a 50/50 basis.

The traditional public performance right was an exclusive right granted to the composer of musical works. The new Canadian public performance right for performers and record companies is a remuneration right, which, like the right of the composers, is funded by broadcasters and other commercial users of recorded music. A tariff proposal is submitted to the Copyright Board of Canada. If users contest the proposal, a hearing is held in which spokespersons for the interested parties and expert witnesses present evidence. The board either approves the proposal or imposes an alternative. Once proclaimed, the tariff for a particular user group, for example, commercial broadcasters, allows any Canadian radio station to play recorded music subject to paying the tariff, even if the particular station did not take part in the hearings. The payout accrues equally to collectives representing the record companies and the performers. As a result of this new right, performers will receive payments under contract from their recording companies and payments from their collective. The recording companies will receive public performance royalty payments as well as revenue from the sales of their products.

The balance of payments effect of a public performance right for performers and record companies was a controversial issue in the long and contested debate that preceded its introduction. Keyes and Brunet (1977, 86–89) recommended avoiding any direct balance of payments effect by extending the public performance right only to Canadian recordings. In contrast, the House of

---

7. Broadcasters are the most important users of the public performance right to music. Others are cable services, background music providers, taverns and restaurants, and cinemas.

Commons Subcommittee on the Revision of Copyright proposed that the right be offered to foreign performers and record companies on the basis of reciprocity (House 1985, 50). Most of the music played over the radio and at other public performances is foreign, mainly American. The Canadian content requirements for the playing of music on radio varies. The current benchmark figure is rising from 30 to 35 percent Canadian. National treatment would have resulted in American performers receiving the lion's share of the royalty fund. The House of Commons Subcommittee on the Revision of Copyright declared that "[a]s a matter of principle, all creators should be protected against unauthorized uses of their intellectual property" (House 1985, 55). Despite this statement of principle, Canadian legislators were unlikely to tax Canadian broadcasters to create a fund that would largely benefit American interests.

As a consequence, the Canadian neighboring rights legislation and that of most other countries are based on material reciprocity rather than national treatment. Reciprocity is consistent with the Rome convention and with neighboring rights plans introduced in a variety of European countries. Canada has joined the Rome convention. In the new legislation, the Canadian minister of industry can rule that a Rome convention country is not eligible for reciprocal treatment if it does not grant a right to remuneration that is comparable in scope and duration with the Canadian right. In addition, the minister can grant access to the performers and record companies of other countries that are parties to NAFTA if requested to do so. There are no conditions in the article giving the minister this power. Although Mexico is covered both as a member of the Rome convention and of NAFTA, Mexican music fills a trivial proportion of Canadian air time. The NAFTA provision sends a message that access to the fund is negotiable with the United States. At the moment, the fund is accessible by performers and record companies from Canada or a Rome country with similar programs.

Until 1995, the United States did not recognize a public performance right for recordings as distinct from the compositions contained in them. In that year, the Digital Performance in Sound Recordings Act created a new exclusive right in sound recordings to perform a recorded performance by a digital audio transmission. An interactive transmission of a digital recording from a site on the Internet requires a license from the recording company. A digital transmission is also deemed to be a copy and is subject to a mechanical right royalty.

The United States refuses to join the Rome convention and has instead supported the negotiation of a new treaty covering the public performance rights of record producers and performers. In the negotiations held under the auspices of WIPO, the United States pressed for national treatment of neighboring rights. Both Canada and the United States are signatories to the WIPO Performances and Phonograms Treaty. In the treaty, the exclusive rights granted performers and record producers are given national treatment.[8] The right to remuneration of performers and producers of recordings is also granted national treatment nominally, but under article 15(3) of the treaty a contracting party may "in a notification deposited with the Director General of WIPO, declare that it will apply the provisions of paragraph (1) only in respect of certain uses, or that it will limit their application in some other way, or that it will not apply these provisions at all." Most countries other than the United States will probably take the steps to nullify the default national treatment on the right to remuneration for performers and producers. The United States may have considered that it could opt for national treatment with respect to the Digital Performance in Sound Recordings Act and establish a favorable strategic position from which to continue to lobby for unconditional national treatment.[9]

Because of the dominance of American popular music internationally, the inflows to the United States would outweigh the outflows under reciprocity and the maintenance of current programs in Europe and Canada (Newmark 1992, 173). The Canadian and European programs would likely be altered if the United States ever adopted a program with support comparable to the European or Canadian regimes, so the gain might be short lived. The Canadian and European governments are gambling that the American antipathy toward compulsory licensing schemes and, more importantly, the political strength of the American broadcasters will prevent the adoption of public performance rights for performers and record companies. Whether as a result of pressures from broadcasters or for other reasons, the Digital Performance in Sound Recordings Act was the thinnest of edges of a lean wedge. As Martin comments:

---

8. Performers have an exclusive right to authorize the public performance right of their unfixed performances, the fixation of their unfixed performances, the right to reproduce the fixation of their performances, the right to distribute their recorded performances, the right of rental, and the right to make them available for interactive downloading. The producers are given the exclusive rights of reproduction, distribution, rental, and downloading. Each member of the convention can decide whether the right to remuneration will accrue to producers or performers. If it is to be shared, the country can opt to determine the split in law.

9. Patry opines: "The Digital Performance Rights Act for sound recordings is an excellent example of a *really* dumbed down bill. It has been so dumbed down that even in the form in which it was introduced, it would have failed to accomplish important United States objectives, such as obtaining reciprocal foreign royalties and letting the United States participate in a proposed new multilateral treaty for sound recordings. Notwithstanding its anemic condition on introduction, the process of running the legislative gauntlet of every piggish private sector roadblock drained it of all life and logic" (1996, 146).

> Due to the very limited protection granted under the Act, the amount
> of royalties, if any, that can be expected to flow across the Atlantic
> under material reciprocity will be *de minimis* for the foreseeable future.
> (1996, 754)

The political calculus in the United States would change if the financial
health of the American recording industry were threatened. The new technologies may pose such a threat by making piracy more difficult to control (Acheson
and Maule 1994f). There is no evidence that piracy to date has threatened the
viability of the recording industry, but there is concern that the combination of
digital taping, digital radio, and the Internet may have a profound effect on the
impact of piracy as well as on the legal distribution of music. If it did, all
countries would be searching for alternative means of channeling revenue from
beneficiaries of recorded music to performers and recording companies.

The neighboring rights initiatives for performers is sometimes justified as
a response to a concern that performers are at a disadvantage in contracting with
record companies. If that is the case, nothing in these plans tends to alleviate the
situation. The demand for performers may be increased, but bargaining power
is unlikely to be altered. There has always been a relatively large group of
performers who report earning little income from performing and make ends
meet with part-time work in the rest of the economy. At the same time there is
a professional core of performers with above-average incomes and a star fringe
with extremely high incomes.[10] That distribution has not changed, and there is
nothing in the Canadian public performance right of performers scheme that
would alter bargaining power. Performers will benefit by less than the revenue
transferred from the broadcasters to the extent that contracts with the record
companies become correspondingly less generous. Record companies benefit
directly from their share of the royalties and indirectly if, as we expect, they end
up paying performers less through their contracts.

That piracy concerns influenced the Canadian public performance right for
performers and record companies initiatives receive some support from the
simultaneous introduction of a blank tape levy. This policy develops an
additional income source for record companies, performers, and songwriters.

---

10. After examining the data, Globerman and Rothman reach a tentative conclusion
that many full-time musicians earn above-average incomes. They observe that the
"stereotype of the starving artist is inappropriate when applied to professional performers
in Canada" (1981, 18–19).

The Blank Tape Levy

Blank tape levies deter piracy by raising the costs of copying. In Canada, as in other countries, the development of analogue tape recorders resulted in substantial reproduction of records and films without the permission of the copyright holder (Keon 1982). Home taping is significant, but the bulk of the damage to commercial interests arises from bootleg production. Statistics on black market activities are crude, but the available estimates provide an idea of the scope of the problem. Table 10 reproduces estimates of the importance of pirated music in different countries made by the International Federation of the Phonographic Industry. Keon, who followed this issue closely in Canada, concluded in 1986 that "analysis of potential compensatory schemes to reimburse the industry for lost revenue is called for" (1986, 171).

TABLE 10. Pirate Sound Recordings, 1997

Country	US$ millions
Russia	375
Brazil	250
China	240
India	100
Italy	90
Mexico	65
Saudi Arabia	35
Malaysia	25
Paraguay	20
Greece	20

Source: International Federation of the Phonographic Industry file
<www.ifpi.org/piracy/global_position.htm>.

While further analysis was undertaken, technology did not stand still. Digital audiotape systems have been developed that create copies as good as originals. Machines that can reproduce compact discs are also available at relatively low prices. The RIAA encountered for the first time a significant number of CD-recordables (CD-R) in the pirate marketplace during 1997. The RIAA states that CD-R hardware costs begin around US$400 and the blank discs are less than US$1. The Internet provides a cheap and increasingly rapid means of distributing music in digital formats, such as MP-3. According to the RIAA, advanced compression technology allows users "to download, and in some cases, upload hundreds of full-length, near CD-quality sound recordings, without the permission of the copyright holder."[11]

The industry has emphasized the potential danger to its revenue sources posed by these new technologies. The recent Task Force on the Future of the Canadian Music Industry (Canada 1996c, i) echoed this warning: "Without new copyright initiatives, digital radio and pay audio services and rapidly expanding use of the information highway threaten the ability of Canadian recording artists and record companies to control the use of their work or to be adequately compensated."

In 1997, the Canadian government legalized the widespread practice of taping for personal use. At the same time, it gave songwriters, performers, and record makers a right to receive remuneration from manufacturers and importers of blank audiotape. In this program, collectives representing these beneficiaries have to file a proposed royalty with the Copyright Board. The board considers the proposal and approves either it or a modified tariff. The revenue generated by the levy on blank audiotape will be split among the collectives representing the three eligible parties in proportions set by the board. The only guidance to the board in its deliberations is that the tariffs be fair and equitable.

There is no equivalent of the Rome convention in this context. As with the public performance right for performers and recording companies, the guiding principle governing access to the Canadian program is reciprocity. In two separate clauses of the act (85[1] and 85[2]), the minister is given discretion to grant access to the funds to parties from other countries, first to those who live in countries that have similar policies and have undertaken to grant Canadians access and second to those who live in countries that do not have such policies but are willing to grant Canadians such rights in their country. There is no special mention of NAFTA countries in these clauses.

The United States has a tax on digital audiotape and tape machines. The tax is 2 percent of the value of a tape machine with a minimum of $1 and a maximum of $8 per machine. The tax on blank tape is 3 percent. Any tape machine sold in the United States must have the serial copy management system or its equivalent. The sale of any means of circumventing this system is prohibited.

Two-thirds of the funds are segregated in a Sound Recordings Fund and distributed to nonfeatured musicians appearing on recordings distributed in the United States, to the featured recording artist, and to those who own the copyright in the record (usually the record companies). One-third is distributed

---

11. RIAA press release, March 5, 1998.

to the music publishers and composers of the recorded songs (shared half and half).

Although the tax base is much more limited than in Canada, the American plan has definite parallels to the Canadian one on the payout side. Some initiative to grant reciprocal access to the Canadian plan by American record companies and performers can be expected. The extent of this access is likely to be contested.

The Qualified Ban on Parallel Imports of Books

Book publishing and distribution have given rise to a series of disputes between Canada and the United States, where geographic proximity enhances interdependency between the two markets (see chap. 13). Canadian publishers that obtain the rights to distribute foreign books in Canada have had to compete with American sources of the same book. Canadian bookstores and libraries have often ordered directly from sources in the United States that offer shorter delivery times, cheaper prices, or both. The Canadian publishers claim that this loss of revenues has reduced their ability to support Canadian authors. The publishers claim that they cross-subsidize Canadian writers with monies earned from the sale of foreign books, although there is no mandatory requirement to do so.

The government has lent a sympathetic ear to this argument. One response is the ban on foreign-owned or controlled companies establishing book publishing or retailing operations in Canada, as discussed in chapter 13. To further insulate the Canadian book distribution system from that of other countries, Canada has recently prohibited the importation of a book "where copies of the book were made with the consent of the owner of the copyright in the book in the country where the copies were made, but were imported without the consent of the owner of the copyright in the book in Canada."[12] This prohibition only applies when the Canadian publisher has an exclusive right to distribute the book in Canada or a part of Canada. A bookstore in Canada that sells or has in its inventory a book that meets the above description will also be in violation of the law and subject to prosecution. As noted in chapter 13, what this legislation will mean in terms of deterring Canadian institutional and commercial book buyers from ordering through the American wholesale system is under discussion between buyers, the industry, and the government.

---

12. Section 27.1 of Bill C–32, An Act to Amend the Copyright Act, 45 *Elizabeth II*, 1996, House of Commons of Canada.

Conclusion

Concerted efforts have been made in the past decade to achieve greater conformity in national copyright laws, more uniform and effective enforcement, and a higher average level of protection. The number of bilateral, regional, and international initiatives in this regard has been remarkable. They continue with more emphasis on influencing the contracting basis of the industries. Neighboring rights have created income rights and obligations to pay royalties that did not exist formerly. Parallel import restrictions strengthen the ability of copyright holders to price discriminate in licensing different national markets. A number of countries, including Canada, have adopted neighboring rights regimes that establish funds to remunerate recording companies, performers on records, owners of audiovisual programs, and broadcasters. The same broadcasters and the cable companies provide, grudgingly, the bulk of the revenues for the funds. At the same time, a set of parallel initiatives—called blank tape levies—have also been introduced widely. They provide another set of funds for the same groups. We interpret these events as a response to a feared, but not yet realized, drying up of traditional sources of revenue for participants in the music industry and to a lesser extent the audiovisual industry.

The United States has opposed these initiatives on the grounds that they shut out their companies and performers, which are creating substantial value for broadcasters and others in foreign markets. The American music market has been extremely dynamic in the absence of neighboring rights. There is little doubt that the countries adopting neighboring rights policies want to reward their own performers and are reluctant to do the same for foreign performers. The press in most of the countries inveighs against the Americanization of their cultures with the same enthusiasm that listeners tune into American songs.

American interest groups attack the Canadian and European public performance rights for performers and producers as offending "fairness." An example of this approach is the testimony before the U.S. House Ways and Means Committee's Subcommittee on Trade of Jack Valenti, the president of the Motion Picture Association of America (MPAA), in which he noted:

> the EC member states and potential EC members—nearly thirty countries—are all, every one, either considering adoption or have adopted levy, rental and even public performance regimes. Just in the days since the NAFTA was announced, the EC has released a draft video levy directive that would banish U.S. copyright owners from any share of royalties collected for the home copying of their movies and TV programs.

Now consider this: 40% to 50% of all the works copied, rented or
performed will be U.S. movies or U.S. television programs...(Valenti
1992, 4)

The Canadian blank tape levy has been attacked by Charlene Barshefsky, the
current U.S. Trade Representative. She has disputed the Canadian claims that
Canada has an exemption for cultural industries under NAFTA and has no
national treatment obligations in this area under the WTO agreement. In the
tradition of the informal trade dispute resolution mechanism, she has called for
discussions on this issue while simultaneously drawing attention to her concerns
about the high levels of imports of Canadian durum and spring wheat.
Discussions on the issue reportedly took place at a two-day trade ministers
meeting attended by Canada, Japan, the EU, and the United States.[13] When she
was appointed and before the formal release of the details of the amendments
covering the Canadian policy on parallel book imports, Ms. Barshefsky also
complained to Canadian officials about that initiative.

In the absence of policymakers believing that the Canadian record industry's
future was in jeopardy, it is difficult to understand from a political economy
perspective why Canada adopted a public performance right for performers and
record companies and a blank tape levy at this time. The Canadian record
companies are profitable, and growing. The radio broadcasters have been
relatively unprofitable, and the advertising market was depressed at the time the
legislation was gaining momentum. The broadcasters are all Canadian
companies. The major record companies are largely foreign. Universal has a
record division and is a Canadian company, but it was foreign owned when the
current program was promoted by successive Canadian governments representing different political parties. There is no evidence that there are too few records
available in Canada, and Canadian recording artists are excelling in the
international market.

If the initiatives are responding to trends affecting the appropriability of
income by the music and audiovisual industries, the United States may have to
adopt similar measures. The Audio Home Recording Act of 1992 is a significant
step in that direction. If this is the case, the reciprocity commitments of other
countries will generate a flow of net payments to the United States and reduce
the amounts distributed to national players. The policies are likely to be amended
in response. The Rome convention only covers neighboring rights, and it is quite
elastic in its restrictions. The convention also lacks a workable dispute resolution
mechanism. The architects of the new WIPO treaty claim that it is not designed
to supersede Rome, but the relationship between the two is not clear. The blank
tape levy schemes have no international governance structure. Integrating

---

13. *Globe and Mail*, May 3, 1997.

neighboring rights obligations and blank tape levies with copyright under the WTO is attractive since the same dispute resolution mechanism could be employed.

Europe has not allowed member countries to impose parallel import restrictions on other members. Until the late 1980s, U.S. law concerning parallel imports was unclear. The legal issue was the extent to which the first-sale doctrine exhausted rights created by copyright law. Decisions handed down by various courts at that time led Stern to conclude that "these decisions converge to bring the hitherto uncertain US law in the field into closer accord with EC principles" (1989, 119). In contrast to the usual thrust of Canadian policy, the conditional ban of parallel imports of books protects foreign rights holders by reinforcing their ability to price discriminate. The foreign rights holder can provide the Canadian licensee with greater monopoly power. The Canadian assumption is that the Canadian licensee does not just pay more for the altered right but that the licensee earns more rents and spends them supporting the publishing of Canadian books. Since NAFTA addressed intellectual property, it is logical to develop a common regional position on parallel imports of copyrighted material as a stepping stone toward consideration of the issue at the international level.

CHAPTER 15

Censorship, Content Classifications, the V-Chip, and Howard Stern

Mad cow disease is to meat what violence is to television programming. In each case consumers want the product in a manner that is neither contaminated nor harmful. Consequently, standards are introduced, phytosanitary measures for food products and conditions for program content. Because both involve restrictions, these measures can be administered in ways that affect trade. The EC, for example, has health standards for beef that the British government views as excessively restrictive in terms of British exports.

The difference between the two is that anyone who is not suicidal agrees that mad cow disease is best avoided. Consumers do not agree on what media content is detrimental to development nor on the best means of adjusting the menu. This disagreement is reflected in different policies across media. Some of these differences reflect the varying ability to exclude targeted groups from harmful content in books, magazines, music, film, and television programming. Others may reflect a perception that the developmental impact of content varies across media. For example, the immediacy and intimacy of television and the movies arguably generate a greater impact on a developing child than does a book.

Censorship, as we use the term, appears in different guises. The state may proscribe some material or the industry may "voluntarily" restrict what it offers, either because producers and distributors share the social concerns of the state or because state regulation is forestalled. In some instances, regulation prohibits access of a target group, for example, children, to particular content. For other content, prohibitions are general. The boundaries dividing what is acceptable and what is not may depend on criteria, such as community standards, that vary across the country, state, or province. The law may allow private possession and personal access to specified content but make illegal its distribution to the public.

Instead of prohibiting, regulation may inform individual or family choices by classifying content. Prohibition or classification requires putting diverse content into a limited set of categories. The crudest partition is binary—acceptable or forbidden. Informational labeling may require much finer distinctions.

Many religious and fraternal groups provide another layer of control in a modern society. They recommend or admonish members not to consume particular movies or books or products produced by specified companies. These guidelines, or in some cases more organized responses like boycotts, do not have the force of law, but failure to comply may weigh heavily on particular members. In some cases, these groups may interfere with the ability of nonmembers to access the content in question, within and sometimes beyond the elastic bounds of the law.

Judgments vary on where the line should be drawn in exercising censorship. The debates on the issue invariably call on scientific evidence about the connections between what people see, hear, and read and what they become. Experts disagree on causal links and the effectiveness of policy alternatives. Most citizens are not fully conversant with the scientific evidence, so public opinion varies even more than informed opinion. For example, in the debate leading to the adoption of a rating scheme for television programs in the United States, the American Medical Association (AMA) made a strong statement on the effects of television violence on children and society:

> For many years, the AMA has actively investigated and analyzed the deleterious effects that TV violence has on children. Since 1976, the AMA has recognized TV violence as a risk factor which threatens the health and welfare of young Americans and the future of our society.[1]

A decade earlier, in discussing the censorship of films, Randall provided a more qualified assessment:

> Worry about erotica or the depiction of violence is a concern that also appears to be reasonably held by many reasonable persons. Unfortunately, there is no conclusive evidence that such portrayal in the movies has or does not have harmful effects; hence, it is impossible to say how justified or unjustified some of the fears may be. (1985, 516)

Government censorship, of which policies toward violence are a part, has a long history in the print, film, and broadcast media as well as in public speaking. Censorship has traditionally focused on sex, sacrilegious material, obscenity, political views, incitements to hate, language, and violence. In recent years, the list has expanded to cover areas in which values were under pressure to change, for example, on sexual orientation and gender roles. Freedom of expression constraints have exerted an uneven discipline on censorship in democratic societies. Each society sets its own standards. Asian leaders, for

---

1. April 8, 1997, submission to FCC regarding CS Docket No. 97–55 by the American Medical Association.

example, talk about Asian standards as being different from those of North America or Western Europe.[2]

Recently, a number of countries has initiated programs to facilitate viewer control of television programming. The combination of a hardware filtering device, the V-chip, and classification requirements are being adopted in North America, throughout Europe, and in some Asian countries. The television classification scheme parallels a similar program that evolved in the North American film industry. Because of the difficulty of determining what rating a film or a television program should receive in a classification scheme, the existing film and new television regulations can also be diverted to serve other ends. The fuzziness of the criteria create a zone of temptation within which protectionist goals can be pursued.

Censorship, Classification, and the Film Industry

In the United Kingdom, municipal fire regulations were introduced at an early stage in the evolution of cinemas because of the danger associated with the combustion of films. These regulations became an instrument for controlling the exhibition of films that were seen to be morally harmful, especially for young persons. Local communities have always been anxious to impose their own standards, as illustrated in the film *Cinema Paradiso* where the parish priest undertakes to preview all the films and cut out the offending parts. These were reassembled in a collage for later viewing.[3]

From the Production Code to the MPAA Rating System

In the United States, Chicago introduced a motion picture censorship ordinance in 1907, and by 1921 seven of the 48 states had censorship legislation. The Supreme Court denied First Amendment protection to the content of films in 1915, when the justices ruled that films were solely articles of commerce. In 1922, as a result of public pressure and the threat of more restrictive legislation, the major studios set up the Motion Picture Producers and Distributors of

---

2. In recognition of differing standards, Rupert Murdoch's Star TV removed the BBC from signals distributed by satellite to viewers in China and HarperCollins withdrew from a book-publishing contract with Chris Patten, the former governor of Hong Kong, because of material allegedly critical of China. The book was subsequently published as *East and West* by Macmillan, 1998.

3. When nudity was first permitted in films shown in Canada, the films were distributed with additional footage of the nude scenes so as to reduce the incentive for projectionists to remove these parts for other use.

America (MPPDA) with a mandate to preview scripts.[4] The MPPDA established a formula for vetting source material.

Difficulties arose with the introduction of sound after 1929, as controls were needed for both visual and audio material. In 1931, there was pressure for a congressional inquiry into film production as a result of the popularity of gangster films associated with the press coverage given to persons like Al Capone. Some argued that there was a link between movie attendance and juvenile crime. By addressing the concerns over the portrayal of violence, which had substantial box office appeal, producers switched to attracting audiences with an increased portrayal of sex.[5]

A Production Code was published but not rigorously enforced until after the Catholic Church formed the Legion of Decency in 1934 and organized boycotts occurred in some major American cities. Joseph Breen was appointed head of the Production Code Administration (PCA). Under his leadership the code became an effective constraint. The PCA had to approve a film before a member studio could release it. No member could exhibit a movie in its theaters that did not bear a PCA seal. The Production Code regulated the content of films along a number of dimensions:

> The basic premise of the code is that the movies as entertainment and as art affect the moral life of a people. Although it is admitted that art in itself may be "unmoral," art as a product of a person's mind and as an influence upon those who come in contact with it is claimed to have "a deep moral significance." (Inglis 1985, 378)

Inglis notes that no proof of this proposition is offered.

The code appealed to natural law as "written in the hearts of all mankind, the great underlying principles of right and justice dictated by conscience" (Inglis 1985, 379). Injustice could be portrayed as long as the instance was clearly an aberration within a system that was basically fair. For example, an individual trial could be depicted as corrupt as long as the court system was presented as just. If the plotline required immoral behavior, the movie would only be approved if other moral elements and a just punishment provided compensation. The moral balance had to be positive. Prevailing prejudices and racial biases were hidden. In order to gain PCA approval the Warner Bros. film *Zola*, which was released on August 11, 1937, "managed to tell the Dreyfus story

---

4. Will H. Hays, a former postmaster general in the Harding administration, was its first president, followed by Eric Johnston and Jack Valenti, a former aide to President Lyndon Johnson, who has been its president since May 1966. The name of the organization has changed over time.

5. Today, many Asian films are notable for their absence of sex and inclusion of violence.

without the word Jew ever being uttered, although Dieterle did highlight the anti-Semitism issue with a bit of telltale camera work, pulling in for a close-up on the word when it appeared on a military document" (Schatz 1988, 214).

Under Breen's guidance, the Production Code developed through interactions among producers and the PCA. Detailed prohibitions or guidelines evolved constraining obscenity, vulgarity, profanity, the expression of unpatriotic sentiments, nudity, suggestive dances, references to alcoholism or drugs, and the use of salacious titles. Repellant subjects such as hangings, surgical operations, the selling of women, brutality, and the branding of animals were not to be shown. Where the plot required, a director had to find a sanitized means of alluding to the controversial activity or subject. For example, a suicide was never shown on screen, but a shot off screen would indicate that it had happened. Standards from other countries were also integrated into the guidelines. American films showed married couples sleeping in single beds to meet a requirement of the British Board of Film Censors (Maltby 1993, 37–72).

The Production Code regulated the advertising and promotion of films. It also deterred the promotion of products within the film:

> Although occasionally high-pressure publicists for national products try to inject their sponsors' wares into films and at times bribe studio employees to achieve their ends, every effort is made to avoid unnecessary close-ups of radios and other items showing the name of the product, outdoor scenes showing advertising signs or billboards, and dialogue mentioning trade names. (Inglis 1985, 388)

After 1942, there was no explicit constraint on exhibition. In 1945, the MPPDA became the MPAA. On May 26, 1952, in *Burstyn v. Wilson*, the Supreme Court confirmed that the First Amendment applied to films. The case involved the censoring of Roberto Rossellini's 40-minute film, *The Miracle,* because its content was deemed sacrilegious. As well as granting a film a First Amendment defense, the court required timely decisions by censors. In the end, the only legal ground for censorship was obscenity. How obscenity was to be determined was vague. In some decisions the Supreme Court established community standards, which it acknowledged would vary among regions of the United States, as the appropriate measure. In others, the Supreme Court sometimes approved decisions on particular films that were binding for the country as a whole. A 1974 example was the unanimous judgment that *Carnal Knowledge* was not obscene, even though it had been judged so in Georgia, presumably through the application of local standards.

With shifting tastes and a restless creative community, the constraints were constantly being tested and altered. In the early 1960s, United Artists broke ranks with other MPAA members and successfully defied the code by releasing Otto Preminger's *The Moon is Blue* and *The Man with the Golden Arm* without the seal of approval (Randall 1985, 524). The PCA made binary decisions. A movie was either approved for everyone or not approved. There were no conditional approvals. The first break in this policy was the introduction in 1966 of an SMA (suitable for mature audiences) label to cover films such as the two Preminger offerings. In 1968, a full rating system was introduced, with films classified in four categories (G, PG, R, and X). The categories depended on defining material suitable for viewers of different ages, and the rating criteria related to theme, language, nudity, sex, and violence:

> Contrary to popular but uninformed notions, violence has been a key factor in ratings. (Many violent films would have been given X ratings, but most of the directors chose, on their own, to revise the extremely violent sequences in order to receive an R rating.) (Valenti 1983, 367)

Currently the American movie rating system classifies a film as G, PG, PG–13, R, or NC–17,[6] with, in some instances, brief informational annotations about why the film received a particular rating. Under, the rating system a producer can assess his or her film as X without submission to the rating agency. The shift in responsibility that accompanied the development of a rating system was significant. The MPAA became a categorizing rather than a censoring agency. Enforcement of the age restrictions for viewing films in different categories was made the responsibility of exhibitors. This responsibility was voluntary, and its effectiveness varied with the intensity of local pressures. Enforcement of the classifications is more difficult for videos. Observance of the voluntary rating scheme is endorsed by the Video Software Dealers Association, an organization of video store operators

The PCA and the subsequent rating system applied to members of the MPAA but were available to independent American and foreign producers. With the PCA, fees rose with the value of the budget of the film. No charge was levied if the film was rejected. Fees for foreign films were one-half the fee charged for comparable American films. Until 1942, a foreign film could not be exhibited in a cinema owned by an MPAA member without certification. In 1938, the

---

6. These symbols are trademarked and can only be used if films are approved by the MPAA. The X designation was never trademarked, and any X rating is now self-imposed. A side effect of the Production Code was an allegation that "through the Code the majors exercised a practical censorship over the whole industry, restricting the production of pictures treating controversial subjects and hindering the development of innovative approaches to drama or narrative by companies that might use innovation as a way of challenging the majors' monopoly power" (Maltby 1993, 69).

MPPDA reported that 98 percent of all the pictures exhibited in the United States were submitted to and approved by the PCA (Inglis 1985, 386).

After 1942, as the majors divested their theater chains, independent cinemas and the art house circuit provided a wider set of exhibition venues for foreign films. The homogenizing of quality through the application of the code to American films created marketing opportunities for foreign films:

> Not all imported films were "art," but many offered a striking alternative to Hollywood's slick products by revealing slices of life and dramatic elements that American films, following the strictures of the Production Code, had failed to develop. Imported films, moreover, were often made more on an artisan and less on a factory basis, and consequently seemed to present more personalized statements than the sanitized and anonymous Hollywood product. Italian neorealist films, the French nouvelle vague, and pictures such as Dreyer's *Ordet* in the mid-1950s, revealed new dimensions of the cinema to American audiences, after which Hollywood's fare seemed anemic and inconsequential in comparison. Not a few foreign films were able to capitalize on sexual content and frankness, which the production Code rendered taboo and which television could not deliver into living rooms."
> (Guback 1985, 477)

The success of this foreign competition was partly responsible for the breakdown of the PCA and the adoption of the rating system.

As long as a favorable rating was an asset in obtaining bookings, the rating system posed a potential barrier to entry for foreign films. Independent and foreign producers regularly charged the MPAA with discriminating against their films when they received a different rating than the producers believed appropriate or commercially advantageous (Randall 1985, 527). Local communities have also used the rating system to punish particular content. Some states tax cinemas or make licensing decisions guided by the ratings of the films exhibited. Some newspapers also refuse to accept advertisements for X-rated films.

Judging the net effect of the self-regulation of film in the United States on foreign trade is as difficult as determining the "moral balance" of a film. The pervasive control of the PCA and easier access to theaters and other distribution windows create opportunities for foreign films. On the other hand, the governance structure of the rating system for films creates a potential for opportunistic behavior by the dominant players in the industry. An analogue would be allowing the American automobile manufacturers to rate foreign cars with respect to difficult to measure criteria such as comfort and road worthiness.

There is no evidence that opportunism has been exercised, but adopting a rating process that is not controlled by one element of the industry would diminish the suspicion of bias.

Film Censorship in Canada

Film distribution is under the jurisdiction of the Canadian provinces. All the larger provinces have a board or government department that approves and rates films. The Maritime Provinces have pooled their efforts and created a common office to exercise this function. The provinces have also cooperated to create a national rating and stickering system for videos. Unlike the PCA, which affected the content of movies as they were produced, the Canadian censorship boards play a more passive role. They assess and categorize movies, mostly foreign, that are seeking permission to be distributed in their jurisdictions.

Censorship in Ontario, Canada's largest province, dates from 1911. Speaking in support of the Theatres and Cinematographs Act (later the Theatres Act), which had been championed by the Social & Moral Reform Association, the premier of the province expressed concern "about the evils inherent in motion pictures and the possible influence on the young." A Censor Board was created and given the power to either permit or reject any film and suspend the license of an exhibitor. In the 1930s the board began to move toward classification. In 1981, a four-category system—Family, Parental Guidance, Adult Accompaniment, and Restricted—was adopted. In the mid-1980s the board was renamed the Ontario Film Review Board (OFRB) and jurisdiction was extended to include videos. Under the current system, 16 short pieces of information may be provided in addition to a rating. For example, the OFRB gave *Crash,* a film directed by the Canadian David Cronenberg, an R rating and attached the informational comments "sexual content" and "violence."

In 1995–96, the board's panels reviewed 3,103 films. Seven percent were rated as Family, 15.7 percent as Parental Guidance, 15.8 percent as Adult Accompaniment, and 59.8 percent as Restricted (1.7 percent were not approved). The last category included mainly adult sex films that contained violence, underage participants, or abusive behavior toward women.

The incidence of censorship varies among the provinces. Alberta is at the laissez-faire end of the spectrum. The last banning of a theatrical film there occurred in the late 1980s. The film *Silent Night Deadly Night* was described as a "Santa Claus slasher film." In Alberta, videos are classified by a separate, industry-administered system. The video of *Silent Night Deadly Night* was not banned but was marketed as "Banned in Alberta!" in the province's video outlets. The board currently acts solely as a classification board. At times producers request that their films be rated more harshly in order to enhance their marketing appeal.

Censorship, Classification, and Television Programming

Broadcasting standards have followed a different evolutionary path in different countries. The regulatory processes usually allow for a public complaint process and include public broadcasters, whereby the state as owner can directly determine what material is broadcast. John Reith, the first director of the BBC, played an active role in determining the type of material broadcast on the British airwaves. There was little chance of having anything offensive broadcast with Reith at the helm. His actions were so restrictive in limiting choice that they contributed to the success of Radio Luxembourg, which broadcast popular music and commercials in English from a location not subject to British regulations, and later to the operation of pirate radio stations located on ships anchored in the North Sea.[7]

In the United States the television industry came under almost immediate pressure to control content.[8] The National Association of Broadcasters (NAB) adopted its first television code in 1952. The code explicitly constrained sexual and violent material. It was attacked on one side by the American Civil Liberties Union as a violation of the First Amendment and on the other by a sequence of politicians determined to establish tougher standards. Concern with violence resulted in a family viewing policy in the mid-1970s, which created a window of time in the evening in which only programs suitable for children would be aired. The family viewing policy was challenged in the courts by the Writers Guild of America in 1976. The District Court ruled that enforcement of the NAB code violated the First Amendment, but the decision was vacated and remanded on appeal because the court was deemed to lack jurisdiction. The Justice Department then brought an antitrust suit, alleging that the NAB code restricted advertising to the detriment of consumers and sponsors. A settlement was reached, and the code became inoperative.

Pressure continued in the 1980s, and a consumer boycott was threatened. In response, the major networks reduced the number of action shows, which were a focal point of the campaign. In 1990, the Television Program Improvement Act was passed, which gave the firms responsible for what appeared on the screens antitrust immunity while they developed joint standards. The NAB drafted a code that was to act as a guideline for broadcasters.

---

7. The rise of Radio Luxembourg in the face of opposition from the public broadcaster and supporting interests in the United Kingdom is documented in Nichols (1983).

8. MacCarthy (1995) provides a detailed account of the history of U.S. self-regulation in television.

Despite this constant agitation, the standards have become more permissive over time. Muto has provided a chronology of the relaxation of constraints on network television. Her list includes such television landmarks as:[9]

1. Arthur Godfrey saying *damn* and *hell* in 1950
2. Ozzie and Harriet Nelson shown in bed together in 1952
3. Yvette Mimieux wearing a bikini in a *Dr. Kildare* episode in 1961
4. the featuring of the first divorced lead characters in *The Odd Couple* in the 1970s
5. the treatment of homosexuality and rape in different episodes of *All in the Family* in the 1970s
6. the beheading of a man in *Shogun* in 1980
7. the discussion of masturbation in a *Seinfeld* episode called "The Contest" in 1992.

As channel capacity increased and more differentiated services became available, the television menu has become increasingly diverse. The milestones that presumably were shocking at the time seem quaint in comparison with the range of content routinely shown on a modern cable system. The First Amendment continued to bar enforcement of an industry code and frustrate those concerned with the impact on children of unsuitable programming. Technology in the form of the V-chip provided another path. Parents could be empowered to control more effectively the programs to be watched by their children. The U.S. Telecommunications Act of 1996 requires that parents be informed about what programming is about to be shown and be provided with blocking technology that will allow them to censor violent, sexual, or other programming that they deemed harmful to their children.

The history of censorhip in film and television indicates that there has always been concern about program content, including the portrayal of violence, and that society has supported governments in introducing a range of control measures.[10] The current V-chip initiative is merely the present manifestation of this debate. We are particularly interested in the cross-border effects of this policy.

---

9. *Wall Street Journal* story by Sheila Muto, reprinted in the *Globe and Mail*, September 18, 1995, A13.

10. While we focus on television content in this section, similar concerns have been expressed and rating systems introduced in relation to computer software, video games and on-line services, while the recording industry informs consumers through labeling (Roberts 1997).

The V-Chip

There are a number of ways to address the issue of television program content. First, with no government intervention, viewers may decide what they and their children watch with minimal information provided about the program content; second, scripts may be previewed before the program is made, a technique similar to the MPPDA's Production Code; third, existing programs may be rated so as to inform viewers as to what to expect; and, fourth, a viewer may program a television set equipped with a device to detect rating information encoded in the program signal about the level of violence or other sensitive categories and block chosen programming.

The V-chip is a detecting and blocking device patented by Tim Collings, a professor of electrical engineering at Simon Fraser University in Burnaby, British Columbia. The V in V-chip stands for viewer control rather than violence. The chip can read rating information inserted into the vertical blanking interval—a recurring moment in signal transmission when content is not being carried. In North America, the V-chip program requires that new television sets be equipped with a blocking device. A viewer will have to invest in either a television set that has the functionality built in or in an add-on.[11] There is a strong incentive to agree on a common standard for the blocking device. Otherwise, television sets will become unnecessarily expensive, particularly in Canada, which has the smaller market.

The blocking device requires a compatible rating classification system. Both Canada and the United States have relied on industry groups to suggest an appropriate set of categories and a process for determining a program's classification. Since programming is licensed internationally and foreign broadcast signals are received directly and retransmitted in other countries, these decisions potentially affect the international licensing and carriage of content.

In Canada, the chip will have to accommodate four systems: the Canadian English system, the Canadian French system, the system for pay and PPV television, and the American system. This requirement could be reduced to three systems if the Canadian English rating system and the American one could be replaced with a common system. In the Canadian field trials, the users strongly supported developing a common English-language system for the two countries.

At one point in the CRTC hearings on the V-chip, there was discussion of an approach whereby Canadian standards would be applied to all signals entering Canadian homes, with distributors required to curtail or scramble any program that contravened the Canadian code. The cable industry opposed any

---

11. In the Canadian system, the cable industry is responsible for making available affordable V-chip devices to subscribers.

approach that would require the curtailment or encryption of American programming, arguing that it could result in a trade dispute.[12]

The governments of the two countries have also considered adding regulations based on the ratings.[13] For example, the right to transmit programming receiving a particular rating can be denied during part of the broadcast day. This measure goes beyond the spirit of the V-chip as empowering the viewer and is using the rating system, designed for its functioning, to impose blanket regulation. For example, some critics of the current system advocate a "safe harbor" time zone in which non-family-oriented programming would be barred. Harmonization of these regulatory measures would also avoid some conflicts.

The process leading to the introduction of the Canadian classificatory scheme is described in table 11. The CRTC has approved a six-level system plus an exempt category that uses descriptive guidelines to evaluate content. The six levels are: Children, Children over 8 years, Family, Parental Advisory, Over 14 Years, and Adults. The exempt category includes news, sports, documentaries, and other informational programming, talk shows, music videos, and variety programming. English-language pay and PPV services will be allowed to continue to use the ratings of the provincial cinema ratings boards for feature films. French-language programming, including pay and PPV, will use the rating system of Quebec's Régie du Cinéma.

The CRTC has restricted programming that contains scenes of violence intended for adult audiences to the 9 P.M. to 6 A.M. period. After 9 P.M. the broadcasters must provide sufficient information about programming to enable parents to make informed choices. The before 9 P.M. safe harbor from violent programming does not apply to broadcasters who have CRTC-permitted substitution rights over programming.

The United States and the V-Chip

In 1996, the U.S. Congress passed the Telecommunications Act, which acknowledges the impact of television on children and calls for "parental choice in television programming."[14] To achieve the latter goal, the act requires that the FCC determine a suitable blocking device and set up an advisory committee to recommend procedures to rate video programs for sexual, violent, and other

---

12. CRTC Public Notice 1996–36, March 14, 1996, para. 2.c.ii.

13. Among the issues that have arisen are how to rate live programs. Another is the rating of series. Should the series receive one rating or should each episode be judged separately?

14. Telecommunications Act of 1996, Pub. L. No. 104–104, 110 Stat. 56 (codified at 15 U.S.C. Secs. 79, 79z–5c, 79z–6, 5714; 18 U.S.C. Secs. 1462, 1465, 2422; and scattered sections of 47 U.S.C. [1996]).

indecent material. On March 12, 1998, the FCC approved the Industry's TV Parental Guidelines, which contain six ratings:

1. TV-Y, which is appropriate for children of all ages
2. TV-Y7, which is suitable for children seven and above
3. TV-G, which is suitable for all ages
4. TV-PG, where parental guidance is suggested because of infrequent coarse language, limited violence, and some suggestive sexual dialogue and situations
5. TV-14, which may be inappropriate for children under 14 because of sophisticated themes, strong language, and sexual content
6. TV-M, which is suitable for "mature audiences only" because of profane language, graphic violence, and explicit sexual content

Additional information is also provided where appropriate, concerning four categories: S (sex), L (coarseness of language), V (violence), or D (suggestiveness of dialogue). An on-screen icon shows the rating to the viewer at the beginning of a show. The TV Parental Guidelines do not rate sports, news, commercials, or promotions.

TABLE 11. Chronology of the Development of the V-Chip in Canada

Date	Event
December 1989	Multiple killings of women at Montreal's École Polytechnique.
November 1992	Petition with 1.3 million signatures calls for a ban on television violence.
February 1993	Formation of Action Group on Violence on Television (AGVOT), an organization representing different components of the Canadian broadcasting industry.
November 1994	The Canadian Broadcast Standards Council (CBSC) rules that the American children's program, "*Mighty Morphin Power Rangers*," violated the Canadian Association of Broadcasters' (CAB) violence code. YTV and the TVA network withdraw the program, while Global Communications Inc., broadcasts a modified version of the program.
April 1995	CRTC announces a public hearing on violence in television programming.
March 1996	The CRTC issues a decision on television violence policy.
July 1996	AGVOT requests an extension. Notes that since the United States is not expected to release its program classification system until February 1997, the delay will facilitate achieving compatibility between the Canadian and United States systems.
April 1997	AGVOT proposes, and CRTC accepts a six-level rating system. Programming which contains scenes of violence intended for adult audiences shall not be telecast before the late evening viewing period, defined as 9 P.M. to 6 A.M.
April 1997	AGVOT reports that major broadcasters will display ratings on-screen by the fall of 1997.

Source: CRTC Public Notices 1995/5, April 3, 1995; 1996–36, March 14, 1996; and 1997–80, June 18, 1997.

The use of the industry-developed guidelines is voluntary, with each broadcaster deciding whether or not to apply the ratings to its programs. BET has chosen not to participate in the TV Parental Guidelines system, while NBC has decided to continue to apply only the six age-based categories.

The FCC has chosen a standard for hardware that is compatible with the approved rating system. Although the FCC has not required that television receiver manufacturers provide for alternative rating systems, it "encourages" providing for additional rating systems to the extent practicable and expressed a belief that the market will allow accommodation of additional rating systems.[15] The use of parental control filters for on-line services has been addressed by firms such as Microsoft, Net Nanny, and Solid Oak Software, which have developed techniques to block unwanted material and provide audit trails. The Platform for Internet Content Selection (PICS) allows users to filter on-line services accessed by personal computers. PICS is described as an open labeling platform that is designed so "any given piece of content on the Internet can be rated essentially an infinite number of different ways by an infinite number of different parties."[16] Thus, the problem of accommodating different rating standards seems to have been resolved for on-line services, while it has yet to be finally worked out for television signals.

The use of different standards among countries may be necessary to accommodate different values. If so, the differences can generate possible trade frictions. Although there are differences between the American and Canadian English classifications, they are small. There is reason to be optimistic that the remaining differences can be resolved through negotiation.

Censorship and "Live" Content

The Howard Stern Case

Live television programs are difficult to rate before the fact, as their content varies widely and cannot readily be controlled. The same holds for radio talk shows. In 1997, Howard Stern's talk show was "imported" by two Canadian radio stations, Q107 in Toronto and CHOM-FM in Montreal. Stern's show has been controversial from its first Canadian broadcast, during which he made denigrating remarks about French Canadians and women and hurled obscenities and insults at listeners in a manner foreign to the traditions of Canadian radio.

---

15. FCC Docket No. 97–206, Adopted: March 12, 1998.

16. Daniel Weitzner, PICS Policy cochairman, at the conference The Jurisprudence of Ratings, Benjamin N. Cardozo School of Law, Yeshiva University, New York, March 25, 1996. The conference proceedings are on videotape on file at the Cardozo Law School Library.

At the time of the launch, several radio industry observers suggested that Stern wouldn't last three months on Canadian radio, as Canadians differ significantly from Americans in this dimension. They predicted that racist or sexist humor would not be commercially successful in the Canadian culture.[17] The evidence is not consistent with these predictions. By early 1998, newspapers were reporting that "Stern's numbers in Toronto constitute the biggest debut he has ever had in any of the more than forty markets that carry his show"[18] and "in Toronto, Stern tripled Q107's ratings to the No. 1 radio morning spot in that market. CHOM in Montreal also had impressive gains."[19] The program also generated a wave of criticism from a number of sources including competitors.[20]

The law in Canada with respect to freedom of speech differs from that of the United States. In America, the show is shielded by the First Amendment. The Canadian Charter of Rights guarantees free speech, but it is subject to "such reasonable limits . . . as can be demonstrably justified in a free and democratic society." Canadian broadcasters are constrained as a condition of license from allowing "obscene or profane language" or comments that are "likely to expose an individual or a group or class of individuals to hatred or contempt" on a variety of bases.

The Canadian Broadcast Standards Council (CBSC) enforces a voluntary broadcasting code of ethics, which the CRTC has sanctioned. The council investigates complaints that these guidelines are not being met. In response to complaints, it released two assessments of Stern's show. The first judged that the program was in violation of the industry's ethics code and the sex-role portrayal code and asked the stations involved to inform the public of the decision and take remedial measures. The second deemed the remedial efforts of Toronto station Q107 ineffective and inadequate. The station was granted a chance to make them effective or it would be expelled from the CBSC. The other shoe would fall when Q107 sought a license renewal before the CRTC. If that

---

17. *Ottawa X Press,* January 15, 1998, 5.

18. *Globe and Mail,* January 9, 1998, A10, A11.

19. The Board of Broadcast Measurement indicated that Q107, which began carrying the Stern show on September 2, 1997, went from 4.1 to 11 percent. That tied the station with CHFI-FM and CHUM-FM (at 12.2 percent) at the top of the FM stations in Toronto. The only station with a larger audience is CFRB-AM with 12.2 percent. The stations hardest hit were CFNY-FM, CISS-FM, and Mix 99 (owned by Standard Radio). CBC Radio One rose from 6.1 to 6.6 percent (*Ottawa X Press,* January 15, 1998, 5).

20. Gary Slaight, who is head of Standard Radio, the owner of two radio stations losing ground to Stern in the Ottawa market, said that "it is incredible that an American morning man has the ability to 'intimidate' Canada's radio industry and regulators. He also feels it's "pathetic" that two large radio chains are incapable of pulling together a home-grown morning show" (*Ottawa X Press,* January 15, 1998, 5).

occurred, the courts would likely be busy sorting out whether this type of programming was or was not protected under the Canadian Charter of Rights.[21]

CHOM-FM succeeded in avoiding a second investigation of its broadcast of the Stern show by censoring it. The station acquired new equipment that allowed seamless editing of the show. In the monitoring period, the cuts in content varied from a few words to entire segments of the show. Two ran as long as 20 minutes. For long pauses, the station uses stop sets—station-generated content such as news, information, and commercials—to maintain continuity. Stern has presumably agreed to have his show broadcast in an edited form in Canada.

The CBSC was not persuaded by what it called the comedic defense—the argument that the Stern show is comedy, distasteful to some listeners but not intended as serious social comment. The decision states: "Sexist, abusive and racist comments, and commentary advocating violence against identifiable groups may well be amusing to some people but, in violating the CAB Codes or the Radio Regulations, 1986, they do not pass the test of broadcast acceptability."

Conclusion

The censorship of content is an ongoing story. Community values are as important in determining the incidence of censorship as are constitutional constraints. In the United States, the First Amendment of the Constitution did not prevent the detailed regulation of film content by the industry for over 20 years. Court cases sometimes lead and sometimes follow public opinion. A decade or so after the 1952 Supreme Court decision granting First Amendment protection to films, the MPAA's production code was replaced with a rating system.

A battery of sources—print reviews, television shows, Internet sites, and word of mouth—enrich the crude information provided by the rating system. There is much wider diversity of content available today than at any previous time in North American history. A large segment of the population in both Canada and the United States may find some of the films that are currently available distasteful, even disgusting, but this majority appears willing to limit regulation to the protection of children and other vulnerable groups in society. This equilibrium may not be stable. Our reading of the history of censorship is that public opinion as to where the boundary should be drawn can swing widely.

Censorship can balkanize the distribution of content within a country and internationally. When reflecting different regional and national values it is a

---

21. The decisions can be found on http://www.cbsc.ca, the first released November 11, 1997, and the second, March 23, 1998.

legitimate interference with commerce. Unfortunately, there is no national consensus. Whatever the strength and stability of the political support for censorship, the boundaries around what is acceptable or not are often imprecise. People sharing the consensus often have different ideas about what should be included and excluded. This fuzziness can be exploited for protectionist purposes. With the current, historically liberal, censorship policies in Canada and the United States, there is less scope for this type of strategic behavior. In Canada's case, there are few, if any, cases of recent censorship that have generated either a noticeable public response or any significant charges that the provincial systems discriminate against foreign films. Similarly, American censorship has not been a trade irritant.

In both countries, censorship has been largely displaced by classification. This substitution raises a more subtle concern with respect to trade—the manipulation of the rating system to discriminate among different films and television programs. Again, there is little evidence of systematic bias in the rating systems in place. The current classification systems only provide crude information and are buttressed by far richer private systems of information, which are more difficult to manipulate because of their lack of structure. The most common manipulation of the current systems appears to be at the trash end of the spectrum, where producers seek a severe rating to exploit the "forbidden fruit" syndrome. The producers want their products to be identified as being on the edge or beyond.

When the concept of a rating system was applied to television and coupled with a blocking device, the potential for trade frictions was enhanced. The policy decisions in Canada and the United States had the potential for affecting trade in hardware as well as a large volume of television programming. The beginning of the policy interaction between Canada and the United States was not promising. The chair of the CRTC gave speeches in the United States outlining the Canadian concern and its intentions to implement a Canadian plan regardless of what the United States did. Despite this beginning, the rhetoric quickly cooled and an informal process of cooperation developed. By early 1996, the CRTC included a number of uncharacteristically moderate statements supporting cooperation in its public notice on policy on violence in television programming. These included:

1.   "[D]ifferences between American and Canadian efforts in either timing or approach are quickly narrowing. The opportunity now exists for both countries to work together to implement a practical and affordable parental control system to combat TV violence."

2. "The Commission is also confident that, even if a North American rating system is not achieved in the near future, the cable industry will work with U.S. border broadcasters and U.S. services delivered by satellite to ensure that their programming is rated in a manner that is compatible with Canadian V-chip technology. The Commission is especially encouraged by the participation of two American broadcasters in the current V-chip trials, and by the willingness of U.S. border broadcasters, as communicated to U.S. trade officials, to participate in a classification system."

3. "In light of these developments and commitments, the Commission is satisfied that, rather than implementing interim measures such as those suggested in Notice of Public Hearing CRTC 1995–5, the industry can move directly to common solutions with the U.S., characterized by a determined and accelerated joint effort to implement a practical and affordable parental control system."[22]

The informal process of conflict resolution has worked well in an area in which there was a common political purpose on both sides of the border. Whether the results of this cooperation will achieve what V-chip supporters seek is moot. The eventual impact of the V-chip initiative is unclear. In part it depends on supportive private developments that enrich the information available to viewers. Critics on both sides of the border have been concerned about the impact of an official system on choices of advertisers as to what programming they will support and the derivative effects on creative freedom. Allan King, the president of the Directors Guild of Canada, has argued that the classification system is bound to cause harm by ignoring context with a personal "First Amendment" plea: "If the 20th century has taught us anything, it is that the suppression of expression destroys freedom."[23] Richard Wolf, the executive producer of NBC's *Law & Order,* claims that advertisers will flee before buying time on shows with ratings for violence or sex. ABC's *NYPD Blue* posted content warnings on its show and found that advertisers were slow to support it. The show sold advertising at lower than the going rates when the airing began. "Only recently has the sale price of an ad represented the value of the show's audience."[24]

22. CRTC Public Notice 1996–36, Ottawa, March 14, 1996.
23. Allan King, *Globe and Mail,* October 13, 1995, op. ed.
24. *Variety,* February 19–25, 1996, 1, 61.

The Howard Stern case has not yet been fully played out.[25] Technology has contributed to the apparent solution—the seamless editing of a "live" show to conform with Canadian standards. If the CBSC becomes a significant filter of content, criticism of its control by Canadian broadcasters is likely to increase. In many ways, this process could be more threatening to the freedoms championed by Allan King and Richard Wolf than the classification system.

---

25. A third complaint about Stern was heard by the CBSC on February 3, 1999. The text of the decision is not yet available.

CHAPTER 16

Film Distribution I

During earlier periods of Canadian history, the state frequently encouraged the development of downstream activities in resource-based industries. For example, provincial governments, which have jurisdiction over resources, mobilized various instruments—the prohibition of the export of logs, the structure of taxes and subsidies, and the terms of access to timber on crown land—to encourage the further processing of wood in Canada. A similar array of policies supported additional treatment and refinement of metals like nickel before their export. In general, the Canadian tariff schedule rose as value was added to a product.

This structure has been largely dismantled as a result of the extensive liberalization of trade in goods that occurred under GATT in the post–World War II period. Like many other countries, Canada had also established an array of measures to protect service industries—finance, telecommunications, cable services, broadcasting, and government-provided services such as mail and the sale of alcohol. In the case of films, the subject of this chapter, the state attempted to promote a downstream activity, film distribution, in order to establish an upstream feature film production industry where none existed. Until the recent Uruguay Round, GATT did not systematically focus on negotiating a mutual reduction of the protective shells around the service industries. When attention did shift to services, GATT followed the groundwork laid by NAFTA and the EU, as discussed in chapters 4 and 5.

Canadian film distribution policy provides an instructive example of a dysfunctional set of government policies that has affected both trade and investment. A part of the informal Canadian film distribution policy structure, which evolved after World War II, was the maintenance of a constant state of tension between the government and the major foreign distribution interests. This process had a cyclical element. Each cycle began with rhetorical agitation over either a vaguely specified failure of the Hollywood majors to provide a nation-building menu of films or a complaint about how they did business. Threats of passing legislation or issuing directives that would be harmful to the commercial interests of the majors often accompanied the rhetoric. Negotiations followed. An agreement was then announced. In the agreement, the threats would materialize in a watered-down form or not at all. The majors would buy the right to go about their business by making a measured commitment to whatever the politicians considered to be supportive of cultural development of Canadians or to change some trade practice.

Nationalist spokespersons usually labeled the cycle-ending agreement as a sellout. With the exception of disputes funneled through the competition policy process, there appeared to be little interest by the policymakers or the media in assessing the efficiency of the threatened policy measures. Neither was there an attempt to determine whether the majors had made a best effort to comply, nor if they had, whether the results were constructive. For example, if more screen hours were dedicated to Canadian films, was anyone in the theaters during these hours?

The interaction was a political ritual rather than a serious attempt to forge policy. Canadian Cabinet ministers, past and present, would line up to recall their encounters with the Hollywood Goliath. The Canadian press would vilify the Hollywood "black hats" and cheer the Ottawa "white hats." Once one agreement was announced, a new cycle began. An inconsistent policy environment emerged from the resulting patchwork of commitments, laws, and directives with grandfathered beneficiaries or targeted exceptions. The process also left a residue of ill will among the parties.

The bilateral focus of this process also created frictions with other countries. Since the ritual began, the nature of the international industry has changed. The Hollywood majors have become international in ownership. These multinational companies own film production facilities, theme parks, exhibition circuits, conventional broadcasting, cable, satellite broadcasting, and electronic manufacturing interests around the world as well as in the United States. Increasingly, their production is not done in-house but by producers under contract. Some decision making has been decentralized to corporate head offices in Japan, Australia, and Canada, despite the management of the film divisions remaining in California. A seasoned Hollywood studio chief at Columbia, Fox, or Universal experiencing a run of bad luck or bad management fears a dismissal notice bearing a Japanese, Australian, or Canadian stamp.

Political rhetoric in Canada and other countries continues to be directed against American studios and exploitive American films. The national adjectives are simply incorrect. The Hollywood majors are divisions of large global corporations that deliver mass-market films across a number of language markets. Ownership by Japanese electronic giants, French banks, Australian press magnates, American media conglomerates, or Canadian liquor interests may affect decisions in subtle ways that cannot be accurately predicted from national stereotypes but more significantly the majors have similar internal systems and cultures shaped by their experience in meeting common challenges. The strength of a major studio resides in knowing:

- how to identify the best resources available internationally
- how to contract and manage effectively their combination
- how to orchestrate and promote an effective release across linguistically and culturally distinct markets
- how to extract the commercial potential of a film across complementary sources of revenue
- how to shift or offset the risk concerning the revenue prospects of their films
- how to generate sufficient volume and commercial quality to develop a brand and a reputation among exhibitors
- how to protect their films from piracy

The distribution function is the critical factor integrating financing, merchandising, and production activities. The theatrical launch and promotion of a high-budget film is orchestrated internationally with an eye to both the immediate box office revenue and the subsequent value of nontheatrical exhibition windows and ancillary revenue sources. The best distributional strategy for a film depends on a number of factors. Many current releases, particularly of star-driven, special-effects dominated, action or other formulaic films, involve coordinated showings on a wide set of screens in many countries. As the breadth of these releases across countries and screens within countries expands, the duration of each showing contracts. The coordination of saturation promotional campaigns and simultaneous access to first-run cinemas in major cities around the world is critical.

When the main promotional campaign concentrates on the English-language media, a non-English-language national or regional film distributor can effectively translate the text of advertising material and adjust the campaign to its customers. A Hollywood major is most likely to subcontract these local adaptations, as the expertise required is distant from its core competence. An English-language distributor limited to a small English-language market cannot offer as much to a major. In some cases, it may adapt advertising to the sensitivities of the local market. In most cases, it places ads that have already been developed and books cinemas, but those are off-the-shelf functions that the major can usually do at least as economically as the regional distributor.

Some films are better released over a longer time frame in which word of mouth feedback compensates for the absence of known stars or directors. Stitched together consortia of national film distributors, each exercising some discretion within their areas, are more competitive in distributing a film under this strategy. They can develop low-budget promotional campaigns in the languages of their areas that are effective in the local culture.

These economic factors inform our discussion of the course of Canadian film distribution policy and its international ramifications. The initial section of this chapter covers a series of agreements reached between the Canadian government and the MPAA,[1] its Canadian offshoot the Canadian Motion Picture Distributors Association (CMPDA), or individual member companies. Table 12 sets out the details of the MPA and its counterpart organization in Canada. These episodes were often initiated by government concerns about the lack of screen time devoted to Canadian films. Various policy suggestions floated by the Canadian government during these iterations are examined in passing. A discussion of interactions with the Hollywood majors under Canadian competition policy follows. This section ends with an examination of the role played by an export cartel registered by the MPA, under the U.S. WP.

TABLE 12. American Film Industry Associations and Canada

- In 1922, the major American firms formed an industry association, the Motion Picture Producers and Distributors of America (MPPDA). The name was changed to the Motion Picture Association of America (MPAA).

- In 1945, the MPAA formed an export cartel, the Motion Picture Export Association of America (MPEAA), registered under the Webb-Pomerene Act of 1918. The name of the MPEAA was changed to the Motion Picture Association (MPA) in 1994.

- Membership of the MPA in 1998 consists of Walt Disney Co., Sony Pictures Entertainment Inc., Metro-Goldwyn-Mayer Inc., Paramount Pictures Corporation, Twentieth Century Fox Film Corp., Universal Studios Inc., and Warner Bros. (MPA Website).

- In Canada, the counterpart organization representing the U.S. majors was the Motion Picture Distributors and Exhibitors of Canada (MPDEC) formed in 1920 and incorporated in 1924. The Canadian Motion Picture Distributors Association (CMPDA) representing many of the same companies was also formed in 1920 and incorporated in 1976. Both organizations appear to exist until 1940 when public reference is made only to the CMPDA. (The version of events recorded by Magder (1993, 57) is not confirmed by officials of the CMPDA.)

- Members of the CMPDA in 1998 include Buena Vista International (a subsidiary of Disney), Columbia, MGM, Paramount, Turner Pictures, Twentieth Century Fox, Universal and Warner Brothers.

In the next chapter we complete the discussion of film distribution measures, which, in addition to negotiated contracts between the majors and the government and antitrust initiatives, have included foreign ownership con-

---

1. We frequently refer to the association representing the Hollywood majors as the MPA, its current shortened form, throughout the episodes described in this and the following chapter.

straints, mandated contractual terms, the reservation of distribution of nonproprietary films to Canadian firms, direct and indirect subsidies, and discrimination among foreign distributors. The links between dubbing and film distribution in Quebec are also explored.

The interactive policy process has sometimes resulted in grandfathering the rights of the Hollywood majors in return for a commitment to support an objective of the government. In these instances, the government has taken away rights from all foreigners and then selectively given them back. In film distribution, the resulting discrimination has created friction with European trading partners. The initiation of an EC complaint to the WTO against Canadian film distribution policy on behalf of Polygram, at the time a Dutch film distributor, discussed in conjunction with the proprietary rights initiative in the next chapter is a manifestation of this aspect of Canadian policy.

The MPA and the Canadian Government

The NFB, an agency of the Canadian government, developed into a successful documentary film producer during World War II. In contrast, Canada entered the post war period with essentially no commercial film industry. In this setting, the Canadian government and the Hollywood majors negotiated the Canadian Cooperation Project (1948 to 1957) in which the Hollywood majors promised:[2]

1.   a short film explaining Canada's trade-dollar shortage
2.   increased coverage of Canada in American newsreels
3.   short films about Canada produced by U.S. film companies
4.   distribution of some NFB films
5.   some Canadian sequences in U.S. feature films
6.   radio messages from U.S. stars about the attractions of vacationing in Canada
7.   distribution of fewer B gangster films in Canada
8.   appointment of a liaison officer for the project

Although some interesting films were shot in Canada under the Cooperation Project, the results were often artificial. Gathercole captures the spirit of the nationalists' reaction: "Hollywood agreed to generate tourism to compensate for our balance of trade deficit by writing Canadian place names into its scripts as in "That bird looks like a Saskatchewan thrush to me" and "The bank robbers musta lit out for Shawinigan, Sheriff" (1983, 29).

---

2. See letter from E. Johnston to J. J. Fitzgibbons, January 21, 1948, quoted in Collins (1979, 35).

Subsequent agreements were more limited in scope and focused on gaining access for Canadian films to cinemas. In the early 1970s, an agreement was reached with the two largest theater chains to increase the screen time devoted to Canadian feature films. The largest chain, Famous Players, was owned by Paramount and the second largest, Odeon, was British owned at the time.[3] The chains were to provide at least two weeks screening time in Canada's three largest cities for every major English-language Canadian feature film. The agreement was renegotiated by Hugh Faulkner in late 1975. The two major chains agreed to provide four weeks of Canadian feature films per year in each theater that they controlled and committed to invest a minimum C$1.7 million in the production of Canadian films (Gathercole 1983, 30). In December 1977 Odeon withdrew from the agreement.[4]

At the same time as negotiating agreements with major exhibition chains, the Canadian government was initiating, or actively considering, other programs designed to change the structure of distribution and exhibition. It is difficult to tell which announcements and proposals were designed to enhance the government's bargaining power and which were serious policy alternatives. One of the less plausible trial balloons was government distribution and exhibition of films. In mid-1972, the Canadian secretary of state announced that the government would either buy or build a theater in the national capital region that would play only Canadian films. He also asked the CFDC to consider the viability of a government-subsidized distribution network.[5] A decade later a task force examining film distribution, exhibition, and marketing considered the acquisition by the government of one of the major chains, buying a selected number of theaters in major cities or leasing cinemas on either a short- or long-term basis. The idea was rejected "in principle" because it "would have the effect of 'ghettoizing' Canadian films."[6]

---

3. The Odeon chain was established by Canadian investors associated with N. L. Nathanson, who had previously worked for Famous Players. It was sold to the British-owned Rank Organization in 1946, which in turn sold it to Michael Zahorchak in 1977. Cineplex, a firm started by Canadians Garth Drabinsky and Nat Taylor in 1977, bought the chain in 1984. In 1987, 50 percent of Cineplex was purchased by MCA-Universal. In 1998, it was merged with Sony's Loews chain to become Loews Cineplex Entertainment. The early years of Odeon are set out in Cox (1979, 47–53) and more recent developments in Magder (1996, 149).

4. The withdrawal by the Canadian-owned chain occurred despite the rapid expansion, from a low base of the production of films in Canada, due in large part to the introduction of a generous tax shelter program. These films were frequently not successful in drawing an audience.

5. The Pelletier speech is reprinted in *Cinema Canada* 3 (July–August 1972).

6. Canada 1983, 19, 24.

The only recent Canadian experience with public film distribution is that of the NFB. The report of the Mandate Review Committee was particularly critical of the board's distribution:

In the 1992–95 period, the NFB's distribution and marketing costs totalled roughly C$70.8 million. These expenditures generated total distribution revenues of C$17.5 million over the three years—meaning that the board spent *almost four times* as much as it made in this area. (Canada 1996d, 177)

The committee advocated "far greater use of private distributors for both its current production and for the exploitation of its extensive library of titles." Recently, the NFB has experimented with in-house distribution of its films through cable facilities. The first phase of this project linked two Montreal universities with the NFB library.[7]

Discriminatory tax initiatives designed to influence distribution were also proposed. In 1977, the then secretary of state suggested a 10 percent levy on the rental revenue of distributors. A rebate would be paid equal to the amount of payments made by the distributors to Canadian filmmakers from distributing their films in Canada and world markets. This policy was never implemented and tax measures have concentrated on production with ties to distribution that are discussed in the next chapter. Competition policy is another "large lever" policy that has affected the distribution activities of the Hollywood majors.

The Hollywood Majors and Canadian Competition Policy

Antitrust issues have featured prominently in the distribution of films in Canada and the United States. In Canada during the 1930s the focus was on a wide-ranging investigation of vertical integration of distributors and cinemas and the terms included in vertical contracts between distributors and unaligned cinemas. The report of Peter White, commissioner under the Canadian Combines Investigation Act, on industry practices and a resulting court case anticipate the issues dealt with in U.S. court cases leading up to the Supreme Court's

---

7. A second experimental phase will provide a video on demand service to about 50 institutions across Canada. Information provided by NFB by telephone October 22, 1998.

Paramount Decision and subsequent consent decrees.[8] The antitrust issues of that time had a significant international dimension, as they have today.

The White Report and Subsequent Trial

White's report and the subsequent court case was in response to a complaint by independent Canadian exhibitors about their lack of access to first-run films of the major studios and to the length of time before they were permitted to show them in their second and subsequent runs. White's report led to an indictment for conspiracy in restraint of trade under the Combines Investigation Act and section 498 of the Criminal Code. Charged were three individuals and 15 corporations (one corporation Tiffany Productions of Can. Ltd. was not served) including the MPDEC which White described as an organization of distributors, except for Paramount's Famous Players cinema chain, and an offshoot of the MPPDA.[9]

The government's case focused on the impact of a variety of contracting practices on the profitability of independent cinemas and distributors, not on Canadian film producers, who virtually did not exist, or consumers. Currently, the Hollywood majors and independent distributors of first-run films use many of the same contracting practices. In his decision Judge Garrow dismissed all the charges and in particular stated that it was "obvious" to him "that there was no attempt at price fixing" either overtly or tacitly (*Rex v. Famous Players*, Ontario Supreme Court, March 18, 1932).

The 1983 Undertakings

Another set of competition policy concerns arose in late 1982, when the Director of Investigation and Research applied to the Restrictive Trade Practices Commission (RTPC) to order Columbia Pictures Industries, Inc., Paramount Productions Inc., Universal Films (Canada), Warner Bros. Distributing (Canada)

---

8. The historic antitrust case *United States v. Paramount et al.* was initiated on July 20, 1938, when a suit was filed charging the majors with combining and conspiring to restrain trade unreasonably and to monopolize the production, distribution, and exhibition of motion pictures. It was settled 10 years later when the Supreme Court decided against the defendants. The 1933 code of Fair Competition for the Motion Picture Industry, which had been signed into law following passage of the National Industrial Recovery Act of June 1933 permitted practices such as block booking, clearance, zoning, and admission price discrimination. For a discussion, see Balio (1993, 18–21, 36).

9. These organizations have their modern-day counterparts in the CMPDA and the MPA (see table 12).

Ltd., United Artists Corporation, and Twentieth Century-Fox Film Corporation[10] to supply commercially valuable films to Cineplex, a small but aggressive chain of Canadian cinemas. Negotiations ensued, and in mid-1983 the director announced that the six defendants had agreed to "certain undertakings" that would significantly change their distribution practices. These revisions of the contracting process between a distributor and a cinema were intended to protect a qualified cinema from being shut out of the first-run market for films.[11]

The distributors agreed to solicit offers for runs of their motion pictures from all creditworthy exhibitors and to grant exhibition rights on a picture by picture and theater by theater basis. Each offer was to be considered on its merits, with comparisons limited to theaters that were in substantial competition with each other. The ability of an exhibiting company to show a film in more than one cinema was not to be taken into account in accepting an offer among competing cinemas. Distributors were to provide all eligible bidders with estimates of the patterns and length of runs. Clearances would be limited to theaters that were in substantial competition with each other. The distributors were also to forbear agreeing not to grant another run of a film unless the new run would significantly reduce the expected audience of the film in the original run. New offers were to be entertained for any subsequent run. With respect to blind bidding, the distributors committed to making screenings available in more locations on as timely a basis as possible. The authorities also recognized the procompetitive aspect of blind booking and did not ban it outright.

After the undertaking's implementation, Cineplex and other small chains and independent cinemas received more open access to the films of the major distributors.[12] In return for their undertakings, the director granted a one-year adjournment of the hearing of his application before the RTPC. The distributors agreed that he could bring back the application at any time within the next year if his monitoring determined that they were not complying. This regime only lasted for a short period before Cineplex took over the Odeon chain. This 1984 takeover transformed Cineplex into Cineplex Odeon, the largest chain in Canada. With the previously small chain gaining significant market share and "in the loop" status, distribution practices regressed towards the pre-undertakings pattern.[13] The matter was not reopened by the director within the subsequent year and no similar initiative has since been taken.

---

10. A seventh firm, Astral Films Limited, was named, but it was not included in the eventual negotiations because it distributed as an agent for Columbia and Twentieth Century-Fox.

11. The agreement is reproduced in Director of Investigation and Research (1984).

12. See Report to the RTPC on the Operation of the Undertakings of the Director of Investigation and Research, March 1984.

13. Magder (1993, 206) describes the reversion to an "entente cordiale."

The MPA as an Export Cartel

Cooperation among the Hollywood majors in their international business has been facilitated by the formation a legal export cartel in 1945. Under the Webb Pomerene Act of 1918, a registered cartel receives immunity from American antitrust laws providing that competition in the domestic market is unaffected. WP cartels need only report the annual value of exports and some minor bits of information to maintain their legal status. The agreements are self-enforcing, that is, the agreements are not enforceable in American courts. Given the low costs of registration, the small number of WP cartels is noteworthy.[14] The stability of the agreements that do exist vary, but many are inactive and the expected life of active agreements is low.[15]

WP agreements differ in coverage. Dick reported the distribution of functions specified in 23 WP cartels that were active in 1962 (1996, 246). Seven of the sampled agreements empowered the WP association to negotiate with foreign governments on behalf of the membership. This has been an important role for the MPA, which describes itself as the "Little State Department" on its web site.

In Europe three members of the MPA—Paramount Pictures, MCA, and MGM—formed a joint distribution agency, United International Pictures (UIP), to distribute their films in Europe and the rest of the world except for the United States and Canada. The European Commission was notified of the agreements creating UIP on February 11, 1982, and on July 12, 1989, gave an exemption from antitrust policies from July 27, 1988, until July 26, 1993. The exemption was granted due to the depressed market situation experienced by this business sector and following the acceptance of a number of changes to the agreements aimed at limiting the restrictive effects of the UIP arrangement.[16] The parties obtained a five-year renewal of the exemption from June 1993, but in 1998 the EU decided that there were insufficient reasons to allow the arrangement to continue. UIP has appealed the preliminary ruling. There is no deadline for a final decision from the commission.[17]

A cartel agreement can lower the costs of marketing internationally. If the American industry has a number of small producers accounting for a small

14. "During the past 20 years, the number of registered WP associations has never exceeded 36, and the number of active cartels has not exceeded 29. Currently, 24 export cartels comprising 249 firms are registered with the Federal Trade Commission (FTC)" (Dick 1992, 97).

15. Dick examined a sample of "111 cartel episodes covering 93 industries and spanning the years 1918–65." He found that the median WP cartel remained active for about 5.3 years (1996, 251).

16. Reported in European Union Notice EU, BIO/98/51, Brussels, February 6, 1998.

17. *Financial Times* (London), February 6, 1998, 1.

percentage of world supply, a WP association would lack the market power to raise world prices. The gains for a cartel of firms in this situation can only be generated by reductions in the costs of international distribution. In contrast a cartel covering a substantial proportion of American exports, which in turn represent a considerable proportion of world supply, typically has the market power to raise prices. The extent to which that power can be realized with a self-enforcing agreement depends on the homogeneity of the product and the stability of its demand.

Dick (1992) examines a sample of sixteen WP cartels that operated intermittently between 1919 and 1970 and finds that the cartels raised export volumes by an average of 15 percent and lowered prices by an average of 7.6 percent in comparison to independent exporting. In only two of the sixteen industries sampled—sulphur and carbon black—were the agreements on balance price raising and quantity restricting.[18] In another empirical study of WP activity, Dick (1997, 1–2) concludes that there are greater returns from cartelization for "non-durable, capital-intensive and standardized products" sold in "export markets with growing world demand and a large United States market share." He notes that many of the agreements in contrast cover "unconcentrated and regionally-based industries, where simple price fixing overseas was an unlikely motive."

The MPA was not included in Dick's 1992 sample. In many ways, it is an anomaly among WP cartels. The MPA members have a large share of world markets and dominate American film exports. Both factors contribute to potential market power. On the other hand films do not have the other attributes that increase a cartel's effectiveness in raising prices. A film is a differentiated product and is long-lasting. Durability weakens market power as the stock of old films compete with new releases. This erosion of market power is mitigated to some extent by licensing rather than sale of films in theatrical markets (Coase 1972; Bulow 1982).

Licensing in copyright-based industries is discriminatory. The reservation price for licensing an already existing film has a lower bound set by the costs of delivering it to the licensee. The upper bound is the value of the particular licence to the user. A licensee in New Zealand pays a lower price for distribution rights to a film than does its British counterpart. The distributor of a film practices what was called "value-of-service pricing" in the regulated railway and

---

18. For these products, Dick estimates that "the (export value weighted) average annual price increase attributable to cartel activity was 6.5 percent and the decline in export volume was 14.6 percent" (1992, 103). In the 1962 data, the WP for sulphur (86.1 percent) had the highest share of WP-assisted exports as a percentage of total U.S. exports for a product group and carbon black was third highest. The second highest was the share of motion pictures and television programs (estimated to be over 80 percent) (1992, 103).

telephone industry, but its market power is restricted by competition from other films and media rather than by a supervisory commission. The demand characteristics of a film affect the pattern of price discrimination over different geographical areas and over different media windows. Novelty within a genre is important in film.[19] The demand price for a second viewing is far less than for a first. The marketing challenge for a distributor is to persuade a movie-goer to buy a ticket to its "promises" of satisfaction.

These factors make an effective ex ante agreement on prices difficult to engineer. Neither setting market shares nor granting members exclusive trading areas outside of the United States makes sense for the MPA. Films are extremely risky and the annual ranking of box office success of films released by individual studios is volatile.[20] This volatility in demand for the product of any one distributor further increases the difficulty of forging a self-enforcing cartel agreement dependent on market shares. What might make sense for a cartel in this industry is to agree to limit the total number of pictures made by each studio. An agreement on the annual number of "lottery tickets" each studio produces is more enforceable than one based on market shares, but there are obvious margins for "cheating". Members have an incentive to improve the chances of their restricted number of lottery tickets by putting more resources into each film than otherwise would occur. Production of films by noncartel members would also expand, as would distribution by means of video and television. An agreement by the Hollywood majors to limit the annual flow of films would not be in the interests of world viewers, although it would help accomplish what appears to be the aim of many governments outside the United States, to expand their domestic film industry. In any case, such an agreement would not be protected against antitrust prosecution in the United States by WP status since it would materially affect the domestic market.

WP status protects a cartel from U.S. antitrust prosecution for activities in foreign markets as long as there are no anti-competitive effects in the domestic market. It does not grant any protection against the competition policy of the countries to which the films are exported. Protection from American antitrust prosecution may make the prosecution of cases in other countries more difficult. A countervailing factor is that WP status signals to antitrust authorities of non-U.S. countries that an export agreement exists. Empirically, antitrust actions in other countries with respect to the activities of American WP cartels are rare.

---

19. "Exporters of relatively unprocessed and homogeneous commodities have been much more likely to establish export cartels than producers of differentiated manufacturing goods" (Dick 1992, 98).

20. Globerman (1987, tables 9 and 10, 43–44) shows the wide variability of the rankings and shares of rental revenues of the major distributors in Canada.

Some of the WP agreements face countervailing buying power in that they sell to only one buyer in each country (Dick 1997, 21).[21] A cartel of exhibitors is often not feasible as a countervailing force because of vertical integration between important exhibitors and the Hollywood majors. For example, a buying cartel of independent Canadian cinematic chains would be ineffective because the two largest exhibition chains are owned by members of the CMPDA. It may be feasible in some countries.[22]

Another dimension of WP associations that is important in assessing the MPA's operations is the limitation placed on membership. Firms that are part of a WP cartel must be American, but there is some dispute about what that means. While foreign-based organizations are not eligible to become members of a WP association, the question is open as to the status of a foreign-owned and/or foreign-controlled firm incorporated in the United States (Fugate 1991, 477–78).

The foreign membership issue has surfaced at different times. In 1992 International Raw Materials (IRM) appealed a District Court decision in a case concerning a WP association consisting mainly of foreign-owned firms that became involved in coordinated activities other than exporting.[23] The Court of Appeals noted "that neither the statute nor the legislative history specifically resolves the question of whether membership in a WP association is limited to American-owned firms" and concluded that "permitting foreign-owned firms that export goods from the United States to participate in such associations" was not inconsistent with the purpose of the WP Act. The opinion further clarified that members of WP associations "are not permitted, either themselves or through subsidiaries, to own, operate, or own stock in corporations or other producers outside the United States if there is any possibility that the markets supplied by such foreign operations might, in the absence of such companies be supplied from exports from the United States."

The issue is relevant to the MPA and of interest in Canada because a number of the members are not American owned. Universal Studios is Canadian-owned. As discussed in the following chapter, Universal, as a

---

21. One example concerns sulphur. British, Australian, and New Zealand buyers formed a countervailing buyers' cartel. The British Restrictive Trade Practices Court in 1963 affirmed its legality on the basis of the supply of sulphur to the United Kingdom being dominated by a WP association of U.S. companies (Davidow 1983, 361).

22. Davidow (1983) cites Fugate (1982, 420–21) as stating that the cartel office in Sweden allowed exhibitors to combine when bargaining with United States export cartels. No such reference appears in Fugate, and we are unable to confirm whether such an instance existed.

23. The IRM case is reported in *West's Federal Reporter,* vol. 978 F.2d, United States Courts of Appeals and Temporary Emergency Court of Appeals (St. Paul, MN: West Publishing Co., 1993), 1318–33.

grandfathered member of the CMPDA, is allowed to distribute nonproprietary films in Quebec while Canadian distributors from other provinces are not. Similarly, when Credit Lyonnais owned MGM, it had a distribution status in Quebec denied to traditional French distributors. Future interactions between the MPA and a national government is altered when one of the MPA companies is owned by nationals. For example, Sony may find itself on the other side of the negotiating table from the Japanese government.

The treatment of cartel arrangements that have cross-border effects are the domain of domestic antitrust authorities. The EU evaluates the operation of foreign cartels in its jurisdiction and may allow or disallow their presence. Canada permits as a defense against price-fixing charges that the arrangement only affects export markets. Canada also has a provision in the Competition Act, section 46(1), that prohibits the implementation of a foreign directive whose purpose is to give effect to a conspiracy entered into outside of the country that, if entered into in Canada, would be contrary to the conspiracy provisions of the act. No WP associations have been challenged to date under this section.

Protocols for cooperation in antitrust matters exist between the United States and Canada, Australia, Germany, and the EU. They follow a model agreement recommended by the OECD and included in the U.S. International Antitrust Enforcement Assistance Act of 1994 (Trebilcock 1996, 90). There have been three cases in which Canadian and American antitrust authorities have conducted simultaneous searches and seizures of information in their respective countries and shared the resulting information (Davidow 1997, 11).

Given the difficulties of agreeing on prices for differentiated products like films, it is unclear what effects the MPA as an export cartel has and why it exists except for lobbying purposes. That the MPA has registered as a WP cartel nonetheless adds credibility to assertions that its success abroad rests on the exercise of monopoly power. These are common. For example, the 1985 Film Industry Task Force stated: "At home, American distributors must abide by rules of fair competition, but in Canada they function as a cartel, and by so doing have relegated Canadian producers and distributors to marginal roles in their own market" (Canada 1985, 17). WP status facilitates the ease with which the majors lobby foreign governments, especially when policies are introduced restricting market access for American films. As discussed in the next chapter, the MPA has negotiated a special status for its members in the Quebec Cinema Act and under the Investment Canada Act with respect to distributing nonproprietary films. These represent accommodations with the federal and provincial governments that do not include other American distributors. The FTC has not taken action against this type of agreement nor have Canadian competition authorities considered it anticompetitive by restricting imports.

CHAPTER 17

Film Distribution II

In this chapter, we continue the analysis of Canadian film distribution policy. Negotiated agreements between the majors and antitrust actions discussed in the previous chapter have been accompanied by other policies. These include reserving for Canadian distributors the right to distribute certain foreign and Canadian films, linkages between dubbing and obtaining the right to distribute films, tax benefits and subsidies to production that are tied to hiring Canadian distributors, and direct subsidies to distribution. At the end of the chapter, we discuss the overall impact of this mix of protective devices and consider a more open policy alternative.

Barring Foreign Distributors from Distributing Nonproprietary Films

In the 1980s, the Canadian and Quebec governments moved to bar foreign distributors from distributing films for which they did not own proprietary rights. Proprietary rights have been defined differently in the various settings in which the issue has arisen. Typically a distributor is deemed to have proprietary rights if it produced the film, provided a substantial proportion of its financing, or acquired world rights after the film was made but before it was released. Significant differences in the impact of this policy can be generated by altering the definition of world rights, identifying the film producer, particularly when the film is a coproduction, and delineating what proportion of financing is substantial. Table 13 lists the various stages of this campaign.

The Quebec Cinema Act

In late 1982, the government of Quebec tabled a Cinema Act that differed radically from prior law. Among its proposals were that all distributors operating in Quebec must be 80 percent Canadian owned, the regulation of terms in distributor/exhibitor contracts and filing of these contracts with the Régie du

Cinéma, and requirements to provide French language versions of films.[1] The Hollywood distributors reacted adversely to these restrictions on their activities, and the U.S. government threatened reprisals through its Quebec consulate.

A political battle followed, which at various stages involved the CMPDA; its parent the Motion Picture Export Association (MPEAA); Jack Valenti, its president; Francis Fox, a former federal minister acting as a mediator; ministers from first a separatist and then a federalist provincial government; and spokespersons for national interest groups. An American boycott of the Quebec market was threatened by the MPEAA.[2] One of the majors, Paramount, did boycott Quebec cinemas for five months.

TABLE 13. The Proprietary Rights Campaign

1. In the early 1980s a campaign to establish a separate distribution right for Canada begins.
2. Beginning in August, 1985, Telefilm requires that a production project have a distribution contract with a Canadian distributor as a condition for granting financial support.
3. The Cinema Act in Quebec limited the right to distribute in Quebec to firms which are 80% Canadian-owned and have their principal establishment in Quebec. MPA members as of January 1, 1987, were exempted. A requirement that all distributors reinvest 10% of gross revenues in Quebec productions was put on hold. An English-language release could only run for sixty days before a dubbed French language version would have to be made available.
4. The Minister of Communications proposed legislation that would create an import licensing scheme whereby foreign distributors would be limited to distributing films they had either produced or for which they had world distribution rights. Revised bill dies in 1988.
5. A 1988 Investment Canada directive limits the distribution of films with nonproprietary rights to Canadian distributors. Majors are exempted.
6. In 1988-89 Telefilm creates fund to subsidize Canadian distributors to acquire Canadian rights of Canadian and foreign films.
7. In 1995, CRTC denies any non-Canadian distributor the right to license a film, for which it did not own proprietary rights to PPV undertakings, carried by Canadian satellite distribution undertakings (with no waiver of the Hollywood majors).
8. In the same 1995 decision, the CRTC establishes compulsory terms for distributing films to PPV undertakings carried by satellite broadcasting undertakings.
9. In 1998, EU initiates a complaint against Canada to the WTO for failing to give Polygram the same treatment as the Hollywood majors with respect to distributing non-proprietary films. Issue is put on hold as Seagram acquires Polygram.
10. In 1998, Alliance, a Canadian distributor, has its general license suspended in Quebec because the principal establishment criterion is deemed not to have been met. After negotiations, license is renewed.
11. In 1998, CRTC suspends the non-proprietary rights and contractual initiatives described in points 7 and 8.

1. If a French-language version of a film exists, at least an equal number of copies of that version must be made available to Quebec cinemas as are released in the original language. If no French version is available, an English-language release can only run for 60 days. If a French version has been commissioned, the non-French copies may be granted a license.

2. See the Trade News section of *Cinema Canada,* October, 1985, which has the headline "Valenti Threatens to Pull-Out if Law Enacted."

Revisions were made in the Quebec legislation before it passed in mid-1983. Among the modifications was the narrowing of the scope of protection to cover only Canadian distributors with their principal establishment in Quebec. The majors, many of them having distributed films in the province for over 60 years, and producers from the rest of Canada who historically had operated in Quebec were restricted to distributing proprietary films. The struggle of interests then focused on defining proprietary rights for the purpose of implementing the act. While this issue was being contested, there was a change of government. The new government continued the negotiations and in 1986 reached an agreement with the majors on a definition of proprietary rights that represented a considerable weakening of the impact of the bill.[3] This agreement applied only to a member of the MPAA distributing in Quebec as of January 1, 1987.[4]

In the negotiations leading to the "Bacon/Valenti" agreement[5] and the resulting amendment of the act, the Hollywood majors were not overly concerned about the 60 day limit for distributing English-language films. With the increasing popularity of wider openings of shorter duration, the limit was a constraint that would not often be binding. With the exemption, a generous definition of proprietary rights, and the generally nonbinding 60 day limit, the American majors have been able to operate largely as they had in the past. The only difference is that they cannot distribute non-English language films in Quebec unless they financed all of their production costs. The inroads made by the classic divisions of the majors in distributing this type of film in the early 1980s came largely at the expense of Quebec distributors and helped trigger the bill. The majors had found this line of business internationally to be less rewarding than anticipated, and the revenue generated from the Quebec market was relatively small.[6] Early in the negotiations the majors declared their willingness to abandon this segment of the business. Relations between the majors and the Quebec government have subsequently become less antagonistic

---

3. To qualify as a producer of an English-language film an MPEAA member had to have "world rights" or incur production, duplication, advertising and promotion costs of C\$4.5 million or at least 50% of the total of these categories. For a non-English language film a member qualifies as producer if either it has world rights, covered all of the production costs or the Minister of Culture considers that the member's investment justifies a special permit.

4. Buena Vista (Disney), which did not distribute in Quebec when the Bill was tabled, gained the same status as the other MPEAA members.

5. Lise Bacon was the Minister of Cultural Affairs in the Liberal Government, elected on December 2, 1985.

6. Houle estimates the effect by calculating how much less revenue the majors would have made had this stipulation been in force in 1985 and 1986. He concludes "that at best, the agreement would have meant a transfer of 0.1% to 0.2% of the Majors' volume of business to Quebec companies" (1987, 21).

than during the negotiations because the majors have contracted for an increasing amount of French-language dubbing in Quebec.

Ironically, the Quebec act discriminates more effectively against English-language distributors from other parts of Canada than against the Hollywood majors. Canadian distribution firms from outside Quebec, which did not have a principal establishment in the province, typically distributed a small number of Canadian and foreign films with significantly lower budgets and promotion than a representative Hollywood film. They were unlikely to have invested sufficiently in the films for which they owned Canadian rights to have acquired world rights. Among the national distributors only those based in Quebec can distribute non-proprietary films in the province. Houle (1994) presents the market shares of the three largest Quebec distribution companies for 1992. Alliance is the largest of these, with a share of 5.1 percent of Quebec box office revenue. As a point of comparison, the largest share of the Quebec theatrical release market held by a major studio in 1992 was the 12.4 percent for Warner Bros. and the smallest was the 1.3 percent for MGM/United Artists. Alliance had its general license for distributing films in Quebec revoked in late 1997. La Régie du Cinéma Quebec ruled that the Quebec-based distribution arm required more independence from the company's other Canadian offices to qualify as a Quebec company under the Cinema Act. Alliance entered into negotiations with the regulator and has been able to reestablish itself as a Quebec distributor.

The Proposed National Cinema Act

The 1983 task force on film distribution, exhibition, and marketing recommended a National Cinema Act, which would license the right to import, distribute, or exhibit films. There would be Canadian-owned and controlled licensees and foreign licensees. Canadian-owned and controlled licensees could import and distribute any motion picture in Canada, but no more than 60 percent could come from one company. Foreign-owned or controlled distributors could only distribute films for which they had "worldwide" distribution rights.

This scheme was not implemented, but in February 1987 the minister of communications proposed the introduction of legislation that would create an import licensing scheme whereby foreign distributors would be limited to distributing films that they had either produced or for which they had proprietary rights. The National Association of Canadian Film and Video Distributors claimed that this would transfer about 7 percent of the majors' revenues to Canadian-owned firms (Magder 1993, 224). Not surprisingly, the association supported the initiative. Due to objections raised by foreign distributors, a revised bill was introduced in June 1988, but it died on the government's order paper when an election was called. The Canadian government's subsequent interaction with the majors included a meeting of the president of the MPAA, Jack Valenti, with the minister of communications, Flora MacDonald. An annex to a congressional brief of the MPAA, entitled "U.S. Film Industry's Trade Crisis in Canada," lists four suggestions made by the MPAA to the minister. These were a screen quota forcing Canadian theaters to reserve at least 10 percent of screen time for Canadian films, a box office levy to finance the making of Canadian films, a tax on blank and pre-recorded videotape (with the funds used for domestic production), and the formation of a Canadian/U.S. Council of professionals from the industry to resolve problems.[7] The quota and tax measures are surprising recommendations from the MPAA and inconsistent with its public stand in recent years. The protection of the Canadian market for rights to independent foreign films contained in the proposed bill was instead solely pursued through investment guidelines administered by Investment Canada.

The 1988 Investment Canada Directive

In 1988, the government issued a directive, limiting any new foreign film distribution business to handling films for which it owned proprietary rights, under the Investment Canada Act. For this purpose, proprietary rights were defined to include any film in which the distributor was a major investor or owned world rights. Neither *major investor* or *world rights* was defined. The Hollywood majors doing business in Canada before 1987 were exempted. There are now two classes of foreign firms in theatrical distribution, those with grandfathered distribution rights and those without.

The 1995 CRTC Decision on Film Rights for Satellite DTH PPV Undertakings

As noted in chapter 12, when the CRTC licensed PPV undertakings for satellite television at the end of 1995, it required them to purchase nonproprietary exhibition rights from Canadian distributors. In doing so, the commission extended the domain of the earlier Investment Canada directive while altering it in two ways. The first concerned the definition of proprietary rights. The CRTC definition required the distribution company to own world rights or to have financed at least 50 percent of the film. The second difference was more substantive. The CRTC did not grant the exemption to the Hollywood majors that the Investment Canada initiative had included.

---

7. *Cinema Canada*, May 1988, 20.

Enforcement of the directive is difficult because the CRTC has jurisdiction over the buyers and not the sellers, but the buyers frequently do not have the information to determine who has or does not have proprietary rights. Another difficulty is the determination of what rights a distributor owns at any particular time. A distributor makes a living by judiciously licensing some rights and selling others. The status of their ownership of rights of a film is generally in flux.

In its 1995 decision, the CRTC also set the terms of the contracts for sharing revenue among the DTH PPV undertakings, the DTH distribution undertaking, and the film distribution company. Although this policy applies to films distributed by either Canadian or foreign firms, the bulk of PPV revenue is generated by proprietary films distributed by the majors. As mentioned in chapter 12, the CRTC justified the policy because it mainly taxed foreign suppliers. The president of the Canadian Association of Film Distributors and Exporters, which represents the Canadian distributors benefiting from the changed policy, is quoted as stating that the amount of money at stake was minimal but what counted was the precedent set by the proprietary rights decision of the CRTC.[8]

The Hollywood majors shared this view. Even without mobilizing the support of the U.S. government they have considerable leverage. Without access to the films for which the majors own proprietary rights, the Canadian satellite PPV services would not be viable, unless the Canadian demand for wrestling specials has been seriously underestimated. The beneficiaries of a failure of these services to offer an attractive menu of films would be sellers of gray market access to American PPV services. It is significant that Allarcom, a licensed Canadian PPV undertaking, asked the CRTC to drop its proprietary rights policy in its application for a license renewal. This request was supported through interventions by both ExpressVu and Star Choice. The CRTC acquiesced and justified the suspension of the mandatory contracting terms on the following basis:

When this condition of licence was first imposed, it was in response to concerns expressed that competition among DTH PPV services could produce a situation in which certain DTH PPV licensees which were also integrated with DTH distributors, could exert market pressures whereby DTH PPV licensees could be required to pay a greater portion of their revenues to foreign rights holders than is currently the case in the cable pay-per-view market. The Commission considered that the 1/3 split would promote market stability by ensuring that no licensee would be unduly pressured to accept escalating program costs.

---

8. *Playback,* March 25, 1996, 1, 4.

The Commission notes there are no integrated DTH/DTH PPV services currently in operation. Furthermore, none of the twelve interveners supported the retention of this condition.

With respect to suspending the nonproprietary rights policy, the commission stated:

> When this condition was imposed, the Commission considered that it would provide support for Canada's film distribution industry. At the time, it was anticipated that less than 10% of the feature films exhibited by a PPV undertaking would be subject to this condition, and the licensee was not opposed to the condition of licence, since it followed this practice with its cable pay-per-view service.[9]

We offer a translation of what some of these statements mean. The mandated prices were introduced because of a fear that Power DirecTV's PPV service would bid up the prices of rights and cause existing Canadian suppliers of PPV services to pay more to the foreign owners of those rights. With Power DirecTV not taking up its license, the other satellite PPV services, which are established players in the Canadian context, were finding it difficult to obtain a supply of suitable films on the mandated terms. This difficulty was penalizing them and their carriers, the licensed Canadian DTH satellite distribution services. Therefore, the mandated shares would no longer apply. The reasons given for withdrawing the restriction on the distribution of films with nonproprietary rights are difficult to understand. On the face of it, the CRTC is saying that withdrawal was justified because the policy was diverting too much business to Canadian distributors and because the PPV distributor no longer thought it was a good idea. We believe that the possibility that attractive proprietary rights films might not be supplied if the non-proprietary restriction on the majors remained in place might also have influenced the commission's decision.

Polygram Dispute

On March 13, 1997, Industry Minister Manley approved the application of Polygram Group Canada Inc. to establish a new film production and distribution business in Canada. Commitments included the spending of the lesser of $20 million or 20 percent of Canadian revenues over the next five years on entertainment, production, and postproduction activities in Canada. As a new foreign owned firm, Polygram would only be able to distribute films for which

---

9. All the passages are from CRTC Decision 98–76, Ottawa, March 13, 1998.

it held proprietary rights and thus was at a disadvantage in competing with the major American firms which were grandfathered under the existing policy. Polygram subsequently complained to the European Commission. After investigation, the commission concluded that Canada's treatment of Polygram was discriminatory and violated Canada's MFN commitment under GATS. The EC made a formal protest to the WTO and began a dispute resolution action by undertaking consultations with the Canadian government.

All WTO member countries are committed to the MFN obligations of the GATS unless they entered exceptions before the agreement was finalized. Canada entered an exception for its film and television coproduction agreements. It did not enter an exception for film distribution, where it has grandfathered certain companies under the Investment Canada directive, as Quebec had done in its Cinema Act. Since Polygram was excluded from enjoying the same rights as the Hollywood majors, it claimed that it was not receiving MFN treatment. The Canadian government's response was that the exception for coproductions was necessary in order that Canada could sign new ones with individual countries in the future. An MFN exception for film distribution was not necessary, as grandfathering is allowed under GATS. Canada also contended that it would treat all new foreign firms, American and other, equally.

Another aspect of Canadian film distribution policy affecting the EC's case was the transferability of the privileged status of a grandfathered major in a takeover. When Viacom acquired Paramount, Investment Canada approved the transaction including the transfer of the grandfathered status, after assessing the "net benefits" to Canada. The EC argued that Polygram, as a Dutch firm, was being granted different treatment from an American firm, Viacom, that had also entered Canadian film distribution after the signing of the WTO agreement.

Events took a new turn when Seagram acquired Polygram in 1998, thereby converting the firm to Canadian ownership and acquiring the same distribution rights as the American majors. As of early October 1998, the WTO had listed the dispute under "pending consultations," meaning that proceedings leading to a dispute panel could be activated at any time.[10]

If foreign investors other than a major that already was grandfathered under the Canadian policy had acquired Polygram's film distribution assets, the complaint could have proceeded in a manner similar to the periodical case discussed in chapter 10. A decision on this matter would have further clarified the boundary between a good and a service. If a film were ruled to be a good, then the policy is contrary to MFN provisions of the GATT, as would be the Canadian coproduction treaties. If it is a service and the Canadian policy is

10. In late October 1998, Seagram announced the sale of Polygram's film library for US$250 million to MGM (*Variety,* October 23, 1998). Seagram actively sought buyers for Polygram's film distribution assets but had not sold them as of April 1, 1999.

deemed to be discriminatory, Canada would be in contradiction of the GATS MFN provisions.

The good-service distinction would also have been an important determinant of the procedure adopted by the EC in proceeding with a formal dispute. If the dispute were taken under the GATT, then the EC itself could decide whether to initiate a complaint; if under the GATS, then all member countries would have had to agree to proceed. It is understood that France was reluctant to pursue the Polygram case. In general, France is supportive of Canada's position on cultural trade matters and its films are presently handled by Canadian distributors. It does not consider that it is harmed by the film distribution policy. If films were to be ruled a good, the EC would also jeopardize its coproduction treaties.

Dubbing

Dubbing extends the market of a film. Prior to the use of sound, translated intertitles were inserted into films to increase their attractiveness in different language markets. With the coming of sound, American distributors used subtitling or produced foreign-language versions of films using local performers. The expense of shooting a film more than once soon encouraged distributors to dub the soundtrack of the original film into different languages.

Germany and France argued that dubbed English-language films were cheap to produce, once the original film had been made, and that this constituted unfair competition for their domestic industries. This was an early version of the argument that American producers dump films in foreign markets. When other countries barred films not dubbed within their borders, American film companies began establishing dubbing studios abroad. In the intervening years, dubbing has become a lucrative source of revenue for local actors, and protection of dubbing is widespread.[11]

In Canada, the French-language film industry has been particularly concerned about and affected by the policies of other countries with respect to dubbing. The 1983 task force commented:

> France, its distributors and television networks, generally do not accept Canadian dubbing, which has the effect of forcing non-Canadian dubbing on Canadian releases in order to avoid the doubling of such

---

11. Mexico has taken a different tack. It's Film Law (article 8) requires that feature films, other than those for educational use or classified as appropriate for all ages, must be exhibited with their original soundtrack. It permits subtitles. For dubbing policies in a number of other countries, see Balio (1993, 32–34).

expenses. The task force recommends that (whether by negotiation or coercion, via customs regulations or other legislative or administrative means), the federal government encourage the dubbing of films in Canada. (Canada 1983, 51)

France protects the dubbing of television programming as well by means of an industrial agreement between the unions and the French dubbing and public broadcasting industry. The agreement, which has been renewed on an annual basis since 1977, stipulates that foreign programming originating outside the EC must be dubbed in France. A recent modification allows for the broadcasting of a specified number of hours annually of programming dubbed by non-EC members.

Quebec's Cinema Act (article 83) regulates the dubbing of foreign films through a number of measures. The main restriction is that if no French-dubbed version of the film is available, temporary licenses for as many copies as requested may be issued for forty-five days from the time the film is first publicly exhibited, unless the authorities determine a shorter period or fewer licenses. In certain circumstances, requests may be made to extend temporary licenses for a further fifteen days.

Thus, if a film is expected to have a first-run release of less than 60 days, it is usually not necessary to dub the film into French. If it has a longer first run and subsequent releases, then the film has to be dubbed into French in Quebec. Although the time restrictions are infrequently binding for a coordinated North American release, the majors extend the reach of successful films by sometimes simultaneous but often delayed releases of dubbed versions in foreign markets. This represents a potential market of some significance for Quebec artists, who understand both the nuances of English-language films and the sensitivities of French-language audiences. In the debate over the Quebec Cinema Act, Millard Roth of the CMPDA noted that half of the 140 releases by the majors in 1987 were dubbed into French.[12] The fact that France requires films released in France be dubbed into French by French artists has reduced the market for Quebec artists able to provide this service. As a counter strategy, the Quebec government has bargained with the majors and granted access to protected parts of distribution in return for dubbing commitments.

Language issues are on-going in related areas. They have surfaced with respect to the language used in video games, the dominance of English on the Internet, and delay in the issuing of software in Quebec because its producer wanted a coordinated release of the program in French-speaking countries that did not coincide with its English-language release. A recent example generating criticism was the release of Windows 95 by Microsoft.

---

12. *Variety,* May 18, 1988, 3.

Direct and Indirect Public Grants to Distributors

The 1983 task force, inter alia, recommended that nonrecourse financing be made available to Canadian distributors "who are *permanently* under-financed and limited in their ability to take risks" (Canada 1983, 55; italics original). In the late 1980s, the Canadian government initiated a Feature Film Distribution Fund to be administered by Telefilm Canada. The available funds have varied between C$15 and C$20 million. Telefilm creates lines of credit for Canadian distributors to cover a portion of their advances to acquire rights and their marketing expenses. The amounts of the various expenditures of the Canadian distributors that successfully applied for funding from Telefilm in 1994–95 are presented in table 14.

Beginning in 1988–89, Telefilm supported Canadian distributors in buying the Canadian rights of Canadian and foreign films. The policy was linked to the rights initiative. One blade of the scissors would exclude foreigners from distributing nonproprietary films in Canada. The other blade would provide Canadian distributors access to the public purse so that they could fill the void. At first, Telefilm supported the minimum guarantees offered by Canadian distributors to obtain rights for Canadian films and nonproprietary foreign films. The relative support of the two types of films are shown in figure 5.

TABLE 14. Coverage by Telefilm of Commitments and Expenses of Canadian Distributors, 1994–95

Type of Expenditure	Distributors' Commitments to Film Producers	Telefilm's Commitment to the Distributors	
	Thousands of C$	Thousands of C$	Percentage
Minimum Guarantees of Canadian Films	14578	10321	71
Marketing Costs of Canadian Films	5464	3280	60
Marketing Costs of Foreign Films	1775	1234	70

Source: Telefilm Annual Report 1994–95.

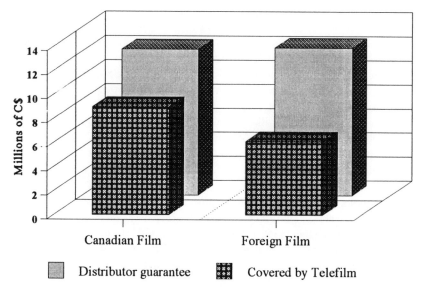

Source: Telefilm Canada Annual Report 1991-92
Fig. 5. Telefilm coverage of distributor commitments, 1991–92

The subsidies fueled more intensive bidding for the Canadian rights of foreign (largely non-American) films. Since the supply of such films was relatively insensitive to the increased demand, prices rose, creating windfall rents for foreign-film owners. The resulting transfers of wealth were not trivial. Yves Dion of Malofilm, a major Quebec distributor at that time, estimated the change in license fees as averaging C$25,000. As a benchmark to judge this figure, the same article in *Variety* reports that the average licensing fee for the Canadian market of a French film is about C$75,000.

> Most executives agree that prices have fallen since Telefilm Canada said last March that distributors could no longer use half of the $C17.5 million Distribution Fund to buy foreign movies.
> They may only use the fund for P&A of foreign films and acquisition of Canadian films. The result has been an end to bidding wars among distributors, which had driven prices of foreign films through the roof.[13]

---

13. *Variety,* August 24, 1992, 23. P&A refers to promotion and advertising expenditures.

As the quotation notes, when the consequences of how the subsidy program was structured became evident Telefilm Canada changed the program.

Currently, the support is targeted at subsidizing the guarantees for Canadian films, but marketing costs are supported regardless of the nationality of the film being distributed in Canada. The average annual amount committed by Telefilm to supporting distribution in the five years from 1990–91 to 1994–95 was just over C$15 million. Between the establishment of the Distribution Fund in 1988–89 and 1995–96, the average advertising budget for Canadian films supported rose from C$114,000 to C$318,000 (Houle 1996, 16). Houle's data also show that for Canadian distributors the advertising expenditures were higher on Canadian productions than on foreign. In part that is accounted for by the spillover effect of advertising in other countries on the non-Canadian films and the availability of advertising material from releases in other countries.

The indirect support for the Canadian distributors is not as visible but is probably more important and costly. The requirement that any project receiving support from Telefilm's Feature Film Fund have a contract for distribution with a Canadian distributor shuts out foreign distributors. The recently introduced provincial and federal tax credit policies also require a Canadian distributor for eligibility. This was not true of the tax shelter regimes that these policies replace.

Caradian producers face no information problem in assessing the capabilities of Canadian distributors. If the Canadian producers thought that the Canadian distributors would do the best job of supporting their films in the domestic market, the Canadian producers would voluntarily place their business with national distributors. That Canadian distributors require both large subsidies and a captive market is indicative of their current inefficiency relative to their competitors.

The Cross-Subsidy Illusion

The indirect and direct subsidies influence the supply price of distribution services in two ways. Restricting supply to Canadian firms increases the supply price at any quantity of distribution services. The direct subsidies to Canadian distributors act in the opposite direction. To these effects proponents of the policies add a third—a cross-subsidy impact on the terms of distribution for Canadian films.

The cross-subsidy argument has two strands. The first maintains that the supply price of distribution for Canadian films will fall because Canadian distributors "spend" profits from the protected distribution of non-proprietary foreign films on supporting Canadian films, that is, Canadian distributors provide the Canadian films with more financial support than would a foreign distributor of similar efficiency. The report of the Film Industry Task Force of

1985 commented that, if foreign distributors were displaced, "Canadian distributors will certainly commit a significant share of their revenues to the financing of Canadian films" (Canada 1985, 332).[14]

There is no convincing evidence that the owners of Canadian distribution firms are willing to dissipate their profits on losing investments in Canadian films. Those that do are unlikely to survive in competition with those that do not. The Canadian distribution firms that have raised money in public offerings have not declared that to be their management strategy. The reality is that Telefilm production subsidies require a Canadian distributor. Canadian distribution firms are unable to respond to this captive market without subsidies from another Telefilm fund. The evidence does reveal that Canadian distributors are willing to spend public funds on Canadian films.

The second strand of the cross-subsidy argument is that Canadian firms are better at distribution than foreign but were kept out of the business through the practices of foreign distributors. Once the market is given to them by the government this latent efficiency will manifest itself. If there are barriers to entry that prevent competent Canadian distributors from displacing incumbents, these should be as visible to the Competition Policy Bureau as to those industry spokespersons who make this argument. If the second strand was correct, why do Canadian firms have to be heavily subsidized when they are the only players allowed to distribute Canadian films financed by Telefilm. Despite its apparent valence in the political arena for more direct and indirect subsidies, the two strands of the cross-subsidy argument with respect to film distribution make little economic sense and are not supported by Canadian experience.

Interpretation

System Competition

Canadian distribution policy is multifaceted. Since the early 1930s, with a pause during World War II, the federal government and more recently the province of Quebec have engaged in a series of strategic interactions with the Hollywood majors. These have followed a pattern of confrontation, threats, and a negotiated solution. This interactive process has focused on access of Canadian cinemas to first run films, the contracting practices of the majors, and access of Canadian films to exhibitors. The negotiations about access for Canadian films has usually been dealt with by direct political negotiation between the large cinema chains and the government. The competition policy authorities have been more involved with the contracting process between distributors and exhibitors.

---

14. See also the report of the Film Industry Task Force (Canada 1983, 13).

The government has supported the view that commercially viable Canadian films have been discriminated against in terms of access to Canadian cinemas. There is little evidence to support the premise. Cinemas will not generally show films that they do not expect to draw an audience. They could not do so and survive. Cinemas depend on a continuous supply of films that they consider to be good risks. In order to support release strategies that generate audiences they have to commit ahead of time and often with little specific information about the film. Mistakes will be made in assessing the prospects of films, given the great uncertainty concerning audience reaction. To minimize the economic costs of mistakes, contracts that share risk have evolved over time. Cinemas also depend on the reputation of the supplier to maintain a flow of good "lottery tickets" and their own business acumen, within the degrees of freedom provided by the contracts, to nurture successes and abandon flops.

A failure of a cinema to book a film that later becomes popular is most likely to occur when a film comes from unexpected sources. When specific cases of failure are cited, they typically refer to a film that is successful in the art house circuit and seeks to cross over to the first-run cinemas. The owners and distributor of the film are often disturbed by the inability of the first run cinema chains to make space for their product. A Canadian example is Francois Girard's now acclaimed *Thirty-Two Short Films about Glenn Gould*, which was a success at the Montreal and Venice film festivals in 1993. Max Films, an established Quebec distributor, complained that they could not get screen time with Cineplex-Odeon before February 1994 because of the queue of American films that Cineplex-Odeon was committed to show. One can understand Max Films concerns, but the problem is a wicked one. A cinema chain could not survive if it breached contracts with concerns that steadily supply a menu of commercially viable films in order to accommodate sporadic cross-overs. As a Canadian firm Cineplex-Odeon presumably was sensitive to Canadian aspirations and knew Canadian audiences.

Crossover of Canadian and other art house films do occur. A cinematic chain operating in Canada, whatever its ownership, would be commercially incompetent if it did not make significant efforts to accommodate crossovers for Canadian films. The evidence is that the cinemas respond reasonably, given their contractual constraints, to the sporadic Canadian film crossovers. For example, in a letter to the *Globe and Mail* of November 13, 1996 Cineplex Odeon's president wrote: "In 1995, Canadian feature films represented 6% of the films exhibited on Cineplex Odeon screens and included all Canadian films which were made available to Cineplex Odeon for possible exhibition."

A monopoly problem can arise when only a few international film distribution systems coexist. Currently, the majors and consortia of regional film distributors provide international distribution services. Alternative means of packaging and delivering content are also developing, as is evident from the importance of such new players as HBO in the United States, Latin America, and Asia, and Canal Plus in Europe. In comparison, policies such as the proprietary rights initiative lessen competition by barring potential players and raise the costs of including Canada in a consortia of distributors.

The Three Tiers of Distribution

The battery of recent film distribution policy measures in Canada ignore the economics of the industry. The Hollywood majors are significant players in financing and distributing high-budget films and extracting value from them internationally. For English-language films that are best launched with a coordinated world promotion campaign and a wide opening, they face little competition. For films that are best released more slowly while word of mouth support develops, more competition exists. Specialized divisions with the majors provide an alternative for the more commercially viable of these films. The Miramax division of Disney is an example of a group that has been successful at identifying the potential of such films. Typically a studio will contract out some of the distribution rights for such films. Miramax, for example, distributes in Canada through Alliance. With these films, one observes more varied alliances of regional distributors than with the more formulaic Hollywood blockbusters. At the third level of theatrical distribution—that of the few films with an interest that is only local or at most national—the Hollywood majors are not competitive. National and local firms have advantages in this segment of the business.

Currently, there is a Canadian presence at all three levels. That one of the majors is now Canadian reflects the growing ability of Canadian capital and management to compete in an open environment, but it is unlikely to affect the national culture in any predictable way. This is true despite the fact that the purchase of Universal by Canadian interests affects statistics, such as the share of the film distribution market held by Canadian firms, more significantly than all of the policies described in this chapter put together. This event should have led to elation among the policy authorities worried about the percentage of films distributed by non-Canadians in Canada. Instead, Statistics Canada has not integrated Universal with Canadian distributors in its statistical series on Canadian versus non-Canadian distribution and shows no enthusiasm to do so. Canadian Heritage officials appear oblivious to the fact that one of the black hats that they aspire to shut out of the Canadian market sits on top of a Canadian head.

To participate in a consortium distributing films of the second type, Canadian distribution firms have to serve a market area of sufficient size to be valued in an international alliance of regional distributors. The sensible areas are English-language North American and French-language markets in the Americas—principally Quebec. The English-speaking market for films in Canada is too small and too similar to the American market to be viable as a separate entity. There is no reason why one or two Canadian firms could not be successful in the North American market either through expansion or merger with an American independent distributor. For the most promising films choosing the second distribution option, the majors will be competitive against independent regional distributors to provide the North American link.[15] Jake Eberts, a Canadian producer who has stitched together effective alliances for distributing a number of films, notes that

> with the exception of a handful of art films, the box office receipts you can generate with a film distributed by a major studio are almost always more than can be generated by an independent. I have tried to stick with the majors in the U.S. ever since. (Eberts and Ilott 1990, 62)

Creating a distinct English-speaking Canadian market adds costs to the consortium approach by unnecessarily fragmenting the coalition. Of course, if Canadian distributors are subsidized sufficiently generously, a separate distribution in Canada could occur voluntarily. A North American distributor would be able to buy the subsidized service at a lower cost than in-house provision. If in a consortium the Canadian market must legally be served by a Canadian firm, subsidies will have to be paid to make the consortium price competitive with that of a grandfathered major. If the current direct support from Telefilm coupled with the indirect requirements of the production funds and the tax credits are accurate indicators of the required subsidy, the program will be very costly. The benefits are negligible. The costs will be higher if the majors are excluded from the nonproprietary market, both because of the subsidies required to do what the majors did at no cost to the Canadian taxpayer but also because of the high probability of retaliation.

---

15. The MPEAA in a Report to the United States Trade Representative: Trade Restrictions Facing the MPEAA Member Companies in Foreign Markets, May 1987 (reprinted in *Cinema Canada* May 1988, 21) reported that two-thirds of the films that their members distributed were made "in-house" and one-third were "pick-ups" that did not grant worldwide distribution rights.

Conclusion

The proprietary rights policy is reminiscent of old-style protectionist develop-mental policies in less developed countries. Check the balance of payments situation in different sectors, and where the country is in deficit initiate import substitution policies. These policies generated stagnation rather than growth. As a package, the current distribution initiatives have also failed. A consultant for the department of Canadian Heritage reports that

> contrary to what has happened in other sectors (videocassette whole-sale, distribution in home entertainment markets), it seems that none of the measures adopted since 1980 (agreement between the Govern-ment of Quebec and the MPEA, Feature Film Distribution Fund, Investment Canada policy, etc.) has had a meaningful impact on the respective shares of the theatrical release market held by Canadian and non-Canadian companies. (Houle 1994, 45)

In our opinion, these policies have failed because they run against the grain of the economic realities of film distribution. They dissipate wealth by orienting Canadian entrepreneurship and skilled people away from competing for an audience here and abroad toward persuading the government to restrain foreign competitors. In doing so they invite the affected countries to retaliate.

We hasten to add that others disagree. Houle, for example, does not derive the same message from the failure, which he has documented, as we do. His conclusion is that Canada should increase rather than reduce protection. In February 1998, the DCH released a paper, "A Review of Canadian Feature Film Policy," accompanied by an invitation to post comments on the department's Internet site. The overwhelming response has been requests for more public funds to be made available for film and television production and distribution. Most industry submissions favor extensions of the tax credit mechanism as opposed to use of the discretionary subsidy programs.

If the contradictions in Canadian policy arising from grandfathering the majors from the Investment Canada directive or the Quebec Cinema Act are removed but the proprietary right initiative is maintained, retaliation is likely. The majors could boycott Canada or delay releases in retaliation for being excluded from participating in the nonproprietary markets, if that is the next step taken by the Canadian government. A total or partial boycott and the resulting spiral of consequences could be very costly to Canada, the majors, and Canadian-American relations. The MPAA has taken private retaliatory actions against a number of countries in the past. For example, it boycotted the United Kingdom after the "Dalton duty" was imposed in 1947, as discussed in chapter 4. More recently the Russian market was boycotted to protest a failure to protect MPAA copyrights.

A significant flaw in the current system is that it encourages such a use of private power. In our opinion, it would be healthy if the federal and provincial governments stopped dealing with the association of the majors as a "Little State Department." Instead the MPA should be granted the status of any other industry association. Its members are subject to Canadian law for their operations in Canada. If a major is involved in breaking those laws, it should be prosecuted. If nothing illegal is occurring, the proprietary right initiative and much of the jawboning are revealed as protectionist measures. If the international nature of the business makes antitrust prosecution difficult, Canada should more diligently pursue closer collaboration with antitrust authorities in other countries as a means of coping with that problem.

Factors that may create cost-saving opportunities for firms in other American industries that have formed WP export cartels are not operative for this industry in Canada. The Canadian government could go on the record as considering continued maintenance of WP status by the MPA members with respect to their operations in Canada a reason for particularly tight competition policy surveillance. The ultimate goal should be to place trade relations within this industry on the same basis as it is for others. In return, the majors should be given government assurance that they will not be harassed either individually or as a group for being commercially successful, as has been frequently the case. Policies should neither discriminate against them nor, as sometimes turns out to be the case under the current approach, for them. International disputes should be dealt with between the respective governments. These steps would contribute to setting the stage for integration of the cultural industries into the international system.

Canadian film distribution policy has ended up discriminating against European firms and not those of the supposed target, the Hollywood majors. The supporters of the protectionist policies within the government talk of an alliance between European countries to support the continuation of inward-looking policies. The Polygram case reflected the reality of the impact of Canada's policies on European interests. France is often cited as a potential ally in maintaining these policies. Perhaps it is rhetorically, but the economics of the French-language film market generates a different imperative. France stands in relation to Quebec in the French-language market as the United States stands in relation to English Canada in the English-speaking market. The French government was hesitant to support the Polygram action by the EC, but French distributors cannot be content that they must subcontract distribution to Quebec-based or Canadian distributors for nonproprietary film distribution in Quebec and Canada. There are also continuing disputes between the French-speaking Canadian and French industries over their respective restrictions against films dubbed in the other language.

CHAPTER 18

Past Lessons and Future Alternatives

In many countries, the policies affecting the cultural industries are markedly different from those in other sectors. Whereas the general trend in economic relations has been to liberalize trade, the policies in the cultural industries have become more restrictive. Part of the explanation lies in the commonly perceived connection between what the different media deliver and the character of the society. Another reason is the persistent dominance of American cultural products. National governments feel vulnerable if the content of what people read, listen to, and watch is not under their control. Their discomfort rises if these media appear to be under the control of institutions in another country with which they have common causes but also contested interests. In this book, we have examined Canadian policies as indicative of the direction, but not the detail, of policies in many countries. The detail of Canadian policies has been presented to convey the complexity of current cultural policy regimes. In order to be able to negotiate a more workable international regime for the burgeoning trade and investment in the cultural industries, each country must be familiar with the policies of other countries. In this concluding chapter we seek lessons for structuring a better international governance structure for the cultural industries from the past and the cases examined in part III.

Lessons from the Past

Historically, protective policies, reflecting the characteristics of their original technologies, developed for each of the media. At the same time technological changes were reducing the costs of distribution and creating an economic imperative to distribute content on a wider and wider basis. Each of the cultural industries responded to the new commercial opportunities within the constraints created by protectionist policy and technology. The publication of books, for example, was spread by licensing the copyright to national publishers or, where permitted, to subsidiary operations of the original publisher. With some technologies, the government could not readily exert control. For example, nonauthoritarian governments could not prevent the spillover of radio and television signals from neighboring countries. Public broadcasters could be created in order to present a national perspective, but they still had to compete with other domestic and foreign signals for the attention of the listener or viewer.

With the development of the computer and the ability to put content into binary formats, transform it, and transport it at low cost, the different media began to converge, at least in the stages before content was delivered to the consumer. Evasion of the patchwork of policies protecting each of the media became easier, and the imperative to distribute internationally was further reinforced. A rapid expansion of national and international distribution of content in every form has resulted. Television signals, magazine and newspaper content, and music are transported by microwave, coaxial cable, fiber, and satellite to all corners of the world. The public has welcomed the choices.

The Dynamic of Protectionist Policies

Governments have continued to try to control access to the wealth of content enabled by technological developments. The gains for consumers of entertainment and information were accompanied by potential losses on the part of some established businesses and government enterprises. These interests also opposed rapid change. The governments acted to cushion the effect on them by slowing down the impact of the new services on the old and, where possible, compensating the losers by granting them valuable rights to provide the new services or to act as gatekeepers for foreign suppliers of such services.

These attempts to insure owners and other stakeholders of established services have been accompanied by efforts to maintain a distinct national menu of content or to tilt the costs of accessing content in favor of particular content. Governments strove to distinguish their country from others, not by allowing their people to distinguish themselves by choosing differently from the universal menu but by crafting a national menu or by rigging the relative prices. The recent technological changes have been so rapid and complex that governments have been unable to "manage" effectively these two concerns. The provision of insurance to existing providers by retarding change has penalized participation in the international opportunities by new and different domestic players. When incumbents were compensated for the potential losses arising from innovation and changed regulations by being granted new rights, they often delayed development of their value because of the effect on the value of their existing assets. In addition, those who owned the rights necessary to bring new services on line at home and to integrate with the international developments were not necessarily those who could develop them with the most energy and skill. The Canadian government has often made these rights costly to transfer, which has further retarded the country's participation in the development phase of the new technologies.

The flexibility needed to establish a presence at a level that would have generated more wealth was absent. An example is the development of cable networks or specialty channels, where Canadian interests failed to take initiatives at a North American level. Despite the earlier and denser cabling of Canada, cable networks from Canada serving both Canada and the United States failed to develop. Instead, the introduction of these services at a national level was slow and costly. A number of Canadian specialty channels, many of them derivative of established American services, were eventually established. Unlike their American counterparts, they concentrated on protecting their right at home from competition rather than looking for opportunities abroad. No American services derivative of Canadian ones were established. A side effect of this inward orientation was the development of a business culture of protection. An impenetrable array of government regulations and interpretations ensued that both lacked transparency and created inconsistencies.

This inward-looking response has contributed to the fact that, after more than 50 years, the American cultural industries continue to dominate international markets in film and television despite the concerted efforts of countries throughout the world to displace American product. American commercial dominance has eroded in a number of industries, for example, the automobile industry, in which trade has been liberalized. Ironically, this is not true for the trade of the cultural industries, for which the United States has favored liberalization but has not obtained it.

Why have the protectionist policies been ineffective in changing American dominance? The cultural industries are inherently international. If a mining company in a small country produces copper and a large country buys its output at the world price, no gain occurs from having access to other markets. If a film producer in a small country makes a successful film, more revenue can be earned from all countries that can be accessed. Protectionist policies for the cultural industries make little economic sense, particularly for a small country. Protection generally reduces wealth, but the effect is more marked in the cultural industries. If the small country is blocked from selling its copper in the large market, it will seek markets elsewhere. The price of its exports will probably be reduced, but the effect will be moderated by expansion of its sales in other markets as other suppliers divert copper to the large market. A film producer barred from its largest foreign market will lose the licensing income from that market. The value of the licenses in other markets is unaffected, as the film is already licensed there and so cannot be diverted to those markets. The revenue from the other markets remains the same, but all the revenue from the large market, which because of size is of dominant importance, is sacrificed.

To reduce the cost of import substitution resulting from protectionist measures, such as content restrictions, the substitute product can be oriented to the international market and sold abroad as well as at home. The ostensible purpose of content policy—to change the menu by adding nationally relevant content—is thwarted. The only difference in the content menu is that international product made nationally has replaced international product made in other countries. If the substitute product is of lower quality or more costly, the country with the content restrictions bears the cost. Its menu of programs is of either poorer quality or more expensive than it would have been without the policy. What does happen, which the Canadian government measures as a success, is that some production migrates from the United States to it. Unfortunately for the government, the process does not stop there. Unless a country is of negligible importance or some other national interest is involved, the United States will retaliate. The cost of import substitution is no longer mitigated by export promotion. The industrial expansion can only be maintained with much larger subsidies than those received before the retaliation.

In short, the success has been limited to gaining a significant but precarious industrial beachhead and not in achieving the vague promise to provide more nationally relevant material. Indeed, the existence of a gap in providing relevant Canadian content is brought into question by observing that the national public and private broadcasters, which have been in existence for half a century or so, have apparently not been able to close it. A nonbeliever in the gap might be excused for asking why, given the budgets over that period, broadcasters have not told the "story" of every town in Canada.[1]

Whether produced in-house or, as is more common, by independent production houses, the dramatic programs on the public and private networks are crafted to travel. What we have demonstrated in our examination of Canadian policies and experiences in each of the cultural industries, except for magazines, is the dynamic stimulus arising from foreign sales. Without export revenues buttressing subsidies, the expansion of Canadian production would have been far less than what has been achieved.

The Canadian experience with television particularly fits the dynamic described. Content restrictions were imposed. Substitute programs were produced in Canada. These programs were similar to the displaced programs. Despite having access to the American market, this expansion in national production required substantial subsidies. If the United States reciprocates by restricting access of Canadian production, the costs of the import substitution, which is currently kept down by simultaneous export subsidization, would

---

1. The hearings before the CRTC in the fall of 1998 reinforced the fact that you can force broadcasters to distribute Canadian programming but you cannot force viewers to watch it, especially in the case of English-language dramas.

escalate significantly. The Canadian industry is extremely vulnerable to such a change in American policy.

An opposite experience has occurred with magazine policy, in which Canada employed two instruments to protect the domestic players. The Canadian advertising market was protected sequentially by income tax provisions and a prohibitive tariff, then by an excise tax to keep split runs out of the market, and now by a prohibition of advertising in split runs. The portfolio of foreign magazines was discriminated against by Canadian postal rates. Under that regime, the Canadian industry as a whole has survived but not prospered. No export promotion policy accompanied these initiatives, and Canada's magazine publishers have not earned much income abroad. Ironically, what has been exported are "Canadian voices telling Canadian stories." For example, two of Canada's most famous short story writers, Mavis Gallant and Alice Munro, have been featured writers in American magazines such as the *New Yorker* for decades.[2] Many of the stories published in these magazines feature life in Montreal and the small towns of English Canada, respectively. Gallant has lived in France since early in her writing career. In her introduction to *Home Truths: Selected Canadian Stories,* she recalls:

> A Montreal collector once told me that he bought Canadian paintings in order to have a unifying theme in the decoration of his house. It means—if anything so silly can have a meaning—that art is neutral adornment, a slightly superior brand of chintz, and that Canadian painters, because they are Canadian, work from a single vision.
>
> Like most of us, the collector probably has a defined range of taste, and he is drawn to painting that happens to fall within its scope. This will not prevent him from showing visitors art that can be seen in good galleries all over Western Europe, not to speak of the United States, and calling it "typically" and even "uniquely" Canadian. He has paid for an exclusive point of view; if art is universal, then he has been cheated.
>
> To dissent would lead into hostile territory. It might be considered un-Canadian, an accusation to which the expatriate writer is particularly susceptible, and will go to some heights to avoid. I have been

---

2. The fly leaf of Alice Munro's *Friend of My Youth*, Mclelland & Stewart Inc. (1991) states: "Every year her writing continues to reach a wider audience, with magazines such as *The New Yorker, Atlantic Monthly,* and several others (represented in this collection) all clamouring for her stories." The same sentence with the addition of *The Paris Review* and the exclusion of the expression in parentheses appears at the beginning of her 1994 book, *Open Secrets,* published by Penguin Books.

rebuked by a consular official for remarking that Rome in winter is not as cold as Montreal; and it surely signifies more than lightheadedness about English that "expatriate" is regularly spelled in Canadian newspapers "expatriot." Whether they know it or not, Canadian artists are supposed to "paint Canadian." (1981, xi)

Both large and small countries need access to foreign markets in order to generate the revenue necessary to support their domestic production. A film producer in the United States may get a large absolute amount of money from foreign markets—theatrical, television, and video—and this may represent half of the total revenues. Because of the small size of the domestic market, a similar producer in English or French Canada will expect to get a much larger share of total revenue from foreign markets and thus has a stronger interest in maintaining access to these markets.

Success achieved in foreign markets supports the domestic industry. It permits producers and distributors to develop their own capabilities and promote the creativity of domestic talent. This redounds to the benefit of local artists and technical personnel and the development of an indigenous culture. The best way to assist domestic industries, cultural and other, is to ensure that they are internationally competitive. The worst way is to condemn them to small domestic markets and to prop them up with subsidies.

The Spin and the Reality of the Protectionist Policies

The protectionist policies for these industries are politically popular. Canadian policies toward the cultural industries are based on the premise that going to the movies, watching television, listening to music, or reading are fundamentally different from other activities. When a Canadian chooses to buy a car, there is no claim that he or she does not know how best to arrange getting from home to work. When the same Canadian and others tune into a foreign-made television program, a statistic is generated that alarms those in charge of Canadian cultural policy. It is of no consequence that the Canadians may be choosing to watch a National Geographic special while forgoing the pleasures of catching a repeat of *Cannibal Girls,* a film that registers on the positive side of the Canadian cultural ledger. In our opinion, the popularity of protectionist policies among voters in general will wane as the dissonance increases between what is promised and what actually occurs. This process may also be accelerated if the political spin that supports these policies loses some of its appeal.

American Dominance

The emphasis on American dominance in public statements is misleading. A more appropriate label would be the dominance of the production and distribution of international content by a system that is also international. The Hollywood and recording company majors have disparate ownership. The "Americans against us" depiction of domination rings particularly hollow in the case of Canada. With Seagram's acquisition of Universal and its purchase of Polygram, the Canadian share of control over the actions of the Hollywood and recording majors exceeds the relative importance of the Canadian market in the world market for films, television programs, or recorded music.

The Hollywood majors have always absorbed creative and marketing talent from everywhere in the world (Acheson and Maule 1994c). In film, they compete to pick up rights for promising pictures initiated by others. In the recording business, they have a stable of artists from around the world under contract. Almost every country tries to influence their behavior in one way or another and in turn is lobbied by them. Each film studio and record label has a brand image. In film, these brands differ and cover a much wider range of product than was true in the days of the PCA.

Canadian Voices Need a Public Space to Tell Canadian Stories

General acknowledgment that what we read, listen to, or watch matters does not justify policies that prohibit or make more expensive content based on criteria that do not relate to the content itself. Unfortunately, this general acknowledgment has created a fog factor that makes the cry "Canadian voices need a public space in which to tell Canadian stories" potent in generating protective policies. Since until very recently all the political parties have supported these policies, their inconsistencies were not raised in political circles. Meanwhile the media benefit from the policies, so their zeal to analyze and explore the basis of these policies and their actual effects has been limited.

In fact only the first part of the mantra has been well served by Canadian policies. Canadian voices are being subsidized and protected. The second part has not been as well served. The incentive under current policies is to obtain as much public help as possible to make product that will be profitable. This means developing the story that generates the most profit in world markets regardless of the nationality of the people or the locations. Sometimes a local story is made more attractive to others if locations and accents are accurate. More often, location is made generic and the "edge" of a story for one audience is dulled in order for it to attract another. In the process a good national story becomes an average international story. This dynamic is revealed by comments made by a successful Canadian entertainment lawyer, Michael Levine, about making a miniseries for television on the history of the Hudson's Bay Company based on a book by Canadian author Peter Newman:

> Now, we could take it and we could plant the entire story in Montreal and on Hudson's Bay and in Winnipeg, and we could tell it from a Canadian viewpoint in a way that I could guarantee that absolutely nobody would have bought it ... The way to do it is to focus on the Orkneys and the Scots and the money men in London and the British Royal Family, so you see it is an international story. (*Globe and Mail*, January 25, 1997, C1)

This change is responsive to economic forces. The effective demand is revealed in licensing fee offers. Mr. Levine is saying that including the Orkneys, the Scots, the London money men, and the British royal family will generate more profit for its creators and producers. In some cases, such alterations will make the difference in the series becoming commercially viable. Attending to the business elements of a production must occur if creative dreams are to be realized. Attending to them inevitably creates compromises for the creative side.

Misinterpreting the Statistics

A small country that has an internationally competitive industry can expect to have only a small share of its domestic market but a similar share of world markets. Together the revenues can be substantial, consisting of, say 2 percent of the domestic market and 2 percent of world markets. The tendency is to consider these situations as leaving little shelf space for domestic product. Policies are then introduced to replace imported with domestic product. Not only does this cause trade frictions, but the results are often programs that neither the domestic nor the foreign audiences patronize.

The statistics collected also frequently fail to reflect the concerns that ostensibly motivated policy. For example, consider the content quotas for television broadcasting. The constraints cover what is on the air and not what is watched. With 50 channels on a cable system, it is possible for a viewer never to watch any "Canadian" program while having all of the Canadian stations meeting their content requirements. It is also possible for a viewer always or mostly to watch "Canadian" shows. The statistics that are routinely reported cover the viewing of individual Canadian and American channels.

Cross-Subsidy

Another misreading of economic forces is embodied in the continuing appeal to the cross-subsidy thesis. This argument maintains that if Canadian firms are protected so as to generate profits they will spend them on unprofitable but politically valued projects. To obtain the desired expenditure the connection has to be enforced through withdrawing the privilege if the condition is not met. Without enforcement, the expenditure is unlikely to occur, and the claim that it does is a means to justify excess profits. If the cross-subsidy argument were correct, the government would not have to apply the detailed regulation that is in place. All broadcasters in Canada are Canadian. By the cross-subsidy argument, they would dispose of profits to support the goals of Canadian policy. Canadian content restrictions would be unnecessary, as would explicit conditions of support for Canadian programming in the terms of a license. In reality, the CRTC requires minimum levels of Canadian content because, in the absence of quotas, the commercial broadcasters would generally show only those programs that have commercial appeal to advertisers. Nor does the concern stop at commercial broadcasters. If the cross-subsidy argument were valid, it would surely not be necessary for the CRTC to hector the CBC, the Canadian public broadcaster, to show more Canadian programs.

The Importance of Ownership

Foreign-ownership constraints are pervasive in the cultural industries. The discretionary alternatives of any ownership are constrained by the costs and demands for product. Within these constraints, owners of different nationalities may not make the same decisions, but how they will differ is almost impossible to determine. Barring national security reasons for national ownership, the case for foreign-ownership constraints is weak. In this area, as in content quotas, Canadian firms have enjoyed the freedom of operating in countries that have weaker controls while maintaining the constraint at home. Canadian newspaper magnates—Lord Beaverbrook, Lord Thomson, and Conrad Black—were and are fond of buying major British newspapers. Canadian cable entrepreneurs have invested profitably in American and British franchises. Their British and American counterparts could not do the same in Canada. Neither England nor the United States have imposed reciprocal ownership constraints, although the

United States has come close to passing legislation that would have imposed foreign-ownership restrictions on cable.

The themes—the "Americans against us," "the benefits of unspecified cross-subsidies," the "Canadian voices need a public space to tell Canadian stories" mantra and the "importance of ownership"—have been cultivated by a mix of industry, bureaucratic, and political interests. This may change. The willingness of national players in the cultural industries to promote protectionist policies will be reduced if access to foreign markets becomes more important than domestic protection. Access abroad is most important for feature film and television programming but is increasingly significant for all the cultural industries except magazine publishing. As the cases discussed in the book indicate, the U.S. government has made it clear in word and in deed that it will respond to any new initiative to extend Canadian protection in these industries. A second factor that may reduce enthusiasm for these policies in the industries themselves is the difficulty of enforcing the protective barriers in the new technological environment.

An Alternative Approach

If Vincent Massey, who chaired the Royal Commission on National Development in the Arts, Letters and Sciences after World War II, were to do the same today, the report would be significantly different from its predecessor. Mr. Massey would probably be surprised at what has transpired since 1951. Some might argue that Canada would not be where it is now without the protectionist policies. We frankly do not know what the net effect of these policies has been. What is clear to us is that continuing with these policies will result in retaliation and the stifling of exports, a major source of success for many of the Canadian cultural industries. The alternative of looking inward and further displacing imports is unattractive for consumers and will lead to an exodus of talent. Continuing to exempt trade in cultural products from international governance is not in the interests of a small country like Canada.

What the rules should be and how they are to be set and administered are complex issues, but the experience drawn from other agreements, especially those involving international trade, may point the way. The WTO contains general safeguard provisions, measures to deal with the circumstances of developing countries, services, intellectual property, and investment. Special arrangements have been crafted for agriculture, textiles, steel, civilian aircraft, financial services, telecommunications, and information technology. Individual commodities have been subjected to treatment through United Nations Conference on Trade and Development, and individual goods have been conditioned by voluntary export and import restraints. Each of these arrangements has been a response to problems faced by particular countries and to the pressure exerted by interest groups (Jackson, Davey, and Sykes 1995, 1160–1204). While they appear to resist the trend toward freer trade, the terms of the arrangements frequently prevent the introduction of further protectionist measures and include procedures that will lead to future liberalization. Thus, standstill and rollback can be part of sectoral agreements. It does not seem beyond the bounds of possibility to design an agreement of mutual benefit that will deal with the circumstances of the cultural industries.

An agreement that encourages outward-looking policies is unlikely to be introduced in isolation. Commitment to such policies requires assurance that other countries are doing the same. National debates on proposed international agreements, as has occurred with the MAI, tend to focus on the obligations imposed on individual countries and the alleged loss of sovereignty. Properly designed, these agreements can result in outcomes of mutual benefit. Each participant accepts obligations while benefiting from the obligations undertaken by others.

What the Trade Disputes Reveal

The trade disputes discussed in part III can be examined from many different perspectives. Linking the issues addressed in these events to the categorization of problems in past trade negotiations is a first step in assessing the role of formal agreements in a more supportive international governance structure. This classification exercise helps identify the pattern of problems and the ability of traditional rules-based remedies to cope with them.

A common issue in the disputes is the right to provide a cultural service in another country. The magazine split-run, CMT, satellite broadcasting, Borders, and film distribution cases are concerned with the denial or threatened denial of the right to operate in Canada. With satellite broadcasting and Borders, a would-be entrant was denied access. With film distribution, CMT, and *Sports Illustrated,* actions were taken to deny foreign suppliers the right to provide services that they had previously been supplying to the Canadian market. The removal of a foreign incumbent often occurs when its activities reveal a profitable niche in the market. CMT is the archetypical example in our cases.

An "import displacement" policy, that transfers a profitable activity from foreign to a politically well-connected set of domestic hands, plays differently in the political arena when services are involved as compared to goods. For goods, a tariff provides a relatively flexible means of experimenting with such policies. A tariff on imported goods reduces their competitiveness, and over time the market share of domestic goods rises. The replacement of quotas with tariffs and the abolition of prohibitive tariffs were important initial steps in the development of a more liberal trade regime for trade in goods. A number of countries have been able to engineer a transition from import-competing policies with respect to goods to more open policies. Gradual reduction of the tariff was accompanied by the market determining which suppliers would provide the imported goods. There is little effective agitation to reverse that trend. For services the equivalent of tariffs are difficult to impose. Sometimes, as is the case with, for example, films, this is because values are not known at the time of entry. When tried, processes designed to circumvent this difficulty have proven unwieldy. An example that has been used with films requires paying a bond at the border, which is refunded if the tariff value, when revealed by box office returns, is below the amount of the bond. In general, the "repatriation" of cultural services developed by foreigners has been pursued through far less flexible and transparent means than the tariff.

Under many of the quotas prevalent in the cultural industries, a political rather than a market decision has determined who will provide the mandated amount of foreign service or, in some cases, the number of foreign suppliers. The CRTC, the Canadian broadcasting regulator, established a list of eligible foreign specialty and pay channels. The criteria for selection are described in such broad terms that almost any decision could be made in an individual case. This informal process of selective protection has been altered by the CMT case. Taking a party off the list will be more difficult in the future, but who will be added remains discretionary. What privileges are conveyed by being on the list also is subject to arbitrary changes through the linkage rules.

Political decisions have also given the Hollywood majors rights that cannot be exercised by a European film distributor and in some instances by a Canadian distributor. Subsequent decisions have made these rights transferable at a negotiated price. In a related area, the Hollywood majors were denied, with considerable fanfare, the rights to distribute nonproprietary films to Canadian digital satellite broadcasting PPV services. In theatrical distribution, they were granted a privileged position for English-language films of this type. Then, with no fanfare, the denial with respect to the PPV distribution services was suspended. By a similarly mysterious process, not only do *Reader's Digest* and *Time,* the original targets in Canada's magazine wars, have rights denied to other foreign magazines, but the former has become Canada's most successful "indigenous" magazine. Emerson claimed that a foolish consistency was the hobgoblin of a small mind. He did not comment on the size of the minds associated with foolish inconsistency.

The cases reveal that the boundaries of the partition of foreign suppliers into insiders and outsiders are often quite rigid. There is no mechanism to ensure that those on the inside are the most efficient of the eligible foreign suppliers. In the CMT case, a foreign insider became temporarily a foreign outsider and was finally transformed into a Canadian insider with access to the Canadian advertising market. Although the partitions between foreign insiders and outsiders are discriminatory and unnecessarily inefficient, they are attractive politically, as they create allies, the insiders, in foreign countries. This reduces the probability of retaliation. In that way, this policy resembles voluntary export restrictions except that the political choice of which foreign suppliers will be favored is not transferred to the foreign government. The rigid partitions are most prevalent in areas of the cultural industries in which the way of doing business has not rapidly changed. Economic costs to them become more severe and difficult to hide when technological change is rapid.

For many services a foreign concern can only compete effectively in the domestic market if it has a commercial presence there. Investment rules are then important in determining the openness of the domestic market. Through exercising discretion as to who will become an insider, the national authorities can tailor the partition to their liking. Foreign-ownership restrictions were important in the magazine, CMT, Borders, and film distribution cases and in the forcing of an increasingly onerous set of obligations on Power DirecTV in the satellite-broadcasting case.

In a number of situations a foreign service with an attractive format can qualify as domestic by taking on Canadian financial partners rather than seeking status as a privileged foreign service. The sharing of its wealth with Canadian partners is the price of admission. The foreign-ownership restrictions help determine this price. The Canadian partners, who are usually knowledgeable about how the system works, "earn" a share of the profit by assisting in obtaining approval. In turn, less of the wealth is passed on to Canadian consumers, as the prices of the service are raised by the reduction in foreign competition. Requiring that Canadians have de facto control as well as own a certain percentage of the supplier adds a very difficult to measure condition that is determined in a closed process. Control as a discretionary filter played an important role in the Borders and CMT cases.

In instances such as the licensing of television programming, quotas are imposed on an activity that does not require a domestic commercial presence. Foreign-ownership requirements protect the broadcasters in Canada while content quotas do the same for domestic producers. Foreign-ownership restrictions also play a role in the latter since a program in which all the key positions are held by Canadians does not qualify as Canadian if the producer is not Canadian. Content limits arose in another guise in the magazine case. The definition of a split run turned on the amount of content that did not appear in a foreign edition. Unlike the television quotas, the nationality of the writers of the content was not definitive. Like the television quotas, what the content contained was irrelevant.

The television or radio music quotas were not featured directly in any of the disputes. Nevertheless, they are a significant potential issue. If the United States were to deny access to Canadian producers to its television or radio markets, many of the Canadian producers would be hurt by more than they benefit from the Canadian measures. The Canadian viewer, advertiser, and broadcaster would face significant adjustments if American programming were cut off and only available through American stations. Their American counterparts would be little affected if Canadian programming were only made available through Canadian stations.

Neighboring rights initiatives, such as the Canadian recognition of public performance rights for performers and record producers and blank tape levies have been proliferating internationally. Their rising importance has revealed a difference of opinion among countries on what should be the guiding principle governing the allocation of the funds collected. The boundary between copyright and neighboring rights is not a bright line. Copyright places considerable reliance on national treatment, while neighboring rights typically incorporate reciprocity in this regard. On this issue, the Europeans and Canadians are on the same page and the United States is more isolated in demanding that national treatment guide both. If the United States accepts reciprocity as the guideline for neighboring rights, that acceptance is likely to be coupled with policy initiatives to adopt at least some neighboring rights. That tie-in would not be welcomed by either Europe or Canada, as it would create adverse balance of payments flows. In this case, the eventual outcome would probably be much less ambitious neighboring rights programs in all countries.

In Canada and a number of other countries, the array of imaginative protectionist measures on access, ownership, content quotas, tariffs, and discriminatory taxes is buttressed by an equally complex set of subsidies and tax breaks. The instrument of competition for footloose film and television productions is special tax treatment. Grants and tax credits are both available to domestic producers. The resulting programs are often licensed internationally. Over time this subsidized production contributes to the development of valuable libraries. The competition among jurisdictions for footloose productions, and to increase the market share of their productions domestically and internationally, has eroded the tax base of the participating countries. In the case of federal countries like Canada, this dissipation has been augmented by competition among the provinces to attract productions.

Canadian postal subsidies were ruled inconsistent with Canada's trade obligations in the magazine case. Otherwise, subsidies did not play a significant role in the cases. Nevertheless, if the international governance of trade and investment in these industries is addressed, we believe that national governments will favor the establishment of enforceable rules to make mutually harmful fiscal wars less probable. Subsidies like quotas are likely to be more important in such negotiations than they were in the cases studied here.

Establishing a responsible set of constraints on subsidies will have to address the boundary between the cultural industries and nonprofit, governmentally supported activities such as museums and art galleries. Subsidies for the arts and humanities in general are provided by all industrialized countries in one way or another. In the United States, public funding has been provided for the National Endowment for the Arts and the National Endowment for the Humanities. Funding in the United States has also been provided for museums and libraries, with the Library of Congress being a heavily subsidized national cultural asset but one that is of value to users from other countries as well. Similar programs occur in Canada and other countries. Because of the diverse forms of cultural funding in different countries and the difficulty of identifying the beneficiaries, it will be hard to reach agreement on what constitutes an allowable subsidy from the viewpoint of a trade agreement. The nonprofit sector is awash with cultural organizations that operate for the public benefit. Arthur Schlesinger Jr. notes that "the most precious institutions in society—our schools, universities, hospitals, clinics, libraries, museums and churches—are precisely those that do not earn their own way" (United States 1997, 5). Except indirectly through attracting tourists and students, these programs do not have a significant international impact and should be separated from the cultural industry programs as far as international governance is concerned.

Antitrust initiatives were important in the history of the film distribution case, and the Canadian competition authorities played a constructive role in the satellite case. We believe that, like quotas and subsidies, the future pressures to coordinate competition policies will be more intense than would be indicated by their relative importance in the cases. In particular, the issue of how price discrimination in licensing copyright should relate to the general treatment of price discrimination is of importance for many national competition policy authorities, including the Canadian. Coordinating the resolution of this issue is particularly important for the cultural industries, which contract on the basis of copyright policy. The lack of coordination is reflected in the provision of the Canadian Copyright Act concerning the parallel importation of books, which differs from American and European law.

Another area of concern to which we have alluded in presenting the background for the film distribution chapters is the activity of export cartels in distribution. One of our themes in this book is the importance of international markets for the cultural industries, not only in mass market content but in specialized niche markets. With this internationalization, the effect of the many mergers taking place in the cultural industries on market power can only be properly assessed and disciplined at a supranational level. A more effective competition policy framework for these industries might also curb ad hoc interferences with contracting. Canadian policies with respect to distributing films to PPV services operating from satellite broadcasters included the arbitrary setting of contractual terms so as to lower the prices paid to foreign rights holders. This discriminatory policy is still operative although currently suspended.

Labor movement is another problem area. As a result of the footloose nature of film and television production, domestic firms often shoot in foreign locations, requiring the cross-border movement of persons. While there will seldom be visa problems for John Travolta, Céline Dion, and Jeremy Irons working in foreign countries, although tax authorities may take a keen interest in their earnings, the ability of technical staff to work abroad is determined by the availability of work permits. Depending on how this procedure is administered, it can be more or less restrictive of this form of service trade. Certainly there are documented examples of film directors who have been held for ransom by foreign officials at the time of permit renewals.

Formal international trade agreements have addressed a number of the dominant issues raised by the cases. The GATS initiated a process for liberalizing market access for services. This initiative has been extended to telecommunications and finance—service sectors with idiosyncratic technologies and regulatory frameworks. The GATS established the principle of transparency in order to facilitate the negotiation and enforcement of MFN treatment in services and levels of market access such as national treatment. With some ingenuity, the replacement of discriminatory quotas or lists for services with more flexible and less discretionary instruments is possible. Given the success of replacing quotas with tariffs in creating a dynamic for liberalization of trade in goods, an equivalent substitution for services is desirable. There have also been promising beginnings in dealing with subsidies in a number of areas, including such difficult sectors as agriculture. Some of these approaches may also help constrain dissipative fiscal competition with respect to tax shelter or credit programs. International initiatives to control restrictive business practices date from the 1940s and the proposed charter for the International Trade Organization, the 1976 OECD Guidelines for Multinational Enterprises, and a 1980 UN resolution on a Set of Multilaterally Agreed Equitable Principles and Rules regarding restrictive business practices. A more recent proposal is a draft International Antitrust Code initiated by a group of mainly German antitrust experts. The subject matter of these approaches tends to include horizontal and vertical agreements and practices, abuse of dominant position, and mergers, which have an international dimension (Jackson, Davey, and Sykes 1995, 1090–1107).

Active discussion of trade and competition issues is currently under way (International Chamber of Commerce, 1998).

The formal arrangements increasingly stress agreement on making policies transparent. Imposition of such a requirement with respect to cultural policies is a necessary condition for progress in developing a better international trading system for the cultural industries. The cases illustrate a number of instances of black box processes in Canadian cultural policy. A good example is the Investment Canada process for determining de facto control. The formal agreements have also contributed to the evolution of a reinforcing set of norms that aid complementary informal processes in resolving disputes.

As well as presenting evidence on the emerging issues, the cases examined throw light on the efficacy of the informal processes in resolving issues. One of these is that the specific antecedents of a dispute can have an important impact on non-rules-based processes of dispute resolution. For example, four decades of noisy diplomacy and emotional politics preceded the *Sports Illustrated* case. Protection of the advertising market was and is the dominant concern. From listening to the political debate, one would have received the impression that cultural content was the issue. This was true whether one tuned in during the 1960s, tne 1970s, or the recent interactions in the *Sports Illustrated* case. The emotional energy from the "Canadian voices telling Canadian stories" theme kept the issue alive politically. There was seldom if ever an attempt to document what content would be displaced by its entry nor why it would not remain viable in the face of competition from stories and writers that lacked a Canadian sensibility. This formulaic process may have been derailed by the complaint of the United States to the WTO, which transferred the dispute from the informal to a formal regime. The latest Canadian initiative and probable American response may perpetuate the drama.

The digital satellite broadcasting case was dealt with through an informal process. Canadian policy denied foreign providers access to a Canadian market, which was being served by no one. Viewers were put on hold while Canadian suppliers were "hothoused" into existence. The low cost of supplying all people in the footprint of a broadcast satellite makes protectionist policies in this area particularly costly, and Canadian viewers may have to wait a long time before receiving a service of similar quality to the signals that have been floating like digital forbidden fruit in the Canadian air for the past five years. When there are no domestic equivalents available at any price, smuggling creates illegal entry into the market. The gray market in digital satellite services remains large. These "imports" pay no tariffs and provide few hostages in the form of Canadian investments and employment.

The informal processes can also lead to a destructive sequence of actions and reactions. This did not occur in the CMT case. This case involved a section

301 submission to the USTR, but a private solution was reached before it had run its course. What did emerge in a couple of the cases was a dangerous strategic politicization of regulatory bodies. In both the CMT and the satellite-broadcasting cases, the FCC became an active instrument of American foreign policy as well as a regulatory body. Similarly, the CRTC initiated the CMT case, orchestrated a Machiavellian score for the satellite broadcasting case before being reined in by the government, and began the V-chip case with a political strut before becoming more constructive and contributing to its resolution.

Finally, the disputes reveal the inadequacy of information on production and trade and the impact of changing technology. Unreliable data were used opportunistically in supporting different positions with little effort to reference sources. Lurking behind all the cases is the threat of convergence and the Internet in delivering content. Any governance structure will have to include a foundation on which solutions to these two sets of issues can be built.

Options for an Agreement

The options for a formal agreement are to include cultural and entertainment goods and services within the framework of the WTO with limited special provisions for particular circumstances. In effect, this route was used in 1947, when the GATT applied to all related items traded as goods but included article IV to address the issue of theatrical screen quotas for films. A second option is to make provision for these industries within regional agreements such as the NAFTA, the proposed Free Trade Agreement of the Americas, and the Asia-Pacific Economic Cooperation Forum. One problem with this is that there will likely be no consistency in the treatment of the same industry within different country groupings. Where a multilateral agreement overlaps with a regional agreement, opportunities are presented for parties to forum shop when a dispute arises, as occurred in the case of *Sports Illustrated.* In addition, most of the cultural industries are international rather than regional in scope.

A third alternative is to develop a sectoral agreement for culture and entertainment, as has been done for telecommunications and financial services. This would permit adapting the terms of the agreement to the special conditions prevailing in the different components of the industry that exist now and will likely come about as a result of increasing use of the Internet and evolving technologies. It would also permit the inclusion of obligations with respect to trade in goods and services, investment flows and commercial presence considerations, copyright concerns, and the movement of persons. Each of these economic dimensions is present in this sector. Failure to address all of them will lead to further border problems as commercial interests shape their organizational and contractual arrangements to take advantage of loopholes and thereby perpetuate the likelihood of trade disputes.

An advisory committee to the Canadian government has proposed a special instrument to accommodate trade and the cultural industries (Canada 1999, 31). If the instrument was separate from the WTO framework, it would mean that this set of economic activities would not be subject to known rules and procedures but to new ones whose impact would only become known over time. We favor examining the possibility of a sectoral agreement for culture within the WTO framework. WTO negotiations frequently embrace a number of contentious issues. The resolution of each is enhanced by the ability to trade concessions among them. A sectoral agreement would be similar to the approach taken for telecommunication services where a reference paper set out the definitions and principles for the sector's peculiarities.[3] Agreement on telecommunications was reached fairly quickly in part because the players knew each other through interaction in the International Telecommunications Union, the companies had worked together on establishing technical standards and the issues did not involve sensitive content matters. We do not foresee that it will be as easy to reach agreement on definitions and principles for cultural goods and services, but feel that this is the most promising way to proceed.

An initial work plan for such an agreement would include:

1. Drawing the boundaries for the inclusion/exclusion of relevant activities in a way that would permit the impact of future technological development to be taken into account.
2. Determining the scope of the agreement with respect to trade in goods, services, investment, intellectual property, and the movement of persons.
3. Identifying factors affecting market access by foreign firms to domestic markets. The list would be both general to the cultural sector and specific to each subsector.
4. Developing a list of subsidies and tax incentives affecting the industry.
5. Developing a list of private actions that affect trade and identifying the scope of antitrust policy to deal with these policies from a trade policy perspective.
6. Examining alternative dispute resolution procedures.

As a target to which the sequence of commitments should aspire, we suggest the following goals: no tariffs and quotas, minimal foreign-ownership restrictions, nondiscriminatory market access, freedom to work, coordinated enforcement of

---

3. See statement by Robert Wolfe to the House of Commons Standing Committee on Foreign Affairs and International Trade, Ottawa, March 2, 1999, 7.

Much Ado about Culture

national antitrust laws, no direct or indirect protection of wholesale or
distribution networks, national treatment in the application of censorship,
national treatment of programming in "safe sanctuary" periods of the day,
subsidies allowed to fill "gaps" in content, national treatment in tax provisions,
and transparency.

Even if a sectoral agreement is not the preferred route, these issues will have
to be addressed. In the absence of an agreement, the informal process of dispute
resolution will prevail with uncertainty as to outcomes and benefits for the more
powerful.

None of the formal approaches will work unless there is a widely held belief
that national culture and the civility of everyday life are enhanced by liberalization and openness. The public debate often seems hostile to these principles
despite the fact that they are extensions of widely held values into commercial
matters. For other areas of trade, the past 50 years of GATT reveal the effect of
a series of decisions based on these principles. They have been pursued over a
broader domain of activities involving less-developed as well as developed
countries, as GATT has evolved to the WTO, a much more complex governance
structure. There has even been progress in extending the principles to agricultural trade. A formal structure has to be supported by a thick set of informal
relationships and protocols of behavior that share the same values. What is
perhaps needed is a catchy mantra that energizes the golden rule of international
commercial relations with the same political potency as nationalism.

Selected Bibliography

Acheson, K. "Political Exchange and Government Policy towards the Canadian Automotive Industry." In *International Trade Policies: Gains from Exchange between Economics and Political Science,* edited by J. S. Odell and T. D. Willett, 253–71. Ann Arbor: University of Michigan Press.

Acheson, K., and C. J. Maule. "The Carrot and the Stick." *Cinema Canada,* September 1988, 17–19.

———. "Trade Policy Responses to New Technology in the Film and Television Industry." *Journal of World Trade,* April 1989a, 35–48.

———. "The Higgledy-Piggledy Trade Environment for Films and Programs: The Canadian Example." *World Competition* 13, no. 2 (1989b): 47–62.

———. "Canadian Content Rules: A Time for Reconsideration." *Canadian Public Policy* 16, no. 3 (1990): 284–97.

———. "Shadows behind the Scenes: Political Exchange and the Film Industry." *Millennium* 20, no. 2 (1991a): 287–307.

———. "It Seemed to Be a Good Idea at the Time." *Canadian Journal of Communication* 16, no. 2 (1991b): 263–76.

———. "The Business Side of an International Television Festival." *Journal of Arts Management, Law, & Society* 22, no. 2 (1992a): 118–33.

———. "Canadian Content Rules for Television: Misleading Lessons for Europe." *The Journal of Cultural Economics* 16, no. 1 (1992b): 13–24.

———. "Risk and the Transfer Cost of a Tax Shelter." *Canadian Tax Journal* 42, no. 4 (1994a): 1082–99.

———. "TV Viewers' Choice: A Tale of Three Cities." *Prometheus* 12, no. 2 (1994b): 189–206.

———. "Understanding Hollywood's Organization and Continuing Success." *Journal of Cultural Economics* 18 (1994c): 271–300.

———. "Review Article: Economics of Film and Television in Australia." *Prometheus* 12, no. 1 (1994d): 94–101.

———. "International Regimes for Trade, Investment, and Labour Mobility in the Cultural Industries." *Canadian Journal of Communication* 19 (1994e): 401–21.

———. "Copyright and Related Rights: The International Dimension." *Canadian Journal of Communication* 19 (1994f): 423–46.

————. "Copyright, Contract, the Cultural Industries, and NAFTA." In *Mass Media and Free Trade,* edited by E. G. McAnany and K. T. Wilkinson. Austin: University of Texas Press, 1996a.

————. "Viewers' Choice: The Effects of Technology, Geography, and Policy." *Canadian Journal of Economics* 29, Special Issue (1996b): 5610–13.

————. "Copyright and Trade Regimes Governing Print, Television, and Film." In *The Cultural Industries in Canada,* edited by M. Dorland, 308–27. Toronto: Lorimer and Co., 1996c.

————. "Canada's Cultural Exemption: Insulator or Lightning Rod?" *World Competition* 20 (September 1996d): 67–90.

————. "Is There Life after Deathstars? Communications Technology and Cultural Relations." In *Big Enough to Be Heard,* edited by F. O. Hampson and M. A. Molot, 95110. Ottawa: Carleton University Press, 1996e.

————. "Culture on the I-Way." *Policy Options* (1996f): 36–39.

————. "Cultural Policies: Canada Can't Have It Both Ways." *Canadian Foreign Policy* (1997a): 65–82.

————. "Cultural Entrepreneurship and the Banff Television Festival." *Journal of Cultural Economics* (Spring 1997b): 321–39.

————. "International Agreements and the Cultural Industries." *North American Outlook* 6, no. 4 (1998a): 7–24.

————. "Copyright, Diversity and the Evolution of Collective Administration." Paper presented at the annual meeting of Canadian Association of Law and Economics, Toronto, 1998b.

Acheson, K., C. J. Maule, and E. Filleul. "Folly of Quotas on Films and Television Programs." *World Economy* 12, no. 4 (1989): 515–24.

Allen, R. "As the World Turns: Television Soap Operas and Global Media Culture." In *Mass Media and Free Trade*, edited by E. G. McAnany and K. T. Wilkinson, 110–27. Austin: University of Texas Press, 1996.

Association of Canadian Publishers. *New Directives, Rethinking Public Policy for Canadian Books.* Toronto: Association of Canadian Publishers, 1995.

————. *Beyond Survival: Forging the Future of Canadian Books.* Toronto: Association of Canadian Publishers, 1997.

Audley, P. *Canada's Cultural Industries: Broadcasting, Publishing, Recording, and Films.* Toronto: James Lorimer, 1983.

————. "Issues Paper IHAC Steering Committee on Canadian Content and Cultural Identity." Report. Paul Audley & Associates, Toronto, 1997.

Bacal, N. "Not Just Another Sequel: The Canadian Motion Pictures Industry after Tax Reform." *Canadian Tax Journal* 36 (May-June 1988): 547–77.

Balassa, B. "Dependency and Trade Orientation." *World Economy* 9 (1986): 259–73.

Balio, Tino. "Surviving the Great Depression." In *Hollywood as a Modern Business Enterprise,* edited by Tino Balio, 13–36. New York: Maxwell Macmillan, 1993.

Bedore, J. "U. S. Film Industry: How Mergers and Acquisitions Are Reshaping Distribution Patterns Worldwide." *Industry Trade and Technology Review,* January 1997, 17–37.

Beebe, J. H. "Institutional Structure and Program Choices in Television Markets." *Quarterly Journal of Economics* 91 (1977): 15–37.

Bernier, I. "Cultural Goods and Services in International Trade Law." In *The Culture/Trade Quandary, Canada's Policy Options,* edited by D. Browne, 108–54. Ottawa: Centre for Trade Policy and Law, 1998.

Bikhchandani, S., D. Hirshleifer, et al. "A Theory of Fads, Fashion, Custom, and Cultural Change in Informational Cascades." *Journal of Political Economy* 100, no. 5 (1992): 992–1026.

Bird, R., ed. *Documents of Canadian Broadcasting.* Ottawa: Carleton University Press, 1989.

Bird, R., M. W. Bucovetsky, et al. *Tax Incentives for the Canadian Film Industry.* Toronto: Institute for Policy Analysis, University of Toronto, 1981.

Boorman, J. *Money into Light—The Emerald Forest: A Diary.* London: Faber and Faber, 1985.

Buchan, Robert J. "Direct Broadcasting Satellite (DBS) around the World—A Canadian Perspective." Speaking notes for the Joint Session of Committees "L" and "Z" of the International Bar Association, Vancouver, September 1998.

Bulow, Jeremy. "Durable Goods Monopolists." *Journal of Political Economy* 15 (1982): 314–32.

Canada. *Investigation into an Alleged Combine in the Motion Picture Industry of Canada.* Ottawa: Department of Labour, 1931.

———. *Report of the Royal Commission on National Development in the Arts, Letters, and Sciences.* Ottawa: King's Printer, 1951.

———. *Report of the Royal Commission on Publications.* Ottawa: Queen's Printer, 1961.

———. *Report of the Senate Committee on the Mass Media.* Ottawa: Queen's Printer, 1970.

———. *Report of the Royal Commission on Newspapers.* Ottawa: Minister of Supply and Services, 1981.

———. *Report of the Task Force on Film Distribution, Exhibition, and Marketing.* Ottawa: Government of Canada, 1983.

———. Combines Investigation Act, *Annual Report for the Year End March 31, 1984.* Ottawa: Consumer and Corporate Affairs Canada, 1984.

————. *Report of the Film Industry Task Force.* Ottawa: Government of Canada, 1985.

————. *Report of the Task Force on the Canadian Magazine Industry: A Question of Balance.* Ottawa: Minister of Supply and Services, 1994.

————. *Report on the Governor in Council Direction Orders to the Canadian Radio-Television and Telecommunications Commission.* Ottawa: Standing Senate Committee on Transport and Communications, June 1995a.

————. *Report of the Policy Review Panel: Direct-to-Home Satellite Broadcasting.* Ottawa: Minister of Canadian Heritage and Minister of Industry, 1995b.

————. Certain Measures concerning Periodicals, First Submission of Canada, Geneva, World Trade Organization, September 26, 1996a.

————. Certain Measures concerning Periodicals, Second Submission of Canada, Geneva, World Trade Organization, November 1, 1996b.

————. "A Time for Action." Industry Task Force on the Future of the Canadian Music, Ottawa, 1996c.

————. New Strategies for Culture and Trade, *Report of The Cultural Industries Sectoral Advisory Group on International Trade,* available on-line at <http://www.infoexport.gc.ca/trade-culture>, 1999.

Canada, Federal Mandate Review Committee. *CBC, NFB, Telefilm, Making Our Voices Heard: Canadian Broadcasting and Film for the 21st Century.* Ottawa: Minister of Supply and Services, 1996.

Canada, Federal Cultural Policy Review Committee. *Report of the Federal Cultural Policy Review Committee.* Ottawa: Department of Communications, Government of Canada, 1982.

Canadian Magazine Publishers Association. *Annual Report, 1994–1995.* Toronto: Canadian Magazine Publishers Association, 1995.

Cebryk, N. D., R. A. Jenness, and M. C. McCracken. *The Canadian Periodical Publishing Industry.* Ottawa: Infometrica, 1994.

Chapters Inc. *Prospectus for Initial Public Offering.* Toronto: Toronto Stock Exchange, 1996.

Clarke, E., and Lorne P. Salzman. "Control in Reality: Identifying Principles of Control in Canadian Communications Law." Paper presented at the Law Society of Upper Canada conference New Development in Communications Law and Policy, Ottawa, Ontario, April 1996.

Coase, R. H. "Durability and Monopoly." *Journal of Law and Economics* 15 (1972): 143–49.

Colina, Enrique. "The Film Critic on Prime Time." In *Cinema and Social Change in Latin America,* edited by Julianne Burton. Austin: University of Texas Press, 1986.

Collins, M. "Cooperation, Hollywood, and Howe." *Cinema Canada* 1979, 34–36.

Collins, Richard. *Culture, Communication, and National Identity: The Case of Canadian Television.* Toronto: University of Toronto Press, 1990.

———. *Broadcasting and Audio-Visual Policy in the European Single Market,* London: John Libbey, 1994.

Comer, Douglas E. *The Internet Book.* Englewood Cliffs: Prentice-Hall, 1995.

Commission of the European Communities. *Interim Report, Realities and Tendencies in European Television: Perspectives and Options.* COM(83), 229 final. Brussels: Commission of the European Communities, 1983.

———. *Television without Frontiers—Green Paper on the Establishment of the Common Market for Broadcasting, Especially by Satellite and Cable.* Communication from the Commission to the Council. Brussels: Commission of the European Communities, 1984.

———. *Green Paper on Copyright and the Challenge of Technology Copyright Issues Requiring Immediate Action.* Communication from the Commission to the Council. Brussels: Commission of the European Communities, 1988.

———. *Directive on the Coordination of Certain Provisions Laid Down by Law, Regulation, or Administrative Action in the Member States concerning the Pursuit of Television Broadcasting Signals (the Television without Frontiers Directive).* Official Journal L 298/1989, 89/552/EEC, 1989.

———. *Directive on Rental and Lending Rights.* Official Journal L 346/1992, 92/100/EEC, 1992.

———. *The Cable and Satellite.* Official Journal L 248/1993, 93/83/EEC, 1993a.

———. *The Term of Copyright Directive.* Official Journal L 290/1993, 93/98/EEC, 1993b.

———. *Audiovisual Policy: Next Steps.* COM (1998), 446 final, 1998a.

———. *The Single Market Review, Impact on Services, Audio-Visual Services, and Production.* Subseries II: vol. 8. Brussels: Commission of the European Communities, 1998b.

Copyright Board of Canada. *Statement of Royalties to Be Paid for the Retransmission of Distant Radio and Television Signals.* Ottawa: Copyright Board of Canada, 1990.

———. *Statements of Royalties to Be Paid for the Retransmission of Distant Radio and Television Signals.* Ottawa: Copyright Board of Canada, 1993.

Cowhey, Peter F., and Jonathan D. Aronson. "The Great Satellite Shootout." *Regulation* (May–June 1985): 27–35.

Cox, Kirwan. "Canada's Theatrical Wars." *Cinema Canada,* 1979, 47–53.

De Sola Pool, I. *Technologies without Boundaries.* Cambridge, MA: Harvard University Press, 1990.

Davidow, Joel. "Cartels, Competition Laws, and the Regulation of International Trade." *New York University Journal of International Law and Politics* 15 (1983): 351–75.

———. "Recent Developments in the Extraterritorial Application of U.S. Antitrust Law." *World Competition* 20, no. 3 (1997): 5–16.

De Vany, A., and R. D. Eckert. "Motion Picture Antitrust: The Paramount Cases Revisited." *Research in Law and Economics* 14 (1991): 51–112.

De Vany, A., and A. D. Walls. "Bose-Einstein Dynamics and Adaptive Contracting in the Motion Picture Industry." *Economic Journal* 106 (1996): 1493–1514.

Dick, Andrew R. "Are Export Cartels Efficiency-Enhancing or Monopoly-Promoting?" *Research in Law and Economics* (1992): 89–127.

———. "When Are Cartels Stable Contracts?" *Journal of Law and Economics* 39 (April 1996): 241–83.

——— "If Cartels Were Legal, Would Firms Fix Prices?" Washington, DC: Economic Analysis Group, Antitrust Division, Department of Justice, 1997.

Dickinson, M., and S. Street. *Cinema and State: The Film Industry and the British Government, 1927–84.* London: British Film Institute Publishing, 1985.

Diebold, William. *The End of the I.T.O.* Essays in International Finance, no. 16. Princeton: Princeton University Press, 1952.

Dreier, Thomas. "Broadcasting and Copyright in the Internal Market: The New Proposal by the EC Commission concerning Cable and Satellite Broadcasts." *European Intellectual Property Review* 2 (1991): 42–46.

Dubinsky, L. "Periodical Publishing." In *The Cultural Industries in Canada,* edited by M. Dorland. Toronto: Lorimer and Co., 1996.

Eberts, J., and T. Ilott. *My Indecision Is Final: The Spectacular Rise and Fall of Goldcrest Films, the Independent Studies That Challenged Hollywood.* New York: Atlantic Monthly Press, 1990.

Eggleston, W. *The Press in Canada.* Ottawa: King's Printer, 1951.

Ernst & Young. *Report submitted to the Task Force on the Future of the Canadian Music Industry: A Study of the Canadian Sound Recording Industry.* Ernst & Young, 1995.

European Parliament. Working Document 1–596/80, 1981.

———. "Report on Radio and Television Broadcasting in the European Community on Behalf of the Committee on Youth, Culture, Education, Information, and Sport." European Parliament Working Document 1–1013/81, 1982.

———. "Report on a Policy Commensurate with New Trends in European Television on Behalf of the Committee on Youth, Culture, Education,

Information, and Sport." European Parliament Working Document 1/1541/83, 1984.

Evans, G. *In the National Interest: A Chronicle of the National Film Board of Canada from 1949 to 1989.* Toronto: University of Toronto Press, 1990.

Fisher, B. S., and R. Steinhardt. "Section 301 of the Trade Act of 1974: Protection for U.S. Exporters of Goods, Services, and Capital." *Law and Policy in International Business* (1982): 569.

Freeman, D. "Sunset Boulevard Revisited." *New Yorker,* June 21, 1993, 72–79.

Fugate, W. L. *Foreign Commerce and the Antitrust Laws.* 3rd ed. Boston: Little, Brown & Co., 1982.

————. *Foreign Commerce and the Antitrust Laws.* 4th ed. Boston: Little, Brown & Co., 1991.

Gadbaw, R. M., and L. A. Kenny. "India." In *Intellectual Property Rights: Global Consensus, Global Conflict?* edited by R. M. Gadbaw and T. J. Richards. Boulder: Westview Press, 1988.

Gallant, M. *Home Truths: Selected Canadian Stories.* Toronto: Macmillan, 1981.

Gathercole, S. "As the Grapefruit Grows: A Short, Critical History of Canadian Film Policy." *Cinema Canada,* March 1983, 29–34.

Globerman, S. *Cultural Regulation in Canada.* Montreal: Institute for Research in Public Policy, 1981.

————. "Economic Aspects of the Operation of Pay-TV in Canada." In *The Introduction of Pay-TV in Canada,* edited by R. B. Woodrow and K. B. Woodside, 121–40. Montreal: Institute for Research on Public Policy, 1982.

————. *Foreign Ownership and Canada's Feature Film Distribution Sector: An Economic Analysis.* Vancouver: Fraser Institute, 1987.

Globerman, S., and M. P. Rothman. *An Economic Analysis of a Performers' Right.* Ottawa: Minister of Supply and Services Canada, 1981.

Goldman, W. *Adventures in the Screen Trade.* New York: Warner Books, 1983.

Grant, Peter. "Copyright: New Developments, New Costs." Paper presented at the conference Copyright: New Developments in Broadcasting and Retransmission, Toronto, Ontario, 1991.

Grenier, L. "Cultural Exemptionalism Revisited: Quebec Music Industries in the Face of Free Trade." In *Mass Media and Free Trade: NAFTA and the Cultural Industries,* edited by E. G. McAnany and K. T. Wilkinson, 306–30. Austin: University of Texas Press, 1996.

Guback, T. H. *The International Film Industry: Western Europe and America since 1945.* Bloomington: Indiana University Press, 1969.

————. "Hollywood's International Market." In *The American Film Industry,* edited by T. Balio, 463–86. Madison: University of Wisconsin Press, 1985.

Hammond, Grant. "The Legal Protection of Ideas." *Osgoode Hall Law Journal* 29, no. 1 (1991): 93–125.

Hirshleifer, D. "The Blind Leading the Blind: Social Influence, Fads, and Informational Cascades." In *The Economics of Human Behavior,* edited by M. Tomassi and K. Ierulli, 188–215. Cambridge: Cambridge University Press, 1995.

Hoekman, B., and C. A. Primo-Braga. "Protection and Trade in Services: A Survey." *Open Economies Review* 8, no. 3 (1997): 235–308.

Hoskins, C., and S. McFadyen. "The Importance of Television International Coproductions and Co-ventures and the Motives of Participants: The Canadian Case." Working Paper, Faculty of Business, University of Alberta, 1992a.

———. "The Mandate, Structure, and Financing of the CBC." *Canadian Public Policy* 18 (1992b): 275–89.

Hoskins, C., S. McFadyen, and A. Finn. *Global Television and Film.* Oxford: Oxford University Press, 1997.

Hoskins, C., and R. Mirus. "Reasons for the U.S. Dominance of the International Trade in Television Programmes." *Media, Culture, and Society* 10 (1988): 499–515.

Hoskins, C., R. Mirus, et al. "U.S. Television Programs in the International Market: Unfair Pricing?" *Journal of Communication* 39, no. 2 (1989): 55–75.

Houle, Michel. "Power Protects." *Cinema Canada,* 139, March 1987, 16–23.

———. *Profile of the Film Distribution and Movie Theatre Industries in Canada (1988 to 1992).* Ottawa: Department of Canadian Heritage, 1994.

———. *Statistical Analysis on the Relevancy of the Canadian Cultural Policy Regarding Distribution.* Ottawa: Department of Canadian Heritage, 1996.

House of Commons Sub-committee on the Revision of Copyright. *A Charter of Rights for Creators.* Ottawa: Minister of Supply and Services, 1985.

Hudson, H. E. *Communication Satellites: Their Development and Impact.* New York: Free Press, 1990.

Inglis, Ruth A. "Self-Regulation in Operation." In *The American Film Industry,* edited by T. Balio, 377–400. Madison: University of Wisconsin Press, 1985.

International Chamber of Commerce. *Report on Competition and Trade in the Global Arena: An International Business Perspective.* Paris, February 1998.

Jackson, J. H. *World Trade and the Law of the GATT; A Legal Analysis of the General Agreement on Tariffs and Trade.* Indianapolis: Bobbs-Merrill, 1969.

———. *The World Trading System.* Cambridge, MA: MIT Press, 1991.

Jackson, J. H., W. J. Davey, and A. O. Sykes Jr. *Legal Problems of International Economic Relations: Cases, Material, and Text.* 3rd ed. St. Paul, MN: West Publishing, 1995.

Jarvie, I. *Hollywood's Overseas Campaign: The North Atlantic Movie Trade, 1920–50.* Cambridge: Cambridge University Press, 1992.

Jeffrey, Liss. "Private Television and Cable." In *The Cultural Industries in Canada,* edited by Michael Dorland. Toronto: Lorimer & Co., 1996.

Johnson, J. R. *International Trade Law.* Concord, ON: Irwin, 1998.

Jones, S. "Mass Communication, Intellectual Property Rights, International Trade, and the Popular Music Industry." In *Mass Media and Free Trade,* edited by E. G. McAnany and K. T. Wilkinson. Austin: University of Texas Press, 1996.

Keon, J. A. *Audio and Video Home Taping: Impact on Copyright Payments.* Ottawa: Minister of Supply and Services Canada, 1982.

————. "Audio Home Recording: Canadian Copyright Implications." *Research in Law and Economics* 8 (1986): 157–74.

Keyes, A. A., and C. Brunet. *Copyright in Canada: Proposals for a Revision of the Law.* Ottawa: Minister of Supply and Services for the Department of Consumer and Corporate Affairs, 1977.

————. "What Is Canada's International Copyright Policy?" *Intellectual Property Journal* 7 (1993): 299–319.

Knelman, Martin. "Claude Jutra in Exile (1977)." In *Documents in Canadian Film,* edited by Douglas Fetherling, 82–88. Peterborough: Broadview Press, 1988.

Knopf, H. P. "New Forms and Fora of Intellectual Property." *Canadian Intellectual Property Review* 5 (1989): 247–74.

Koenigsberg, F. "United States Copyright after Berne—The Most Significant Catalyst in 100 Years." *Logos* 2, no. 2 (1991): 68–72.

Kowall, J. "Foreign Investment Restrictions in Canadian Television Broadcasting: A Call for Reform." *University of Toronto Faculty of Law Review* 50, no. 1 (1992): 61–95.

Krutilla, J. V. "Conservation Reconsidered." *American Economic Review* 57 (1967): 777–86.

Lardner, James. "Annals of Law: The Betamax Case: Part I." *New Yorker,* April 6, 1987, 45–70.

————. "Annals of Law: The Betamax Case: Part II." *New Yorker,* April 13, 1987, 60–81.

Liebowitz, S. J. *Copyright Obligations for Cable Television: Pros and Cons.* Ottawa: Minister of Supply and Services, 1980.

Litvak, I. A., and C. J. Maule. *Cultural Sovereignty: The Time and Reader's Digest Case in Canada.* New York: Praeger, 1974.

———. "Bill C–58 and the Regulation of Periodicals in Canada." *International Journal* (Winter 1980): vol. 36, 70–90.

Liu, X., and K. Acheson. *Assessing Vertical Constriants in Motion Picture Contracts.* CIORU 98–02. Ottawa: Carleton University, 1998.

Lorimer, Rowland. "Book Publishing." In *The Cultural Industries in Canada,* edited by M. Dorland. Toronto: Lorimer and Co., 1996.

MacCarthy, Mark M. "Broadcast Self-Regulation: The NAB Codes, Family Viewing Hour, and Television Violence." *Cardozo Arts & Entertainment Law Journal* 13, no. 3 (1995): 667–96.

Magder, T. *Canada's Hollywood: The Canadian State and Feature Films.* Toronto: University of Toronto Press, 1993.

———. "Film and Video Production." In *The Cultural Industries in Canada,* edited by M. Dorland. Toronto: Lorimer and Co., 1996.

Maltby, Richard. "The Production Code and the Hays Office." In *Hollywood as a Modern Business Enterprise,* edited by Tino Balio, 37–72. New York: Maxwell Macmillan, 1993.

Martin, Rebecca F. "The Digital Performance Right in the Sound Recordings Act of 1995: Can It Protect U.S. Sound Recording Copyright Owners in a Global Market?" *Cardozo Arts & Entertainment* 14 (1996): 733–72.

McIlroy, James. "American Enforcement of Intellectual Property Rights." *Journal of World Intellectual Property* 1, no. 3 (1998): 445–64.

Morris, P. *Embattled Shadows: A History of Canadian Cinema, 1895–1939.* Montreal: McGill-Queen's University Press, 1978.

Motion Picture Association. *Trade Barriers to Exports of U.S. Filmed Entertainment.* Washington, DC: Motion Picture Association, 1998.

Newmark, Linda A. "Performance Rights in Sound Recordings: An Analysis of the Constitutional, Economic, and Equitable Issues." In *Copyright Law Symposium: Number Thirty-Eight,* 141–80. New York: Columbia University Press, 1992.

Nichols, R. *Radio Luxembourg, the Station of the Stars.* London: Allen and Co., 1983.

Nolan, M. "An Infant Industry: Canadian Private Radio, 1919–36." *Canadian Historical Review* 70 (1989): 496–518.

Nordicity Group, Ltd. "Canadian Exports in the New Economy: The Canadian Film and Television Production Industry." Preliminary Report prepared for the Canadian Film and Television Association, Ottawa, 1996.

OECD. *Services: Statistics on International Transactions, 1970–1993.* Paris: OECD, 1994.

Ontario Reports, Cases determined in the Supreme Court of Ontario, the Court of Appeal for Ontario and the High Court of Justice for Ontario, 1932 307–349.

Orf, Ewald. "Television without Frontiers—Myth of Reality." *European Intellectual Property Review* 8 (1990): 270–74.

Owen, B. M., and S. S. Wildman. *Video Economics.* Cambridge, MA: Harvard University Press, 1992.

Parker, J. "PLR in a Copyright Context." *IFLA Journal* 23, no. 4 (1991): 299–304.

Patry, William F. "Copyright and the Legislative Process: A Personal Perspective." *Cardozo Arts & Entertainment* 14, (1996): 139–52

Plant, A. "The Economic Aspects of Copyright in Books." *Economica* 1 (1934): 167–95.

Poddar, S., and M. English. *Private Financing of Certified Canadian Films: A Review of Current Arrangements and Options for the Future.* Toronto: Ernst & Young, 1994.

Porter, Vincent. *Beyond the Berne Convention.* London: John Libbey, 1991.

Pratley, Gerald. "Film in Canada (1955)." In *Documents in Canadian Film,* edited by Douglas Fetherling, 82–88. Peterborough: Broadview Press, 1988.

Prescott, Peter. "The Origins of Copyright: A Debunking View." *European Intellectual Property Review* 12 (1989): 453–55.

Rabinovitch, V. "The Social and Economic Rationales for Canada's Domestic Cultural Policies." In *The Culture/Trade Quandary, Canada's Policy Options,* edited by D. Browne, 25–53. Ottawa: Centre for Trade Policy and Law, 1998.

Raboy, M. *Missed Opportunities.* Montreal: McGill-Queen's University Press, 1990.

———. "Public Television." In *The Cultural Industries in Canada,* edited by M. Dorland, 178–99. Toronto: Lorimer and Co., 1996.

Randall, Richard S. "Censorship: From *The Miracle* to *Deep Throat.*" In *The American Film Industry,* edited by T. Balio, 510–36. Madison: University of Wisconsin Press, 1985.

Reynolds, B. "How to Avoid Getting Ripped Off." *Canadian Musician* (1989): 44–48.

Richardson, B. "Perspectives on Cultural Sovereignty and Trade Protectionism: An American's Perspective." *North American Outlook* 6, no. 4 (1998): 41–45.

Roberts, Diane. "On the Plurality of Ratings." *Cardozo Arts and Entertainment Law Journal* 15, no. 1 (1997): 105–34.

Schatz, T. *The Genius of the System.* New York: Pantheon, 1988.

Smith, D. A. "Collective Administration of Copyright: An Economic Analysis." *Research in Law and Economics* 8 (1986): 137–52.

Smith, Milton L. *International Regulation of Satellite Communication.* Dordrecht: Nijhoff, 1990.

Steiner, P. O. "Program Patterns and Preferences and the Workability of Competition in Radio Broadcasting." *Quarterly Journal of Economics,* (May 1952): vol. 66, no. 2, 194–223.

Stern, R. H. "Some Reflections on Parallel Importation of Copyrighted Products into the United States and the Relation of the Exhaustion Doctrine to the Doctrine of Implied Licence." *European Intellectual Property Review* 4 (1989): 119–27.

Stigler, George J. "United States vs. Loew's Inc.: A Note on Block Booking." *Supreme Court Review* (1963):152–57.

———. "A Theory of Oligopoly." *Journal of Political Economy* 72 (1964): 44–61.

Straw, W. "Sound Recording." In *The Cultural Industries in Canada: Problems, Policies, and Prospects,* edited by M. Dorland, 95–117. Toronto: James Lorimer & Co., 1996.

Thompson, K. *Exporting Entertainment—America in the World Film Market, 1907– 1934.* London: BFI Publishing, 1985.

Towse, Ruth. Book review in *Journal of Cultural Economics,* vol. 21, no. 4, 1997, 355–60.

Trebilock, M. J. "Competition Policy and Trade Law—Mediating the Interface." *Journal of World Trade* 30, no. 4 (1996): 71–106.

Trilling, C. "Anne of Red Hair." *New Yorker,* August 5, 1996, 56–62.

United States. *Canada: Certain Measures concerning Periodicals, First Submission of the United States.* Geneva: World Trade Organization, 1996a.

———. *Canada: Certain Measures concerning Periodicals, Second Submission of the United States.* Geneva: World Trade Organization, 1996b.

———. *Creative America: A Report to the President.* Washington, DC: President's Committee on the Arts and the Humanities, 1997.

Valenti, Jack. "The Movie Rating System." In *The Movie Business Book,* edited by Jason E. Squire, 362–72. New York: Simon and Schuster, 1983.

———. "The North American Free Trade Agreement among Mexico, Canada, and the U.S. Is Fatally Flawed." Motion Picture Export Association of America, Inc., 1992.

West's Federal Reporter. United States Courts of Appeals and Temporary Emergency Court of Appeals, vol. 978 F.2d., 1318–33. St. Paul, MN: West Publishing Co., 1993.

Whitehead, Stephen. "CRTC Regulation of U.S. Direct-to-Home Satellite Services." Ottawa, 1994.

Wildman, S. S., and S. E. Siwek. *International Trade in Films and Television Programs.* Cambridge: Ballinger Publishing, 1988.

Wincor, Richard. *From Ritual to Royalties.* New York: Walker and Co., 1962.

World Trade Organization. *Canada—Certain Measures concerning Periodicals: Report of the Panel.* WT/D531/R. Geneva: World Trade Organization, 1997a.

————. *Canada—Certain Measures concerning Periodicals: Report of the Appellate Body.* WT/D531/AB/R. Geneva: World Trade Organization, 1997b.

————. *Electronic Commerce and the Role of the Word Trade Organization.* Special Studies 2. Geneva: World Trade Organization, 1998.

Yule, A. *Fast Fade: David Puttnam, Columbia Pictures, and the Battle for Hollywood.* New York: Delacorte Press, 1989.

Index

STUDIES IN INTERNATIONAL TRADE POLICY

Studies in International Trade Policy includes works dealing with the theory, empirical analysis, political, economic, legal relations, and evaluations of international trade policies and institutions.

General Editor: Robert M. Stern

John H. Jackson and Edwin Vermulst, Editors. *Antidumping Law and Practice: A Comparative Study*

John Whalley, Editor. *Developing Countries and the Global Trading System.* Volumes 1 and 2

John Whalley, Coordinator. *The Uruguay Round and Beyond: The Final Report from the Ford Foundation Project on Developing Countries and the Global Trading System*

John S. Odell and Thomas D. Willett, Editors. *International Trade Policies: Gains from Exchange between Economics and Political Science*

Ulrich Kohli. *Technology, Duality, and Foreign Trade: The GNP Function Approach to Modeling Imports and Exports*

Stephen V. Marks and Keith E. Maskus, Editors. *The Economics and Politics of World Sugar Policies*

J. Michael Finger, Editor. *Antidumping: How It Works and Who Gets Hurt*

Horst Herberg and Ngo Van Long, Editors. *Trade, Welfare, and Economic Policies: Essays in Honor of Murray C. Kemp*

David Schwartzman. *The Japanese Television Cartel: A Study Based on* Matsushita v. Zenith

Alan V. Deardorff and Robert M. Stern, Editors. *Analytical Perspectives and Negotiating Issues in the Global Trading System*

Edwin Vermulst, Paul Waer, and Jacques Bourgeois, Editors. *Rules of Origin in International Trade: A Comparative Study*

Alan V. Deardorff and Robert M. Stern, Editors. *The Stolper-Samuelson Theorem: A Golden Jubilee*

Kent Albert Jones. *Export Restraint and the New Protectionism: The Political Economy of Discriminatory Trade Restrictions*

Alan V. Deardorff, James A. Levinsohn, and Robert M. Stern, Editors. *New Directions in Trade Theory*

Robert Baldwin, Tain-Jy Chen, and Douglas Nelson. *Political Economy of U.S.–Taiwan Trade*

Bernard M. Hoekman and Petros C. Mavroidis, Editors. *Law and Policy in Public Purchasing: The WTO Agreement on Government Procurement*

Danny M. Leipziger, Editor. *Lessons from East Asia*

Tamin Bayoumi. *Financial Integration and Real Activity*

Harry P. Bowen, Abraham Hollander, and Jean-Marie Viaene. *Applied International Trade Analysis*